EIGHT PLAYS

Eight Plays

Performance Texts

ARTHUR SCHNITZLER

Translated from the German
by William L. Cunningham and David Palmer

NORTHWESTERN UNIVERSITY PRESS
EVANSTON, ILLINOIS

Northwestern University Press
www.nupress.northwestern.edu

Printed in the United States of America

10 9 8 7 6 5 4 3 2 1

ISBN-13: 978-0-8101-1932-1 (cloth)
ISBN-10: 0-8101-1932-3 (cloth)
ISBN-13: 978-0-8101-1933-8 (paper)
ISBN-10: 0-8101-1933-1 (paper)

Library of Congress Cataloging-in-Publication Data
Schnitzler, Arthur, 1862–1931
[Plays. English. Selections.]
Eight plays : performance texts / Arthur Schnitzler ; translated from the German by William L. Cunningham and David Palmer.
p. cm.—(European drama classics)
Includes bibliographical references.
ISBN 0-8101-1932-3 (cloth : alk. paper)—ISBN 0-8101-1933-1 (pbk. : alk. paper)
1. Schnitzler, Arthur, 1862–1931—Translations into English. I. Cunningham, William L. 1939– II. Palmer, David, d. 2000. III. Title. IV. Series.
PT2638.N5A2 2006
832.9—dc22 2006009871

⊗ The paper used in this publication meets the minimum requirements of the American National Standard for Information Sciences—Permanence of Paper for Printed Library Materials, ANSI Z39.48-1992.

~ CONTENTS ~

TRANSLATOR'S NOTE

What began as a collaborative effort resulting in a successful performance of Arthur Schnitzler's *Roundelay* at the University of Louisville Belknap Student Theater evolved into a congenial faculty collaboration between David Palmer and myself that lasted some twenty years. As an undergraduate, David had acted in that play and, as a professional actor, was likewise familiar with *Anatol.* The following introduction, based on the program notes for our individual plays, highlights our intent: to make Schnitzler's major plays accessible to American audiences and theater groups. While providing some context and overview, we wished the plays to speak for themselves, much as they resonated to us throughout our efforts.

We intended our translations as a tribute to our professors Wolfgang Michael and George Schulz-Behrend at the University of Texas in Austin, where David earned his bachelor's degree and I my doctorate. David's untimely death cut short not only a career but also an association of uncommon grace and richness. The following plays are presented in his memory and in honor of our mutual mentors: *Besten Dank!*

William L. Cunningham

TRANSLATORS' INTRODUCTION

Like his fellow Viennese medical colleague and friend Sigmund Freud, Arthur Schnitzler (1862–1931) represents and typifies the final flowering of the multiethnic and multicultural Hapsburg Empire, with its vibrant professional life. The son of a Jewish physician who was actually able to obtain a professorship at the University of Vienna, Schnitzler likewise trained in medicine and received his degree there in 1895. His first major play, *Anatol,* was successfully performed in 1893 and was followed two years later by *Liebelei,* which secured Schnitzler's reputation. Like that of his fellow Viennese dramatist Hugo von Hofmannsthal (1874–1929), Schnitzler's ability and accomplishment are enhanced by a profound distrust of language, a theme which informs and unifies both writers' plays and narrative works. Both writers repeatedly demonstrate how language can be a means of self-deception and a tool for misleading others, a note poignantly struck by Klara Eckold at the conclusion of *An Hour of Recognition:* "Words lie."

In content as well as depth of psychological insight, the plays translated in this volume represent the full spectrum of Schnitzler's dramatic achievement from 1886 to 1915. While representing Austrian drama at its best, the plays transcend their origin and milieu, the fading years of the Hapsburg monarchy. In many respects, they are strikingly modern, notably in the candid expression of sexuality. Despite the apparent decadence and frivolity of many of Schnitzler's characters, his ironic subjectivity and painful awareness of human transience present us with conflicts that are both theatrical and existential, trivializing not only the sordid, pathetic individual, so frequently a male, but also hopes of change, much less of revolution. In falling back on clichés, his protagonists often evoke despair, the sense of the ultimate futility of human endeavor, which came to be associated with the Theater of the Absurd. At the same time, the uneasy melancholy so typically Austrian and Baroque looms behind Schnitzler's Impressionistic variations and repetitions. In their varying combinations of content and manner, his plays defy facile classification, enabling them to overcome the very transitoriness they so frequently celebrate.

For American audiences since 1912, when the *New York Dramatic Mirror* proclaimed John Barrymore's performance in the title role to be his best role to date, the seven scenes of *Anatol* (1888–92) rank among Schnitzler's best-known works (see Reinhold Urbach, *Arthur Schnitzler,* translated by David Daviau, New York: Frederic Ungar , 1973, pp. 53–54). The author himself, however, grew to particularly dislike them, since their undeservedly frivolous reputation resulted in some critics labeling him a bon vivant. At first glance, the series of scenes seems dominated by Anatol's blatant, overbearing male chauvinism, brutal treatment apparently accepted by at least some of the women. The wry remarks and subtle mockery offered by Anatol's friend and confidant Max, however, not only infuse the scenes with considerable humor but also allow the audience critical distance on Anatol's pretensions. As in Schnitzler's later, more mature works, the ironic subjectivity noted above, a deeper seriousness, and even an existentialist angst loom behind the surface decadence, undercutting its flippancy. As is typical of Schnitzler's subsequent writings, some if not all of the women in *Anatol* are revealed to be far stronger and more emotionally complex than their would-be victors, exposing male vanity and pride as mean and pathetic.

Seven scenes traditionally constitute the *Anatol* cycle: "A Question for Fate," "Christmas Shopping," "An Episode," "Jewels of Memory," "A Farewell Supper," "Agony," and "Anatol's Wedding Morning." Our translation also offers the original version of "Anatol's Wedding Morning" (1888) and, as an appendix, two additional scenes: "Anatol's Delusions of Grandeur" and "The Adventure of a Lifetime," the earliest (1886) entry in the Anatol series. Theater groups or directors performing the play have traditionally been free to include all seven scenes or to present just a selection. We hope our addition of the two supplementary scenes and of the original ending will add to the range of performance options. Likewise left to individual interpretation is whether, in that original version of "Anatol's Wedding Morning," the "Herr Kalmon," with whom Anatol's bride has eloped, is one and the same as "young Ralmen," whom Anatol identifies as "my bride's youthful love." In "Anatol's Delusions of Grandeur," we have taken the liberty of changing Fräulein Hanischek's forename from Barbara to Agnes, to make the humor more readily comprehensible to American audiences. Otherwise we have tried to remain faithful to the original.

As critics such as Martin Swales have observed, *Interlude,* written in 1896 as *Liebelei* (literally, "flirtation"), is the closest Schnitzler came to writing a Viennese tragedy (*Arthur Schnitzler,* Clarendon: Oxford, 1971, pp. 181–200). The play is ranked among his more successful works, although, standing in the shadow of *Roundelay* of 1896–97, it ultimately seems unable to transcend its cultural milieu. In contrast to the relatively Impressionistic style of the later play, with its more rapid pace, succession of characters and settings, and occasionally farcical overtones, the concentrated emotional focus on Fritz, Christine, and her father imparts greater psychological depth and intensity to *Interlude.* Unlike the less fully developed figures of *Roundelay,* the three characters evince universal resonance and tragic dimensions. Whether or not Fritz's death itself is tragic, parallels have been noted between him and Everyman. Whatever the validity of Swales's objection to the melodramatic endings in acts 2 and 3, Schnitzler directs our attention to the stage itself, especially at the very conclusion, much as Fritz does at the end of act 1. Despite full consciousness of their lives' transitory nature, all three characters affirm the beauty and validity of this world, the very tension which informs and sustains Vienna's still vibrant Baroque traditions and milieu.

Written in 1896 to 1897 as *Reigen, Roundelay* demonstrates Schnitzler's strengths, while providing grounds for his detractors. The ten dialogues and attendant sexual encounters resulted in charges of obscenity being brought against the author, who was acquitted in a six-day trial. The furor over such allegedly pornographic content notwithstanding, the play treats human sexuality honestly and straightforwardly, which earned the writer the title of Austrian Boccaccio. With their frenetic eroticism, the ten couples bring to mind the Middle Ages, in particular the Dance of Death. Freud admired Schnitzler's command of depth psychology, with the characters' unabashed openness. Produced in France under the title of *La Ronde* (as it is also known in the English-speaking world), the play was adapted for film by Max Ophuls in 1950 with the same title, a distinction already accorded *Interlude* in 1931. The scenes are also known in English under the more literally rendered title of *Hands Round.*

While not overtly Viennese, *The Green Cockatoo* (1899) evinces, like the rest of Schnitzler's oeuvre, a superficial decadence and explores in particular the conflict between reality and illusion, a theme that fascinated earlier Austrian dramatists such as Franz Grillparzer as well as Schnitzler's contemporary Hugo von Hofmannsthal. While the antithesis plays a major role in medieval and Baroque art throughout the German-speaking areas, as well as in other European cultures, it received particular emphasis in Vienna. As in Schnitzler's other works, superficially frivolous "reality" is counterpoised by an intense seriousness that, in *The Green Cockatoo,* is amplified by the magnitude and significance of the historical events looming behind and threatening the individual: the scene is set in Paris, on July 14, 1789. A sense of melancholy transience dominates the apparently revolutionary drama, relativizing the milieu of eighteenth-century France just as much as that of late nineteenth-century Vienna. The juxtaposition of personal squalor and revolution—a revolution that will destroy idealists as well as the decadent nobility and Prospère's sordid troupe of actors—results in mutual trivialization. Both the acting troupe and the aristocrats, as individuals, are overcome by sexual passion, but all of them are about to be overwhelmed by the revolution, which in turn will result in senselessness and failure. Thus the concluding cry of "Long live freedom" is absurdly ironic, for the proclaimers are in fact imprisoned by sexual desire, jealousy, greed, or ambition. Schnitzler was by no means glorifying revolution, contrary to the opinion of the Berlin censors, who altogether banned *The Green Cockatoo,* and the Viennese authorities, who suppressed it after just six performances at the Imperial Theatre. As in his explicitly Viennese plays, Schnitzler lays bare the universal human fears of sex, death, and loneliness, and the yearning to overcome the transitory nature of human existence. As Martin Swales has pointed out (*Arthur Schnitzler,* p. 278), Schnitzler's French characters, like the participants in *Roundelay* and Fritz and Theodor in *Interlude,* fall back on clichés, which Christine in the latter play could not bear and which, for the audience, produce despair, or a sense of ultimate grotesqueness, the fusion of comedy and tragedy that later became a hallmark of the Theater of the Absurd. As in *Roundelay,* the increasingly rapid pace heightens the confusion and blurs the differences between the individual characters. The intense dramatic tension results in a very "theatrical" and frequently performed play. In its rapid pace and its parade of characters *The Green Cockatoo* offers a parallel to *Roundelay.*

Even briefer than the relatively short *Green Cockatoo, The Last Masks* (1901–2) presents themes which inform Schnitzler's later and longer as well as better-known works: notably, aging and the accompanying increase of loneliness. Beyond initial bantering, sexual tension is limited to the recounting of past events. The sexual passion and jealousy of *Cockatoo* and *Roundelay* have been transformed into the desire for revenge, which resonates in Schnitzler's narrative as well as dramatic works. *The Last Masks* is one of the relatively few plays involving the author's own medical profession. The compassionate Dr. Halmschlöger may be seen as a tribute to a colleague, if not the writer's own father, and a forerunner of Professor Bernhardi, in the play of the same name. Despite its narrative economy, the single act casts ironic glances at both the literary and medical professions. The play also continues the recurrent tensions found in Schnitzler's earlier writings: the tensions between illusion and reality, infidelity versus loyalty, social pretext and pretense versus individual feeling and honesty, life and death.

While continuing the underlying tensions between illusion and reality and between social pretext and pretense versus individual feeling and honesty, *Countess Mitzi* (1907) further emphasizes Schnitzler's focus on loneliness and aging, augmented by sexuality. The latter emphasis is by no means restricted to the protagonist of the title, whose past, present, and future provide an ironic twist to the theme of a family reunion, as is evident in the subtitle: "Comedy in One Act." As in other plays included in this volume, women are portrayed as emotionally stronger and are endowed with greater resiliency, insight, and self-awareness than men. Despite some focus on the creative person, in particular a woman, the drama voices social criticism about how Mitzi, from the upper class, can survive as "the other woman" and as an unwed mother, forced by social convention to abandon her child. The hypocrisy is heightened by implicit comparison with women of the lower classes, who are even more exploited and crushed. Thus the piece looks not merely at a bygone past, but poses continuing questions. The scope of action onstage is limited, however, a characteristic which increasingly restricts the appeal and accessibility of Schnitzler's later, in particular his more lyric, plays for contemporary American audiences.

The tendency just noted applies in particular to *Professor Bernhardi* (1912), which presents expansive theoretical perspectives on topics of significance in the dramatist's era as well as our own: social and medical obligations, professional ambition, tolerance, and, in particular, anti-Semitism. As in the earlier plays, the crux of the action centers on personal integrity and social responsibility, with an implicit, underlying tension between illusion and reality. Although an illegal abortion is the basis for the dramatic impulse, the bulk of the play involves extensive discussions of legal, political, and journalistic issues, as well as religious and medical questions, all of which comes at the expense of external action. A more modern public, especially in the United States, isn't so accustomed to such an emphasis on the stage. On an even more pragmatic level, the limited presence of women in the early twentieth-century medical community, as foreshadowed by *The Last Masks,* results in only one such role in this play. For the above reasons, we have offered only the first of the five acts, which in itself is complete, except for the question of the protagonist's fate. The latter, like that of the Countess Mitzi in the play of the same name, is resolved on a lightheartedly ironic note, as evident in the play's subtitle, *A Comedy,* which we have accordingly omitted. Within this one act, Schnitzler presents a strikingly critical view of the latter days of the Danubian Empire and chillingly anticipates the Hapsburg collapse, the Holocaust, and the crises which continue to afflict Europe and humankind almost a full century later.

Despite its concentration on a Viennese middle-aged bourgeois household, *Hour of Realizing* (1915) presents the recurring tensions found in the preceding plays: illusion versus reality, the creative individual versus middle-class collective conformity, authenticity versus hypocrisy. Aging and loneliness are further emphasized. Like numerous other women, such as the Countess Mitzi, Klara Eckold is shown to be stronger, more sensitive, and possessing greater integrity than the men who would dominate her. Her departure at the conclusion of the play recalls that of Nora in Henrik Ibsen's *A Doll's House,* albeit Schnitzler's protagonist is older and more sophisticated. As in the other plays, men are revealed as weak, petty, vindictive, and obsessed with revenge. The background of continuing struggles in Bosnia rings disturbingly relevant in the latter years of the twentieth and first years of the twenty-first centuries.

David Palmer's sudden, untimely death occurred while we were at work on *Hour of Realizing;* his copy of the script was found among his papers. His colleague in theater arts, Professor Stephen C. Schultz, graciously looked over the complete manuscript and offered helpful, thought-provoking suggestions.

The plays translated in this volume were intended both for performance and for reading, by students in courses on German literature in English translation and by anyone interested in theater, regardless of background. We wished to make the plays accessible and able to be read or staged without benefit of program notes or footnotes. While trying to maintain fidelity to the original as far as possible, we aimed at a natural, readily comprehensible style of speech.

Thus repetitions—a particular characteristic of Impressionist writing—have sometimes been deleted and minor modifications made to avoid wordiness, awkwardness, or stilted diction. On occasion, we also made small alterations to lines that simply would not "play" well or that were unclear. In the belief that Schnitzler's literary and psychological mastery ultimately speaks for itself, we have on the whole resisted the temptation to modify, much less omit, portions in the plays offensive to our own sensibilities. However, we have reduced the rather frequent use of "my child" by male characters when addressing women. In attempting to convey the Austrian ambiance, we have retained references to Viennese landmarks such as Josefstadt Theater and to specific locations provided these were sufficiently clear from the context. Otherwise, we have generalized the references, the Augarten Bridge, for example, becoming "a bridge over the Danube." In *Roundelay,* strict adherence to the German would require that the Actress's perfume be reseda or mignonette, but since the plant is scarcely known in the United States, we have substituted jasmine, similarly fragrant and erotic. Our desire to capture something of the German-language original, as well as the lack of suitable alternatives, prompted retention of "Herr," "Frau," and "Fräulein." For the most part, Schnitzler's punctuation and his fondness for ellipsis have been observed, even when the actor's entire speech consists of ". . . ?" (which might be interpreted as a quizzical look), ". . . !" (a triumphant glance), or ". . ." (a pause, a pregnant silence). Stage directions likewise correspond as closely to the original as possible, allowing, as the playwright intended, maximum flexibility in productions.

We wish to thank our students and colleagues at the University of Louisville who have encouraged our efforts over the years. Particular gratitude is due the late Professor Leon V. Driskell for his encouragement, advice, and support and to his colleague Professor Thomas A. Van of the English Department. We are also indebted to Louisville's most illustrious intellectual son, Justice Louis D. Brandeis, and to Professor Edmund Schlesinger, who donated the 1912 Berlin

Fischer edition on which our performance translations are based. The *Roundelay* script was based on a successful production at the University of Louisville, and we extend our thanks to all who were involved in that staging. We are grateful to Northwestern University Press for graciously agreeing to consider our project for publication, and we would like to convey our thanks especially to Susan Harris, Anne Gendler, and Rachel Delaney, for their help and understanding and their patient replies to our numerous questions. A final expression of gratitude is due to Professor Stephen C. Schultz of the Theater Arts Department at the University of Louisville and to our long-suffering families.

W. L. C.
D. P.

EIGHT PLAYS

Anatol

Characters

Anatol

Max, *Anatol's confidant*

Cora, *an unmarried seamstress*

Gabriele, *a married woman*

Bianca, *a circus equestrienne*

Emilie, *an unmarried girl*

Waiter at the Hotel Sacher

Annie, *an actress*

Else, *a married woman*

Franz, *Anatol's servant*

Ilona, *an actress*

Herr Winkler, *father of Anatol's fiancée*

~

Vienna, turn of the twentieth century

A QUESTION FOR FATE

[ANATOL*'s room.*]

MAX: I truly envy you, Anatol . . .

[ANATOL *smiles.*]

MAX: Well, I must tell you I was stunned. Until now I've really regarded the whole thing as a fairy tale. But now that I've seen it . . . how she fell asleep before my eyes, how she danced when you told her she was a ballerina, and how she wept, when you told her her lover was dead—and how she pardoned a criminal, when you made her a queen . . .

ANATOL: Yes, yes.

MAX: I see there's a magician inside you!

ANATOL: In all of us.

MAX: Uncanny.

ANATOL: I can't agree with that. . . . No more uncanny than life itself. No more uncanny than many things we've arrived at over centuries. Just how do you think our forbears felt when they suddenly heard that the earth rotates? They must all have gotten dizzy!

MAX: Yes. . . . But that applied to everyone.

ANATOL: And if we were to discover springtime anew! . . . We wouldn't believe that either! In spite of the green trees, in spite of the blooming flowers, and in spite of love.

MAX: You're misguided, that's all drivel. Along with that animal magnetism . . .

ANATOL: Hypnotism . . .

MAX: No, that's another matter. I could never ever let myself be hypnotized.

ANATOL: Childish! What does it matter if I bid you fall asleep, and you lie down quietly?

MAX: Yes, and then you tell me, "You are a chimney sweep," and I climb into the fireplace and get sooty! . . .

ANATOL: Well, those are just pranks. . . . The big thing about it is the scientific utilization. But alas, we're simply not that far along.

MAX: How's that . . . ?

ANATOL: Well, how do I, who was able to transport that girl into a hundred different worlds, how do I then bring myself into another world?

MAX: Isn't that possible?

ANATOL: I've already tried it, to tell the truth. I stared at this diamond ring for several minutes and implanted the idea into myself: "Anatol! Fall asleep! When you awaken, the thought of that woman who drives you mad will have vanished from your heart."

MAX: Well, when you awakened?

ANATOL: Oh, I didn't fall asleep at all.

MAX: That woman . . . that woman? . . . So you're still . . . !

ANATOL: Yes, my friend! . . . I'm still! I'm unhappy, I'm wild about her.

MAX: So you're still . . . in doubt?

ANATOL: No . . . not in doubt. I know that she's deceiving me! While she hangs on my lips, while she strokes my hair . . . whenever we're in a blissful moment . . . I know that she's deceiving me.

MAX: Delusion!

ANATOL: No!

MAX: And your proof?

ANATOL: I sense it . . . I feel it . . . therefore I know it!

MAX: Strange logic!

ANATOL: Those females are always being unfaithful to us. It's quite natural for them . . . they just don't know it. . . . Just like I have to read two or three books at the same time, those women have to have two or three love affairs.

MAX: She loves you after all?

ANATOL: Infinitely . . . but that's irrelevant. She's being unfaithful to me.

MAX: And with whom?

ANATOL: Do I know? Perhaps with a prince who maybe followed her on the street, perhaps with a dilettante poet from a house in the suburbs who maybe smiled out of the window at her when she went by in the early morning!

MAX: You're a fool!

ANATOL: And what kind of reason would she have not to be unfaithful to me? She's like all the others, she loves life and doesn't reflect. If I ask her, "Do you love me?"—she says yes—and she is speaking the truth. And if I ask her, "Are you being faithful to me?"—she says yes again—and again she's speaking the truth, because she doesn't remember the others at all—at least not in that moment. And has a woman ever answered you, then, "My dear boyfriend, I'm being unfaithful to you"? And where are we to derive any certainty then? And if she's being unfaithful to me—

MAX: So maybe she is, after all!—

ANATOL: Then it's pure chance. . . . In no way does she think, "Oh, I must be loyal to him, my dear Anatol" . . . in no way . . .

MAX: But if she does love you!

ANATOL: Oh, my naive friend! If that were a reason!

MAX: Well?

ANATOL: Why am I not faithful to her? . . . I certainly do love her, after all!

MAX: Yes indeed! But . . . a man!

ANATOL: That stupid old phrase! We're always wanting to persuade ourselves that women are different than we are in that respect! Yes, some . . . those whom their mother locked up, or those who have no spirit. . . . We're quite the same. If I tell a woman, "I love you, only you"—I don't feel that I'm telling her a lie, even if I rested on the breast of another woman the night before.

MAX: Yes . . . you!

ANATOL: I . . . yes! And perhaps not you? And her, my adored Cora, perhaps not her? Oh! And it puts me into a frenzy. If I got down on my knees before her and said, "My darling, my dear child—everything is forgiven you in advance—but tell me the truth," what good would it do me? She would lie, as she did before—and it would get me no further than before. Not one has ever implored me, "For heaven's sake, tell me . . . are you really being faithful to me? Not a word of reproach if you're not, but the truth! I have to know." . . . And how did I respond? . . . I lied . . . calmly, with a blissful smile . . . with the purest conscience. I thought, "Why should I distress you?" And I said, "Yes, my sweet angel! Faithful unto death." And she believed me and was happy!

MAX: Well, then!

ANATOL: But I don't believe it and I'm not happy! I would be, if there were some infallible means of getting those foolish, sweet, hateful creatures to speak or to find out the truth in some other way. . . . But there isn't any, other than chance.

MAX: And hypnosis?

ANATOL: What?

MAX: Well . . . hypnosis . . . This is how I mean it: you get her to fall asleep and then you say, "You must tell me the truth."

ANATOL: Hmm . . .

MAX: You must. . . . Do you hear . . .

ANATOL: Strange! . . .

MAX: It must work, after all. . . . And then you go on to ask her . . . Do you love me? . . . Someone else? . . . Where do you come from? . . . Where are you going? . . . What's the other man's name? And so forth.

ANATOL: Max! Max!

MAX: Well . . .

ANATOL: You're right. . . . One could be a magician! One could conjure forth a word of truth out of a woman's mouth . . .

MAX: Well, then! I see you're saved! Cora is certainly a suitable medium . . . this very evening you can know if you've been deceived . . . or if you're a . . .

ANATOL: A god! . . . Max! . . . I embrace you! . . . I feel as if I've been liberated . . . I'm a completely different man. I have her in my power . . .

MAX: I'm really curious . . .

ANATOL: What's that? Do you perhaps doubt?

MAX: Ah yes, others aren't allowed to doubt, just you . . .

ANATOL: Certainly. . . . When a husband steps out of the house where he has just discovered his wife with her lover, and a friend comes up to him and says, "I think your wife is deceiving you," he won't answer, "I've just come to that conclusion" . . . but "You're a scoundrel and . . ."

MAX: Yes, I'd almost forgotten that it's the first duty of friendship to let one's friend keep his illusions.

ANATOL: Just be quiet . . .

MAX: What is it?

ANATOL: Don't you hear her? I know the sound of those steps, even when they're just in the vestibule.

MAX: I don't hear anything.

ANATOL: Already so close! . . . In the hall . . .

[*He opens the door.*]

Cora!

CORA: Good evening! Oh, you're not alone . . .

ANATOL: Friend Max!

CORA [*entering*]: Good evening! Why this darkness? . . .

ANATOL: Ah, it's still just twilight. You know I love that.

CORA [*stroking his hair*]: My little poet!

ANATOL: My dearest Cora!

CORA: But I'll put on the light all the same. . . . You'll permit me.

[*She lights the candles in the lamps.*]

ANATOL [*to* MAX]: Isn't she delightful?

MAX: Oh!

CORA: Well, how are things going? For you, Anatol—and for you, Herr Max?—Have you been chatting long?

ANATOL: For half an hour.

CORA: Well then. [*Taking off her coat and hat*] And about what?

ANATOL: About this and that.

MAX: About hypnosis.

CORA: Oh, here we go again with hypnosis! All that can make one quite foolish.

ANATOL: Well . . .

CORA: Say, Anatol, I'd like you to hypnotize me sometime.

ANATOL: I . . . you . . . ?

CORA: Yes, I imagine that can be very pretty. That is—if you would do it.

ANATOL: Thank you.

CORA: If a stranger did it . . . no, no, I wouldn't want that.

ANATOL: Well, my darling . . . if you want, I'll hypnotize you.

CORA: When?

ANATOL: Now! At once, on the spot.

CORA: Yes! Good! What do I have to do?

ANATOL: Nothing more, my dear child, than to stay quietly seated in the armchair and then to be so good as to fall asleep.

CORA: Oh, I'll be so good!

ANATOL: I'll position myself here in front of you, you'll look at me . . . now . . . just look at me . . . I'll stroke your forehead and over your eyes. So . . .

CORA: Well now, and what then . . .

ANATOL: Nothing . . . you simply have to want to fall asleep.

CORA: You know, when you stroke me over the eyes like that, I feel quite strange . . .

ANATOL: Quiet . . . don't talk. . . . Sleep. You're already quite tired.

CORA: No.

ANATOL: Yes! . . . A little tired.

CORA: A little, yes . . .

ANATOL: Your eyelids are getting heavy . . . very heavy, you can barely lift your hands anymore . . .

CORA [*softly*]: Really.

ANATOL [*goes on stroking her forehead and over her eyes, monotonously*]: Tired . . . you're quite tired . . . fall asleep now, my dear child. . . . Asleep.

[*He turns to* MAX, *who watches admiringly, and gives an expression of victory.*]

Sleep . . . Now your eyes are firmly closed . . . You can't open them any longer . . .

[CORA *tries to open her eyes.*]

ANATOL: It won't work . . . you're sleeping . . . just go on sleeping calmly. . . . So . . .

MAX [*tries to ask him something*]: You know . . .

ANATOL: Calmly. [*To* CORA] . . . Sleep . . . soundly, sleep deeply.

[*He stands for a time in front of* CORA, *who breathes calmly and sleeps.*]

So . . . now you can ask.

MAX: I just wanted to ask if she's really sleeping.

ANATOL: You see she is. . . . Now let's wait a few moments.

[*He stands in front of her, looks at her calmly. Long pause.*]

Cora! . . . You'll answer me now. . . . Answer. What is your name?

CORA: Cora.

ANATOL: Cora, we're in the forest.

CORA: Oh . . . in the forest . . . how beautiful! The green trees . . . and the nightingales.

ANATOL: Cora . . . Now you'll tell me the truth in all things. . . . What will you do, Cora?

CORA: I'll tell the truth.

ANATOL: You'll answer all my questions truthfully, and when you awaken, you will have forgotten everything! Do you understand me?

CORA: Yes.

ANATOL: Now sleep . . . sleep calmly. [*To* MAX] So I'll go ahead and ask her . . .

MAX: Anatol, just how old is she?

ANATOL: Nineteen. . . . Cora, how old are you?

CORA: Twenty-one.

MAX: Ha ha.

ANATOL: Shhh . . . that's certainly extraordinary. . . . You can see from that . . .

MAX: Oh, if she had only known what a good medium she is!

ANATOL: The suggestion worked. I'll go on asking her.—Cora, do you love me . . . ? Cora . . . do you love me?

CORA: Yes!

ANATOL [*triumphing*]: Do you hear that?

MAX: Now then, the main question, whether she is faithful.

ANATOL: Cora! [*Turning around*] That question is foolish.

MAX: Why?

ANATOL: One can't ask like that!

MAX: . . . ?

ANATOL: I've got to form the question differently.

MAX: But I think it's precise enough.

ANATOL: No, that's just the mistake, it's not precise enough.

MAX: How's that?

ANATOL: If I ask her, "Are you faithful?" she'll take it in the broadest possible sense.

MAX: Well?

ANATOL: Perhaps she'll include her whole . . . past. . . . Possibly she'll think about a time when she loved someone else . . . and she'll answer no.

MAX: Well, that would also be quite interesting.

ANATOL: I think . . . I know Cora met others before me. . . . She once told me herself, "Yes, if I had known that someday I would meet you . . . then . . ."

MAX: But she didn't know.

ANATOL: No . . .

MAX: And as for your question . . .

ANATOL: Yes. . . . This question . . . I find it crude, at least in that form.

MAX: Well then, pose it something like this: "Cora, have you been faithful to me since the time you've known me?"

ANATOL: Hmm . . . That might be something. [*In front of* CORA] Cora! Have you been . . . ? That's also nonsense!

MAX: Nonsense?!

ANATOL: I ask you . . . just imagine how we got to know each other. We didn't sense that we would come to love each other so madly. Those first days we both regarded the whole thing as something passing. Who knows . . .

MAX: Who knows . . . ?

ANATOL: Who knows if she didn't begin to love me—only after she stopped loving someone else? What did she experience the day before I met her, before we spoke our first words to each other? Was it possible for her just to break away like that, without much ado? Or did she maybe *have to* drag along someone else from her past, I say, like an old chain behind her for days and weeks?

MAX: Hmm.

ANATOL: I want to go on even further. . . . The first time it was certainly just a mood of hers—like with me. Neither of us could look at it any differently, we didn't demand anything from each other than a fleeting, sweet happiness. What can I reproach her for, if she committed any wrong during that time? Nothing—nothing at all.

MAX: You're being characteristically gentle.

ANATOL: No, by no means, I just think it's ignoble to take advantage of a momentary situation in that way.

MAX: Well, that's surely a noble intent. But I want to help you out of that embarrassment.

ANATOL: . . . ?

MAX: You ask her as follows: "Cora, since you've loved me . . . have you been faithful to me?"

ANATOL: That sounds very clear in fact.

MAX: . . . Well?

ANATOL: But it's by no means clear.

MAX: Oh!

ANATOL: Faithful! What does that actually mean: faithful? . . . Picture for yourself . . . yesterday she was riding on the train, and a gentleman sitting across from her touched the tip of her foot with his. But surely one mustn't rule out that she'll see even that as a breach of faith, thanks to her characteristically refined sensitivity no doubt associated with her being a hypnotic medium. Hypnosis raises that perceptive ability to an infinite level, of course.

MAX: Well, listen to that!

ANATOL: All the more so when she became acquainted with my perhaps somewhat exaggerated views through the conversations we were sometimes accustomed to having on that theme. I myself told her, "Cora, even when you simply take a look at another man, even that is being unfaithful to me!"

MAX: And what did she do?

ANATOL: And she, she laughed in my face and said just how could I believe that she would look at another man.

MAX: And you still believe—?

ANATOL: Things do happen—picture it yourself—a pushy fellow follows her in the evenings and presses a kiss on the back of her neck.

MAX: Well—that . . .

ANATOL: Well—that's surely not impossible—after all!

MAX: Then you don't want to ask her.

ANATOL: Oh still—after all . . .

MAX: Everything you've brought up is nonsense. Believe me, women don't misunderstand us when we ask them about their faithfulness. If you were now to whisper to her in an affectionate, lovesick voice, "Are you being faithful to me . . . ?" she won't think about the tip of any gentleman's foot, nor about any pushy fellow's kiss on her neck—but she'll think only about what we commonly understand by unfaithfulness. That still gives you the advantage of being able to pose further questions, if her answers are insufficient. That would have to clear up everything.

ANATOL: So you really want me to ask her . . .

MAX: I? . . . You certainly wanted to!

ANATOL: Something else has just occurred to me, you see.

MAX: What, in fact . . . ?

ANATOL: The unconscious!

MAX: The unconscious?

ANATOL: I believe in unconscious states, you see.

MAX: Really.

ANATOL: Such states can originate on their own, but they can also be produced, artificially . . . by a narcotic or by intoxicating means.

MAX: Don't you want to explain yourself more clearly . . . ?

ANATOL: Visualize a room in twilight, with the right atmosphere.

MAX: In twilight . . . with the right atmosphere . . . I'm visualizing.

ANATOL: She's in this room . . . and so is someone else.

MAX: Yes, but how did she get there?

ANATOL: I want to leave that open for the time being. There are certainly pretexts . . . Enough! Such a thing can occur. Well—a couple of glasses of Rhine wine . . . a characteristically sultry atmosphere weighing heavily on it all, the smell of cigarettes, scented tapestries, the faint glow of a glass chandelier and red curtains—solitude—quietness—just the whispering of sweet words . . .

MAX: . . . !

ANATOL: Well, others have succumbed to that before! Better and calmer than she is!

MAX: Oh well, I just can't see how that fits with the concept of faithfulness, to accompany someone to such a chamber.

ANATOL: Such mysterious things do happen . . .

MAX: Well, my friend, you do have the solution to one of those mysteries which have shattered the most brilliant male minds before you; you need only speak, and you will know everything you want to know. One question—and you will find out if you are one of the few who are loved *exclusively.* You can find out where your rival is, find out how he succeeded in his victory over you—and you don't say this exactly!—You get to ask one question to fate! But you don't pose it! You torment yourself days and nights, you'd give up half your life for the truth. Now it lies before you and you won't bend down to pick it up! And why not? Because it might just occur that a woman you love is really like you feel they all should be—and because you prefer your illusion a thousand times more than the truth. Enough of playing, then. Awaken this girl and let it be enough for your pride to know that you could have accomplished—a miracle!

ANATOL: Max!

MAX: Well, maybe I'm wrong? Don't you know yourself that all the things you told me earlier were evasions, empty phrases with which you could delude neither me nor yourself?

ANATOL [*swiftly*]: Max . . . Just let me tell you, I want to, yes, I do want to ask her!

MAX: Ah!

ANATOL: But don't be angry with me—not in front of you!

MAX: Not in front of me?

ANATOL: If I have to hear that dreadful thing, if she answers me, "No, I was not faithful"—then I alone should be the one to hear it. To be unhappy and unfortunate—that is only half of it. To be pitied—that is all of it! . . . I don't want that. You are, after all, my best friend, but precisely for that reason I don't want your eyes looking on me with that expression of pity which tells an unfortunate one just how wretched he is. Perhaps it's something else as well—perhaps I'm ashamed in front of you. You'll certainly find out the truth, after all—you've seen this girl with me today for the last time, if she has deceived me! But you shouldn't hear it at the same time I do, that's what I couldn't endure. Do you understand that . . . ?

MAX: Yes, my friend [*pressing his hand*], and I'll also leave you alone with her.

ANATOL: My friend! [*Escorting him to the door*] I'll call you back in less than a minute!—

[MAX *exits.*]

ANATOL [*stands in front of* CORA . . . *looks at her for a long time*]: Cora!—

[*He shakes his head, walks around.*]

Cora!—

[*He gets on his knees in front of her.*]

Cora! My sweet Cora!—Cora! [*Arising resolvedly*] Wake up . . . and kiss me!

CORA [*arises, rubs her eyes, grabbing him around the neck*]: Anatol! Did I sleep a long time? . . . Well, where's Max?

ANATOL: Max!

MAX [*coming from the adjacent room*]: Here I am!

ANATOL: Yes . . . you slept for a rather long time—you were also talking in your sleep.

CORA: For God's sake! I didn't say anything wrong, did I?—

MAX: You just answered his questions.

CORA: Well, what did he ask?

MAX: Thousands of things! . . .

CORA: And I always answered? Always?

ANATOL: Always.

CORA: And may one know what you asked?—

ANATOL: No, one may not! And tomorrow I'll hypnotize you again!

CORA: Oh no! Never again! After all, that's witchcraft. One is asked questions and doesn't know anything about it after waking up.—I must have prattled pure nonsense.

ANATOL: Yes . . . for example, that you love me . . .

CORA: Really.

MAX: She doesn't believe it! That's very good!

CORA: But look here . . . I certainly could've also told you that while awake!

ANATOL: My sweet angel!

[*They embrace.*]

MAX: My dear sir and my dear lady . . . adieu!—

ANATOL: Are you going so soon?

MAX: I must.

ANATOL: Don't be angry that I'm not escorting you.—

CORA: Good-bye!

MAX: Not at all. [*At the door*] One thing is clear to me: that women also lie during hypnosis. . . . But they're happy—and that is the main thing. Adieu, dear children.

[*They don't hear him, since they are locked in a passionate embrace.*]

[*Curtain*]

CHRISTMAS SHOPPING

[*Christmas Eve, six o'clock. Light snowfall in the streets of Vienna.*]

ANATOL: My lady, my lady . . . !

GABRIELE: What? . . . Ah, it's you!

ANATOL: Yes! . . . I'm pursuing you!—I can't stand to see the way you're dragging all those things!—Just let me take your packages!

GABRIELE: No, no, thank you!—I'll just carry it all myself!

ANATOL: But I ask you, my lady, just don't make it so very hard for me, if for once I want to be gallant.

GABRIELE: Well—that one thing there . . .

ANATOL: But that's certainly nothing at all . . . Just give me . . . So . . . that . . . and that . . .

GABRIELE: Enough, enough—you're too generous!

ANATOL: If one can be that sort of person just for once—it's truly such a pleasure!

GABRIELE: But you demonstrate your gallantry only in the street and—when it's snowing.

ANATOL: . . . And when it's late in the evening—and when it happens to be Christmas—eh?

GABRIELE: Why, it's a sheer miracle to see you for a change!

ANATOL: Yes, yes . . . you mean that I haven't paid you even one visit this year—

GABRIELE: Yes, I do mean something like that!

ANATOL: My lady—I'm not making any visits at all this year—none at all! And—how are things going for your fine husband?—And what are your dear little ones doing?—

GABRIELE: You can spare yourself such questions!—I'm well aware all that interests you very little!

ANATOL: It's uncanny to meet someone who knows people so well!
GABRIELE: I know—you!
ANATOL: Not as well as I would wish!
GABRIELE: Refrain from such remarks! Will you—?
ANATOL: My lady—I can't do that!
GABRIELE: Then give me back my little packages!
ANATOL: Don't be angry—don't be angry!!—You see, I'm behaving myself again . . .

[*They walk alongside each other silently.*]

GABRIELE: Surely you can say something or other!
ANATOL: Something or other—yes—but your censure is so severe . . .
GABRIELE: Just tell me something. Well, we haven't seen each other for such a long time now . . . What are you actually doing?
ANATOL: As usual, I'm doing nothing!
GABRIELE: Nothing?
ANATOL: Nothing at all!
GABRIELE: That's too bad for you!
ANATOL: Well . . . That doesn't make much difference to you!
GABRIELE: How can you claim that?
ANATOL: Why am I squandering my life?—Who's at fault?—Who?
GABRIELE: Give me the packages!—
ANATOL: I certainly didn't blame anyone. . . . Not anyone in particular . . .
GABRIELE: No doubt you go for walks all the time?
ANATOL: Walking! You put such a contemptuous tone into that! As if there were anything more beautiful!—That word implies something splendidly unpredictable!—By the way, it doesn't apply to me at all today—today I'm busy, my lady—exactly like you!—
GABRIELE: How's that?
ANATOL: I'm also buying Christmas presents!—
GABRIELE: You?!
ANATOL: I'm just not finding anything proper!—In the process I've been standing at all the shopwindows in all the streets every

evening for weeks now!—But the merchants have no taste and no inventive genius.

GABRIELE: That's exactly what the buyer must have! When one has as little to do as you, one reflects, one does the inventing oneself—and orders the presents in advance, during autumn.—

ANATOL: Ah, I'm not the person for that! Does one even know in autumn to whom one will be giving something at Christmas?—And two hours from now we're back to the Christmas tree—and I still haven't the slightest notion, not the slightest—!

GABRIELE: Shall I help you?

ANATOL: My lady . . . You are an angel—but don't take the little packages away from me . . .

GABRIELE: No, no . . .

ANATOL: So one may say angel!—That's beautiful—angel!—

GABRIELE: Would you kindly be silent?

ANATOL: I'm quite calm again, really.

GABRIELE: So—give me some sort of hint. . . . For whom should your gift be appropriate?

ANATOL: That is . . . hard to say, actually . . .

GABRIELE: For a lady, naturally?!

ANATOL: Well, yes—as—I've already said, you know people well!

GABRIELE: Oh come now . . . what kind of lady?—A real lady?

ANATOL: . . . Now first we must come to some agreement about that concept! If you mean a lady of high society—then it's not completely true . . .

GABRIELE: So . . . of common society? . . .

ANATOL: Good—let's say of common society.—

GABRIELE: Actually, I should've imagined that . . .

ANATOL: Just don't be sarcastic!

GABRIELE: I certainly do know your taste. . . . It's probably one of them from the streetcar line again—thin and blond!

ANATOL: Blond—I admit . . . !

GABRIELE: . . . Yes, yes . . . blond . . . it's remarkable that you always get involved with such lower-class ladies—always!

ANATOL: My lady—it's not *my* fault.

GABRIELE: Refrain from that—sir!—Oh, it's also just as well that you stay with your kind . . . it would be quite wrong for you to leave the scenes of your triumphs . . .

ANATOL: But what should I do then—it's only out there that I'm loved . . .

GABRIELE: Are you understood then . . . out there?

ANATOL: By no means!—But you see . . . only in common society am I loved; in high society—I'm just understood—you certainly know . . .

GABRIELE: I don't know anything at all . . . and I don't want to know anything further!—Come here . . . that is just the right shop there . . . let's buy something there for your common lady . . .

ANATOL: My lady!—

GABRIELE: Oh well . . . just look . . . there . . . That small jewel case with three different perfumes . . . or this one here with six soaps . . . Exotic Herb . . . Chypre . . . Jockey Club—that should be something after all—shouldn't it?!

ANATOL: My lady—that's not *nice* of you!

GABRIELE: Or wait, here . . . !—Do look . . . This little brooch with the six artificial diamonds—just think—six!—Just look how that glitters!—Or this delightful little bracelet with the heavenly pendants . . . Ah—one even represents a veritable Moor's head!—That should have a huge effect . . . in the lower-class world! . . .

ANATOL: My lady—you're mistaken! You don't know these girls—they're different from what you imagine . . .

GABRIELE: And there . . . ah, how delightful!—Do come closer—well—what do you say to that hat?! The shape was extremely stylish . . . two years ago! And the feathers—how those things do flutter—don't they?! That should make a colossal stir—out there!

ANATOL: My lady . . . we never spoke about there . . . and by the way, you're also probably underrating their taste out there . . .

GABRIELE: Right . . . you're really making it difficult—well, just come to my aid—give me a hint—

ANATOL: How shall I . . . ?! No doubt you would only give a superior smile—in any case!

GABRIELE: Oh no, oh no!—Just enlighten me . . . ! Is she vain—or modest?—Is she large or small?—Does she have a passion for bright colors . . . ?

ANATOL: I shouldn't have accepted your kindness!—Why, you're mocking!

GABRIELE: Oh no, I'm listening, really!—Just tell me something about her!

ANATOL: I don't dare to—

GABRIELE: Go ahead, dare to! . . . How long have you . . . ?

ANATOL: Let's stop that!

GABRIELE: I insist on that!—How long have you known her?

ANATOL: For—some time!

GABRIELE: Don't just let me interrogate you this way. . . . Tell me the whole story . . . !

ANATOL: There's just no story to tell!

GABRIELE: But what about where you got to know her, and how and when and just what kind of person she is—I'd like to know that!

ANATOL: Fine—but it's boring—and I'm telling you so!

GABRIELE: It'll certainly interest me. I'd really like to find out something about this world for once!—Just what kind of a world is it?—I just don't know anything about it!

ANATOL: You also wouldn't understand anything about it!

GABRIELE: Oh, sir!

ANATOL: You have such a summary contempt for everything which isn't in your sphere!—Very unjust.

GABRIELE: But I'm really so teachable!—They really don't tell me about anything from that world!—How am I supposed to know it?

ANATOL: But . . . you have this vague feeling that—they'll take from you out there. A quiet hostility!

GABRIELE: Now please—they'll not take away anything from me—if I want to keep it.

ANATOL: Yes . . . but if you don't want something or other for yourself . . . it still annoys you if someone else gets it, doesn't it?—

GABRIELE: Oh—!

ANATOL: My lady . . . That's so like a woman! And because it's so like a woman—it's probably extremely noble and beautiful and profound, too . . . !

GABRIELE: Just where do you get your irony!!

ANATOL: Where do I get it?—I want to tell you. Once I was kind too—and full of trust—and there was no scorn in my words. . . . And I quietly endured many a wound—

GABRIELE: Just don't start getting sentimental!

ANATOL: Those honorable wounds—of course!—A "no" at the right time, even from the most beloved lips—I could get over that.—But a "no" when the lips were saying "perhaps!" a hundred times—when the lips were smiling "it may be" a hundred times,—when the tone of voice was sounding like "certainly" a hundred times—such a "no" turns a person into—

GABRIELE: We really wanted to buy something!

ANATOL: A "no" like that turns a man into a fool . . . or a cynic!

GABRIELE: . . . You really wanted to . . . tell me something—

ANATOL: Fine—by all means, if you want me to tell you something . . .

GABRIELE: Certainly I want that! . . . How did you get to know her . . . ?

ANATOL: Lord—simply the way one gets to know somebody!—In the street—at a dance—in a bus—beneath an umbrella—

GABRIELE: But—you surely know—I'm interested in this specific case. We do want to buy something for this specific case!

ANATOL: Over there, in . . . "common society," there just aren't any specific cases . . . actually, there aren't any in high society either . . . All of you are just so typical!

GABRIELE: My dear sir! Now you're starting—

ANATOL: Well, that's nothing insulting—not at all!—I'm just a type, too!

GABRIELE: And what kind, then?

ANATOL: A thoughtless melancholic!

GABRIELE: . . . And . . . and I?

ANATOL: You?—quite simply: a fashionable woman!

GABRIELE: So . . . ! . . . And she!?

ANATOL: She . . . ? She . . . a sweet young girl!

GABRIELE: Sweet! Nothing less than "sweet"?—And I—just a "fashionable woman"—

ANATOL: An angry fashionable woman—if you insist . . .

GABRIELE: So . . . just tell me now about the . . . sweet young girl!

ANATOL: She's not fascinatingly beautiful—she isn't especially elegant—and she's by no means brilliant . . .

GABRIELE: Well, I certainly don't want to know what she *isn't*—

ANATOL: But she has the soft grace of an evening in spring . . . and the charm of an enchanted princess . . . and the spirit of a girl who knows how to love!

GABRIELE: That kind of spirit apparently is very widespread . . . in your common world! . . .

ANATOL: You can't project yourself into that world! . . . They kept too many secrets from you when you were a little girl—and they've said too much to you since you've been a young woman! . . . This has resulted in your naive views—

GABRIELE: But nevertheless you've heard—I want to be enlightened . . . I really do believe you about the "enchanted princess"!—But tell me about what the enchanted garden looks like, in which she resides—

ANATOL: Of course you mustn't imagine a sparkling salon there, where the heavy portieres descend—with bouquets of dried flowers in the corners, trinkets, shining towers, subdued velvet, and the affected semidarkness of a dying afternoon.

GABRIELE: I really don't want to know what I'm *not* supposed to imagine.

ANATOL: So—picture it—a small room in twilight—so small—with painted walls—and yet somewhat too light as well—a couple of old, cheap engravings with faded inscriptions hanging here and there.—A hanging lamp with shade.—When it turns evening, the window offers a prospect on chimneys and roofs sinking into the darkness! . . . And—when springtime comes, then the garden across the street will blossom and smell so sweet . . .

GABRIELE: How happy you must be to be already thinking about May at Christmas!

ANATOL: Yes—*there* I'm even happy at times!

GABRIELE: Enough, enough!—It's getting late . . . we wanted to buy something for her! . . . Perhaps something for the room with the painted walls . . .

ANATOL: Nothing is needed there!

GABRIELE: Of course . . . for her!—I do believe that!—But for you—yes, for you! I'd like to decorate the room quite properly, in your style!

ANATOL: For me?

GABRIELE: With Persian carpets . . .

ANATOL: But I ask you—there?!

GABRIELE: With a hanging vase of bent red-green glass . . . ?

ANATOL: Hmm!

GABRIELE: A couple of vases with fresh flowers?

ANATOL: Yes . . . but I also want to take her something—

GABRIELE: Ah yes . . . it's true—we have to decide—no doubt she is already waiting for you?

ANATOL: Absolutely!

GABRIELE: She's waiting?—Tell me . . . just how does she welcome you?

ANATOL: Ah—the way one simply welcomes somebody.—

GABRIELE: She hears your steps outside on the stairs . . . right?

ANATOL: Yes . . . at times . . .

GABRIELE: And is standing at the door?

ANATOL: Yes!

GABRIELE: And grabs you around the neck—and kisses you—and says . . . What does she say then . . . ?

ANATOL: Just what one says in such cases . . .

GABRIELE: Well . . . for example!

ANATOL: I don't know any examples!

GABRIELE: What did she say yesterday?

ANATOL: Ah—nothing special . . . it sounds so simple when you don't hear the tone of her voice with it . . . !

GABRIELE: I really want to imagine that too: well—what did she say?

ANATOL: . . . "I'm so glad that I have you again!" . . .

GABRIELE: "I'm so glad"—that what?

ANATOL: "That I have you again!" . . .

GABRIELE: . . . That's actually pretty—very pretty!—

ANATOL: Yes . . . it's affectionate and honest!

GABRIELE: And she is . . . always alone?—You can see each other undisturbed like that?!—

ANATOL: Oh well—she lives by herself—she's quite alone—no father, no mother . . . not even an aunt!

GABRIELE: And you . . . are everything for her . . . ?

ANATOL: . . . Possibly! . . . Today . . .

[*Silence.*]

GABRIELE: . . . It's getting so late—do you see how empty the streets are already so empty . . .

ANATOL: Oh—I've held you up!—You must have to go home.

GABRIELE: Of course—of course! They're already expecting me!—Just how are we going to do it about that present . . . ?

ANATOL: Oh—I'll just find some trifle or other . . .

GABRIELE: Who knows, who knows?—And I just have it in my head that I . . . that I . . . want to select something for your . . . for this . . . girl . . . !

ANATOL: But I ask you, my lady!

GABRIELE: . . . I'd like most to be there when you take her the Christmas present! . . . I've such a desire to see the little room and the sweet girl!—She really doesn't know what a good situation she has!

ANATOL: . . .

GABRIELE: But now give me the little packages!—It's getting so late . . .

ANATOL: Yes, yes! Here they are—but . . .

GABRIELE: Please—wave to that coach there, coming toward us . . .

ANATOL: Such a hurry all of a sudden?!

GABRIELE: Please, please! [*Waving*] I thank you . . . ! But now what are we going to do about the present . . . ?

[*The coach has stopped, he and she stand still; he starts to open the door of the coach.*]

GABRIELE: Wait! . . . I would like to give her something too . . .

ANATOL: You . . . ?! My lady, you too . . .

GABRIELE: Whatever?!—Here . . . take . . . these flowers . . . quite simply, these flowers . . . ! It's to be nothing more than a greeting, nothing further. . . . But . . . you must present her something with that.—

ANATOL: My lady—you're so kind—

GABRIELE: Promise me you'll deliver it to her . . . and with the words I want to impart to you now—

ANATOL: Certainly.

GABRIELE: Do you promise me?

ANATOL: Yes . . . with pleasure! And why not?

GABRIELE [*having opened the door of the coach*]: Then tell her . . .

ANATOL: Well . . . ?

GABRIELE: Tell her: "These flowers, my . . . sweet girl, are sent you by a woman who can perhaps love just like you and who didn't have the courage to . . ."

ANATOL: My . . . lady?!—

[*She has climbed into the coach.—The coach rolls away, the streets have grown almost empty of people. He gazes after the coach for a long time, until it has turned around a corner. . . . He stands still a while longer, then he looks at his watch and hurries off swiftly.*]

[*Curtain*]

AN EPISODE

[MAX's *room, kept quite dark; dark red portieres. A door in the background, center stage. A second door to the left of the audience. In the middle of the room is a large writing desk; on it a shaded lamp, books, and papers. A tall window to the right. In a secluded corner to the right a fireplace with a blazing fire, two low armchairs in front, a dark red fire screen casually set alongside.*]

MAX [*seated in front of the desk and reading a letter while smoking a cigar*]: "My dear Max! Here I am again. Our company is staying here three months, as you've no doubt read in the newspaper. The first evening is for friendship. I'll be at your house this evening. Bibi" . . . Bibi . . . so Bianca . . . Well, I'll be expecting her.

[*Someone knocks.*]

Could that be her already . . . ? Come in!

ANATOL [*enters gloomily, carrying a large package under his arm*]: Good evening!

MAX: Ah—what have you brought?

ANATOL: I'm seeking asylum for my past.

MAX: How am I to understand that?

[ANATOL *holds out the package toward him.*]

MAX: Well?

ANATOL: Here I'm bringing you my past, my whole youthful life. Take it into your home.

MAX: With pleasure. But won't you please explain yourself further?

ANATOL: May I sit down?

MAX: Certainly. And by the way, why are you in such a festive mood?

ANATOL [*has sat down*]: May I light up a cigar?

MAX: Here! Take them, they're from the latest crop.

ANATOL [*lighting up one of the cigars offered him*]: Ah—excellent!

MAX [*pointing to the package* ANATOL *has put onto the desk*]: And . . . ?

ANATOL: This youthful life cannot be lodged in my house anymore! I'm leaving the city.

MAX: Ah!

ANATOL: I'm beginning a new life, for the time being. To do that I must be free and alone, and therefore I disengage myself from the past.

MAX: So you have a new sweetheart.

ANATOL: No—it's just I no longer have the old one for the present . . . [*quickly breaking off and pointing to the package*]—my dear friend, I let all this trumpery rest at your house.

MAX: Trumpery, you say—! Why don't you just burn it?

ANATOL: I can't.

MAX: That's childish.

ANATOL: Oh no, that's just my kind of faithfulness. I can't forget any of them I loved. When I rummage through these leaves, flowers, and locks of hair this way—you'll have to permit me to come over here sometimes just to rummage—then I'm at their side again, then they live again and I'm adoring them anew.

MAX: So you want to provide yourself a place to rendezvous with old sweethearts in my dwelling . . . ?

ANATOL [*scarcely listening to him*]: Sometimes I've such thoughts . . . If only there were a way of commanding them all to appear again! If only I could conjure them up out of the void!

MAX: This void could be various kinds of things.

ANATOL: Yes, yes it might be . . . imagine that if I were to pronounce a certain word . . .

MAX: Perhaps you'll find an effective one . . . for example, "one and only darling"!

ANATOL: So I'll call: One and only darling . . . ! And now they come, the one from some small cottage in the common world, another from the ostentatious salon of her fine husband—one from the hat check of her theater—

MAX: Several!

ANATOL: Several—fine . . . one from the women's clothing store—

MAX: One from the arms of a new sweetheart—

ANATOL: One from the grave . . . one from here—one from there—and now they're all here . . .

MAX: You'd better not pronounce that word. This gathering could get uncomfortable, since they may have stopped loving you—but none has stopped being jealous.

ANATOL: Very prudent. . . . Therefore rest in peace.

MAX: But now that calls for finding a place for this stately packet.

ANATOL: You'll have to spread it out.

[*He tears open the package, revealing neat packets held together by ribbons.*]

MAX: Ah!

ANATOL: It's all nicely arranged.

MAX: By names?

ANATOL: Oh no. Every packet bears some inscription or other: a verse, a word, a remark recalling for my memory the whole experience. Nobody's name—for in the end each of them could be named Marie or Anna.

MAX: Go ahead and read.

ANATOL: Will I know you all again? Many a packet lies here for years without my even looking at it.

MAX [*taking one of the little packages in his hand, reads parts of the inscription*]: "Mathilde, so delightfully beautiful . . . impetuously charming . . . Let me clasp you . . . kiss your neck . . . wondrously sweet . . . ! . . ." Isn't that a name, after all—? Mathilde!

ANATOL: Yes, Mathilde.—But that wasn't her name. All the same, I kissed her neck.

MAX: Who was she?

ANATOL: Don't ask. She lay in my arms, that suffices.

MAX: So away with that Mathilde.—A very thin packet, by the way.

ANATOL: Yes, there's only one lock of hair in it.

MAX: No letters at all?

ANATOL: Oh—not from that one! It would've been terribly difficult for her. But where would we wind up if all the women wrote us letters! So away with that Mathilde.

MAX [*reads from another packet*]: "All women are, in one respect, the same: they become insolent when caught in a lie."

ANATOL: Yes, that is true!

MAX: Who was this one? A weighty packet!

ANATOL: Eight pages of pure lies! Away with it.

MAX: And was she also insolent?

ANATOL: When I pointed it out to her. Away with her.

MAX: Away with the insolent, lying woman.

ANATOL: No aspersions. She lay in my arms—she's sacred.

MAX: At least that's a good reason. So, to go on. [*Reading from another packet*] "To fan away bad spirits, my dear sweet treasure . . . I think of your fiancé . . . and I must give a smile, for there are things that are far too wild . . ."

ANATOL [*smiling*]: Ah yes, that's the one.

MAX: Ah—just what's in there?

ANATOL: A photo. Of her and her fiancé.

MAX: Did you know him?

ANATOL: Naturally, otherwise I wouldn't have smiled. He was a dolt.

MAX [*seriously*]: He lay in her arms, he's sacred.

ANATOL: Enough.

MAX: Away with the wild, sweet child, complete with ridiculous fiancé. [*Taking a new packet*] What's this? Just one word?

ANATOL: Which one then?

MAX: "Slap."

ANATOL: Oh, now I remember.

MAX: That was no doubt how it concluded?

ANATOL: Oh no, how it started.

MAX: Ah yes! And here . . . "It's easier to change the direction of a flame than to kindle one."—What does that mean?

ANATOL: Well, I changed the direction of the flame, someone else kindled it.

MAX: Away with the flame. . . . "She always brought her curling iron."

[*He looks at* ANATOL *questioningly.*]

ANATOL: Oh yes, she simply always brought her curling iron—always prepared. But she was very pretty. By the way, I have just a piece of her veil.

MAX: Yes, it feels like that. . . . [*Reading further*] "How did I lose you?" . . . Well, how did you lose her?

ANATOL: I don't exactly know that. She was gone—out of my life, suddenly. I assure you that sometimes happens. It is as when you leave an umbrella somewhere and you only remember many days later. . . . Then you no longer know when and where.

MAX: Adieu, lost woman. [*Reading another packet*] "You were a dear, sweet creature—"

ANATOL [*continuing dreamily*]: "Girl with the pricked fingers."

MAX: That was Cora—wasn't it?

ANATOL: Of course—you knew her, of course.

MAX: Do you know what's become of her?

ANATOL: I ran into her again later—as a master carpenter's wife.

MAX: Truly!

ANATOL: Yes, that's the way seamstresses with pricked fingers end up. They find love in the city and marriage in the common world . . . there was a darling!

MAX: Farewell—! And what's this? . . . "Episode"—isn't there anything in here? . . . Dust!

ANATOL [*taking the wrapper in his hand*]: Dust—? This was once a flower!

MAX: What does that mean: "Episode"?

ANATOL: Ah nothing, a mere thought. It was just an episode, a novel of two hours . . . nothing! . . . Yes, dust!—It's actually sad that nothing else is left behind from so much sweetness—isn't it?

MAX: Yes, that's certainly sad . . . but how did you arrive at that word? Couldn't you have written it on all of them?

ANATOL: Yes, indeed, but I was never conscious of it in those days. When I was with this one or that, it frequently lay on my lips, especially in the earlier times, when I still thought so very much of myself, it lay on my lips:—"You poor child—you poor child—!"

MAX: Why?

ANATOL: Well, I considered myself one of the intellectually mighty. I ground them—those ladies and girls—beneath my brazen feet which I tramped over the earth. Universal law, I thought—I must trample you all.

MAX: You were the strong gale sweeping away the blossoms . . . weren't you?

ANATOL: Yes! I stormed along like that. Thus I simply thought "you poor, poor child." Actually I was deceiving myself. Today I know I don't belong to the mighty, and that's what's so sad—I've accommodated myself to that. But in those days . . . !

MAX: Well, and the episode?

ANATOL: Yes, she too was simply one of . . . She was one of the people I found on my way.

MAX: And ground into the earth.

ANATOL: Do you see, when I consider it, it seems to me I really did grind her into the earth.

MAX: Ah!

ANATOL: Yes, just listen. It's actually the most beautiful of all the things I've experienced. . . . I can't tell you, not at all.

MAX: Why not?

ANATOL: Because the event is as ordinary as can be. . . . It's . . . nothing. You can in no way sense the beautiful nature of it. The mystery of the whole matter is that I experienced it.

MAX: Well—?

ANATOL: So I was sitting there in front of my piano . . . It was in the little room I inhabited in those days . . . evening . . . I've known her for two hours . . . My green and red hanging lamp is burning—I mention the green and red lamp, that's also part of it.

MAX: Well?

ANATOL: Well! So I'm at the piano. She is—at my feet, so that I couldn't reach the pedal. Her head is lying in my lap and her tangled hair glistens green and red from the lamp. I'm improvising on the piano, but just with my left hand, she's pressed my right hand to her lips . . .

MAX: Well?

ANATOL: Always your expectant "Well . . . ?" Actually there's nothing further . . . So I've known her for two hours, I also know I'll probably never see her again after this evening—she's told me that—and at the same time I feel I'm loved madly at this moment. That envelops me so completely—the entire atmosphere was intoxicating and smelled so sweetly of this love. . . . Do you understand me?

[MAX *nods.*]

—And again I had this foolish thought: you poor—poor child! I was so clearly conscious of the episodic nature of this event. While I felt the warm breath from her mouth on my hand, I was already experiencing the whole thing in my memory. She too had been one of those I had to trample. That very word occurred to me, this dry word: Episode. [*Pointing to the packet*] And at the same time I was somehow eternal. . . . I also knew the "poor child" could never get this hour out of her memories—I knew this to be so in her case. One often feels that way, of course: tomorrow morning she will have forgotten me. But this was something different. I meant the world to this girl there at my feet, I felt that with the kind of holy, imperishable love with which she enveloped me. One can sense that, that's not to be taken from me. At this moment she could surely think of no one but me—just me. But for me she was already past, fleeting, the Episode.

MAX: What was she then, actually?

ANATOL: What was she—? Well, you knew her. We got to know each other one evening at a lively gathering, but you knew her already, as you told me at the time.

MAX: Well, who was she then? I knew lots of women already. You certainly depicted her as a fairy-tale figure in the light of your lamp.

ANATOL: Yes—she wasn't that in life. Do you know what she was—? Now I'm just destroying the whole mystique.

MAX: So she was—?

ANATOL [*smiling*]: She was—from—from—

MAX: From the theater—?

ANATOL: No—from the circus.

MAX: Is that possible!

ANATOL: Yes—it was Bianca. I didn't tell you before that I met her again—after that evening I didn't care at all about her.

MAX: And do you really believe that Bibi loved you—?

ANATOL: Yes, she's the one! Eight or ten days after that festival we met on the street. . . . The following morning she had to go to Russia with her whole troupe.

MAX: So it was high time.

ANATOL: Of course I knew it, now everything has been destroyed for you. You've not yet arrived at the mystery of love.

MAX: And how is the riddle of women resolved for you?

ANATOL: In the atmosphere.

MAX: Ah—you use semidarkness, your green and red lamp . . . your piano playing.

ANATOL: Yes, that's it. And that makes life so diverse and so variable that one color can change the whole world for me. What would this girl with the glistening hair have been for you, for a thousand others, what would this lamp have been for you all, this lamp which you mock?! A circus equestrienne and a red and green glass with a light behind it! Of course the magic is gone then; no doubt one can live then, but one will never live through something. You all grope your way brutally into some adventure with open eyes, but with closed minds, and it remains colorless! But thousands of lights and colors flash up out of my soul and I can certainly feel what all of you just—enjoy!

MAX: A veritable magical spring, your "atmosphere." All whom you love plunge down into it and bring up a strange air of adventure and the unexpected in which you become enraptured.

ANATOL: Take it that way, if you want.

MAX: Well, as for your circus equestrienne, you can hardly convince me that she felt the same thing as you, beneath the green and red lamp.

ANATOL: But I sensed what she felt in my arms!

MAX: Well, I knew her too, your Bianca, and better than you did.

ANATOL: Better?

MAX: Better because we didn't love each other. For me she's not the fairy-tale figure, for me she's one of the thousand fallen women that a dreamer's fantasy loans new virginity. For me she's nothing better than hundreds of others who spring through hoops or appear in short skirts in the final quadrille.

ANATOL: So . . . so . . .

MAX: And she was nothing more. I haven't overlooked anything that was in her. You, on the contrary, saw what was not in her. Out of the rich and beautiful life of your soul you projected your fantastic youth and fervor into her empty heart, so the light of *your* light was what sparkled back to you.

ANATOL: Of course. That's also happened to me at times. But not that time. I certainly don't want to make her better than she was. I was neither the first nor the last . . . I was—

MAX: Well, what were you? . . . One of many. She was the same in your arms as in those of others. Woman in her highest moment!

ANATOL: Why did I reveal this to you? You haven't understood me.

MAX: Oh no. You have misunderstood me. I just wanted to say you may have sensed the sweetest magic, while it meant the same for her as many previous times. Well, did the world have a thousand colors for her?

ANATOL: You knew her very well?

MAX: Yes, we frequently met each other at the lively gathering to which you once accompanied me.

ANATOL: That's all it was?

MAX: That's all. But we were good friends. She had wit, we liked to chat with each other.

ANATOL: That's all it was?

MAX: That's all . . .

ANATOL: . . . And even then . . . she did love me.

MAX: Don't we want to read further . . . ? [*Taking a packet in his hand*] "If I just knew what your smile means, you with eyes of green . . ."

ANATOL: . . . By the way, do you know that her whole troupe is back in town again?

MAX: Certainly, and she as well.

ANATOL: As you say.

MAX: Quite definitely. And I'll even see her this evening.

ANATOL: What? You? Do you know where she's staying?

MAX: No. She wrote me that she's coming to my house.

ANATOL [*jumping up from the armchair*]: What? And you're just now telling me?

MAX: How does it concern you? After all, you want to be—"free and alone."

ANATOL: Hold on!

MAX: And then there's nothing sadder than warmed-over magic.

ANATOL: You mean—?

MAX: I mean you should be careful about seeing her again.

ANATOL: Because she could once again become dangerous for me?

MAX: No—because it was so beautiful that time. Go home with your sweet memories. I wouldn't try to re-create the experience.

ANATOL: You can't seriously believe I should forgo a reunion that comes so easily.

MAX: She's wiser than you. She didn't write to you. . . . Besides, she may even have forgotten you.

ANATOL: Nonsense.

MAX: You think that's impossible?

ANATOL: That makes me laugh.

MAX: Not everyone's memory gets its mood from the elixir of life which gives your memory such eternal freshness.

ANATOL: Oh—but that time!

MAX: Well?

ANATOL: It was one of those immortal times.

MAX: I hear steps out in the hallway.

ANATOL: Here she is at last.

MAX: Go, withdraw through my bedroom.

ANATOL: I'd be a fool to do that.

MAX: Go—why do you want the magic destroyed for you?

ANATOL: I'm staying.

[*Knocking is heard at the door.*]

MAX: Go! Go quickly!

[ANATOL *shakes his head.*]

MAX: Then position yourself over here, so that she at least doesn't see you right away—over here . . .

[*He shoves him over to the fireplace, so that he is partly covered by the screen.*]

ANATOL [*supporting himself on the mantelpiece*]: It doesn't bother me.

[*More knocking.*]

MAX: Come in!

BIANCA [*entering sprightly*]: Good evening, dear friend. Here I am again.

MAX [*stretching out his hands to her*]: Good evening, dear Bianca, it's nice of you, really nice!

BIANCA: Then you did receive my letter? You're the very first—in fact the only one.

MAX: And you can imagine how proud I am.

BIANCA: And what are the others doing? Our Hotel Sacher gathering? Does it still exist? Will we again meet after each evening's performance?

MAX [*assisting her in removing her wraps*]: But there were evenings when you weren't to be found.

BIANCA: After the performance?

MAX: Yes, when you disappeared right after the performance.

BIANCA [*smiling*]: Ah yes . . . How nice when it's put like that—without the slightest jealousy! One also needs friends like you . . .

MAX: Yes, yes, one does.

BIANCA: Friends who love without tormenting you.

MAX: That was surely seldom the case for you!

BIANCA [*perceiving* ANATOL*'s shadow*]: You're not alone after all.

[ANATOL *steps out, bows.*]

MAX: An old acquaintance.

BIANCA [*putting her lorgnette to her eyes*]: Ah . . .

ANATOL [*stepping closer*]: Fräulein . . .

MAX: What do you say to this surprise, Bibi?

BIANCA [*somewhat embarrassed, visibly searching among her memories*]: Ah really, we do know each other . . .

ANATOL: Certainly—Bianca.

BIANCA: Naturally—we know each other very well . . .

ANATOL [*seizing and holding on to her right hand with both hands, clearly worked up*]: Bianca . . .

BIANCA: Just where was it we met . . . just where . . . ah yes!

ANATOL: Do you remember . . .

BIANCA: Of course . . . Right . . . it was in St. Petersburg . . . ?

ANATOL [*swiftly letting go of her hand*]: It was . . . not in St. Petersburg, Fräulein . . .

[*He turns to leave.*]

BIANCA [*nervously to* MAX]: What's wrong with him? . . . Have I insulted him?

MAX: There, he's slinking away . . .

[ANATOL *has disappeared through the door in the background.*]

BIANCA: Well, what does that mean?

MAX: Well, didn't you recognize him?

BIANCA: Recognize . . . yes, yes. But I don't quite know where or when did we . . . ?

MAX: But Bibi, it was Anatol!

BIANCA: Anatol—? . . . Anatol . . . ?

MAX: Anatol—piano—hanging lamp . . . such a red and green . . . here in the city—three years ago . . .

BIANCA [*touching her forehead*]: Where were my eyes then? Anatol! [*Running over to the door*] I have to call him back . . . [*Opening the door*] Anatol! [*Running out, behind the set into the staircase*] Anatol! Anatol!

MAX [*stands there smiling, having followed her up to the door*]: Well?

BIANCA [*entering*]: He must be down in the street already. May I?! [*Quickly opening the window*] There he goes down there.

MAX: Yes, there he is.

BIANCA [*calls*]: Anatol!

MAX: He can no longer hear you.

BIANCA [*gently stamping her foot on the floor*]: What a pity. . . . You must apologize to him for me. I've hurt him, the dear, good person.

MAX: So you do remember him after all?

BIANCA: Well, certainly. But . . . he looks confusingly like someone in St. Petersburg.

MAX [*reassuringly*]: I'll tell him that.

BIANCA: And then, when you don't think about somebody for three years and suddenly he's standing there—you can't remember everything, can you?

MAX: I'll close the window. There's a cold breeze coming in.

[*He closes the window.*]

BIANCA: I'll still see him while I'm here, won't I?

MAX: Perhaps. But I want to show you something.

[*He takes the wrapper from the desk and extends it to her.*]

BIANCA: What's that?

MAX: That's the flower you wore that evening—that evening.

BIANCA: He kept it?

MAX: As you see.

BIANCA: So he loved me?

MAX: Ardently, immeasurably, eternally—like all of these.

[*He points to the packets.*]

BIANCA: Like . . . all of these! . . . What does that mean? Are those only flowers too?

MAX: Flowers, letters, locks of hair, photographs. We were just about to put them in order.

BIANCA [*in an irritated tone*]: Within various headings.

MAX: Yes, obviously.

BIANCA: And which one do I come under?

MAX: I believe . . . under this one!

[*He throws the wrapper into the fireplace.*]

BIANCA: Oh!

MAX [*to himself*]: I'm avenging you as well as I can, friend Anatol . . . [*Aloud*] Then, and now don't be angry . . . Come sit down with me over here, and tell me something about the last three years.

BIANCA: Now I am quite disposed! To be received like this!

MAX: I'm your friend after all. . . . Come, Bianca . . . tell me something!

BIANCA [*letting him pull her down into the armchair beside the fireplace*]: What, then?

MAX [*alighting across from her*]: For example, about the someone "similar" in St. Petersburg.

BIANCA: You are insufferable!

MAX: So . . .

BIANCA: But what do you want me to tell you?

MAX: Just begin. . . . Once upon a time . . . well . . . once upon a time there was a large, large city . . .

BIANCA [*peevishly*]: A large, large circus was playing there.

MAX: And also there was a petite, petite artiste.

BIANCA [*laughing softly*]: Who jumped through a large, large hoop . . .

MAX: Do you see . . . It's already working!

[*The curtain begins to descend very slowly.*]

Every evening in a private box . . . well . . . every evening in a private box sat . . .

BIANCA: Every evening in a private box sat a handsome, handsome . . . Ah!

MAX: Well . . . and . . . ?

[*Curtain has descended.*]

JEWELS OF MEMORY

[EMILIE*'s room, fitted out in moderate elegance. Evening twilight. Open window with prospect onto a park. The top of a tree towers up at the window, with scarcely any foliage left.*]

EMILIE: . . . Ah . . . This is where I find you—! And in front of my desk . . . ? Just what are you doing? You're rummaging through the drawers? . . . Anatol!

ANATOL: I had every right—and I *was* right, as we now see.

EMILIE: Well—what did you find—? Your own letters?

ANATOL: What?—And this here—?

EMILIE: This here—?

ANATOL: These two little stones . . . ? The one is a ruby and this other dark one?—I'm not familiar with either of them, they're not from me . . . !

EMILIE: . . . No . . . I had . . . forgotten . . .

ANATOL: Forgotten? . . . They were so safely hidden, there in the corner of this lowest drawer. You'd better confess right now, instead of lying the way women all do. . . . So . . . you're silent? . . . Oh, that cheap indignation. . . . It's so easy to be silent when one is guilty and destroyed. . . . Well, I want to go on searching. Where have you hidden the rest of your jewelry?

EMILIE: I don't have any more.

ANATOL: Well—

[*He begins to tear open the drawers.*]

EMILIE: Stop searching . . . I swear to you I don't have anything.

ANATOL: And this . . . why is this here?

EMILIE: I was wrong . . . perhaps . . . !

ANATOL: Perhaps! . . . Emilie? We're on the eve of the day when I wanted to make you my wife. I truly believed everything past was erased. . . . Everything. . . . You and I together threw the letters, the fans into the fireplace, the ten thousand trifles reminding me of the time before we knew each other. . . . You and I together did all that. . . . The bracelets, the rings, the earrings . . . we gave them away, threw them away, they flew over the bridge into the river, through the window into the street. . . . Here you lay before me and swore to me . . . "Everything is past—and only in your arms have I sensed what love is . . ." Naturally I believed you . . . because we believe everything women tell us, which makes us happy, from the first lie on . . .

EMILIE: Am I supposed to swear to you anew?

ANATOL: What good does it do? . . . I'm finished . . . finished with you. . . . Oh how well you played that! Feverishly you stood here before the flames, as if you wanted to wash away every spot from your past, and you stood here before the glowing remains of the paper and ribbons and trinkets. . . . And how you sobbed in my arms that time we strolled along the riverbank and threw that expensive bracelet down into the gray water where it sank immediately . . . how you cried then, tears of purification, of regret. . . . Such a stupid comedy! Don't you see that everything was in vain? That I mistrusted you even then? And that I was rummaging around there with good reason? . . . Why don't you speak? . . . Why don't you defend yourself? . . .

EMILIE: Because you just want to leave me.

ANATOL: Even so I want to know what these two stones mean. . . . Why did you keep precisely *these*?

EMILIE: You don't love me anymore . . . ?

ANATOL: The truth, Emilie . . . I want to know the truth!

EMILIE: What for, if you don't love me anymore?

ANATOL: Perhaps something or other lies hidden in the truth.

EMILIE: Well, what?

ANATOL: Something to help me . . . understand the matter. . . . Do you hear, Emilie, I've no desire to regard you as a wretched woman!

EMILIE: You're pardoning me?

ANATOL: You're supposed to tell me what these stones mean!

EMILIE: And then you want to pardon me—?

ANATOL: This ruby: what does it mean and why have you kept it—?

EMILIE: . . . Will you listen to me calmly then?

ANATOL: . . . Yes! . . . But go ahead and speak . . .

EMILIE: . . . This ruby . . . it comes from a locket . . . it . . . fell out . . .

ANATOL: And who was this locket from?

EMILIE: That doesn't matter. . . . I only had it on a . . . on a certain day around—on a simple chain . . . around my neck.

ANATOL: From whom did you get it—?!

EMILIE: That's irrelevant . . . from my mother, I believe. . . . Do you see, if I were now as wretched as you believe, I'd tell you I kept it because it was from my mother—and you'd believe me. . . . But I kept this ruby because it . . . fell out of my locket on a day whose memory . . . is dear to me . . .

ANATOL: . . . Continue!

EMILIE: Ah, it's so easy when I can just tell you—Tell me, would you laugh at me, if I were jealous of your first love?

ANATOL: What's that supposed to mean?

EMILIE: And even so, that memory is something sweet to me, one of the pains which we seem to enjoy. . . . And then . . . that day is significant . . . when I got to know the feeling which binds me—to you. Oh, one must have *learned* what love is, to love as I love you! . . . Had we found each other when love was something new, who knows, we might have gone on past each other without realizing. . . . Oh, don't shake your head, Anatol, that's the way it is, and you once said so yourself—

ANATOL: I myself—?

EMILIE: Perhaps it is just as well that way, as you said, and first we both needed to be ready for this height of passion!

ANATOL: Yes . . . when we love a fallen woman we're always ready with some such consolation.

EMILIE: To be quite open with you, this ruby represents the memory of the day . . .

ANATOL: . . . Then say it . . . say it . . .

EMILIE: You know already . . . yes . . . Anatol . . . the memory of *that* day. . . . Ah . . . I was a stupid creature . . . sixteen years!

ANATOL: And he was twenty—and large and dark! . . .

EMILIE [*innocently*]: I don't know any more, my darling . . . I just remember the forest rustling around us, the spring day laughing above the trees . . . ah, I remember a ray of sunshine breaking forth amid the thicket and glittering above a multitude of flowers—

ANATOL: And you don't curse the day which took you from me, before I knew you?

EMILIE: Perhaps it gave me to you. . . . No, Anatol . . . however it may be, I don't condemn that day, and I also hate to lie to you that I ever did. . . . Anatol, you surely know—that I love you as no one ever—and as you've never been loved . . . but even if your first kiss made every hour I experienced meaningless—even if every man I encountered faded from memory—can I nevertheless forget the moment which made me a woman?

ANATOL: And you claim to love me—?

EMILIE: I can scarcely remember the features of that man's face, I no longer know how his eyes looked—

ANATOL: But you do know that you breathed the first joyous sighs in his arms . . . that this ardor first overflowed into your heart from his, which made a knowing woman out of the girl so full of misgivings, and you do know you cannot forget him in your thankful soul! And you don't realize that this confession must drive me wild, that suddenly you've roused up this whole slumbering past! . . . Yes, once again I'm reminded that you can still dream of kisses other than mine and that when you close your eyes in my arms, perhaps some other image than mine arises before them.

EMILIE: How you misunderstand me! . . . You're right, of course, if you think we should separate . . .

ANATOL: Well—how am I supposed to understand you then . . . ?

EMILIE: Just how well-off those women are, who know how to lie! No . . . you men can't bear it, the truth . . . ! Just tell me one thing more: why were you always asking it of me? "I would pardon you everything, just not a lie!" . . . I can still hear how you said it . . . And I . . . I, who confessed everything to you, who made herself so humble before you, so wretched, who screamed into your face: "Anatol, I am a lost woman, but I love you . . . !" None of the stupid evasions which other women are always making use of came over my lips.—No, I declared it: Anatol, I loved the life of pleasure, I was lustful, hot-blooded—I sold myself, gave myself away—I'm not worthy of your love. . . . Do you also remember that I told you that before you kissed my hand for the first time? . . . Yes, I wanted to flee from you, because I loved you, and you pursued me . . . you begged for my love . . . and I didn't want you, because I didn't venture to stain you, the man whom I loved more, you, whom I loved differently—ah, the first man I loved . . . ! And then you took me, and I was yours! . . . How I shuddered . . . trembled . . . wept. . . . And you lifted me up so high, you gave everything back to me again, piece by piece, which they had taken from me . . . in your impetuous arms I surely became what I had never been: pure . . . and happy . . . you were so noble . . . you could pardon . . . And now . . .

ANATOL: . . . And now . . . ?

EMILIE: And now you're simply driving me away again, because after all I'm just like the others—

ANATOL: No . . . no, you're not that.

EMILIE [*gently*]: What do you want then . . . ? Am I supposed to throw it away . . . that ruby . . . ?

ANATOL: I'm not noble, oh no . . . very, very petty . . . throw it away, this ruby . . . [*Gazing at it*] It fell out of the locket . . . it lay in the grass—among the yellow flowers . . . a ray of sunshine fell on it . . . there it lay glittering . . .

[*Long silence.*]

—Come, Emilie . . . it's getting dark outside, we want to go for a walk in the park . . .

EMILIE: Won't it be too cold . . . ?

ANATOL: Oh no, there's already the sweet smell of awakening spring . . .

EMILIE: As you wish, my darling!

ANATOL: Yes—and *this* little stone . . .

EMILIE: Ah this . . .

ANATOL: Yes, this little black one here—and what about *that* one—what about it . . . ?

EMILIE: Do you know what kind of stone that is . . . ?

ANATOL: Well—

EMILIE [*with a proud, covetous look*]: A black diamond!

ANATOL [*arising*]: Ah!

EMILIE [*keeping her look riveted on the stone*]: Rare!

ANATOL [*with suppressed rage*]: Why . . . hmm . . . why did you . . . keep that one?

EMILIE [*simply keeps looking at the stone*]: That one . . . that one is worth a quarter million! . . .

ANATOL [*crying out*]: Ah! . . .

[*He throws the stone into the fireplace.*]

EMILIE [*screams*]: What are you doing!! . . .

[*She bends down and takes the fire tongs, with which she hurriedly pokes around in the embers, in order to seek out the stone.*]

ANATOL [*looking at her for a few seconds while she kneels with glowing cheeks in front of the open fire, then calmly*]: You whore!

[*He exits.*]

[*Curtain*]

A FAREWELL SUPPER

[*A private dining room at the Hotel Sacher.* ANATOL, *standing near the door, is giving orders to the* WAITER. MAX *is reclining in an armchair.*]

MAX: Well—will you be finished soon—?

ANATOL: . . . Right away, right away!—So, is everything understood?—

[*The* WAITER *exits.*]

MAX [*as* ANATOL *comes back into the middle of the room*]: And—if she doesn't come at all?!

ANATOL: Just why "not at all!"—Now—now it's ten o'clock!—She simply isn't able to be here yet!

MAX: The ballet has been over for a long time now!

ANATOL: I ask you—until she removes her makeup—and changes her clothes!—Incidentally, I want to go over there—and wait for her!

MAX: Don't spoil her!

ANATOL: Spoil?!—If you only knew . . .

MAX: I know, I know, you treat her brutally. . . . As if that weren't a kind of spoiling too.

ANATOL: I wanted to say something quite different!—Yes . . . if you only knew . . .

MAX: Well just go ahead and say it . . .

ANATOL: I'm feeling very festive!

MAX: You finally want to get engaged to her—?

ANATOL: Oh no—much more festive!

MAX: You're marrying her tomorrow?—

ANATOL: No, how superficial you are!—As if there weren't any spiritual festivities which have nothing to do with all this external trumpery.

MAX: So—you've discovered a secluded corner of your soul which you weren't aware of until now—correct? As if she would understand any of that!

ANATOL: You're making clumsy guesses . . . I'm celebrating quite simply . . . the end!

MAX: Ah!

ANATOL: A farewell supper!

MAX: Well . . . and what am I supposed to—?

ANATOL: You are supposed to shut the eyes of our love.

MAX: Please don't make tasteless comparisons!

ANATOL: I've been delaying this supper for a week now—

MAX: Then at least you'll have a good appetite today . . .

ANATOL: . . . That is . . . we've been eating supper with each other every evening . . . this week—but—I didn't find the word, the right one! I didn't dare . . . you have no idea how nervous that makes a person!

MAX: For what purpose do you actually need me?! Am I supposed to be your prompter—

ANATOL: You're supposed to be there for all eventualities—to stand by, along with me, if it's necessary—to mitigate—reassure—make it understandable.

MAX: Wouldn't you first like to inform me why all that is supposed to happen—?

ANATOL: With pleasure! . . . Because she bores me!

MAX: So, some other woman is amusing you then—?

ANATOL: Yes . . . !

MAX: So . . . so . . . !

ANATOL: And what a woman!

MAX: What type?!

ANATOL: None at all! . . . Something new—something unique!

MAX: Oh well . . . only toward the conclusion does one arrive at the type . . .

ANATOL: Imagine a girl—how shall I say it . . . three-quarter time—

MAX: You do still seem to be under the influence of the ballet!

ANATOL: Yes . . . I just can't help you now . . . she reminds me so much of a ceremonious Viennese waltz—sentimental cheerfulness . . . smiling, impish melancholy . . . that's just her nature. . . . A tiny sweet little blond head, you know . . . so . . . well, it's hard to describe! One becomes so warm and content around her. . . . When I bring her a bouquet of violets, there's a tear in the corner of her eye . . .

MAX: Try it with a bracelet sometime!

ANATOL: Oh my dear friend—that wouldn't work in her case—you're mistaken—believe me . . . I wouldn't like to have supper *here* with this girl. . . . The simple little café is for her, the cozy place—with the tacky decorations and the minor officials at the next table!—Each of these past evenings I've been at such a place with her!

MAX: What?—But you just said that you and Annie—

ANATOL: Yes, that's the way it is too. Every evening this week I've had to eat supper twice: once with the one I wanted—and once with the one I wanted to be free of. . . . Unfortunately I have yet to succeed with either of the two . . .

MAX: Do you know?—Why not take Annie to one of those simple cafés—and the new little blond to the Hotel Sacher . . . and perhaps it will work!

ANATOL: Your lack of understanding of this comes from the fact that you don't know the new one yet. She is modesty itself!—Oh, I tell you—a girl—you should see what she does when I want to order a better wine . . . what she does!

MAX: A tear in the corner of her eye—correct?

ANATOL: She won't allow me—under no condition whatsoever! . . .

MAX: So lately you've been drinking domestic wine—?

ANATOL: Yes . . . before ten o'clock—then champagne, naturally . . . Life is like that!

MAX: Well . . . excuse me . . . life isn't like that!

ANATOL: Just picture the contrast! But now I've enjoyed it to the full!—It's once again a case where basically I feel that my disposition is enormously honest—

MAX: So! . . . Ah!

ANATOL: I can't continue this duplicity any longer . . . I'm losing all self-respect . . .

MAX: You!—I'm the one, I, I . . . you certainly don't need to put on any show for me!

ANATOL: Why—since you're already here . . . But seriously . . . I can't feign love when I no longer feel anything!

MAX: You can only feign if you do still feel something . . .

ANATOL: I told Annie candidly, right then—right then, at the very beginning . . . when we swore each other eternal love: Do you know, dear Annie—whoever of us senses one fine day that it's coming to an end—will say to the other straight out . . .

MAX: Ah, you agreed upon that at the moment you each swore eternal love . . . very good!

ANATOL: I told her repeatedly—We don't have the slightest obligation toward each other, we're free! When our time is up, we'll simply part—but no deception—I abhor that!

MAX: Well, then it'll go very smoothly after all—today!

ANATOL: Smoothly! . . . Now that I am to say it, I don't trust myself. . . It'll certainly hurt her after all . . . I can't bear any crying.—In the end I'll fall in love with her all over again, if she cries—and then I'll still be deceiving the other woman!

MAX: No, no—but no deception—I abhor that!

ANATOL: If you're here, it will be much more spontaneous! . . . A breath of cold, healthy cheerfulness emanates from you, in which the sentimentality of farewell must congeal! . . . One can't cry in front of you! . . .

MAX: Well, I'm here in any case—but that's all I can do for you. . . . Persuade her?—No, no . . . not that—it would be against my convictions . . . you're too nice a person . . .

ANATOL: Look, dear Max—perhaps you could to a certain extent. . . . You could tell her she isn't losing so very much in me after all.

MAX: Well—that still might work—

ANATOL: That she'll find hundreds of others—who are more handsome—wealthier—

MAX: More prudent—

ANATOL: No, no—please—no exaggerations—

[*The* WAITER *opens the door.* ANNIE *enters, wearing a raincoat she has thrown on, with a white boa; she is carrying yellow gloves in her hand, a strikingly wide hat clapped negligently on her head.*]

ANNIE: Oh—good evening!

ANATOL: Good evening, Annie! . . . Excuse me—

ANNIE: One can depend on you! [*Throwing the raincoat aside*]—I look around me on all sides—right—left—nobody there—

ANATOL: Fortunately you don't have far to come!

ANNIE: One keeps one's word!—Good evening, Max!—[*To* ANATOL] Well—meanwhile you could have at least sent word . . .

ANATOL [*embracing her*]: You don't have a corset on?

ANNIE: Well—perhaps I'm supposed to get all dressed up—for you?—Well excuse me—

ANATOL: That would be agreeable to me—only you must beg Max's pardon!

ANNIE: But why?—it surely doesn't bother *him*—*he's* not jealous! . . . So . . . so . . . eat—

[*The* WAITER *knocks.*]

Come in!—Today he knocks.—That doesn't occur to him as a rule!

[*The* WAITER *enters.*]

ANATOL: You will serve!

[*The* WAITER *exits.*]

ANNIE: You weren't there today—?

ANATOL: No—I had to—

ANNIE: You didn't miss much!—They were all asleep today . . .
MAX: Just what kind of act came before yours?
ANNIE: I don't know . . .

[*They sit down at the table.*]

. . . I went to my wardrobe—then onto the stage—I wasn't concerned about anything . . . anything! . . . By the way, I've got something to say to you, Anatol!

ANATOL: Really, my dear child?—Something very important—?
ANNIE: Yes, rather! . . . Perhaps it will surprise you . . .

[*The* WAITER *serves up the food . . .*]

ANATOL: Then I'm really very curious! . . . I also . . .
ANNIE: Well . . . just wait . . . this isn't something for him to hear—
ANATOL [*to the* WAITER]: Go . . . we'll ring!

[*The* WAITER *exits . . .*]

Well, then . . .

ANNIE: —Yes . . . my dear Anatol . . . it will surprise you. . . . Why, on the other hand! It won't surprise you at all—it shouldn't surprise even you . . .
MAX: Pay raise?
ANATOL: Now don't interrupt her . . . !
ANNIE: Right—dear Anatol . . . Say, are those Ostend or Whitestable?
ANATOL: Now she's talking about the oysters again! They're Ostend!
ANNIE: I thought so. . . . Ah, I have a passion for oysters. . . . Actually that's the only thing one can eat every day!
MAX: Can?!—Should! Must!!
ANNIE: Right! I say so myself!
ANATOL: So you want to inform me of something very important—?
ANNIE: Yes . . . it certainly is important—indeed, very important!—do you remember a certain remark?
ANATOL: Which one—which one?—But after all I can't know which remark you're referring to!

MAX: He's right about that!

ANNIE: Well I'm referring to the following . . . Wait . . . just what was it—"Annie," you said . . . "we don't ever want to deceive each other . . ."

ANATOL: Yes . . . yes . . . well?!

ANNIE: Never deceive! . . . Better to tell the whole truth right away . . .

ANATOL: Yes . . . I meant . . .

ANNIE: But if it's too late?—

ANATOL: What are you saying?

ANNIE: Oh—it's not too late!—I'm telling you just in time—just barely in time. . . . Perhaps tomorrow it would be too late!

ANATOL: Have you lost your mind, Annie?!

MAX: What?

ANNIE: Anatol, you must go on eating your oysters. . . . Otherwise I won't say anything . . . anything at all!

ANATOL: What does that mean?—"You must"—!

ANNIE: Eat!!

ANATOL: But you must tell me . . . I will not bear this kind of joking!

ANNIE: Well—we did agree that we should tell each other quite calmly—if it should come to this. . . . And now it's simply coming to this—

ANATOL: What are you saying?

ANNIE: I am saying that today, alas, I'm having my final supper with you!

ANATOL: Will you perhaps show me the kindness of—explaining yourself more fully?!

ANNIE: It's over between us—it has to be over . . .

ANATOL: Yes . . . now tell me—

MAX: This is superb!

ANNIE: What do you find superb in it?—Superb—or not—that's the way it is *now*!

ANATOL: My dear child—I still don't quite understand. . . . You've no doubt received an offer of marriage . . . ?

ANNIE: Ah, if only it were the case!—But that wouldn't be any reason to let you go.

ANATOL: To let me go?!

ANNIE: Well, I suppose it just has to come out.—I'm in love—Anatol—furiously in love!

ANATOL: And may one ask with whom?

ANNIE: . . . Tell me, Max—why on earth are you laughing then?

MAX: It's too droll!

ANATOL: Just let him go on. . . . The two of us need to speak with each other, Annie!—You do owe me an explanation . . .

ANNIE: Well—I'll certainly give it to you. . . . I've fallen in love with someone else—and I'll say it to you straight out—because that's what we agreed on . . .

ANATOL: Indeed . . . but what the devil—with whom?!

ANNIE: Indeed, dear child—you must not get coarse!

ANATOL: I demand . . . I demand quite decidedly . . .

ANNIE: Please, Max—ring—I'm so hungry!

ANATOL: And now that too!—An appetite!! An appetite during such a parley!

MAX [*to* ANATOL]: Well, she's *really* having supper today!

[*The* WAITER *enters.*]

ANATOL: What do you want?

WAITER: Someone rang!

MAX: Go on serving!

[*While the* WAITER *clears off the table . . .*]

ANNIE: Yes . . . as for Catalini, she's going to Germany . . . that's been agreed upon . . .

MAX: So . . . and they're letting her go without ado?

ANNIE: Well . . . without ado—actually one can't say that!

ANATOL [*stands up and walks back and forth in the room*]: Where's the wine then?!—You! . . . Jean!!—You're asleep today, so it seems!

WAITER: If you please—the wine . . .

ANATOL: I don't mean the one which is on the table—you can well imagine that!—I mean the champagne!—You know that I want to have it on the table right at the start!

[*The* WAITER *exits.*]

ANATOL: . . . I'm asking for an explanation, after all!

ANNIE: One just shouldn't believe a single thing from you men—not a single thing—pure and simple! When I think how beautifully you set that forth for me: when we feel that it's coming to an end—then we'll say so to each other and part in peace—

ANATOL: Now if you'll just tell me after all—

ANNIE: Well this is what you mean—peace!

ANATOL: But dear child—you'll understand, after all, that it does interest me—who—

ANNIE [*slowly sipping the wine*]: Ah . . .

ANATOL: Drink up . . . drink up!

ANNIE: Well, you've probably been—for such a long time now—

ANATOL: As a rule you drink it right down—

ANNIE: But, dear Anatol—I'm also taking leave from Bordeaux wine now—who knows for how long!

ANATOL: Confound it anyhow!—What kind of stories are you telling me there?! . . .

ANNIE: Now there'll be no more Bordeaux . . . and no oysters . . . and no champagne!

[*The* WAITER *enters with the next course.*]

—And no *filets aux truffles*!—All that is gone now . . .

MAX: Good Lord—you have a sentimental stomach! [*Since the* WAITER *is serving*]—may I hand it to you?—

ANNIE: I thank you very much! . . . Now then . . .

[ANATOL *lights himself a cigarette.*—]

MAX: Aren't you eating any more?

ANATOL: Not for the time being!

[*The* WAITER *exits.*]

. . . So, now I would just like to know who the lucky man is!

ANNIE: And if I go and tell you his name—you certainly won't know any more then—

ANATOL: Well—what sort of person is he? How did you get to know him? What does he look like—?

ANNIE: Handsome—as handsome as he can be! That's everything, of course . . .

ANATOL: Well—that certainly seems to be enough for you . . .

ANNIE: Certainly—there won't be any more oysters then . . .

ANATOL: We know that already . . .

ANNIE: . . . And no champagne!

ANATOL: But good grief—he'll no doubt have additional characteristics, other than that he can't pay for your oysters and champagne—

MAX: He's right about that—that isn't a real occupation after all . . .

ANNIE: Well, what harm is it—if I love him?—I'll forgo everything—this is something new, something I've never experienced yet.

MAX: But do you see . . . in a pinch, even Anatol could have offered you a bad meal!—

ANATOL: What is he?—A clerk?—A chimney sweep—?—A traveling oil salesman?—

ANNIE: Why, you child—I'll not let him be insulted!

MAX: Well, just say what he is after all!

ANNIE: An artist!

ANATOL: What kind?—Probably trapeze?! For your kind that is certainly something—From the circus—isn't he? A trick rider?

ANNIE: Stop that name calling!—He's a colleague of mine . . .

ANATOL: So—an old acquaintanceship? . . . Someone you've been with daily for years—and also with whom you've probably been deceiving me for some time now!—

ANNIE: Then I wouldn't have said anything to you!—I relied on your word—that's why I'm confessing everything to you now, before it's too late!

ANATOL: But—you're already in love with him—God knows for how long—And in spirit you've been deceiving me for a long time—

ANNIE: You can't forbid me that!

ANATOL: You're a . . .

MAX: Anatol!

ANATOL: . . . Do I know him?—

ANNIE: Well—he probably hasn't caught your attention . . . he just dances in the chorus. . . . But he'll advance—

ANATOL: How long . . . have you been fond of him—?

ANNIE: Since this evening!

ANATOL: Don't lie!

ANNIE: It's the truth!—Today I felt . . . that it's my destiny . . .

ANATOL: Her destiny! . . . Do you hear, Max—her destiny!!

ANNIE: Yes, something like that can also be destiny!

ANATOL: Do you hear—but I want to know everything—I have a right to that! . . . At this moment you're still my sweetheart! . . . I want to know since when these things have been going on . . . how it began . . . when he dared!—

MAX: Yes . . . you really should tell us that . . .

ANNIE: That is what one gets for being honest . . . Truly—I should've done it the way Fritzel did with her baron—he still doesn't know anything today—and so she's been having that thing with the lieutenant from the hussars for three months now!

ANATOL: He'll catch on too, that baron certainly will!

ANNIE: That's certainly possible! But you would never have caught on to me, never!—I'm much too clever for that . . . and you're much too stupid!

[*She pours herself a glass of wine.*]

ANATOL: Will you stop drinking!

ANNIE: Not today!—I want—to get tipsy!—As it is, it's the last one . . .

MAX: For a week!

ANNIE: Forever!—For I'll stay with Karl because I really like him—because he's fun-loving, even if he has no money—because he won't torment me—because he's a sweet, sweet—dear fellow!

ANATOL: You didn't keep your word!—You've been in love with him for a long time now!—That's a stupid lie, that one about this evening!

ANNIE: Then don't believe me, for all I care!

MAX: Well, Annie . . . Just tell us the story . . . tell us everything—or nothing at all!—If you want to part from each other in peace now—you must do that for him, after all, for his sake, for Anatol's . . .

ANATOL: Then I'll tell you something as well . . .

ANNIE: Well . . . it began like this . . .

[*The* WAITER *enters . . .*]

ANATOL: Just tell me—just tell me . . .

[*He sits down alongside of her.*]

ANNIE: It's been about fourteen days now . . . or longer, he gave me a couple of roses then—at the back exit door. . . . I had to laugh!—He looked quite timid in doing that—

ANATOL: Why didn't you tell me anything about that—?

ANNIE: About that?—Well, then I would have had a lot to tell!

[*The* WAITER *exits.*]

ANATOL: So, go on—go on!

ANNIE: . . . Then at rehearsals he was always slinking around me so strangely—well—and I noticed that—and at first I was annoyed—and then I was glad—

ANATOL: Extremely simple . . .

ANNIE: Well . . . and then we talked—and then I liked everything about him so much—

ANATOL: What did you talk about then?—

ANNIE: Everything possible—how they threw him out of school—and how he was supposed to have gone into an apprenticeship—well—and how the theater blood in him began to stir . . .

ANATOL: So . . . and I never heard anything about all that . . .

ANNIE: Well . . . and then it came out that we lived two houses away from each other when we were children—we were neighbors—

ANATOL: Ah! Neighbors!—That's touching, touching!
ANNIE: Yes . . . yes . . .

[*She drinks.*]

ANATOL: . . . Go on!
ANNIE: Why should I go on then?—I've already told you everything! It's my destiny—and I can't do anything—against my destiny . . . and . . . against . . . my destiny . . . I . . . can't . . . do . . . anything . . .
ANATOL: I want to know something about this evening—
ANNIE: Well . . . what—

[*Her head sinks down.*]

MAX: Why, she's falling asleep—
ANATOL: Wake her up!—Put the wine out of her reach! . . . I have to know what happened this evening—Annie—Annie!
ANNIE: This evening . . . he told me—that he—likes—me!
ANATOL: And you—
ANNIE: I told him—that I'm glad—and because I don't want to deceive him—I'm telling you adieu—
ANATOL: Because you don't want to deceive *him*!!—So not for my sake—? . . . For his sake?!
ANNIE: So what?—I just don't like you any longer!
ANATOL: Well fine!—Fortunately all that doesn't bother me anymore . . . !
ANNIE: So?!
ANATOL: I too am in the pleasant situation—of being able to forgo your further charm!
ANNIE: So . . . so!
ANATOL: Yes . . . yes!—For a long time now I haven't really loved you! . . . I love someone else!
ANNIE: Ha ha . . . ha ha . . .
ANATOL: For a long time now! Just ask Max there!—Before you came—I told him!

ANNIE: . . . So . . . so . . .

ANATOL: For a long time now! . . . And this other woman is a thousandfold better and lovelier . . .

ANNIE: So . . . so . . .

ANATOL: . . . She's a girl for whom I'd give up a thousand women like you with pleasure—do you understand—?

[ANNIE *laughs.*]

ANATOL: Don't laugh!—Ask Max: there—

ANNIE: It's just too funny!—That you want me to believe that now—

ANATOL: It's true, I'm telling you—I swear to you that it's true! I haven't loved you for a long time now! . . . I didn't even think of you while I was alone with you—and when I kissed you, I thought of her!—Her!—Of her!—

ANNIE: Well—then we're even!

ANATOL: So!—You think so?!

ANNIE: Yes—even! That's really quite nice!

ANATOL: So?—We're not even—oh no—not at all!—That's not one and the same at all . . . what you experience . . . and I! My story is somewhat less—innocent . . .

ANNIE: . . . What?—[*Becoming more serious*]

ANATOL: Yes . . . my story sounds a little different—

ANNIE: But why is your story different—?

ANATOL: Well—I—I deceived you—

ANNIE [*stands up*]: What?—What?!

ANATOL: I deceived you—as you deserve it—day for day—night for night—I was coming from her when I met you—and was going to her when I left you—

ANNIE: . . . Detestable . . . That is . . . detestable!!

[*She goes to the coatrack, throws on her raincoat and boa—*]

ANATOL: One can't go too fast with your kind—otherwise you'll get ahead! . . . Well, fortunately I have no illusions . . .

ANNIE: There it's plain to see again!—Yes, it is!!

ANATOL: Yes . . . it's plain to see, right? Now it's plain to see!

ANNIE: That a man like you is a hundred times more ruthless than any woman—

ANATOL: Yes, it's plain to see!—I was so ruthless . . . yes!

ANNIE [*having wound the boa around her neck, now taking hat and gloves into her hand, goes over and stands in front of* ANATOL]:—Yes . . . ruthless!—I certainly didn't tell you . . . that before!

[*She tries to leave.*]

ANATOL [*following her*]: What?!

MAX: Just let her go then!—Why, surely you wouldn't stop her!—

ANATOL: "That!"—you didn't tell me?—What the?!—That you . . . That you . . . that—

ANNIE [*near the door*]: I would never have told you that . . . never! . . . That only a man can be so ruthless—

WAITER [*enters with a custard*]:—Oh—

ANATOL: Go to the devil with your custard!

ANNIE: What!? Vanilla custard!! . . . So!—

ANATOL: You still dare!—

MAX: Just let her!—After all she has to give up custard—forever—

ANNIE: Yes . . . along with such delights!—The bordeaux, the champagne—the oysters—and quite especially you, Anatol—!

[*She suddenly walks away from the door with a vulgar smile, goes to the cigarette box standing at the full-length mirror, and stuffs a handful of cigarettes into her pocket.*]

Not for me!—I'm taking these to him!

[*She exits.* ANATOL *starts after her, then stands still near the door.*]

MAX [*calmly*]: Well . . . you see . . . That went quite well! . . .

[*Curtain*]

AGONY

[ANATOL*'s room, evening twilight beginning. The room is empty for a while, then* ANATOL *and* MAX *enter.*]

MAX: Well . . . I've been through all this with you before!

ANATOL: Stay a little while.

MAX: But am I not disturbing you?

ANATOL: I'm asking you to stay! I simply have no desire to be alone—and who knows if she's even coming!

MAX: Ah!

ANATOL: Seven times out of ten I've waited in vain!

MAX: I wouldn't stand for that!

ANATOL: And sometimes you have to believe the excuses—ah, sometimes they're even true.

MAX: All seven times?

ANATOL: What do I know! . . . I'm telling you there's nothing more horrible than being the lover of a married woman!

MAX: Oh no . . . I would like even less to be her husband!

ANATOL: It's been going on now—for how long—?—Two years—no!—more! It was already that long at Mardi Gras—and it's now the third "springtime of our love" . . .

MAX: So what's wrong?!

ANATOL [*has thrown himself down into an armchair at the window, still wearing his overcoat and carrying his cane*]:—Ah, I'm tired—I'm nervous, I don't know what I want . . .

MAX: Take a trip!

ANATOL: Why?

MAX: To cut short the end of it!

ANATOL: What does that mean—the end of it!?

MAX: I've seen you like this sometimes before—the last time you remember how you couldn't decide when to let go of a certain stupid creature who wasn't even worth your pains.

ANATOL: You mean I don't love her anymore . . . ?

MAX: Oh! Now that would be wonderful . . . if that were true, you wouldn't be suffering any longer! But now you're going through something much worse than death—and this is the deadly part.

ANATOL: You have such a way of telling a person pleasant things!—But you're right—it is agony!

MAX: There's just something consoling in talking about it. And for that we don't even need philosophy!—We don't even need to be grand and universal—it's more than enough to delve down into the uttermost depths of a particular situation.

ANATOL: You make it seem quite a pleasure.

MAX: That's just the way I mean it.—But all afternoon down at the Prater amusement park I saw it in you—you were already as pale and boring as possible.

ANATOL: She wanted to go there today.

MAX: But you were glad we didn't meet her coach because you no longer have that smile you greeted her with two years ago.

ANATOL [*standing up*]: Just how does that happen!—Tell me, just how does that happen—?—So this is what's in store for me once more—this gradual, slow, unspeakably sad fading away?—You have no idea how I dread that—!

MAX: That's just why I say: take a trip!—Or have the courage to tell her the whole truth.

ANATOL: What? And how?

MAX: Well, quite simply that it's over.

ANATOL: We needn't be so very proud about such kind of truth. After all, it's just the brutal candor of a worn-out liar.

MAX: Of course! Rather than part with a swift resolve, you prefer to hide behind a thousand ruses when it's no longer the same as before. But why?

ANATOL: Why, because we don't believe it ourselves! Because in the midst of this endless tediousness and agony, there are strange, deceivingly luminous moments in which everything flourishes more beautifully than ever before . . . ! Never do we yearn more for happiness than in these final days of love—and we don't want to look behind the mask, whenever there's a mood or an ecstasy or a void disguising itself as happiness . . . Then comes the moment you're *ashamed* to have believed all the sweetness is over—then you beg for forgiveness for so much, without putting it in words.—You get so worn out by the fear of dying—and suddenly life is back again—more heated, more glowing than ever—and more deceptive than ever!—

MAX: Now don't forget this: the end often comes earlier than we suspect!—Often happiness begins to die with the first kiss.—Haven't you heard of people who are severely ill but think themselves healthy up to the last—?

ANATOL: I am not one of those happy people!—That's for certain!—I've always been a hypochondriac when it comes to love. But maybe my feelings weren't even as sick as I believed—but all the worse!—Sometimes it seems as if I have the evil eye . . . It's just that my gaze is directed inwardly, and my happiest feelings wither before it.

MAX: Then you must simply be proud of your evil gaze.

ANATOL: Oh no, I do envy the others! Do you know—the happy people for whom every bit of life is a new victory!—I always have to make up my mind to finish something, but I keep stopping—I consider, I take rests, I drag along—! It's the same thing other people overcome with ease, even while experiencing it . . . for them, it is one and the same thing.

MAX: Don't envy them, Anatol—they don't overcome things, they just go past them!

ANATOL: Isn't that also happiness—?—At least they don't have this strange feeling of guilt which is the secret of the pains we have in parting.

MAX: What guilt is that?

ANATOL: Didn't we have the obligation to put into the couple of years or hours we loved them the eternity we promised them? And yet we could never do it! Never! We part from every woman with this consciousness of guilt—and our melancholia is nothing but a quiet admission of that. It's merely our final honesty!—

MAX: Our first honesty at times . . .

ANATOL: And it all hurts so much.—

MAX: My dear friend, these long-lasting relationships just aren't good for you. . . . You have too delicate a nose—

ANATOL: How am I supposed to understand that?

MAX: Your present state always drags along quite a heavy load of your unassimilated past. . . . And now the first years of your love are beginning to rot, and your soul doesn't have the wondrous power to completely eliminate them.—And what's the natural result—?—That the stench of the rotting surrounds even your healthiest, most flourishing hours right now—and the poisoned atmosphere of your present is beyond saving.

ANATOL: That may well be.

MAX: And therefore this jumble of past and present and future is always within you, as constant, indistinct transitions! For you, the past isn't a simple, fixed fact, disengaging itself from the moods in which you experienced it—no, your moods lie heavily over all that; they just grow more pale and wilted—and die out.

ANATOL: Oh, well. And those painful moods which so often enter my best moments come from that atmosphere.—I'd like to get away from them.

MAX: I find to my utter astonishment that nobody is secure against sometimes having to say something first-rate! . . . So now I have something on my tongue: be strong, Anatol—get over it!

ANATOL: But you're laughing when you say that! . . . It's possible I would be able to do that!—But I lack something far more important—the need!—I feel I'd be losing so much if one fine day I were to find myself "strong"! . . . There are so many sicknesses and just one healthy condition—! . . . One always has to be as healthy as the other people—but one can also be sick in a way quite different from everyone else!

MAX: Isn't that just your vanity?

ANATOL: And even if it is?—Again you know full well that vanity is a fault, don't you—? . . .

MAX: I infer from all this that you just don't want to take a trip.

ANATOL: Perhaps I will take a trip—fine, then!—But I have to *surprise* myself with that—there mustn't be any purpose involved—a purpose ruins everything!—That's what's horrible about such things, that you—have to pack a trunk, send for a cab—tell the driver—to the station!

MAX: I'll attend to all that for you! [*Since* ANATOL *has rushed to the window and looked out*]—So what's wrong?—

ANATOL: Nothing . . .

MAX: . . . Ah yes . . . I completely forgot.—I'm going now.

ANATOL: . . . Do you see—once again I'm feeling—?

MAX: . . .

ANATOL: That I adore her!

MAX: There's a very simple explanation for that, namely this: that you really do adore her—at this moment!

ANATOL: Farewell, then—don't order the cab yet!

MAX: Don't be so high-spirited about it! The express train for Trieste isn't leaving for four hours—you can send for the baggage later—

ANATOL: Thanks very much!

MAX [*at the door*]: I can't possibly depart without an aphorism!

ANATOL: How's that?

MAX: Women are a mystery!

ANATOL: Oh!!

MAX: Just let me finish! Women are a mystery! So to speak! But what kind of mystery would we be for women, if only they were sensible enough to think about us?

ANATOL: Bravo, bravo!

[MAX *bows and exits.*]

[ANATOL *is alone for a while, walks back and forth in the room, then sits down facing the window, smokes a cigarette. The sounds of a violin are heard from the upper floor—break—steps are heard in the corridor . . .* ANATOL *becomes attentive, stands up, puts the cigarette in an ashtray, and walks toward* ELSE, *just as she enters, deeply veiled.*]

ANATOL: At last!—

ELSE: It's already late . . . yes, yes!

[*She removes her hat and veils.*]

—I couldn't come any earlier—couldn't possibly!—

ANATOL: Couldn't you have let me know?—Waiting makes me so nervous!—But—you're staying?

ELSE: Not long, dear angel—my husband—

[ANATOL *turns away, annoyed.*]

ELSE: Look—how you're acting again! I can't do anything about that!

ANATOL: Oh well—of course, you're right!—That's simply the way it is—and one has to acquiesce . . . Come, my darling—over here! . . .

[*They step to the window.*]

ELSE: I might be seen!

ANATOL: It's so dark—and the curtain hides us here! It's so annoying that you can't stay long!—I haven't seen you for two days now!—And it was only for a couple of minutes the last time!

ELSE: So do you love me—?

ANATOL: Ah, you surely know that—you're everything for me, everything! . . . To be alone with you always—

ELSE: I'm quite happy being here with you too!

ANATOL: Come . . . [*Pulling her beside him onto the armchair*]—Your hand! [*Drawing it to his lips*] . . . Do you hear the old man playing up there?—Beautiful—isn't it—?

ELSE: My darling!

ANATOL: Ah yes—to be with you like this at Lake Como . . . or in Venice—

ELSE: I went there on my wedding trip—

ANATOL [*with suppressed annoyance*]: Did you have to say that now?

ELSE: But after all, you're the only one I love! The only one I have ever! Never anyone—not even my husband—

ANATOL [*folding his hands*]: I ask you!—Can't you picture yourself unmarried at least for a few seconds?—Just sip the charm of this moment—just imagine the two of us alone in the world . . .

[*The clock strikes.*]

ELSE: How late is it—?

ANATOL: Else, Else—don't ask!—Forget there are others—after all, you're here with me!

ELSE [*tenderly*]: Haven't I already forgotten enough for you?—

ANATOL: My darling—[*kissing her hand*]

ELSE: My dear Anatol—

ANATOL [*softly*]: Well, just what is it now, Else—?

[ELSE *gestures with a smile that she must leave.*]

ANATOL: You mean?

ELSE: I must be off!

ANATOL: You must?

ELSE: Yes.

ANATOL: Must—? Now—now—?—Go then!

[*He withdraws from her.*]

ELSE: One can't talk with you—

ANATOL: One can't talk to me! [*Pacing back and forth in the room*]—And you don't understand how this sort of life is driving me to a frenzy?—

ELSE: And that's my thanks!

ANATOL: Thanks, thanks!—Thanks for what?—Haven't I given you as much as you've given me?—Do I love you less than you love me?—Do I make you less happy than you make me?—Love—insanity—pain—! But thankfulness?—How does that stupid word come into it?—

ELSE: So, no thanks at all—not a bit do I get from you?—I, who sacrificed everything for you?

ANATOL: Sacrificed?—I don't want any sacrifice—and if it was a sacrifice, then you never loved me.

ELSE: And now that, too? . . . I don't love him—I, who am betraying my husband for him—I, I—don't love him!

ANATOL: Now I didn't say that!

ELSE: Oh, what have I done!

ANATOL [*stopping in front of her*]: Oh, what have I done!—That splendid remark is simply the last straw!—What you have done? I want to tell you . . . seven years ago you were a stupid teenager—then you married a man because one simply must.—You took your wedding trip . . . you were happy . . . in Venice—

ELSE: Never once!—

ANATOL: What?—Didn't he kiss you—didn't he embrace you?—Weren't you his wife?—Then you came back—and then you became bored—that's understandable—you are beautiful—fashionable—and a woman—! And he is quite simply a blockhead! Then came the years of flirting . . . I assume it was only flirting!—You say you haven't loved anyone else before me. Well, that can't be proved—but I assume that, because the contrary would be unpleasant for me.

ELSE: Anatol! Flirting! Me!

ANATOL: Yes . . . flirting! And what does it mean to be flirtatious? To use both lust and deceit!

ELSE: I did that?—

ANATOL: Yes . . . you!—Then came the years of struggle—and you vacillated!—Shall I never experience my grand romance?—You became more and more beautiful—your husband more and more boring, stupid, and ugly . . . ! Finally it was inevitable—you took yourself a lover. By chance I am this lover!

ELSE: By chance . . . you!

ANATOL: Yes, I, by chance—for if I weren't here—it would simply have been another!—You felt yourself unhappy in your marriage or not happy enough—and you wanted to be loved. You played the coquette with me a bit, some drivel about *la grande passion*—and then as you looked at one of your girlfriends riding past you in her coach, or perhaps as you looked at a flirt in a private box beside you, you simply thought: why shouldn't I have some pleasure too!—And so you became my sweetheart!—You did that!—That's all—and I don't see why you use such grand phrases for this little adventure.

ELSE: Anatol!—Anatol!—Adventure?!—

ANATOL: Yes!

ELSE: Take back what you said—I implore you!—

ANATOL: And what is there for me to take back—what else would you call it—?

ELSE: Do you really believe that—?

ANATOL: Yes!

ELSE: Well—then I must go!

ANATOL: Go—I'm not keeping you.

[*Pause.*]

ELSE: You're sending me away?

ANATOL: I—send you away—And two minutes ago you said—"I must be off!"

ELSE: Anatol—And I must—! Don't you understand that—

ANATOL [*resolvedly*]: Else!

ELSE: What?

ANATOL: Else—you do love me—? Then say it—

ELSE: I am saying it—Then for heaven's sake—what kind of proof do you really demand from me—?

ANATOL: Do you want to know—? Fine!—Perhaps I'll be able to believe you if you love me . . .

ELSE: Perhaps?—Now you say that!

ANATOL: You do love me—?

ELSE: I adore you—

ANATOL: Then—stay here with me!

ELSE: What?—

ANATOL: Flee with me—All right?—with me—to another city—to another world—I want to be alone with you!

ELSE: What's gotten into you—?

ANATOL: What's "gotten into" me—? The only natural thing—All right!—Just how can I let you go away—back to him—how have I ever been able to do it?—All right—how can you bring yourself to do it—you! who "adore" me!—How can you? Scorched by my kisses, how can you go from my arms, back to that house which has become foreign to you, now that you belong to me?—No—no—we've just accommodated ourselves to it like this—we haven't considered how monstrous this is! It's impossible to continue living like this—Else, Else, you're coming with me!—Well . . . you're silent—Else!—To Sicily . . . to wherever you want—across the sea for all I care—Else!

ELSE: But what are you saying?

ANATOL: Nobody between us any longer—across the sea, Else!—and we'll be alone—

ELSE: Across the sea—?

ANATOL: Wherever you want! . . .

ELSE: My dear, cherished . . . child . . .

ANATOL: Are you hesitating—?

ELSE: Look, dearest—why do we really need to do that—?

ANATOL: What are you saying?

ELSE: To go away—it's surely not necessary . . . After all, we can see each other in Vienna almost as often as we want—

ANATOL: Almost as often as we want.—Yes, yes . . . we . . . don't need to go at all . . .

ELSE: Those are flights of fancy . . .

ANATOL: . . . You're right . . .

[*Pause.*]

ELSE: . . . Angry—?

[*The clock strikes.*]

ANATOL: You must go!

ELSE: . . . For heaven's sake . . . it's gotten that late . . . !

ANATOL: Well—just go . . .

ELSE: Until tomorrow—I'll be here with you at six o'clock!

ANATOL: . . . As you wish!

ELSE: You're not kissing me—?

ANATOL: Oh yes . . .

ELSE: I'll make you well again . . . tomorrow!—

ANATOL [*accompanying her to the door*]: Adieu!

ELSE [*near the door*]: One more kiss!

ANATOL: Why not—here!

[*He kisses her; she leaves.*]

ANATOL [*comes back into the room*]: With that kiss I've now made her into what she deserves to be . . . into one more! [*Shaking himself*] Stupid, stupid . . . !

[*Curtain*]

ANATOL'S WEDDING MORNING

[*Tasteful*ly *arranged bachelor's quarters: the door at the right leads to the entryway; the door at the left, bordered with curtains, leads to the bedchamber.* ANATOL, *in morning attire, enters on tiptoes from the left and closes the door softly. He sits down on the chaise longue and presses a button; bell rings.* FRANZ *appears from the right and goes to the left door, without noticing* ANATOL.]

ANATOL [*doesn't notice the servant at first, then runs after him and prevents him from opening the door*]: Why are you slinking around like that? I didn't even hear you!

FRANZ: What do you wish, sir?

ANATOL: The samovar!

FRANZ: But of course.

[*He exits.*]

ANATOL: Softly, you blockhead! Can't you walk more gently? [*Tiptoes to the left door, opening it a little*] She's still asleep! . . . She's still asleep!

FRANZ [*entering with the samovar*]: Two cups, sir?

ANATOL: But of course!

[*Doorbell rings.*]

. . . Look outside! Just who can that be this early in the morning?

[FRANZ *exits.*]

ANATOL: Today I'm definitely not in the mood to get married. I would like to call it off.

[MAX *enters, as* FRANZ *opens the door to the right.*]

MAX [*cordially*]: My dear friend!

ANATOL: Shh . . . Quiet! . . . One more cup, Franz!

FRANZ: But there are two cups already!

ANATOL: One more cup, Franz—and out.

[FRANZ *exits.*]

Well . . . and now, my dear friend, what brings you here at eight in the morning?

MAX: It's ten!

ANATOL: Then what brings you here at ten in the morning?

MAX: My forgetfulness.

ANATOL: Speak more softly . . .

MAX: But why? Are you nervous?

ANATOL: Yes, very!

MAX: But you shouldn't be nervous today.

ANATOL: So what do you want then?

MAX: You know I'm to be the official witness at your wedding today, your charming cousin Alma is to be the other witness.

ANATOL [*without emotion*]: Get to the point.

MAX: Well—I forgot to order the bouquet and at this moment I don't know what color Fräulein Alma's dress will be. Will she be in white, pink, blue, or green?

ANATOL [*annoyed*]: Certainly not green!

MAX: Why certainly not green?

ANATOL: My cousin never wears green.

MAX [*piqued*]: How could I know that!

ANATOL [*annoyed*]: Don't shout so! That all can be settled quietly.

MAX: So you don't have any idea what color she will be wearing today?

ANATOL: Pink or blue!

MAX: But they are very different.

ANATOL: Ah, pink or blue is quite irrelevant.

MAX: But it's certainly not irrelevant for my bouquet!

ANATOL: Then order two, and you can put the one in your lapel.

MAX: I didn't come here to listen to your bad jokes.
ANATOL: I'll be making an even worse one at two o'clock today!
MAX: You're certainly in a good mood on your wedding day.
ANATOL: I'm nervous!
MAX: You're keeping something secret from me.
ANATOL: Nothing!

[ILONA*'s voice from the bedroom:* Anatol!]

[MAX *looks in surprise at* ANATOL.]

ANATOL: Excuse me a moment.

[*He goes to the bedroom door and disappears for a moment.* MAX *gazes after him wide-eyed.* ANATOL *kisses* ILONA *without* MAX *seeing it, closes the door, and crosses back to* MAX.]

MAX [*indignantly*]: One doesn't do such a thing!
ANATOL: Hear me, dear Max, and then judge.
MAX: I hear a female voice and judge: you're starting early to deceive your wife!
ANATOL: Sit down and listen to me, you'll soon speak differently.
MAX: Never. I'm certainly no model of virtue, but such a thing . . . !
ANATOL: You don't want to listen to me?
MAX: Tell me then! But be quick, I'm invited to your wedding.

[*Both sit.*]

ANATOL [*sadly*]: Ah yes!
MAX [*impatiently*]: So.
ANATOL: So . . . So yesterday evening was the rehearsal dinner at my future in-laws' home.
MAX: I know, I was there!
ANATOL: Yes, right, you were there. There was quite a crowd of people there! They were in very high spirits, drinking champagne, pronouncing toasts . . .
MAX: So was I . . . to your happiness and good fortune!
ANATOL: Yes, you were too . . . to my happiness and good fortune! [*Pressing his hand*] I thank you.

MAX: You did already, yesterday.

ANATOL: So they were in very high spirits until midnight—

MAX: I know.

ANATOL: For a moment it seemed as if I were happy.

MAX: After your fourth glass of champagne.

ANATOL [*sadly*]: No—only after the sixth. . . . It's sad and I can scarcely comprehend it.

MAX: We've talked enough about that.

ANATOL: Even that young fellow was there who I know for certain was my bride's youthful love.

MAX: Ah, young Ralmen.

ANATOL: Yes—he's a kind of poet, I think. One of those who seem destined to be the first love of so many women but never to be their last.

MAX: I wish you would come to the point.

ANATOL: Actually, I was quite apathetic toward him, in fact I smiled about him. . . . The gathering broke up at midnight. I took leave of my bride with a kiss. She even kissed me . . . coldly . . . I was shivering as I proceeded down the stairs.

MAX: Aha . . .

ANATOL: This one and that one were still congratulating me near the gate. Uncle Edward was drunk and embraced me. A doctor of jurisprudence was singing a university students' song. The youthful love, I mean the poet, disappeared with pinned-up collar in a side alley. Someone was teasing me. Now I would certainly have walked up and down the rest of the night in front of my beloved's windows. I smiled scornfully. . . . It had begun to snow. People gradually dispersed . . . I was standing alone . . .

MAX [*pityingly*]: Hmm . . .

ANATOL [*more warmly*]: Yes, standing alone in the street—in the cold winter night while the snow whirled around me in large flakes. It was to a certain extent . . . gruesome.

MAX: I ask you—just tell me where you went?

ANATOL [*grandly*]: I had to go to—to the masquerade!

MAX: Ah!

ANATOL: You're astonished, correct—?

MAX: Now I can picture what follows.

ANATOL: Certainly not, my friend—as I stood there like that in the cold winter night—

MAX: Shivering . . . !

ANATOL: Freezing! Then it hit me like a tremendous pain that from now on I would no longer be a free man, that I must say farewell forever to my sweet, wild bachelor's life! I said to myself this is the last night you can come home without being asked "where were you?" . . . The last night of freedom, of adventure . . . perhaps of love!

MAX: Oh!—

ANATOL: And so I stood in the midst of the tumult. Silk and satin dresses rustled all around me, eyes glowed, masks nodded, sparkling white shoulders smelled sweetly—the whole carnival pulsated and raged. I hurled myself into this bustling chaos and let it rage over my soul. I had to absorb it, had to bathe myself in it! . . .

MAX: Get to the point. . . . We don't have time.

ANATOL: I am being shoved like that through the crowd, and after my head gets intoxicated, my breath gets intoxicated with all the perfumes floating around me. It all streamed in on me as never before. The Lenten carnival was offering me a personal, yes, a very personal farewell festival.

MAX: I'm waiting for the third intoxication . . .

ANATOL: It did come . . . the intoxication of the heart . . . !

MAX: Of the senses!

ANATOL: Of the heart . . . ! Oh well, of the senses. . . . Do you remember Katharine . . . ?

MAX [*loudly*]: Oh, Katharine . . .

ANATOL: Psst . . .

MAX [*pointing to the door of the bedroom*]: Ah . . . is she the one?

ANATOL: No—not exactly. But she was there—and also a delightful brunette lady whose name I'm not mentioning . . . and that blond little Lizzie of Theodore's—but Theodore wasn't there—and so on. I recognized them all in spite of their masks—by the voice, the walk, by some movement or other. But strangely . . . there was only one I didn't recognize right away. I was pursuing her or she was pursuing me. Her figure was so familiar. In any case, we were constantly meeting: at the fountain, at the buffet, beside the stage box . . . constantly! Finally she had my arm and I knew who she was! [*Pointing to the bedroom door*] Her.

MAX: An old acquaintance?

ANATOL: Don't you get it, my good fellow? After all, you know what I told her six weeks ago, when I got engaged . . . the old fairy tale: I'm taking a trip, I'm coming back soon, I'll love you eternally.

MAX: Ilona . . . ?

ANATOL: Psst . . .

MAX: Not Ilona . . . ?

ANATOL: Yes—but that's why you must be quiet! So you're back again, she whispers into my ear. "Yes" is my quick-witted reply. When did I come?—This evening.—Why hadn't I written earlier?—No postal connection.—Where then?—Inhospitable village.—But now . . . ?—Happy, here again, been faithful.—I too—I too—Blissfulness, champagne, and again blissfulness.—

MAX: And again champagne.

ANATOL: No—no more champagne.—Ah, then, as we went home in the coach . . . as before. She was leaning on my breast. Now we never want to separate again—she said . . .

MAX [*standing up*]: Wake up, my friend, and see that you get to the end.

ANATOL: "Never separate"—[*Standing up*] And I'm getting married at two o'clock today!

MAX: To another.

ANATOL: Oh well, one always marries another.

MAX [*looking at the clock*]: I believe it's high time.

[*He makes a movement signifying that* ANATOL *should remove* ILONA.]

ANATOL: Yes, yes, I'll just see if she's ready.

[*He walks to the door, stands still in front of it, turns to* MAX.]

Isn't it actually sad?

MAX: It's immoral.

ANATOL: Yes, but also sad.

MAX: Just go do it.

[ANATOL *walks to the door of the adjoining room.*]

ILONA [*sticking out her head; then stepping out, wrapped in an elegant domino robe*]: Why, it's only Max!

MAX [*bowing*]: Only Max.

ILONA [*to* ANATOL]: And you're not saying anything at all.—I thought it was a stranger, otherwise I'd have been here with you much sooner. How's it going, Max? What do you say to this rogue?

MAX: Yes, that he is.

ILONA: Six weeks I've been crying for him. . . . He was . . . just where were you?

ANATOL [*with a grand movement of his hand*]: There, where—

ILONA: Didn't he write to you either? But now I've got him back again. [*Taking his arm*] . . . Now there's no more going away . . . no more being apart. Give me a kiss!

ANATOL: But . . .

ILONA: Ah, Max doesn't count. [*Kissing* ANATOL] Now what a face you're making! . . . But I'll pour the tea for the two of you and one for myself, if I may.

ANATOL: Please . . .

MAX: Dear Ilona, unfortunately I can't accept the invitation to have breakfast with you . . . and I also don't understand . . .

ILONA [*sets about working with the samovar*]: What don't you understand?

ANATOL: Actually Anatol should also . . .

ILONA: What should Anatol—?

MAX [*to* ANATOL]: Actually, you should already—

ILONA: What should he?

MAX: You should already be in formal dress!

ILONA: Ah, don't be ridiculous, Max, we're staying home today, we're not moving from here . . .

ANATOL: Dear child, unfortunately that won't be possible . . .

ILONA: Of course that will be possible.

ANATOL: I'm invited . . .

ILONA [*pouring tea*]: Decline it.

MAX: He can't decline.

ANATOL: I'm invited to a wedding.

[MAX *makes motions urging him on.*]

ILONA: Ah, that's quite irrelevant.

ANATOL: That's not quite irrelevant—for I'm the toastmaster, so to speak.

ILONA: Your lady loves you.

MAX: Actually that's a secondary point.

ILONA: But I love him and that's the main point. . . . Don't keep interrupting me!

ANATOL: My child . . . I must be off.

MAX: Yes, he must be off—believe him—he must be off.

ANATOL: You must excuse me for a couple of hours.

ILONA: Now kindly sit down . . . How many lumps of sugar, Max?

MAX: Three.

ILONA [*to* ANATOL]: And you . . . ?

ANATOL: It's really high time.

ILONA: How many lumps?

ANATOL: You know that . . . always two lumps—

ILONA: Whipped cream, rum?

ANATOL: Rum—you know that too!

ILONA: Rum and two lumps of sugar. [*To* MAX] That man has principles!

MAX: I must go!

ANATOL [*softly*]: You're leaving me alone?

ILONA: You will finish your tea, Max!

ANATOL: My child, I must change my clothes now—!

ILONA: For God's sake—just when is this miserable wedding?

ANATOL: In two hours.

ILONA: Of course you're invited too?

MAX: Yes!

ILONA: Another toastmaster?

ANATOL: Yes . . . he is one too.

ILONA: Just who is getting married?

ANATOL: You don't know him.

ILONA: Well, what's his name then? It can't be a secret.

ANATOL: It's a secret.

ILONA: What?

ANATOL: The marriage ceremony is taking place in secret.

ILONA: With toastmasters and bridesmaids? Now, that's nonsense!

MAX: Just the parents aren't allowed to know anything.

ILONA [*sipping her tea; calmly*]: Boys, you're lying to me.

MAX: Oh I beg you!

ILONA: God knows where you two are invited today! . . . But nothing will come of it—Naturally you can go where you want, dear Max—but this one is staying.

ANATOL: Impossible, impossible. I can't be absent from the wedding of my best friend.

ILONA [*to* MAX]: Shall I give him leave to go?

MAX: Dearest, dearest Ilona—you must—

ILONA: Well, which church is this wedding taking place in?

ANATOL [*uneasily*]: Why do you ask?

ILONA: I want to at least see this event.

MAX: But that won't do . . .

ILONA: Well, why not?

ANATOL: Because this wedding is taking place in a completely . . . in a completely underground chapel.

ILONA: But doesn't a path lead to it?

ANATOL: No . . . that is—naturally a path leads to it.

ILONA: I'd like to see this bridesmaid of yours, Anatol. That is to say, I'm jealous of this lady. One hears stories of toastmasters and their bridesmaids getting married afterward. Do you understand, Anatol—I don't want you getting married.

MAX: Well, what would you do then . . . if he did get married?

ILONA [*quite calmly*]: I would disrupt the marriage ceremony.

ANATOL: —Really—?

MAX: And just how would you do that?

ILONA: I'm not sure yet. Probably a great commotion in front of the church door.

MAX: That's trite.

ILONA: Oh, I'd be sure to come up with a new refinement.

MAX: What, for example?

ILONA: I would arrive the same way as a bride—wearing a myrtle wreath—now wouldn't that be inventive?

MAX: Extremely . . . [*Standing up*] I must go now . . . adieu, Anatol!

ANATOL [*standing up, resolvedly*]: Excuse me, dear Ilona, but I must change my clothes now—it's high time.

FRANZ [*entering with a bouquet*]: The flowers, sir.

ILONA: What kind of flowers?

FRANZ [*looking at* ILONA *with an astonished and somewhat friendly expression on his face*]: . . . The flowers, sir.

ILONA: You still have Franz?

[FRANZ *exits.*]

But didn't you want to get rid of him?

MAX: Sometimes that's so difficult.

[ANATOL *holds the bouquet in his hand, wrapped in tissue paper.*]

ILONA: Let me see what kind of taste you have!

MAX: The bouquet for the bridesmaid?

ILONA [*throwing off the tissue paper*]: Why, this is a bride's bouquet!

ANATOL: My God, they sent me the wrong bouquet . . . Franz, Franz!

[*He quickly exits with the bouquet.*]

MAX: The poor bridegroom will receive his bouquet.

ANATOL [*entering again*]: He's already run off, that Franz.—

MAX: And now you must excuse me—I must go.

ANATOL [*accompanying him to the door*]: But what am I supposed to do?

MAX: Confess.

ANATOL: Impossible.

MAX: Well, in any case, I'll come back again, as soon as I can—

ANATOL: I implore you—please do!

MAX: And the color of the dress . . .

ANATOL: Blue or red—I've got such a feeling—Farewell!—

MAX: Adieu, Ilona!—[*Softly*] I'll be back in an hour!

[ANATOL *reenters the room.*]

ILONA [*falling into his arms*]: At last! Oh how happy I am.—

ANATOL [*mechanically*]: My angel!

ILONA: How cold you are.

ANATOL: After all, I just said: my angel.

ILONA: But must you really go off to this stupid wedding?

ANATOL: In all seriousness, darling, I must.

ILONA: But do you know, at least I could come with you in your coach up to the bridesmaid's home . . .

ANATOL: Now what's getting into you? We can meet each other this evening, and after all you must go to the theater today.

ILONA: I'll cancel it.

ANATOL: No, no, I'll pick you up.—Now I must put on the dress coat. [*Looking at the clock*] How the time passes. Franz, Franz!

ILONA: Well, what do you want?

ANATOL [*to* FRANZ *as he enters*]: Did you get everything ready in my room?

FRANZ: You mean the morning coat, the white tie, sir—

ANATOL: Oh well—

FRANZ: I'll immediately see to it, that—

[*He goes into the bedroom.*]

ANATOL [*walking back and forth*]: Say—Ilona—this evening then—after the theater—right—?

ILONA: I'd really like to stay with you today.

ANATOL: Now don't be childish—now I also have—obligations, you certainly realize that!

ILONA: I love you, I don't realize anything more.

ANATOL: But of course it's necessary.

FRANZ [*coming out of the bedroom*]: Everything has been gotten ready, sir.

[*He exits.*]

ANATOL: Good.

[*He goes into the bedroom and continues speaking from behind the door, while* ILONA *remains onstage.*]

I mean, of course it's necessary that you realize that.
ILONA: So you're really changing your clothes?
ANATOL: But I can't go to the wedding like this.
ILONA: Just why are you going?
ANATOL: Are you starting that again? I must.
ILONA: So, this evening.
ANATOL: Yes. I'll wait for you at the stage door.
ILONA: Just don't be late!
ANATOL: No—but why should I be late?
ILONA: Oh just remember, once I waited a whole hour after the theater.
ANATOL: Really? I don't remember.

[*Pause.*]

ILONA [*walks around in the room, taking a look at the ceiling and walls*]: Say, Anatol, isn't that a new picture you have there?
ANATOL: Yes. Do you like it?
ILONA: I just don't understand anything about pictures.
ANATOL: It's a very beautiful picture.
ILONA: Did you bring that along?
ANATOL: What do you mean? From where?
ILONA: Well, from your trip.
ANATOL: Yes, correct, from my trip. No, actually it's a present.

[*Pause.*]

ILONA: Say, Anatol.
ANATOL [*nervously*]: How's that?
ILONA: Just where were you?
ANATOL: I already told you that.

ILONA: No, you didn't say a word.

ANATOL: I told you that last night.

ILONA: Well, I've forgotten it then!

ANATOL: I was in the vicinity of Bohemia.

ILONA: So what was there for you to do in Bohemia then?

ANATOL: I wasn't in Bohemia, just in the vicinity—

ILONA: Ah yes, no doubt you were invited to go hunting.

ANATOL: Yes, I was shooting rabbits.

ILONA: For six weeks?

ANATOL: Yes, without interruption.

ILONA: Why didn't you tell me adieu?

ANATOL: I didn't want to distress you.

ILONA: Do you know, Anatol, I think you wanted to jilt me.

ANATOL: Ridiculous.

ILONA: Well you certainly tried it once before.

ANATOL: Tried—yes, but I didn't succeed.

ILONA: How's that? What are you saying?

ANATOL: Oh well, I wanted to break away from you, you do know that.

ILONA: But that's nonsense, you just can't break away from me!

ANATOL: Ha ha!

ILONA: What are you saying?

ANATOL: Ha ha, I said.

ILONA: Now don't laugh, my darling, you did come back to me that time.

ANATOL: Oh well—that time.

ILONA: And this time too—you simply love me.

ANATOL: Unfortunately.

ILONA: What—?

ANATOL [*yelling*]: Unfortunately!

ILONA: Do you know, you're very courageous when you're in another room. You wouldn't say that to my face.

ANATOL [*opens the door, sticking his head out*]: Unfortunately.

ILONA [*going over to the door*]: What does that mean, Anatol?

ANATOL [*behind the door again*]: That means that this simply can't go on like this forever!

ILONA: What?

ANATOL: It can't go on like this, I'm saying, it can't last forever.

ILONA: Now I'm laughing: ha ha.

ANATOL: What?

ILONA [*tearing open the door*]: Ha ha.

ANATOL: Close it!

[*Door is closed again.*]

ILONA: No, my darling, you love me and you can't leave me.

ANATOL: Do you think so?

ILONA: I feel it.

ANATOL: So you honestly think I'll lie at your feet through all eternity.

ILONA: You won't marry—I know that.

ANATOL: You must be insane, my child. I love you—that's nice, of course—but we're not joined for eternity.

ILONA: Do you think I'll ever give you up at all?

ANATOL: But you'll have to do it sometime.

ILONA: Have to? But when?

ANATOL: When I get married.

ILONA [*pounding on the door*]: And just when will that be, my darling?

ANATOL [*scornfully*]: Oh soon, my darling!

ILONA [*more worked up*]: But when?

ANATOL: Stop that pounding. A year from now I'll long since be married.

ILONA: You fool!

ANATOL: Incidentally, I could even get married in two months.

ILONA: No doubt some woman is already waiting!

ANATOL: Yes—now—some woman is waiting right now.

ILONA: So in two months?

ANATOL: I have a feeling you doubt . . .

[ILONA *laughs.*]

ANATOL: Don't laugh—I'm getting married in a week!

[ILONA *bursts out laughing even more brightly.*]

ANATOL: Don't laugh, Ilona!

[ILONA *sinks laughingly onto the sofa.*]

ANATOL [*near the door, stepping out in a dress coat*]: Don't laugh!
ILONA [*laughing*]: When are you getting married?
ANATOL: Today.
ILONA [*looking at him*]: When—?
ANATOL: Today, my darling.
ILONA [*standing up*]: Anatol, stop joking!
ANATOL: But this is serious, my child, I'm getting married today.
ILONA: You really are crazy?
ANATOL: Franz!
FRANZ [*coming in*]: Sir—?
ANATOL: My bouquet!

[FRANZ *exits.*]

ILONA [*standing threateningly in front of* ANATOL]: Anatol . . . !

[FRANZ *brings the bouquet.* ILONA, *turning around, rushes toward the bouquet with a shout.* ANATOL *quickly takes it out of* FRANZ'*s hand;* FRANZ *exits, slowly and smilingly.*]

ILONA: Ah!!—So it's true.
ANATOL: As you see.

[ILONA *tries to tear the bouquet out of his hand.*]

ANATOL: Just what are you doing?

[*He has to seek refuge from her; she runs after him, around and through the room.*]

ILONA: You wretch, you wretch!

[MAX *enters with a bouquet of roses in his hand and stands still in the door, disconcerted.*]

ANATOL [*has found refuge by standing on an armchair, holding his bouquet high in the air*]: Help me, Max!

[MAX *hastens toward* ILONA, *holding her back; she turns to him, wrests his bouquet out of his hand, throws it onto the floor, and tramples it underfoot.*]

MAX: Ilona, you really are insane. My bouquet! Now what am I supposed to do!

[*Bursting out in violent weeping,* ILONA *sinks down onto a chair.*]

ANATOL [*still on the armchair, embarrassed, at a loss for words*]: She provoked me . . . Yes, Ilona, now you are weeping . . . naturally . . . Why did you laugh in my face . . . ? She scoffed at me—do you understand, Max? . . . She said . . . that I wouldn't have the nerve to get married . . . well . . . the fact remains I am getting married—just to be contrary.

[*He begins to climb down from the armchair.*]

ILONA: You hypocrite, you deceiver.

[ANATOL *gets up on the armchair again.*]

MAX [*has picked up his bouquet*]: My bouquet!

ILONA: I was aiming for his. But you don't deserve any better either.—You're an accessory.

ANATOL [*still standing on the armchair*]: Now be reasonable.

ILONA: Yes—you men always say that when you've driven a woman insane! But now you'll see something! It will be a fine wedding! Just you wait . . . [*Getting up*] Meanwhile, adieu!

ANATOL [*having jumped down from the armchair*]: Where are you going—?

ILONA: You'll see.

ANATOL AND MAX: Where are you going?

ILONA: Just let me go!

ANATOL AND MAX [*barring her exit*]: Ilona—what do you want—Fräulein Ilona—what do you want—?

ILONA: Let me go! . . . Let me go.

ANATOL: Be sensible—calm down—!

ILONA: You're not letting me out of here.—What . . . [*Running around in the room, throws the tea service off the table in a rage*] [ANATOL *and* MAX *at a loss.*]

ANATOL: Now I ask you—is it necessary to get married when one is loved *so very* much!

[ILONA *sinks down brokenhearted onto the couch, weeps. Pause.*]

ANATOL: Now she's calming down.

MAX: We must go . . . and I without—a bouquet.—

FRANZ [*coming into the room*]: The coach, sir.

[*He exits.*]

ANATOL: The coach . . . The coach—just what am I to do? [*Goes over to* ILONA, *stepping behind her, kissing her hair*] Ilona!—

MAX [*from the other side*]: Ilona—

[*She continues weeping quietly, with a handkerchief in front of her face.*]

Just go now and rely on me.—

ANATOL: I really must go—but how can I . . .

MAX: Go . . .

ANATOL: Will you be able to get her out of here?

MAX: I'll whisper in your ear during the ceremony . . . "Everything is in good order."

ANATOL: I have one fear—!

MAX: Just go now.

ANATOL: Ah . . .

[*He turns to leave, comes back again on tiptoes, presses a soft kiss on* ILONA*'s hair, exits quickly.*]

MAX [*sits down across from* ILONA, *who is still weeping, holding her handkerchief in front of her face; looking at the clock*]: Hmm, hmm.

ILONA [*looking around, as if awakening from a dream*]: Where is he . . . ?

MAX [*taking her by the hands*]: Ilona . . .

ILONA [*getting up*]: Where is he . . . ?

MAX [*not letting go of her hands*]: You wouldn't find him.

ILONA: But I want to.

ANATOL: You are reasonable after all, Ilona, you certainly don't want any big commotion . . .

ILONA: Let me—

MAX: Ilona!

ILONA: Where is the wedding taking place?

MAX: That's beside the point.

ILONA: I want to go there, I must go there!

MAX: You will not do that . . . why, what's gotten into you!

ILONA: Oh this scorn! . . . This deception!

MAX: It's neither one thing nor the other—it is simply life!

ILONA: Just be quiet—you—and your phrases.

MAX: You are being childish, Ilona; otherwise you would realize that it is all in vain.

ILONA: In vain—?!

MAX: It's just nonsense . . . !

ILONA: Nonsense!—?

MAX: You would make yourself ridiculous—that's all.

ILONA: What—some more insults!

MAX: You will find consolation!

ILONA: Oh how poorly you know me!

MAX: Yes, if he were to go to America.

ILONA: What does that mean?

MAX: If he were really out of your reach?

ILONA: What does that signify?

MAX: The main point is—that you are not the one who has been deceived!

ILONA: . . . !

MAX: One could leave the other one and return to you!

ILONA [*with a wild, joyful expression in her face*]: Oh . . . if that were . . .

MAX: You are noble . . . [*pressing her hand*]

ILONA: I want to get revenge . . . that's why what you said makes me happy.

MAX: You are one of those women "who bite when they love."

ILONA: Yes, I am one of those.

MAX: Now you appear to me as quite grand.—Like a woman who would like revenge on us for her whole sex.

ILONA: —Yes—Yes . . . I want that . . .

MAX [*standing up*]: I just have time yet to drive you to your home. [*To himself*] Otherwise another misfortune will happen.—[*Giving her his arm*] Now say farewell to these rooms!

ILONA: No, my dear friend—not farewell. I will be coming back!

MAX: Now you think yourself a demon—and actually you are only a woman after all! [*In response to a discontented movement of hers*] . . . But that is enough too . . . [*Opening the door for her*]—If you please, my Fräulein?—

ILONA [*turning around once more before walking out, with affected grandeur*]: Auf Wiedersehen! . . .

[*She exits with* MAX.]

[*Curtain*]

ORIGINAL VERSION OF "ANATOL'S WEDDING MORNING" (1888)

Written in London in 1888, the original version of "Anatol's Wedding Morning" differs from the scene as it appears on pages 76–94. The two versions open in the same way, with the setting of the scene and Anatol's initial exchange with Franz.

ANATOL [*doesn't notice the servant at first, then runs after him and prevents him from opening the door*]: Why are you slinking around like that? I didn't even hear you!
FRANZ: What do you wish, sir?
ANATOL: The samovar!

[FRANZ *opens the door and exits,* HERR WINKLER *then walks in.* ANATOL *goes toward him; composedly.*]

ANATOL: Oh, my dear Papa!

[HERR WINKLER *is taken aback at the word "Papa."* MAX *bows, makes a move to leave.*]

HERR WINKLER: Stay.—I'd like you to stay.
ANATOL: Don't you want to have a seat, Papa?
HERR WINKLER: Don't keep saying "Papa!"
ANATOL [*to himself*]: He knows—!
HERR WINKLER: My dear, young friend—
MAX: Friend?—
ANATOL: You're putting me on tenterhooks. Please talk, Papa.
HERR WINKLER: Don't say "Papa" to me—I'm not that.
ANATOL [*fearfully*]: But in a few hours . . .

HERR WINKLER: Not ever!—Are you ready to hear the worst? Oh, my daughter—my daughter!

MAX: Please go ahead and explain yourself! You see Anatol is quite beside himself.

ANATOL: That I am, sir!

MAX: Tell us what's wrong with your daughter.

HERR WINKLER: I don't know . . . I don't know!

ANATOL: What . . . just what . . . ?

HERR WINKLER: I don't know—she has gone away!

MAX: Eloped!

HERR WINKLER: Sir, a Fräulein von Winkler does not elope!

ANATOL: Oh—of all days to go away!

HERR WINKLER: Just last night, on the post coach.

ANATOL: It certainly looks like she's just fleeing from me.

HERR WINKLER: I was afraid you'd take it like that.

MAX: It looks rather like she's fleeing to someone else.

ANATOL [*gloomily*]: With someone else.

HERR WINKLER: Who told you—

ANATOL: Herr Kalmon has abducted your daughter.

HERR WINKLER: You know that too?

ANATOL: I had a suspicion! A suspicion!

MAX: Can't you give my friend further particulars?

ANATOL: I request them at once.

HERR WINKLER [*to* ANATOL]: Thank you for staying calm.

ANATOL: Yes indeed, Papa.

[HERR WINKLER *jerks.*]

ANATOL: Herr Kalmon's Papa, I am calm.

MAX: Tell us.

HERR WINKLER: As if I knew all that much myself! I only know that she was, to my surprise, missing for breakfast at seven. You understand, I was hoping to have breakfast with her today. I asked the maid, but my daughter was already gone at seven. This reassured me.

MAX: Reassured you?

ANATOL: How could it?

HERR WINKLER: I thought perhaps she had gone to confession.

[ANATOL *laughs bitterly.*]

HERR WINKLER: Oh well, sometimes young girls are so high-strung. And I waited.

MAX: How long?

HERR WINKLER: It got to be eight and then nine. I had breakfast alone.

MAX: The poor father!

ANATOL: Go on, go on!

HERR WINKLER: The hairdresser came, she waited with me. The dressmaker came, she waited with me and the hairdresser. Finally the florist came, they all waited with me. I walked back and forth in the room, I went out to the staircase, I looked out one of the windows. I had the consoling thought: if she doesn't come from one side, she'll come from the other. She didn't come from any side! At ten a telegram came from Linz. I trembled. Here it is, read it.

ANATOL: I can't! Max!

MAX [*reading*]: "We await your blessing in the Hotel at the Sign of the Crab. Telegraphic response paid for. Alexandra and Kalmon."

ANATOL [*bitterly*]: Ha!

MAX [*to* HERR WINKLER]: And now? Your blessing?

ANATOL [*likewise to* HERR WINKLER]: You have already had it sent by telegram?

MAX: I regard it as very generous of Herr Kalmon to pay for your blessing in advance.

HERR WINKLER: Ah, Herr Kalmon—that wretch! "Telegraphic response paid for"—that's my daughter's style!

ANATOL: I would have played a pathetic role, had I showed up there with my bouquet at noon—and Fräulein Alexandra didn't even think it necessary to let me know!

HERR WINKLER: Just don't be so hard on her! The poor child . . . after all, she couldn't think of everything.

ANATOL: And the wedding guests? And the banquet? And the caterers?

HERR WINKLER: I fled from that, and I'll go back late this afternoon to pack my bag and go away.

FRANZ [*entering*]: A telegram.

ANATOL [*tearing it out of his hand*]: "Don't love you, would have been unhappy, esteem you nevertheless. Don't be angry. Send me pardon. Alexandra."

MAX: Telegraphic response paid for?

ANATOL: Not even that!

HERR WINKLER: Do you understand, my friend, that I can do no more?

MAX: There'll be nothing left for you to do except send her your pardon.

ANATOL: Pardon her? Not ever!

HERR WINKLER: But I ask you, what do you want to do?

ANATOL: I don't know yet.

[*He walks back and forth.*]

HERR WINKLER [*to* MAX]: What will he do?

[MAX *shrugs his shoulders.*]

ANATOL: I will pardon her.

HERR WINKLER: I thank you!

ANATOL: But I'll know where to find Herr Kalmon!

HERR WINKLER: You want to steal her husband?

MAX: Calm yourself, Herr von Winkler; like you, my friend will also go away. How quickly one forgets.

HERR WINKLER: You will be noble!

ANATOL: Yes indeed!

HERR WINKLER: You are pardoning her?

ANATOL [*giving him his hand*]: This is for your daughter and Herr Kalmon.—Your Château d'Iquem will be served tonight?

HERR WINKLER: Of course it will be.

ANATOL: And your Rhine wine, vintage '36?

HERR WINKLER: Yes.

ANATOL: I was almost afraid I'd pardoned Herr Kalmon too quickly.

FRANZ [*entering*]: My lord, the coach is ready.

ANATOL: I no longer have need of it.

HERR WINKLER: I'll be using it right away, if it's already here. Now farewell, my friend.

ANATOL: Depart in peace.

HERR WINKLER [*moved*]: Farewell.

[*He exits.*]

ANATOL: What now?

MAX: I find it quite charming that Fräulein Alexandra reached this conclusion before she married you.

ILONA [*entering quickly*]: Well, what's going on?

ANATOL: My child, I'm not going to the wedding, we're staying together.

ILONA: What?

ANATOL: Yes, and even more! Can you take a quick vacation?

ILONA: Right away.

ANATOL: Well, I'm inviting you to go to Italy with me this evening.

ILONA: You're an angel! First-class compartment?

ANATOL: Already ordered.

MAX: He thinks of everything!

[FRANZ *enters.*]

ANATOL: What do you want, you rogue?

FRANZ: I wanted to remind my lord—

ANATOL: Never mind, never mind! I'm not going anywhere.

FRANZ: So I may unpack?

ANATOL: Of course not. I am traveling, as was arranged.

ILONA: Franz! Send this telegram for me.

ANATOL: Let me see it!

ILONA: Don't be nosey!

ANATOL: But after all, I am allowed—?

ILONA: You don't trust me.

ANATOL: Trust who? I wish to see it . . . I wish to know what it is!

ILONA: After all, I gave it to Franz, so it's not for any rival.

ANATOL: Franz—out of here! He's still standing here.

[FRANZ *exits.*]

ANATOL: That's just it: you want to mollify me!

[*He wrests it from her and reads.*]

Oh! Oh!

MAX: What's going on? May one read it? "Herr Kalmon, Linz, Hotel at the Sign of the Red Crab. We pardon you. Anatol and Ilona."

ANATOL: You heard!

ILONA: Every word!

ANATOL: And—?

ILONA: And am not at all angry with you.

MAX: You're magnanimous!

ILONA: By no means. We quickly pardon unfaithfulness where love is not involved. Now confess: you're really glad she eloped.

ANATOL: I could almost love her for it.

MAX: And the telegram?

ANATOL: Will be dispatched! They'll find out about it at the Red Crab.

ILONA: That we're happy!

MAX: That you two are witty.

ANATOL: No, that there is someone to be envied more than the woman who deceives, namely, the man who finds consolation for it.

[*Curtain*]

Anatol: Two Supplementary Scenes

The two pieces that follow are not part of the Anatol series as it is generally known. "Anatol's Delusions of Grandeur," which Schnitzler intended as an alternative to "Anatol's Wedding Morning," features the aging Anatol. "The Adventure of a Lifetime" not only offers the earliest version (1886) of the Anatol *sequence but also presents many of the basic conflicts in compressed form, thereby lending itself to performance on its own. These two less frequently published scenes, together with the seven "canonical" ones, offer theatrical groups a complete spectrum of possibilities for performance: one or more of the scenes may be omitted, as seems feasible or appropriate.*

ANATOL'S DELUSIONS OF GRANDEUR

Characters

Anatol

Max, *Anatol's confidant*

Baron Diebl

Annette

Flieder, *a musician*

Berta

[*The garden of a pleasant inn, the facade of which occupies most of the background. A broad veranda runs along the entire facade. Two staircases lead from the inn to the garden. In the remaining background, not filled by the inn, a gentle, hilly landscape is visible, just starting to sink into twilight.—While the area to one side of the house is situated in the wing, the area to the other is exposed and in it a path is visible, lined with poplar trees and leading directly up to the lattice gate of the garden. As in the garden, separate tables and chairs are on the veranda, all of them empty except where* ANATOL *and* MAX *are seated on the veranda, smoking cigarettes.*]

ANATOL: Don't you remember, my dear Max, how we sat here last time?

MAX: Now that was surely a long while ago!

ANATOL: Yes . . . in those days I happened to need a setting like this . . . with its unpretentiousness and gentility. . . . I needed this country road with its trite poplars . . . those meadows over there with their soft green . . . the hills nearby, disappearing into the red glow of evening . . .

MAX: And today?

ANATOL: Today I love that background for its own sake—

MAX: Is this your last love?

ANATOL: No . . . just a new kind of love, whose turn it is right now, which means love for things as they are—

MAX: Oh . . . ?

ANATOL: For nature as nature . . . for the hills as hills . . . for cigars as cigars . . . for a Persian sofa as a Persian sofa . . . whereas up until now I only loved things for their connections with people.

MAX: So now you're finished with us poor folks?

ANATOL: Oh no! My friends—you in particular—I still do love you.

MAX: Well don't believe that! I'm always here just for your cues.

ANATOL: If that was the case . . . that's changing now, my dear friend. I fear that's also a sign of approaching age. Lately I've been noticeably interested in the opinions of others.

MAX: Ah!

ANATOL: I can listen, I become attentive . . .

MAX: Is that why you've sought me out again after all this time?

ANATOL: I had such a deep need to speak with you again! It's as if I had to prattle off my last will and testament to you!

MAX: Oh go on . . . what kind of posing is that! Sentimentalities!

ANATOL: No . . . I'm quite serious . . . the end, my dear friend! My heart is drawing up its last will!

MAX: Is that what's making you sad?

ANATOL: No, oh no.—I no longer want to be loved—I don't want that.

MAX: Well, you'd know how to yield to that.

ANATOL: No . . . I don't want to lose my last illusion!

MAX: Which one is that?

ANATOL: That the young fellows have nothing to fear from us. That's one illusion I've arduously preserved.

MAX: You certainly never had them before—such illusions! Surely you don't believe that! You were always a virtuoso when it came to jealousy!

ANATOL: That may well be! I'm just speaking at random . . . it occurred to me like that . . . ! By the way, do you have anything against my asserting the opposite of what I said a minute ago?

MAX: Oh, I expected that!

ANATOL: At times I do want to be loved again, after all! Quite simply, everything is over, my dear Max, isn't it—

MAX: You're still not tired of yearning?

ANATOL: How could that be? I only understood the art of gaining as much experience as possible from externals, at very little expense . . . and now sometimes my whole past seems so paltry—and then again so remarkably rich at times . . .

MAX: There you go with our horrible habit of always wanting to have measurements!

ANATOL: You're right, that's wrong! And one certainly can't rely on memory . . . it tells lies, it has moods . . . and then what do we ourselves actually know about our adventures? We and women—we certainly are on different paths with our yearning! I've asked them all: "Haven't you loved someone before me?"—And they all asked me: "Will you love someone after me? . . ." We always want to be her first love and she wants to be our last!

MAX: Of course . . . of course!

ANATOL: The other day I saw that little girl, Annette, the one who's running around with the violinist. . . . Delightful, I tell you . . .

MAX: Well, and?

ANATOL: That Flieder fellow is young, amiable, gifted, whereas I'm . . . well, different in all possible respects, certainly no longer young, almost gray . . .

MAX: Well, what about that Annette?

ANATOL: She's flirting!

MAX: Well?

ANATOL: With me . . . with me, if you please! It's annoying! She goes walking with that young person, hanging on his arm in the manner of very young women . . . with ecstatic, idiotic, immoral eyes. I come by . . . the eyes stop being ecstatic, they fix on me, they're no longer idiotic, but sweet and crafty . . . but they remain immoral . . .

MAX: Now why are you suddenly telling me about Annette?

ANATOL: It went through my mind like that. I think there's no possibility at all of feeling secure! You see, however well we know a woman, we can only know how she loves us, and never . . . how she could love someone else! Therefore it's no guarantee when a woman idolizes us with tears in her eyes and swoons with affection, which so often makes us gullible. . . . Perhaps she's adoring someone else at the same time, as a quite different woman . . . thoughtless, graceful, and impetuous . . .

MAX: So you think that little Annette is playing sentimental with Flieder?

ANATOL: Playing?—Is!!—Well, women themselves imagine they're just playacting because now they feel like this, and now like that. And that amazes them. And often there's no trace of playacting in it.—They're not even lying, as often as we believe . . . it's just their realities are changing on them every minute . . .

MAX: How quiet it is here! That's certainly a pleasure!

ANATOL: Yes, it's too bad we have nothing to recover from! This would be just the right kind of evening quiet with which to get over such pains!

MAX: Well, who has ever gotten over a pain that's so real?

ANATOL: Ah, over every one of them! Every time I've experienced that, it's been so banal I finally came to distrust mine as well. That was my last and deepest pain!

MAX: And thus consolation itself becomes painful . . .

ANATOL: Might that perhaps be true? Just think how much a solitary walk, an hour of reflection, a poem written from the soul can accomplish at times!

MAX: Oh, solitude seems to be over for us now . . . do you hear?

ANATOL: What . . . ?

MAX [*looking over the railing; sound of coaches rolling*]: Why they're already rounding the corner and rushing this way, straight this way!

ANATOL: Just how many coaches are there?

MAX: Two . . . three . . . Good Lord, but they're rushing! Here comes one more over the crossing . . .

ANATOL: Directly toward us?

[*Sound of coaches, horses' hooves.*]

MAX: Gentlemen and ladies. Ah, just look! They're waving their handkerchiefs!

ANATOL: Acquaintances?

[*The coaches drive past on the country road and stop at the imaginary back of the building. "Good evening, gentlemen!" can be heard from one of the coaches.*]

ANATOL: Good evening! Who is it, then?

MAX: One of them was Baron Diebl. Ah, in the last coach . . . just look, Berta!

ANATOL: What?! Is she still enjoying herself?

MAX: She still is! And when I think she's been doing that for twenty years!

ANATOL: In those days she was sixteen!

MAX: It's good that one can't see into the future after all.

ANATOL: Why?

MAX [*pointing toward the street*]: Because this picture would already have occurred to you!

ANATOL: Oh Lord . . . we aren't spared these pictures, they're just not as exact!—By the way, have you already excluded those other women?

MAX: Not quite exactly.

ANATOL: That noise!

MAX: Well, they're probably not coming to us! They'll sit down in the salon and then they won't disturb us any further!

ANATOL: That's Baron Diebl . . . he's still alive!

MAX: Don't you sometimes still get together with him and his party?

ANATOL: Oh no, I've never associated much with them. They make me nervous, those people. You see, one converses with them only when one's drunk. But I've never been drunk . . .

MAX: Well, they're certainly very happy in their way!

BARON DIEBL [*entering*]: Good evening, greetings to you both! I recognized you from the street!

ANATOL: Good evening!

MAX: Good evening!

BARON DIEBL: So one has to come out here to find you!

ANATOL: Well, not exactly!

BARON DIEBL: So where have you been hiding? Been away?

ANATOL: I've been here!

BARON DIEBL: So you've become a hermit!

ANATOL: I've stayed a hermit!

BARON DIEBL: Oh! [*To* MAX] What do you say, dear friend—he's stayed that way! He's of the opinion that he always was.

MAX: Yes, that's the way I understood it!

BARON DIEBL: But then I must request you not to be like that! You were once a very jolly fellow. And I'm sure you still are!

ANATOL: I was never a jolly fellow.

BARON DIEBL: Really! Well, today you have the chance to be one!

ANATOL: You're too kind!

BARON DIEBL: Yes, both of you! You'll be meeting some acquaintances, almost nobody you don't already know!

ANATOL: You're really too generous—but we're in the process of starting home.

BARON DIEBL: Starting home?! Don't be ridiculous! You'll have the time of your life! Imagine who is here! Aside from Berta . . . for she's always here. So just listen: Juliette! You do know her?

MAX: The French woman?

BARON DIEBL: Yes, picture it, and he—her husband—is making a trip around the world! Isn't that convenient for her!

MAX: Oh Lord, a woman could even deceive a man while he is driving to the suburbs . . .

BARON DIEBL: Ah, very good . . . you're right about that! [*To* ANATOL] He thinks the ladies will take advantage of any opportunity!

ANATOL: Yes, yes, I understood him!

BARON DIEBL: But you didn't laugh! One is supposed to laugh at a joke! So, what was I saying . . . Juliette! Yes, then Rosa, who has gotten horribly proud. It's to my credit that she came along at all! You wanted to know why she has gotten proud?

ANATOL: No . . .

BARON DIEBL [*to* MAX]: Not you either?

MAX: Oh yes. Why has Rosa gotten so horribly proud?

BARON DIEBL: It's not known for sure . . . it's just rumored: too many crowns in his coat of arms!

MAX: Oh.

BARON DIEBL: Yes, say no more about that! Then "Fräulein" Hanischek is with—quite recent—is just now making her debut!

MAX: "Fräulein" Hanischek? That's simply dreadful!

BARON DIEBL: "Fräulein" is just her nickname for now. She is called that! But then her first name is even worse. Just guess. Well . . .

ANATOL: But how am I supposed to figure out her first name?

BARON DIEBL: Agnes! And not only that, she still doesn't have a nom de guerre . . . She might even be christened today.

MAX [*still quite startled*]: Agnes! Agnes!!

BARON DIEBL: Well, what do you two say to that? Agnes! I would just like to know how her lovers have managed with that name! And picture poor Fritz Walten, who's got her now . . . he hasn't come up with any other name yet, poor devil! He still has to keep on calling her Agnes! But you two aren't even asking me who else is here?

MAX: Yes, if you please, who else is here?

BARON DIEBL: Tell me first if you two want to come.

ANATOL: As far as I'm concerned, dear Baron, I'm simply not in the mood for it.

BARON DIEBL: What? Am I really supposed to believe that you can no longer get in the mood for such a thing?

ANATOL: But is it so very inconceivable that one just isn't so inclined?

BARON DIEBL: Ah, blasé!

ANATOL: I've no desire to converse about it, I don't have your gift for being cheerful.

BARON DIEBL: I've seen you cheerful that way before!

ANATOL: Then you misunderstood me. In any case, I've had my cheerfulness . . . but never that of others!

BARON DIEBL: Well, everyone is as cheerful as he can be.

ANATOL: Yes, and on behalf of those waiting below, I thank you very much!

BARON DIEBL: Ah, perhaps we're not delicate enough when it comes to the fairer sex . . .

ANATOL: Well, what do they mean to people like you?

BARON DIEBL: To hear you talk, one would think the kind of women you've loved are quite different from the ones we ordinary people . . .

ANATOL: Certainly . . . for I was the one who loved them! Or do you really believe I lead the same life as the rest of you, as you, sir? You believe our adventures were the same because they looked alike from the outside. . . . The rest of you seek the flirt in every woman . . . and I sought the woman in every flirt!

BARON DIEBL: It only follows that I didn't need to seek as long . . .

ANATOL: And that you were frequently mistaken!

BARON DIEBL: And you were mistaken every time . . . like everyone who worships the ladies!

ANATOL: I do not worship them!

MAX: Oh yes! You worship that which you bestow on them. That's artistic vanity!

ANATOL: And therefore the amateurs of love don't even comprehend me!

BARON DIEBL: Well then, practice your artistry among us today!

ANATOL: That can't always be done . . .

BARON DIEBL: Perhaps there is someone after all who could interest you today.

ANATOL: That "Fräulein" Hanischek?!

BARON DIEBL: Oh no! Something quite special . . . a girl as young and beautiful as a goddess! Among us today for the first time!

ANATOL: Alone?

BARON DIEBL: Oh no . . . with him . . . with Flieder!

ANATOL: With whom?!

BARON DIEBL: With that Flieder fellow from the opera.

ANATOL: Ah, Annette?

BARON DIEBL: Yes. He . . . as jealous as a fool—enough to make you die laughing—she . . . enchanting, naive, almost!

ANATOL: Give her my greetings!

BARON DIEBL: So even that doesn't attract you? Well, how is one to entice you then? Say, Max, could he seriously be in love? [*To* ANATOL] Or are you yearning for something quite wonderful, untouched . . . for a woman who doesn't know anything at all about life and love? Am I not right, Max? Well wait! Next time we'll bring along a virgin for you!

ANATOL: Not necessary. I make virgins for myself!

BARON DIEBL: Oh, but sometimes that might have its difficulties!

ANATOL: Isn't that the only ambition in love?

MAX: No, just the only one that can't be fulfilled!

ANATOL: To make the others forgotten, as if they've never been.

BARON DIEBL: Yes, but imagine if this effort weren't even necessary . . .

MAX: If one has nothing, nothing at all to pardon . . .

ANATOL: One always has something to pardon.

MAX: Even if one is the first?

ANATOL: Yes, that it perhaps could have been someone else. Indeed, where one is the first, one has perhaps even more to pardon than in other cases . . . oneself!

BARON DIEBL: We can't deal with this gentleman today.

ANATOL: Don't let that bother you, Max!

MAX: Do you want to stay here alone?

ANATOL: For a while yet. Perhaps you'll still find me here when you come back.

MAX [*to* BARON DIEBL]: Well, then I'd like to walk with you for a few moments.

BARON DIEBL: So, auf Wiedersehen, my melancholy Anatol!

ANATOL: Adieu!

[BARON DIEBL *and* MAX *exit.* ANATOL *lights himself a cigarette, looks across the railing of the veranda into the twilight—then takes his hat and cane and is about to leave. The door opens and* ANNETTE *steps onto the veranda.*]

ANNETTE: Herr Anatol!

ANATOL: . . . ?

ANNETTE: Oh, you were about to leave?

ANATOL: Fräulein Annette, it is you?

ANNETTE: Yes, it's Fräulein Annette! They sent me for you . . .

ANATOL: So you're really here with these people?

ANNETTE: Yes, the Baron did tell you that!

ANATOL: Of course, of course . . .

ANNETTE: Then why are you so sad?

ANATOL: Sad?

ANNETTE: Why don't you want to join us? It's so nice! If you were there, it would be even nicer!

ANATOL: I just can't understand why you're here!

ANNETTE: But why?

ANATOL: I don't understand how one can find happiness among people . . . and even more so, how one can associate with people at all . . .

ANNETTE: What . . . you don't understand that? Then you're just exactly like him!

ANATOL: But why?

ANNETTE: He really doesn't understand it either. You wouldn't believe how he shuns being seen with me!

ANATOL: Ah!

ANNETTE: He's always wanting to be alone with me . . .

ANATOL: But that goes without saying!

ANNETTE: Well, you know, at times I really do like to go walking with him, for I love nature . . .

ANATOL: Really!

ANNETTE: Oh, very much!

ANATOL: But you also like people, don't you? A fun-loving get-together, with singing and drinking!

ANNETTE: Oh yes . . . I prefer that even more.

ANATOL: And does he know that?

ANNETTE: He certainly must know it.

ANATOL: Do you tell him that?

ANNETTE: What should I tell him?

ANATOL: Well, perhaps something like this: "My friend, I love you very much, but solitude makes me very sad . . . and I want to have fun."

ANNETTE: But look, if I told him that bluntly, it would hurt him . . . he's so jealous of everything! Sometimes I'm not even allowed to laugh!

ANATOL: Well, then do it now, where he can't hear you.

ANNETTE: Yes . . . but now I don't feel like it.

ANATOL: Sooo!

ANNETTE: And just when I do feel like it, I'm not allowed to! Why, only the other day . . .

ANATOL: Well, why do you hesitate, then?

ANNETTE: I've stayed too long with you, they'll get impatient . . .

ANATOL: But come on and tell me.

[*He draws her beside him on the bench, holds her hand; she looks at him, then smiles flirtatiously.*]

Now, what was it about the other day?

ANNETTE: Well, at one point the other day I wanted to laugh but wasn't allowed to . . . then he spoke for so long and was so funny that the tears came to his eyes . . .

ANATOL: Well?

ANNETTE: Just think—a man who cries. He better not do that again.

ANATOL: You told him that?

ANNETTE: Oh no, I simply suppressed laughing, as much as I could . . .

ANATOL: My dear child!

ANNETTE [*flirtatiously*]: Do you really like my hand so much?

ANATOL: You probably don't love him very intensely . . . as deeply as he would like to be loved . . . you should make that clear to him . . .

ANNETTE: Kiss my hand!

ANATOL: But why . . .

ANNETTE: Well, then let go of it . . .

ANATOL [*kisses her hand, brief pause*]: Yes, then you would have to tell him . . .

ANNETTE: But what . . .

ANATOL: That what he's demanding isn't love, that you can't love him like that . . .

ANNETTE: Well, then he'd surely be unhappy!

ANATOL: But that's good!

ANNETTE: I certainly do love him . . . but I don't want any emotion, no, no, not any emotion! [*Jumping up*] Oh no . . . I've completely forgotten why I came here! You're supposed to come along downstairs now!

ANATOL: My dear child, I would rather chat alone with you here . . .

ANNETTE: We can also chat alone downstairs.

ANATOL: Oh, what would he say?

ANNETTE: But we will be speaking very softly.

ANATOL: That would hardly reassure him . . .

ANNETTE: Are you coming downstairs, then?

ANATOL: What affectionate eyes you have when you ask . . .

ANNETTE: I can't be resisted, can I?

ANATOL: Perhaps you can, after all!

ANNETTE [*suddenly, with hands raised*]: Come!

ANATOL: But my child!

ANNETTE [*quite suddenly at his feet*]: Anatol, come!

ANATOL: What's gotten into you?

ANNETTE: After all, one can play a bit of comedy!

ANATOL: Good that you at least admit it.

ANNETTE: But if it were the truth?

ANATOL: Stand up, if you please!

ANNETTE [*standing up*]: And I'm leading you downstairs with me . . . and you'll sit down beside me . . . and . . .

ANATOL: I can see it! You're using me to make him jealous . . .

ANNETTE: But why? Don't you believe I like you?

ANATOL: You're a little bit too much of a flirt, Annette!

ANNETTE: You're saying that because you don't believe me.

[*She takes a flower from her breast, kisses it, and gives it to* ANATOL.]

Is this also flirting?

[*At this moment,* BARON DIEBL, FLIEDER, *and* BERTA *appear.*]

BARON DIEBL: Well, what is it, Annette? We wanted to gain a man and we're losing one more woman!

ANNETTE: I don't believe it will do any good.

FLIEDER: You've probably not tried everything yet!

ANATOL: Herr Flieder! Oh . . . Berta!!

BERTA: Yes, it's me. And, if you please, come with us. Will you say no to my request?

ANATOL: Such graciousness, such kindness!

BERTA: Yes . . . an old love never dies!

ANATOL: I'm coming, I'm coming . . . I can't resist any longer!

BERTA: Don't you want to take my arm?

[*The others go on ahead.*]

ANATOL: One moment, Berta! I have to ask you something!

BERTA: Yes . . . well, what's wrong, my old Anatol?

ANATOL: Just how long has it been since I last talked to you?

BERTA: Do you still remember how long it has been?

ANATOL: The last time was years and years ago . . .

BERTA: But what are you thinking!

ANATOL: Ah well . . . of course we've been seeing each other . . . we've also been talking . . . yes, yes . . . but when was it just the two of us?

BERTA: What do you mean?

ANATOL: We've chatted like old acquaintances who've lived their whole loves separately. . . . What we once meant to each other has simply disappeared from our memory . . .

BERTA: Oh, I recall very well . . .

ANATOL: You still remember?

BERTA: But you silly little fool . . . I've never forgotten anyone!

ANATOL: How young, how young we were in those days! And I don't know how it happens . . . it seems as if today I'm seeing you again for the first time since our last kiss! . . . In all those very long years since then . . . what actually happened to you?

BERTA: Well, things went quite well for me.

ANATOL: Of course I continued to meet you here and there . . . but what happened to you? Do you know it hardly ever occurred to me whenever I encountered you . . . that she . . . she was once my sweetheart . . .

BERTA: Very flattering!

ANATOL: Actually, it's indeed fortunate . . . for I honestly worshipped you . . .

BERTA: Oh, I remember, I remember!

ANATOL: Doesn't it suddenly appear to you again, so clearly, that distant time?

BERTA: Oh, I still remember everything . . .

ANATOL: Ah!

BERTA: For example . . . just wait . . . how you paraded in front of my window!

ANATOL: Ah! You still think about that?

BERTA: Yes, it was so funny!

ANATOL: Hmm . . . many things may well have seemed funny to you, in those days . . .

BERTA: Oh no, you were so sweet!

ANATOL: Ah, come now! Now let's start by telling each other everything!

BERTA: Everything?

ANATOL: Yes, everything! I still have so much to ask you!

BERTA: I just don't understand you at all . . . that occurs to you today?

ANATOL: Well, I just told you: I'm seeing you today for the first time, and it seems to me as if we separated that last time without saying everything. . . . There were so many riddles in your eyes . . . even your smile was so peculiar . . . and then . . .

BERTA: Well, and what else?

ANATOL: You found consolation so quickly . . .

BERTA: Oh well . . .

ANATOL: What?

BERTA: And you did too! Now please . . . after all, we both knew that it had to be over sometime . . .

ANATOL: You knew it?

BERTA: Well, what do you think? That we're supposed to believe unquestioningly what you men tell us?

ANATOL: But at that time . . . at that time, when you were still practically a child . . .

BERTA: Oh, good lord, I was always shrewd . . .

ANATOL: And when we swore each other eternal love . . . you always knew that really . . .

BERTA: Well . . . and you? Perhaps you wanted to marry me?

ANATOL: But after all, we worshiped each other!

BERTA: Well, well . . . but that certainly doesn't mean we have to lose our heads . . . !

ANATOL: Yes, yes . . .

BERTA: Shall we go inside now?

ANATOL: But please . . . it's so beautiful here . . . this evening breeze is so gentle . . .

BERTA: Ah! Are you still like that?

ANATOL: Like what?

BERTA: Well, that you're so poetic.

ANATOL: Because I find the breeze gentle?

BERTA: Do you see how I still remember everything . . . ? You also brought me poems sometimes . . .

ANATOL: So . . . I don't think about that anymore!

BERTA: One time I read one of them with Flora . . . do you still think about Flora, the blonde?

[*She laughs.*]

ANATOL: Well, so why are you laughing?

BERTA: She recited it . . . you remember . . . with lots of pathos, and she imitated your eyes too . . .

ANATOL: My eyes?

BERTA: Yes, those big, soulful eyes!

ANATOL: So . . . do I have such soulful eyes?

BERTA: Oh, we could read all kinds of things in them!

ANATOL: Even jealousy?

BERTA: Why do you ask that?

ANATOL: Hmm . . . I'm just remembering a certain evening when we went to the theater together . . .

BERTA: We went there often!

ANATOL: Well, I'm remembering a very definite evening. It was at an operetta and a fashionable gentleman with a full grizzled beard was sitting beside us, and he was staring at you . . .

BERTA: Now really!

ANATOL: He was staring at you, as if he knew you . . .

BERTA: Ah, that was that Frenchman . . . a big man.

ANATOL: Yes, yes, a Frenchman! You knew him?

BERTA: Yes . . . no!

ANATOL: Yes, yes! You didn't tell me that at the time!

BERTA: Oh well, at the time. But you were so jealous!

ANATOL: Yes, because he kept staring at you!

BERTA: Well, what could I do about that?

ANATOL: Where did you know him from?

BERTA: Well, what can I say? Just what do you want from me? I think I'm meeting an old friend, and now he's taking advantage like a lover!

ANATOL: You'd better answer me. I still recall just exactly . . . I still recall . . . how you tried to reassure me that evening! The words are still in my ear!

BERTA: The words?

ANATOL: And the look with which you told me, "Ah, but now you're even jealous of that old man there!"

BERTA [*laughs*]: And he wasn't all that old!

ANATOL: So you lied to me, you simply lied to me in those days!

BERTA [*furiously*]: One has to, one just has to!

ANATOL: . . . ?

BERTA: But you men just draw lies out of us, you just force us to lie!

ANATOL: I always begged you just to tell the truth!

BERTA: Yes, with your words! But it's in the look, the look!

ANATOL: What's in the look?

BERTA: Just this: "Lie to me . . . lie to me!"

ANATOL: What kind of nonsense is that!

BERTA: Don't you see I'm right? You'd still be grateful to me today, if I had lied to you!

ANATOL: So you knew that Frenchman?

BERTA: Well, you could see it.

ANATOL: And when I said, "You're flirting," you got ugly!

BERTA: After all, one can't confess everything to someone like you!

ANATOL: No doubt because I tormented you too much?

BERTA: Yes, you did, but I didn't care!

ANATOL: And your grave look, the tears, when I reproached you?

BERTA: So, I cried?

ANATOL: Tears one doesn't remember can't have been genuine!

BERTA: Whenever I was sad, you got so affectionate. I already knew that about you!

ANATOL: And therefore . . .

BERTA: Well, was it so wrong of me that I wanted you to be affectionate?

ANATOL: Well then, flirtatious, untruthful, an actress . . . you were all that?

BERTA: You did tell me that a thousand times, in those days!

ANATOL: Yes, it's just I didn't believe it!

BERTA: But after all, darling! It was beautiful in those days, wasn't it . . . ? So I gladly pardoned your tediousness!

ANATOL: What? I was tedious too?

BERTA: Oh well, you know . . . there were times like that . . . You had such moods! And then you wracked your brain over nothing but old stories . . . and you had to go over everything hundreds of times. . . . Sometimes it was quite twisted, quite crazy . . .

ANATOL: Well . . . !!

BERTA: Oh, but sometimes it was very beautiful too, oh yes, very poetic . . .

ANATOL: But most of it was tedious and ridiculous!

BERTA: Oh, I could always tell what you meant . . . even when it was nonsense.

ANATOL: So those dreamy looks of yours, with their seemingly sweet harmony, drifting their way toward me, were just nothing . . . but reserve?

BERTA: But you just kept on talking like that . . .

ANATOL: . . . that eternal, frivolous, uncomprehending reserve . . .

BERTA: You've always said that—"I don't understand you!"

ANATOL: And I didn't even believe it!

BERTA: I understood you quite well! You men just imagine that we don't understand you . . .

[BARON DIEBL *and* MAX *enter.*]

BARON DIEBL: It's beginning to get lively downstairs! Right now, they're involved with the question of Fräulein Hanischek's christening!

BERTA: Ah, then I must go down. I've thought of such a delightful name for her . . .

ANATOL: One more moment, Berta!

BERTA: Well, quickly, quickly!

ANATOL: Go!

BERTA: Such a fool!

[*She exits with* BARON DIEBL.]

MAX: Well, what did you want?

ANATOL: To pose a final question which she surely could have answered for me now.

MAX: Well, what did you want to ask her?

ANATOL: Just imagine, I had such a sudden desire to have Berta tell me the story of our love! In those days she laughed in my face, flirted with others, hardly understood me, and probably deceived me as well . . .

MAX: Well, what else? A woman like that . . .

ANATOL: Yes, but what she seemed to me at the time! How was one to know it then? What skill in dissembling! And at that time she was also . . . at that time, of course . . . she was like that before her first kiss! One's experiences are certainly so incidental! Her first lover cannot take any more pride in his conquest of her than her last!

MAX: Oh well . . . Do you want to leave now?

ANATOL: Then she must have spoken the truth just now? Perhaps for her time has changed, shifted, and falsified the images of the past! Perhaps she really did understand me back then, and today she just thinks she does!

MAX: Such a melancholy brooder you are! Now you're going to fret all over again about this woman you'd forgotten for twenty years—?

ANATOL: It's foolish . . . it's sick! But my frivolity has turned to melancholy. I'm dragging all my memories around with me . . . and some days I spread them out . . .

MAX: Like a bag of pearls . . .

ANATOL: And nothing but artificial ones!

MAX: But what if one woman were genuine?

ANATOL: What good would it do her? Like the others, she'd have to bear the curse of mistrust! You can't tell them apart—impossible! And who knows, perhaps I once loved the woman who really did understand me, and I could have been happy . . . and I didn't dare. . . . Are you coming with me?

[*They exit down the steps.* ANNETTE *comes in quickly, looks around.*]

FLIEDER [*following her*]: Where did they go? Where?

ANNETTE: Are you back again?

FLIEDER: I just knew it, you were attracted back up here!

ANNETTE: Just what are you saying? Just who are you talking to?

FLIEDER: What do you want on the veranda?

ANNETTE: To be alone with you!

FLIEDER: With me?

ANNETTE: I just knew you were following me!

FLIEDER: Well?

ANNETTE: Earlier I was so upset that you weren't paying me enough attention. And if you hadn't followed me . . . I wouldn't believe you loved me any longer . . .

FLIEDER: Do you believe it now?

ANNETTE: Do I believe . . . my sweetheart!

FLIEDER: Let me tell you something, darling: let's go!

ANNETTE: What . . . ?

FLIEDER: Yes. Let's not go back to those people down there, downstairs . . . Let's go . . . alone . . . to your place . . .

ANNETTE: But so soon? [*Distracted*] Look, there he goes . . .

FLIEDER [*very annoyed*]: Who?

ANNETTE: Well, Anatol . . . and Max!

FLIEDER: But why are you looking out there? Why does that interest you?

ANNETTE: But one can't help noticing things, after all!

FLIEDER: But not when I'm telling you about my love! And you chose to notice him of all people!

ANNETTE: Still jealous after all?

FLIEDER: . . . ?

ANNETTE: But my sweet little angel . . . jealous of such an old man!!

[*Curtain*]

THE ADVENTURE OF A LIFETIME

A Comedy in One Act

Characters

Anatol

Max, *Anatol's confidant*

Cora

Gabriele

[*A simple room, furnished in unaffected taste: bookcase, desk, cupboard, chairs, etc., an armchair beside the desk.—Just one door, in the background.*]

MAX [*reading aloud*]: "—and as he spoke these words, his head sank backward"—[*looking at* ANATOL, *who is staring into space*]—"his head sank heavily backward."—Say, Anatol!

ANATOL [*as if awakening*]: Ah!

MAX: It seems to me you're not even listening!

ANATOL: Oh, certainly!—Only in the last few moments my thoughts were wandering. Excuse me! But just go on reading now.

MAX: No. You're already worn-out and distracted. You must listen when I am reading from my own novellas!—Why, it's already getting dark.—

ANATOL: Oh, I'll put on some lights right away. [*Lighting several candles*] But you must go on reading.—

MAX: Tomorrow—or, if you want, later on this evening, but not now.—Do you like the story so far?

ANATOL: Quite well, up to the disappearance of the countess.—

MAX: —Of the baroness.—

ANATOL: Fine, of the baroness. One's quite anxious to know the outcome and waits for something truly remarkable to happen.—And from that point on—

MAX: Well—

ANATOL: From that point on—I was no longer listening—I was somewhere else.—

MAX: May one ask where?

ANATOL: Oh, my friend,—you could figure that out!

MAX: Your riddle allows for two solutions—one is called Cora, the other—Gabriele!

ANATOL: You're making a bad joke when you name those two in one breath!

MAX: Well, then I don't understand you!

ANATOL: Because you want to do everything in clichés. Because you can't break away from the old prejudice that there is only love—do you understand—love. After all, there are a thousand kinds of love.

MAX: Yes! And—

ANATOL: Well, if there are so many kinds of love, why shouldn't a person be able to feel two kinds of love at the same time?

MAX: That's a nice aphorism. Who said it?

ANATOL: I did!

MAX: So you will prove to me that you can love Cora as well as Gabriele!

ANATOL: Certainly!

MAX: Well?!

ANATOL: Listen! What is Cora to me?—

MAX: A pastime.—

ANATOL: Please do not interrupt me. Cora is—my sweetheart! I worship her, she is delightful, amiable, devoted, whimsical, and has—between you and me—the most beautiful neck I've ever kissed. She brings a sweet, carefree atmosphere into this small room that continually enchants and seduces me. The rustle of her dress, the music of her voice, the touch of those small white hands with their fingertips pricked by needles have become something my nerves have need of. And everything my senses demand I find in this amiable creature. In her arms I don't think: "These lips learned kissing from someone else." But part of her charm comes from the fact that she has some things to forget and others she must make me forget. That charm of hers overpowers me and transforms our quiet evenings into a fairy tale. This is further intensified by the power of my own feelings.—

MAX: How fortunate!

ANATOL: And now—Gabriele! What is Gabriele to me?

MAX: A foolish mistake!

ANATOL: Oh please! Gabriele is the adventure of a lifetime!

MAX: Ah!

ANATOL: She is *la grande passion*—which eventually must make me either ineffably happy or wretched.—

MAX: What does that mean, *la grande passion*?

ANATOL: *La grande passion*! Well, it's called that when one must strive somewhat longer to . . .

MAX: And—just as long as one has not yet attained the conquest.

ANATOL: Oh, you're mistaken—and if you really had the eyes of a young poet—

MAX [*proudly*]: But I do!

ANATOL: —then you would understand, seeing it with those eyes—you would've had to see that glance Gabriele let fall on me from her private box in the theater the other day, on me, who was sitting alone below—

MAX: —Alone, in the first row between a lieutenant of the guards and my humble self in a suffocatingly full house.—

ANATOL: Yes, yes, all right!—From that look you would've had to see what the two of us mean to each other, Gabriele and I.

MAX: Well, I'll admit she flirted with you.

ANATOL: Quiet! She loves me—and, what's more—she understands me. In this young woman I see the companion of my endeavors and ideals—only she will make me into a true poet.

MAX: But when?

ANATOL: Well, I can certainly tell you that.—She will come here to me!

MAX: Oh!

ANATOL: Do you see! That evening, when she leaves this garret—

MAX: —on the second floor—

ANATOL: —and leaves, I will have experienced the adventure of a lifetime!

MAX: And you believe that this inaccessible, regal woman will come here to you?

ANATOL: I know it. I've felt it.—The other evening, as we were dancing at the masked ball in the palace, I felt her lips on my cheeks.

MAX: By chance!

ANATOL: But one doesn't bite by chance.

MAX: Ah yes!

ANATOL: Then we took a stroll together.—"Can't I ever speak to you undisturbed?" I asked her.—"Can't I ever tell you, far from these insensitive people, how very much I love you?"—She looked at me with her deep eyes—"You love me, Anatol?! You, Anatol!!" It was the first time she called me that—then she went on speaking. "But they can see me. And you know, Anatol, that my husband—" Then I said, "There are places, secluded places, where nobody can see you."—She replied, "You shouldn't have said that, Herr Anatol!"

MAX [*in the same tone*]: Because I know it.

ANATOL: If you please, Max!—In departing she whispered to me, "Yours!" Nothing but this word, but it told me everything—that same instant I was gazing into her eyes.

MAX: The adventure of a lifetime!—It's just as well that one believes it only as long as one hasn't experienced it!

ANATOL: Why?

MAX: Because otherwise one couldn't find life interesting anymore, after that adventure. What else in our existence could captivate us, if we were really convinced that the most beautiful part of life is over? Men like you expect the adventure of a lifetime a hundred times over, because they live to see it a hundred times over. Then they aren't satisfied and go on waiting.

ANATOL: Nice! Who says that?

MAX: I do!

ANATOL: But you're wrong, and you're doing me a great injustice! I feel my passion for Gabriele is the most tremendous thing ever to befall me.

MAX: Is Cora coming here to you today?

ANATOL: What's that question supposed to mean?

MAX: Nothing but what the words imply.

ANATOL: Oh well! But—

MAX: Despite the fact that you love Gabriele—

ANATOL: Certainly, and since, as I think I've already explained to you, there are a thousand kinds of love—

MAX: You could then harbor nine hundred and ninety-nine other larger and smaller raptures in your heart.

ANATOL: Well—surely that's theoretically possible.

MAX: I have a disclosure for you.

ANATOL: Then I'm anxious to hear—

MAX: —that what you're experiencing may just not be one love, but two infatuations.

ANATOL: Once again I see that you don't comprehend my spirit.

MAX: That's it—you have spirit, but no character, and that's the reason.—A person with spirit is able to have passion, is able to get worked up, perhaps be lovesick, but only a person with character is able to love!

ANATOL: Very beautiful, but again not true.

MAX: We'll never reach an agreement, if you think you can simply refute me with a denial.

ANATOL: Oh! It doesn't occur to me to want to dissuade you from your views—just go—parade in front of some teenager's window, disdain the other women and imagine that you have character.

MAX: Teenager or not, that's immaterial. The only thing that's certain is that we love *one;* all the others are—

ANATOL: But there are no others. [*With pathos*] There are just women!

MAX: Ha ha! You are precious! With such principles—one doesn't experience the adventure of a lifetime! For that to happen, the whole world must sink before us and around us, we are alone among millions—we do not hear the raging of everyday life, as it incessantly tumbles down around us.

CORA [*entering at the door*]: I knock once—then twice, nobody says, "Come in," the door isn't opened—so I have to let myself—

ANATOL [*going toward her*]: Cora, dearest Cora!

CORA [*kissing him on the mouth*]: There! Good evening, Max!

[MAX *walks over to her, kisses her hand.*]

CORA [*to* ANATOL, *pointing toward* MAX]: Is he staying?

ANATOL: I hope he won't deprive us of the pleasure of his company.

MAX: Certainly not—or for a few minutes at most.—But are the two of you dining at home then?—

CORA: Yes, Anatol, let's stay home.—It's raining outside, let's have supper brought to the room—shall we?

ANATOL: As you will, my darling!

CORA [*to* MAX]: You were leaving?

MAX: For half an hour! I must go home to see about some letters I'm just expecting. Auf Wiedersehen!

[CORA *and* ANATOL *accompany him to the door,* MAX *exits.*]

ANATOL [*to* CORA]: You still have your umbrella in your hand.—

CORA: It's all wet! Look!

[*She opens it up, drops fall down; with a smile she puts the opened, dripping umbrella into a corner.*]

ANATOL: And your coat!

CORA: Help me!

[*He assists her in taking off her coat, kisses her. She embraces and kisses him.*]

Ah!

[*She sits down on the sofa while he hangs up her coat.*]

Come, sit down with me!

ANATOL: So, here I am! How long since I've seen you!

CORA: Since yesterday evening!

ANATOL: Much too long, my child. [*Grasping her hands*] Don't you want to take off your gloves?—

CORA [*unbuttoning her gloves, as he draws them off her hands*]: Doesn't it make more sense to stay at home for now, rather than go over to the inn, where there are so many people who smoke and stare?—

ANATOL: The smoking would bother me less than the staring, but I do find the staring unpleasant.

CORA: Jealous?

ANATOL: But you know I am.—

CORA: I just find it very unnecessary.

ANATOL: Well, that would be the last straw if you regarded my jealousy as justified! But let's not talk about that.—What did you do all day?

CORA: Ah, I have so much to do. Look! [*Pointing to her fingertips*] My fingers are all pricked!

[ANATOL *kisses her fingertips.*]

CORA: Right now I'm overloaded with work. If it weren't for the evenings with you—I'd hardly know what I was put on this earth for.—

ANATOL: My darling!

CORA: Well, who shall we send?

ANATOL: For what?

CORA: Well, to get supper!

ANATOL: Yes, who?

CORA: For God's sake, just don't send your high-class neighbor's maid, the maid who was so generous as to go the other day. That was just horrible. Those sardines in rancid oil, those dried-up, ordinary cold cuts, and that boney old chicken!

ANATOL: And the wine!

CORA [*shaking herself*]: Sour!—

ANATOL [*grandly*]: I will get our supper myself!

CORA: Ah!

ANATOL: What does her ladyship command?

CORA: Ah, let *me* go, otherwise they'll palm off all kinds of things on you.—

ANATOL: Remain sitting, your ladyship. Your little feet should not be exposed to another soaking.—

CORA: But what will you bring?

ANATOL [*parrying her with a superior smile*]: They'll not palm anything off on me! [*While putting on his coat*] Meanwhile, just set the table, my darling! Three places—don't forget that Max is coming. Also prepare the tea urn—cigarettes are up there.—

CORA: Cigarettes too?

ANATOL: Cigarettes too!—So!—Yes, the wineglasses!

CORA: *The* wineglass!

ANATOL: But what do you mean?—

CORA: Well, you smashed the other wineglass to pieces!

ANATOL: Then we'll drink the wine out of water glasses, that's even more stylish!—Now, have I forgotten anything else?—No!—Adieu, my darling!

[*He kisses her, is about to exit.*]

CORA: Without an umbrella! In *that* rain!

ANATOL [*turning around again*]: Ha ha! Without an umbrella!—[*Becoming serious*] It occurs to me just now—it's been sitting in the café since the day before yesterday!

CORA: Well, take mine!—

ANATOL: Yours! [*Covering himself as well as* CORA *with the umbrella, their kiss is heard, but not seen*] Adieu!—

[*He exits.*]

CORA [*at the door*]: Auf Wiedersehen!—So!—Well, let's set the table. But first, a cigarette!

[*She climbs onto a chair, takes cigarettes from the cupboard, puts one in her mouth, and jumps down.*]

Where's the lighter, then?—Ah, here! [*Lights the cigarette while laying out the tablecloth, plates, and place settings*] That cigarette has a strong bite, though.—It is definite then, I'm lovesick for Anatol.—And actually that's something very grand. These young poets want to be loved quite differently than—the lieutenants, for instance!—Well, all that certainly lies behind me, thank goodness! Ah, these young poets! It's not enough that you love them, but you also have to have a passion for them.—These knives are quite blunt—I'll have to take them to be sharpened tomorrow.—But what good does it do?—I really do have a passion for him! For his blond head, his stupidities, his forebodings, even for his friend, that little Max.—A hole in the napkin—he probably wrapped a burning cigar in it, in his absentmindedness.—Sometimes I believe I'm too fun-loving for him—I laugh, and he gets annoyed! Oh, it seems these fine, young poets like to see tears in the eyes of the ladies they love.—So!—

[*The cigarette smoke rises into her eyes.*]

Away with you!—

[*Throws it at the fireplace. A knock at the door.*]

A good joke of Anatol's. He shall just knock.

[*Knocking again.*]

[*As if to herself*] Come in!

GABRIELE: It's me!

CORA [*jumps*]: Who's that?!—

GABRIELE: It's me, Herr Anatol, open the door!

CORA: A woman's voice! Who can that be?!

GABRIELE: It's me!

CORA [*with a sudden resolve*]: Come in!

GABRIELE [*enters, veiled, fashionably dressed in black; recoiling*]: Oh, I beg your pardon, I've got the wrong address.

CORA [*cunningly*]: Certainly not, if you're looking for Herr Anatol!

GABRIELE: Then this is his apartment?—

CORA: This room—indeed.—

GABRIELE: He is not at home?—

CORA: He will be coming back right away.—

GABRIELE: So.—

[*She starts to leave.*]

CORA [*with a sudden resolve*]: Oh, just wait patiently, if you please; you are expected—probably.—

GABRIELE: Me . . . how do you know that?

CORA: Oh— [*Hesitatingly*] You see, I'm the daughter of Herr Anatol's landlady—and he asked me to lay the table with two settings.

GABRIELE: Two settings?—How could he know that?

CORA [*quickly*]: Oh, he doesn't need to know anything. Herr Anatol foresees everything.—

GABRIELE: He foresees everything.—[*To herself*] I feel quite uneasy here.—

CORA: But doesn't the lady want to have a seat until Herr Anatol returns?

GABRIELE: I would really prefer to leave!

CORA: Oh—please—stay—you would no doubt meet Herr Anatol on the stairs.—

GABRIELE [*to herself*]: This girl—[*Aloud*] Where did he go, then?

CORA: He's getting supper.

GABRIELE: What?

CORA: I mean for the two of you.

GABRIELE: But my dear, what are you saying? Surely that all is a mistake.—

CORA: Oh, no—he just foresaw it.—He told me today: "Fräulein Cora, I know for certain she's coming this evening!"—

GABRIELE [*in an undertone*]: What's this?—Could he have taken those few words I dropped the other day as binding?

CORA: And now you're here, as he foresaw.

GABRIELE [*to herself*]: Did he understand me before I understood myself?

CORA: Don't you want to take off your coat? [*To herself, as she removes the mantilla from* GABRIELE, *who stands lost in thought*] How sweet that smells . . . what kind of perfume?!—I'd like to kill her!

GABRIELE [*turning around*]: Yes, but what are you doing?

CORA [*pointing to the mantilla*]: I took the liberty!—Oh, Herr Anatol will be so happy to find you here!

GABRIELE: Give me my coat, I must leave!

CORA [*to herself*]: Just what's wrong with her?

GABRIELE [*about to go to the door*]: Steps.—

CORA: It's nothing—I heard nothing—but he'll be here in a moment.

GABRIELE: I can't go back out there!

CORA [*to herself*]: She's trembling. She's a lady—a married lady . . . !

GABRIELE [*throws herself onto an armchair*]: Then I'll wait for him!

[CORA *stands behind her.*]

CORA [*to herself*]: And I'm not even allowed to strangle her!—

GABRIELE: —Fräulein!—My dear!

CORA: What do you wish?—

GABRIELE: Herr Anatol has been living here for a long time now?—

CORA: Oh, a long time now.—My mother rented him this tiny little room two years ago. A respectable, modest gentleman.—

GABRIELE [*turning around to* CORA]: So!—

CORA: Yes!

GABRIELE: And you?—

CORA: I take care of the domestic things.—

GABRIELE: Then I've disturbed you?—

CORA [*going over to the table*]: Yes, that's right—in setting the table.—

GABRIELE: But what are you doing?—There are three places.

CORA: Oh, how I'm so distracted!

[*She clears the table, throwing one napkin into the corner.*]

GABRIELE [*getting up*]: Oh, if only my husband hadn't gone to Paris!

CORA [*rearranging the table*]: What was madam saying about Paris?

GABRIELE: Oh, nothing, nothing!—[*To herself*] Just what does that woman want?—It all seems so suspicious to me.—

CORA [*to herself*]: If only I could smash that glass on the floor!

GABRIELE [*to herself*]: But I do love him!—I do love him!

CORA [*to* GABRIELE]: He's certainly staying away a long time.

GABRIELE: How does it happen that he's getting the supper himself?

CORA: For you!

[*They both look each other in the face and approach each other.*]

GABRIELE [*recoiling*]: Footsteps!

CORA: Yes, this time for sure.—

[*Quiet, steps, and the clearing of a throat.*]

CORA: It's him!

GABRIELE: It's him!

ANATOL [*pushing open the door with the umbrella, enters with bottles and packages*]: So—well, indeed! And with that rain! [*Seeing the two women standing at each side of the door, dumbfounded*] Gabriele!—

[*Pause. Both women look at him; he tries to put his hands to his head but is prevented by the packages.*]

Allow me to take off my coat.—

[CORA *assists him.*]

Oh, please—please.—

[CORA *puts the things aside.*]

GABRIELE: You see, Herr Anatol, I keep my word!—

ANATOL [*looks around to* CORA, *then taking* GABRIELE*'s hand and kissing it*]: I thank you, Frau Gabriele!

CORA: I took the liberty, Herr Anatol, of receiving the lady in your absence.—

ANATOL: I thank you, Fräulein Cora—[*To* GABRIELE] I just have to take off my coat.—

[*He walks past* CORA, *who is clearing away the packages from the table.*]

It's not what you think, Cora!—

CORA: Be quiet, Herr Anatol, you blackguard you!

GABRIELE: Herr Anatol!—I don't know what's wrong with you!—Such a reception!

ANATOL: Well, here I am again—I'm here with you, Frau Gabriele. [*Kissing her hand*] Do sit down—come, Frau Gabriele!

GABRIELE: What's the matter, Herr Anatol! You're agitated?

ANATOL: It's your presence, Frau Gabriele! It's your presence—Gabriele.

GABRIELE: Why doesn't that girl just go away?

ANATOL: Oh, you don't know her, Frau Gabriele—she's an angel!

GABRIELE: Adieu, then, sir, something's going on here I cannot fathom!

ANATOL: For God's sake, Frau Gabriele, don't be rash—you see—she's only my chambermaid—so to speak—

GABRIELE [*softly*]: You are confused, sir—you are lying.—

ANATOL [*softly*]: Gabriele—that hurts.

CORA: I'll be finishing up right away. Oh, such food Herr Anatol has brought back.—

ANATOL: Well, do you hear that, Frau Gabriele?

GABRIELE: If that girl really is your landlady's daughter, why doesn't she leave us?—

ANATOL: Oh, and how happy I would be to be alone with you, Frau Gabriele.—

GABRIELE [*withdrawing her hand from his grasp*]: That's not what I meant.

CORA: Does Herr Anatol have anything else to command?

ANATOL [*suddenly in good spirits*]: No, you can go, Fräulein Cora!

CORA [*flinching, then to herself*]: Just you wait, Anatol.—[*Aloud*] No, I can't go yet, I still have to wait for Herr Max, after all.—

GABRIELE: Max? Now just who is that?

ANATOL: For heaven's sake, Gabriele—have patience for just one moment. I want to tell this stupid creature—Max—Max is her sweetheart—probably a sergeant—one moment.

[*He hurries over to* CORA.]

GABRIELE [*draping her coat around her shoulders*]: Oh, how severely I'm being punished.

ANATOL [*to* CORA]: I beg you, Cora, just be quiet for an instant.

CORA: Go ahead, Herr Anatol! Tomorrow morning I'll throw acid in your face!

ANATOL: As if I cared—although you'd be wrong to do that, but just listen, Cora—

[GABRIELE *attempts to go out the door.*]

ANATOL [*to her*]: What are you doing, Frau Gabriele? I implore you—stay—you've misunderstood my agitation!

GABRIELE: Let me go—I'm leaving!

ANATOL: Then you'll find out that I'm a man, Frau Gabriele! [*Locking the door*] You're staying!

[GABRIELE *sinks down onto an armchair and weeps.*]

ANATOL [*to* CORA *again*]: So listen, Fräulein Cora.—

CORA: You heel!

ANATOL: This lady—I hardly know her—at a ball—a couple of words—which she misunderstood—

GABRIELE: You are locking me in, Herr Anatol—

ANATOL: Just a minute—just a minute—

CORA: Go to her, Herr Anatol.—

ANATOL: As if I cared. [*Going to* GABRIELE] I implore you, Frau Gabriele—pardon me.—I locked the door because I dreaded that my happiness would leave me again and I'd be as wretched as before.—[*Turning around;* CORA *has sat down at the table*] Yes, I love you, Frau Gabriele—and the explanation of all my confusion comes from the fact that—it's only random circumstances—this girl—the door there—

[*Knocking is heard.*]

GABRIELE [*leaps up*]: Someone's knocking!

CORA: Someone's knocking!

ANATOL [*without emotion*]: Someone's knocking!

MAX [*outside*]: Well, just what's going on—now open up!

[*Quiet in the room.* MAX *knocks louder and louder.*]

Well, do you want to open up?

CORA [*going to the door, to herself*]: He left the door unlocked and still it wouldn't open.—

GABRIELE: For heaven's sake, what are you doing?

CORA: I have to open the door, after all.—

GABRIELE [*to* ANATOL, *witheringly*]: It's the sergeant.—

[CORA *opens the door,* MAX *enters.*]

MAX: Good evening!

[*He looks around, astonished, bows before the stranger.*]

Good evening! [*Softly to* CORA] What's this?

CORA [*likewise*]: He deceived me!

MAX [*to himself*]: Ah—so that's Gabriele—Good evening! Anatol!—Won't you be so kind as to introduce us?—

ANATOL: If you please—with great pleasure.—His name is Max, most gracious lady.

MAX: I am delighted to make this chance acquaintance—

GABRIELE [*standing up and turning her back to him*]: Now will you let me go, Herr Anatol?

[MAX *shrugs his shoulders and crosses to* CORA.]

ANATOL: But Gabriele! Why—

GABRIELE: I am not accustomed to the company of sergeants.—

ANATOL: He's in mufti, after all.—

GABRIELE: He is not this girl's sweetheart, that's just not true—you are lying, Herr Anatol!

ANATOL: All right, then. He's not. But he is one of my friends.

GABRIELE: Ah!

ANATOL: Well, can I help it that he had to come over this evening?! After all, he didn't know any more than I did—

GABRIELE: Oh how bitterly I have deluded myself.—

ANATOL [*sees* CORA *speaking with* MAX, *and notices that* MAX *is trying to soothe* CORA]: I didn't deserve that!

GABRIELE: What?—Just remember, Herr Anatol, how you described to me one of your evenings. "I sit"—you said—"in my room alone with my books, my writings—I have no friend who understands me, no girl who loves me."—While telling me this, you looked at me. . . . Don't look at me like that, with those deceitful eyes of yours.—

ANATOL [*looking around repeatedly*]: Deceitful? I, deceitful!—Well, then—this is a friend—this is a girl.—Yet is this a friend who understands me?—or a girl who loves me?—This is an everyday acquaintance—and a kind of chambermaid you chance to find with me—the one, because he's visiting me; the other, because she's tidying up. Don't you comprehend, Frau Gabriele, that I still feel alone among these people—

CORA [*until now being held back by* MAX *with difficulty, walking over to the couple*]: Supper is on the table.

ANATOL: So? Fräulein Cora, have you set four places?—

GABRIELE: What, Herr Anatol, you believe that I'll be staying here?—

ANATOL: I hardly dare to ask you to. I would almost like to suggest that we talk somewhere else—

CORA: Ah, why shouldn't we all dine together?

GABRIELE [*with a sudden resolve*]: Yes, why shouldn't we all dine together?

ANATOL: —All of us together! [*To himself*] There's no salvation now! [*To* GABRIELE] If you please!—

[*She sits down.*]

[*To* CORA] If you please!—

CORA: I thank you!

ANATOL [*to* MAX]: If you please! [*Softly*] What do you say to that!—

MAX: You're doomed!
ANATOL [*furiously*]: Sit down!

[*The three sit and stare at each other;* ANATOL *wearily drops down on the armchair. Order of places:* ANATOL *facing the audience,* GABRIELE *to his right,* CORA *to his left,* MAX *with his back to the audience.*]

MAX: Will you allow me to pour the wine, Anatol?

[*He pours.*]

CORA [*to* MAX]: So—don't fill mine all the way, Max.
GABRIELE [*to* ANATOL]: This strange chambermaid who is dining with you, Herr Anatol, and your friend—
ANATOL: Oh, she's an insolent one!
MAX [*pouring wine for* GABRIELE]: Allow me—?
GABRIELE: Away with that!—I'm not drinking it.—
CORA: But Herr Anatol has distinguished himself today! Cold Rhenish salmon!—sardines!—caviar!
MAX: I'll take some of the salmon.—
CORA: Give me some of that too, after all.—
ANATOL [*to* GABRIELE]: Take some salmon, my lady!
MAX: Perhaps you prefer the sardines.
GABRIELE: Take that away.—
MAX [*to* ANATOL]: Well, so say something then.—
ANATOL: My dear guests!
MAX: What, a speech!?—Yes, fun!—Make a toast!

[GABRIELE *gets up and tries to leave.*]

ANATOL [*going after her*]: What? You want to leave? Frau Gabriele, you still don't believe me?
MAX: Besides, there are people on the stairs right now.—
GABRIELE [*slowly returning to her place*]: Ah!
CORA [*to* MAX]: I can't take it any longer, I'm suffocating.—
ANATOL [*standing*]: I had a request for a toast.—
MAX: Bravo!—
CORA: Fill my glass, Max.

MAX [*to himself*]: If only one of these women would just leave!

ANATOL: But to what, dear ladies, am I supposed to raise my glass?

GABRIELE: —Ladies?

MAX: An untenable position!

CORA: Just go on speaking, Herr Anatol!

ANATOL: Ah, there are so many things to which one can raise one's glass!

MAX: Very true!

ANATOL: There is, for example, freedom, brotherliness, love—

CORA AND GABRIELE [*arising at the same time*]: Love!

ANATOL [*quickly*]: And hate!

CORA and GABRIELE [*sitting down quickly*]: Hate!

MAX: One doesn't drink to hate.—

ANATOL [*with pathos*]: Would anyone deny me that?—Esteemed party companions! I drink to—hate!

MAX: It's crazy, but I can't blame him for it.—

ANATOL [*to* GABRIELE]: Perhaps some sardines?

GABRIELE: Now that is just too much, sir. I could pardon you your embarrassment, but not your mockery.—

CORA: What does she want? Is she suddenly getting a temper?

ANATOL: But Gabriele!—

CORA [*to* MAX]: He's grabbing her by the hand!

MAX: He certainly has to!

GABRIELE [*to* ANATOL]: Let me go now, Herr Anatol.—

CORA [*to* MAX]: Where's an empty plate?—

MAX: Here! Perhaps you want some of the salmon?—

CORA: Just give it here—this plate! [*Getting up and throwing it to the floor*] There!

GABRIELE: What?

ANATOL: Cora, what are you doing, dear?

GABRIELE: Dear! And she also smashes your plates to bits, Herr Anatol? I know enough.—

CORA: Yes, you know everything!

ANATOL: But my esteemed ladies—just be quiet for a moment, so I can explain.—

CORA: There's nothing here to explain!—Listen, sir! I'm in a rage—furious! But surely not because I love you, but because I despise you!—Here by chance is something that could still remind me of you. [*Taking her bracelet and hurling it to the floor*] So—there it is—you'll not see me again, Herr Anatol—farewell.—

ANATOL: Never again?

CORA [*having thrown her coat around her shoulders and taken umbrella and hat in hand—threateningly*]: One more time, at the most!

ANATOL: Oh yes!—[*To himself*] The acid!

GABRIELE: I'm sorry my husband has gone to Paris!

MAX [*consolingly*]: He'll come back again!

[CORA *is about to exit.*]

ANATOL [*to* MAX]: I beg you—follow her! She might do harm to herself.—

MAX: Don't worry—but I'll escort her just the same.—

ANATOL: Quickly, quickly! [*Softly*] But talk her out of the acid at least.—

MAX [*has taken hat and overcoat*]: Madam, I hope that we'll soon—

[GABRIELE *turns away indignantly.*]

ANATOL: Just stop your impudence and leave—

[MAX *quickly exits.* GABRIELE *has been standing benumbed, suddenly sees herself alone with* ANATOL *and tries to escape; he holds her back. Pause.*]

ANATOL [*affectedly*]: Finally alone!

GABRIELE: You should let me go, Herr Anatol.

ANATOL: Not before you've heard me, Frau Gabriele.—

GABRIELE: I don't want to hear you.—

ANATOL: Not before you've pardoned me.—

GABRIELE [*laughing*]: Incidentally, you're stupid as well.

ANATOL [*injured*]: It seems, madam, that you're intent on hurting me.

GABRIELE [*astonished*]: Ah, don't you know as well—sir—that I find you incredible.—

ANATOL: Gabriele!

GABRIELE: Now will you let me depart in peace, Herr Anatol?—

ANATOL: You love me, Gabriele—I know it—you'll not leave me.

GABRIELE: I love you?—You?!—

ANATOL: Such indignation tells me more than a thousand terms of affection could confess.—Yes [*grasping her hand*]—from the shaking of your fingertips, from the trembling of your lips, from the intoxicated look with which you aim to destroy me and yet which can only make me happy . . .

GABRIELE [*trying to extricate herself from him, in a rage*]: You are impudent—I want to leave!

ANATOL: Because you love me!

GABRIELE: I would like to kill you!

ANATOL: Because you love me!

GABRIELE: I hate you!

ANATOL: Because you love me!

GABRIELE: I am indifferent to you.—

ANATOL: You are mistaken, madam, for you adore me.—

GABRIELE [*wringing her hands*]: Oh, for this creature's sake I wanted to—ah—my husband—

[*She shakes herself.*]

ANATOL: I implore you, let's not talk about your fine spouse now—be so gracious, Frau Gabriele, as to listen to me.—[*Keeps on holding her hands*]

GABRIELE: I wouldn't be listening to you, if I didn't have to—

ANATOL: Do you know who that girl was, who left just now?

GABRIELE: Your sweetheart, Herr Anatol!

ANATOL: No, Gabriele!—It was—my past!

GABRIELE: Ah, lovely! Now you're even getting allegorical.—

ANATOL: Every young person has a past—some have several even, and I was no better than the others.—Life plays with us, Gabriele, but it plays so ingeniously! Before it lets us find the real treasure, it fools us with counterfeit jewels, which please us, as long as we are children! Yes, Gabriele! I confess with complete candor—life has played much with me, and many a counterfeit jewel has pleased me.—

GABRIELE: If you only knew how repugnant you are to me with your—phrases.—

ANATOL: You would not be the noble soul—that you are—if you've misunderstood me.—[*More ardently*] Gabriele—everything you've seen and heard still reels before you—and therefore I pardon you, that you don't understand at first.—

GABRIELE: Let me go, sir.—

ANATOL [*falls at her feet, holding on to her hands*]: Don't go—oh, don't go from me!—But don't you understand that you, only you, are the one I love to the point of insanity—that everything, everything lies far, far behind me and that it's nothing but shadows projecting out of a hazy past into a flourishing present. It' s not easy to wipe away all those shadows at once—they push their way forward, they insist on their dark, old power; they would gladly imagine themselves real, just as they were before—but finally they fade away completely.—

GABRIELE: Your "shadows" smash plates to bits and call you "Anatol dear!"

ANATOL: You don't want to understand me!—You want to tear apart my heart! Do you believe that I—could have fallen at her feet the way I have at yours?—There are hundreds of Coras, but just one Gabriele—there are hundreds of interludes, but just one passion—life has thousands of experiences, but just one adventure—the adventure of my lifetime—is you, Gabriele!

GABRIELE: Enough, don't block my way any longer.—

ANATOL: Gabriele!

GABRIELE: I know you can speak well—for only through your fine speeches have you been able to insinuate yourself into the depths of my heart. The way you spoke, I had to believe you.—I truly imagined I was the only one.—

ANATOL: You are.—

GABRIELE: Oh, I could have pardoned you hundreds of other things—for all I care, ten ballerinas or whatever—but this girl is here with you at home—I don't pardon you that! I had no claim on the fire of your youth—sir! Yet I did have a claim on your heart, since you lay at my feet. But now you've lied to me and nothing of all that I—unfortunately—felt for you, nothing, nothing is left at all, but a little anger and a great deal of regret.—So!—And now will you let me go?

ANATOL: Gabriele!

GABRIELE: I beg you, no more unnecessary efforts. And since, as you no doubt see, you can't convince me that you love me, then at least show some tact by no longer detaining a woman who is indifferent to you.—

[ANATOL *tries to speak.* GABRIELE *makes a parrying gesture.*]

ANATOL [*steps back, pointing to the door*]: My lady! The way is clear!

[GABRIELE *quickly goes to the door, opens it, and exits. Pause.*]

ANATOL [*alone, walks back and forth in the room, sits down at the table, gets up again, annoyed*]: Oh!—

MAX [*entering*]: So, here I am.—

ANATOL: What?—Back already?—

MAX: I met Frau Gabriele on the stairs—I take it that means—

ANATOL [*with melancholy*]: Max!

MAX: She was quite annoyed.—Yes, yes!

ANATOL: —And Cora?

MAX: She quickly dismissed me and got into a coach to go home.—Why, it's just pouring out there.—

ANATOL: Well, what did she say then?

MAX: Never wants to see you again—and so forth. Nothing particular.—She's given up on the acid.

ANATOL: What does she want then?

MAX: Only revenge.—Oh well—since she's simply through with you.—

ANATOL: Yes, yes—I'll just go shoot myself.

MAX [*sitting down at the table*]: May I?—as for me there's simply no reason to do without supper.—

ANATOL: Oh, if you please.—

MAX: But tell me, what else happened here then?—

ANATOL: Past—lost.—

MAX: The adventure of your lifetime!—Ha ha!—

ANATOL: Don't laugh—I don't feel like joking at all.

MAX: Hold on—come here—let's drink.—

ANATOL [*slowly approaching him*]: Ah!

MAX: Let's drink to ourselves and that which is yet to come, to high-spirited times.—My dear Anatol, youth is the true adventure of human life—and—enjoy yourself—we, after all, we are in the center of life!—

ANATOL [*standing at the table;* MAX *has put the glass into his hand; wearily*]: For all I care.—No!—I'll never get over it.

MAX [*laughing*]: But friend!

ANATOL: At least not tonight.—

MAX: But soon!

ANATOL: I just don't know how I am to break out of this mood.—

MAX: New love . . .

ANATOL [*looking at him*]: New love?

MAX: Well of course; there, take your glass and clink it with mine. After all, it's so simple, my Anatol! You just have to look—for another one.—

ANATOL [*laying his hand on* MAX*'s shoulder*]: *Another* one?—[*Drinks, puts glass down vehemently; quite despairing*] Two!

[*Quick curtain*]

Interlude

Characters

Fritz Lobheimer, *a young man*

Theodor Kaiser, *a young man*

Mitzi Schlager, *a clerk in a women's clothing store*

Christine, *Weiring's daughter*

Gentleman

Catherine Binder, *the wife of a garment worker*

Hans Weiring, *a violinist at the Josefstadt Theatre*

Lina, *Catherine's nine-year-old daughter*

In addition, the voice of Fritz's manservant is heard offstage.

~

Vienna, turn of the twentieth century

ACT ONE

[FRITZ's *room. Elegant and comfortable.* THEODOR *and* FRITZ *enter.* THEODOR *carries an overcoat on his arm, takes off his hat, but keeps his cane in his hand.*]

FRITZ [*calling offstage*]: Then no one called?

SERVANT'S VOICE: No, sir.

FRITZ [*entering*]: Should we go ahead and send the carriage away?

THEODOR: Of course, I thought you had already done that.

FRITZ [*crossing to door*]: Send the carriage off. Oh, and . . . as a matter of fact you can go now, too. I won't need you anymore today. [*To* THEODOR] Why don't you put your things down?

THEODOR [*at desk*]: Here are a couple of letters for you.

[*He throws his topcoat and hat on a chair but keeps his cane.*]

FRITZ [*goes quickly to desk*]: Ah! . . .

THEODOR: Well, well! You look really upset.

FRITZ: From Papa. [*Opens the other*] From Lensky.

THEODOR: Don't let me disturb you.

[FRITZ *glances through the letters.*]

THEODOR: What does Papa have to say?

FRITZ: Nothing special. I'm supposed to spend a week with them out on the estate later this spring.

THEODOR: A very sensible idea. I'd like to send you there for six months.

[FRITZ, *at desk, turns to him.*]

THEODOR: Certainly!—Horseback riding, fresh air, dairymaids . . .

FRITZ: Look, there aren't even any dairy farms in that part of the country.

THEODOR: Well, anyway. You know what I mean . . .

FRITZ: Do you want to come with me?

THEODOR: But I can't.

FRITZ: Why not?

THEODOR: My dear fellow, I've got my comprehensive exams to take! If I went along, it would just be to keep you there.

FRITZ: Listen, don't you worry about me.

THEODOR: What you need, I'm convinced, is just some fresh air—I could see that today. Out there in the fresh, green of springtime, you became your old, lovable and pleasant self again.

FRITZ: Thanks.

THEODOR: And now you're just falling apart. That dangerous atmosphere is closing in on us again.

[FRITZ *seems irritated.*]

THEODOR: You just don't know how relaxed you were out there. You were even in good spirits. Just like the good old days. And the other day, when we were out with those two adorable girls, you were really very charming. But now that's all over . . . and you find it absolutely necessary to think of . . . [*with irony*] "that woman."

[FRITZ *stands, annoyed.*]

THEODOR: You don't know me, my friend, I don't intend to stand for this any longer.

FRITZ: My God, such energy!

THEODOR: Oh, I'm not saying you have to [*ironically again*] forget "that woman." All I want, dear Fritz, is for this unfortunate business—which keeps me so worried about you—to mean no more to you than an ordinary adventure. Look, if you'd just stop adoring that woman, you'd be surprised to find someday that you really "like" her. And only then you will come to see that she's not an enchantress at all, but just a very lovely young woman with whom you can have a good time, just as you can with any other girl who's pretty and has a lively personality.

FRITZ: Why do you say "worried about me"?

THEODOR: Oh, you know why. I'm always worried that the two of you will run away together. I can't hide the fact that I'm constantly worried that you'll run off with her some fine day.

FRITZ: Do you mean that? . . .

THEODOR [*after a pause*]: That's not the only danger.

FRITZ: You're right, Theodor. There are other dangers as well.

THEODOR: Just don't do anything foolish.

FRITZ [*to himself*]: There are other dangers . . .

THEODOR: What's the matter? You've got something really specific in mind.

FRITZ: Oh no, nothing specific. [*With a glance out the window*] After all, she was mistaken once before.

THEODOR: How come . . . what? I don't understand.

FRITZ: It's nothing.

THEODOR: What is it? I do wish you'd talk sense.

FRITZ: It's just that sometimes lately she's . . . seemed frightened.

THEODOR: Why? There must be a reason.

FRITZ: There is no reason. Just nerves—[*ironically*] Perhaps it's a guilty conscience.

THEODOR: You say she was mistaken once before—

FRITZ: Well, yes. And maybe again today.

THEODOR: Today? Now, what's all this about?

FRITZ [*after a short pause*]: She thinks . . . we're being watched.

THEODOR: How's that?

FRITZ: She has nightmares . . . actually, they're real hallucinations. [*At the window*] She looks through the crack in the curtains here, sees someone standing over there on the corner and thinks . . . [*Interrupting himself*] Do you think it's at all possible to recognize someone's face from this distance?

THEODOR: Hardly.

FRITZ: That's just what I say. But that's the terrible thing about it. . . . She doesn't dare go out. She gets all worked up and weeps hysterically . . . She says she'd like to die with me—

THEODOR: Of course.

FRITZ [*short pause*]: Today I had to go down and see.—Very casually, I went down as though I were just going out—of course there wasn't a familiar face in sight . . .

[THEODOR *remains silent.*]

And that's most reassuring, isn't it? People just don't sink into the ground, do they? . . . Well? Answer me!

THEODOR: What kind of answer do you want from me? Of course, people don't sink into the ground. But they do sometimes hide in doorways.

FRITZ: I looked in all of them.

THEODOR: I'm sure you must have looked very innocent to anyone watching.

FRITZ: There wasn't anyone there. I tell you, she was hallucinating.

THEODOR: All right. But that ought to teach you to be more cautious.

FRITZ: Anyway, I'd have noticed if he were suspicious. I dined with them just yesterday, after the theater—with both of them—it was so cozy and pleasant—it's just ridiculous.

THEODOR: I beg you, Fritz. Give up this whole damned business. Do it for my sake. I have nerves too, you know. I know you're not the sort of fellow who can just run from this sort of situation, and that's why I've made it easy for you—given you the chance to get involved with another . . .

FRITZ: You don't mean . . . ?

THEODOR: Well? Didn't I take you with me a couple of weeks ago on my date with Mitzi? And didn't I ask her to bring along her prettiest girlfriend? Now, you don't deny that you liked that little . . . ?

FRITZ: Of course, I did—she's charming . . . so charming. You have no idea how I've longed for affection like that, without all the problems . . . for someone sweet, quiet, and agreeable . . . with whom I can recover from all of life's irritations and torments.

THEODOR: That's it, exactly! Recovery! That's the most important thing. Women are there to help us recover. . . . That's why I'm so against those so-called interesting women. Women aren't there to be "interesting," but just pleasant. You should look for your happiness where I've always looked for, and found, mine. Where there are no big scenes, no dangers, no tragic complications; where there are no particular problems at the beginning and no anguish at the end—where you receive your first kiss with a smile and you part ever so gently and tenderly.

FRITZ: Yes, that's it.

THEODOR: Women are fortunate in their robust humanity. Why are we so compelled to turn them into either angels or enchantresses?

FRITZ: She really is a dear thing, though—so devoted and good. Sometimes I almost think she's too good for me.

THEODOR: You know, you're hopeless! If you intend to take this affair seriously too . . .

FRITZ: But I wasn't thinking of that. We're in agreement: Recovery.

THEODOR: If so . . . then I'm washing my hands of you. I've had enough of your tragic love affairs. They bore me. And if you mean to come at me with that famous conscience of yours—I'll give you my simple principle for these situations: Better it were me to be her lover than another fellow. Because that other fellow is going to be there as sure as fate.

[*The doorbell rings.*]

FRITZ: Now, who could that . . .

THEODOR: Just go and see. There you go again turning pale! Just calm down now. It's those two sweet girls.

FRITZ [*pleasantly surprised*]: What? . . .

THEODOR: I took the liberty of inviting them over today.

FRITZ [*going out*]: Well, why didn't you tell me? I've sent my servant away.

THEODOR: That makes it all the cozier.

FRITZ [*offstage*]: Well hello there, Mitzi.

[MITZI *enters carrying a parcel;* FRITZ *follows.*]

FRITZ: And where's Christine? . . .

MITZI: Oh, she'll be here soon. [*To* THEODOR] Well hello there, Ted.

[THEODOR *kisses her hand.*]

You'll have to excuse us, Herr Fritz. Theodor did invite us over. . . .

FRITZ: Of course, it was a wonderful idea. Theodor did forget one thing, though.

THEODOR: Theodor didn't forget anything. [*Taking the parcel from* MITZI] Did you bring everything I put on your list?

MITZI: Of course I did. [*To* FRITZ] Where can I put this?

FRITZ: Just give it to me. For now, we'll just put it here on the sideboard.

MITZI: I did bring something extra that you didn't write down, Ted.

FRITZ: Give me your hat, Mitzi.

[*He takes her hat and boa and puts them on the piano.*]

THEODOR: What's that?

MITZI: A mocha cream torte.

THEODOR: You and your sweet tooth!

FRITZ: So tell me, why didn't Christine come with you?

MITZI: She's accompanying her father to the theater first, then she'll come here on the streetcar.

THEODOR: Such an affectionate daughter . . .

MITZI: She certainly is, especially since they've been in mourning.

THEODOR: Oh, who died?

MITZI: The old gentleman's sister.

THEODOR: Ah, her aunt!

MITZI: She was a spinster and had lived with them for a long time—and now he just feels very lonely.

THEODOR: Christine's father is the little man with short gray hair, isn't he?

MITZI [*shaking her head*]: No, he has long hair.

FRITZ: Where do you know him from?

THEODOR: Lensky and I went to the Josefstadt Theatre the other day, and I got a look at the cello players.

MITZI: But he doesn't play the cello, he plays the violin.

THEODOR: Oh, really? I thought he played the cello.

[MITZI *laughs.*]

But that's not funny. How was I supposed to know?

MITZI: You've got a beautiful place here, Herr Fritz. Just beautiful. What's the view of?

FRITZ: That window looks out over Straw Lane, and in the next room . . .

THEODOR [*suddenly*]: Now tell me, why are you two being so formal? You could just call him Fritz.

MITZI: We'll get better acquainted over supper.

THEODOR: Such strong principles. But that's reassuring . . . And how is your dear mother doing?

MITZI [*turning to him with a troubled expression*]: You won't believe it. She has . . .

THEODOR: A toothache—I know, I know. Your mother's always got a toothache. She should just go to a dentist.

MITZI: But her doctor says it's just rheumatism.

THEODOR [*laughing*]: Well, then. If it's just rheumatism . . .

MITZI [*with a photo album in her hand*]: You have so many beautiful things here! . . . [*Leafing through the book*] Who is this? . . . Oh, is this you in your uniform, Herr Fritz? Were you in the military then?

FRITZ: Yes.

MITZI: In the dragoons! Were you in the yellow or the black?

FRITZ [*smiling*]: The yellow.

MITZI [*lost in a dream*]: The yellow dragoons.

THEODOR: There she goes getting all dreamy again. . . . Hey, Mitzi, wake up!

MITZI: So, now you're a lieutenant in the reserves?

FRITZ: That's right.

MITZI: I bet you look handsome in your fur hat.

THEODOR: Such extensive knowledge! By the way, Mitzi, I was in the military too, you know.

MITZI: Were you in the dragoons too?

THEODOR: Yes.

MITZI: Well, how come you never told anyone that?

THEODOR: I wanted to be loved for myself alone.

MITZI: Listen, Ted. Next time we go out together, you'll have to wear your uniform.

THEODOR: Anyway, I'll be going on maneuvers in August.

MITZI: Good Lord. By August—?

THEODOR: That's right—eternal love doesn't last that long.

MITZI: Who thinks of August in May? Isn't that right, Herr Fritz?—Say, why did you run away from us last night?

FRITZ: How's that?

MITZI: You know, after the theater?

FRITZ: You mean Theodor didn't extend my apologies to you both?

THEODOR: Of course I did.

MITZI: What good are your apologies to me . . . or rather to Christine? When a promise is made, it should be kept.

FRITZ: Actually, I'd much rather have been with you . . .

MITZI: Honestly?

FRITZ: But that wasn't possible. You saw I was with some acquaintances in their box. And afterward I just couldn't get away . . .

MITZI: Sure, you couldn't get away from those pretty ladies. You think we didn't see you from the gallery?

FRITZ: I saw you, too . . .

MITZI: You were sitting back in the box.

FRITZ: Not all the time.

MITZI: But most of the time. You were sitting behind a lady in a black velvet dress, and you kept peering forward [*imitating him*] like this.

FRITZ: You were really watching me closely.

MITZI: Of course, it's none of my concern, but if I were Christine . . . How come Theodor has time after the theater? How come he doesn't have to go and dine with some acquaintances?

THEODOR [*proudly*]: That's right, how come I don't have to go dine with acquaintances? . . .

[*Doorbell rings.*]

MITZI: That's Christine.

[FRITZ *hurries out.*]

THEODOR: Do me a favor, Mitzi.

[*She looks at him questioningly.*]

Forget your military reminiscences—at least for a time.

MITZI: But I don't have any.

THEODOR: Well, you didn't learn all that stuff from the officer's manual.

[CHRISTINE *enters, carrying flowers;* FRITZ *follows.*]

CHRISTINE [*slightly embarrassed*]: Good evening. Are you glad we came?—You're not angry, are you?

FRITZ [*exchanging greetings; then to* CHRISTINE]: Don't be silly. Sometimes Theodor is just cleverer than I am.

THEODOR: Well, is your papa already playing his violin?

CHRISTINE: Oh, yes. I accompanied him over to the theater.

FRITZ: So Mitzi told us.

CHRISTINE [*to* MITZI]: And then Catherine held me up for a while too.

MITZI: Oh no, not that hypocrite.

CHRISTINE: She's not a hypocrite. She's been very nice to me.

MITZI: But that's what you think about everyone.

CHRISTINE: Why should she be hypocritical with me?

FRITZ: Who is this Catherine?

MITZI: She's married to a garment worker, and she's always getting irritated about anyone who's younger than she is.

CHRISTINE: But she's still young herself.

FRITZ: Let's just forget Catherine. What have you got there?

CHRISTINE: Just some flowers I brought for you.

FRITZ [*taking them, kisses her hand*]: You're a little angel. Wait, we'll put them in a vase. . . .

THEODOR: Hold on, you've no feeling for such occasions. Flowers should just be strewn randomly about the table—of course, after it's been set. Actually they should be made to just fall from the ceiling—but that wouldn't work either.

FRITZ [*laughing*]: Well, hardly.

THEODOR: In the meantime, I suppose we should put them in water after all.

[*He puts them in a vase.*]

MITZI: Well my children, it's getting dark!

[FRITZ *has helped* CHRISTINE *off with her coat; she takes off her hat, and he puts coat and hat away.*]

FRITZ: We'd better light the lamp now.

THEODOR: The lamp?—Nonsense! We'll light candles. That'll look much nicer. Come along and help, Mitzi.

[THEODOR *and* MITZI *light candles around the room, while* FRITZ *and* CHRISTINE *talk.*]

FRITZ: Well, my darling. How are you doing?

CHRISTINE: I'm fine, now . . .

FRITZ: Well, and other times?

CHRISTINE: I've longed to see you so.

FRITZ: We just saw each other yesterday.

CHRISTINE: Of course, but only at a distance. [*Shyly*] You know, it wasn't nice of you to . . .

FRITZ: I know, Mitzi already told me. But you're being childish as usual. I couldn't get away. Surely you must understand that.

CHRISTINE: Yes . . . but Fritz . . . just who were those people in the box with you?

FRITZ: Just acquaintances of mine. It doesn't really matter what their names are.

CHRISTINE: Well, who was the lady in the black velvet dress?

FRITZ: My dear child, I never remember women's dresses.

CHRISTINE [*coaxingly*]: Oh, come on.

FRITZ: That is, I do remember them sometimes. For instance, I remember very well the dark gray blouse you were wearing the first time we met—and that black and white outfit you had on last night at the theater.

CHRISTINE: I'm also wearing it today!

FRITZ: So you are. But it looks much different from a distance . . . no, seriously. And that locket—I recognize that too.

CHRISTINE [*smiling*]: When was I wearing it?

FRITZ: Let me see . . . I know, it was that time we went for a walk in the park—by the old fort where all those children were playing.—Wasn't it?

CHRISTINE: That's right. . . . So you do think of me sometimes.

FRITZ: Quite often, my child.

CHRISTINE: Not as often as I think of you. I think of you all the time—all day long. I'm only happy when I see you.

FRITZ: Don't we see each other often enough?

CHRISTINE: Often . . .

FRITZ: Of course. But we won't see each other as much during the summer. . . . For instance, I might be going out of town for a couple of weeks, what would you say to that?

CHRISTINE [*alarmed*]: What do you mean—do you want to go out of town?

FRITZ: No . . . but it is possible that I might get an impulse to be by myself for a week or so . . .

CHRISTINE: But why?

FRITZ: I just said it's possible. I know myself . . . I get those impulses. And sometimes you might not want to see me for a few days, too. . . . I'd understand that.

CHRISTINE: Fritz, I'll never feel like that.

FRITZ: Well, you never know.

CHRISTINE: I do know . . . I love you.

FRITZ: And I love you too . . . very much.

CHRISTINE: But you're everything to me, Fritz. For you I could . . . [*breaks off*]—no, I can't imagine a time when I wouldn't want to see you. As long as I live, Fritz—

FRITZ [*interrupting*]: Please, I'm asking you, my child . . . You shouldn't say things like that . . . I don't like such big words. Let's not talk about always . . .

CHRISTINE [*sadly*]: Don't be alarmed, Fritz. I know it's not forever.

FRITZ: Now, don't misunderstand me, my child. It is possible [*laughing*] that someday we may discover that we just can't live without each other—but we have no way of knowing that now, do we? We're only human after all.

THEODOR [*pointing to candles*]: Be so kind as to take a look. Now, doesn't that look much better than a silly-looking lamp?

FRITZ: You're right. You have a real feeling for these occasions.

THEODOR: By the way, my children. Why don't we start thinking about supper?

MITZI: Oh, yes! Come on, Christine! . . .

FRITZ: Just a minute, I'll show you where to find everything.

MITZI: First of all, we'll need a tablecloth.

THEODOR [*in a comic accent*]: You mean, a "table-clawt."

FRITZ: I beg your pardon?

THEODOR: Oh, don't you remember that fellow at the Orpheum? "Dat eez de table-clawt," "dat eez de peez of metal," and "dat eez a leetle piccolo."

MITZI: Say, when are you going to take me to the Orpheum? You promised you would just the other day. And when we go, we'll take Christine and Herr Fritz too.

[FRITZ *hands her the tablecloth.*]

And then we'll be the acquaintances in your box.

FRITZ: Yes, yes.

MITZI: And then the lady in the black velvet dress can go home alone.

FRITZ: It's so silly the way you two keep going on about the lady in black.

MITZI: Oh, we don't keep going on about her . . . so, now what . . . the silverware?

[FRITZ *shows her where it is.*]

Good—and the plates? . . . yes, thank you . . . now, we can take care of the rest by ourselves. Go on, you're just bothering us.

THEODOR [*is now lying on the sofa; as* FRITZ *approaches*]: If you don't mind . . .

[MITZI *and* CHRISTINE *set the table.*]

MITZI: Have you ever seen the picture of Fritz in his uniform?

CHRISTINE: No.

MITZI: You've got to see it. It's so chic.

[*They continue talking.*]

THEODOR [*on the sofa*]: You know, Fritz, evenings like this are my passion.

FRITZ: Yes, it is nice.

THEODOR: I just feel so relaxed. Don't you?

FRITZ: Oh, sure. I wish I could always feel like this.

MITZI: Oh, Herr Fritz, is there any coffee in this thing?

FRITZ: Yes. . . . You should go ahead and light the burner, because it takes that thing a good hour to finish . . .

THEODOR [*to* FRITZ]: You know, I'd give you ten of your so-called enchantresses for a sweet little creature like that.

FRITZ: There's no comparison.

THEODOR: We hate the very women we love, and love only the women who are indifferent to us.

[FRITZ *laughs.*]

MITZI: What's going on? We'd like to hear too.

THEODOR: It's not for your ears, children. We're just philosophizing.

[*To* FRITZ] Even if we were seeing them tonight for the last time, we'd still be in good spirits, wouldn't we?

FRITZ: The last time . . . There's always something so depressing about that. Good-byes are always so painful, even when you've been looking forward to them for such a long time.

CHRISTINE: Oh Fritz, where are those little forks?

FRITZ [*going to the sideboard*]: Here they are, darling.

[MITZI *has come over and is running her fingers through* THEODOR*'s hair.*]

THEODOR: You pussycat, you.

FRITZ [*opening* MITZI*'s package*]: Oh, this is magnificent . . .

CHRISTINE [*to* FRITZ]: You've arranged everything so nicely!

FRITZ: Yes . . .

[*He arranges the things* MITZI *has brought on the table.*]

CHRISTINE: Fritz . . . don't you want to tell me?

FRITZ: Tell you what?

CHRISTINE [*very shyly*]: Who the lady was?

FRITZ: No. Now don't get me angry. [*More gently*] Look, we did both agree about that. No questions asked. But that's the nice thing about it. Whenever I'm with you the world disappears. And I don't ask you anything either.

CHRISTINE: You can ask anything.

FRITZ: But I don't. There's nothing I want to know.

MITZI [*returning*]: Good Lord, you've messed everything up. Here let me . . . [*taking over arranging the food and plates, and so forth*]

THEODOR: Fritz, have you got anything to drink in the house?

FRITZ: Yes, there's bound to be something.

[*He goes into the entryway.*]

THEODOR [*rises and looks at the table*]: Good . . .

MITZI: I don't suppose there's anything else we need!

FRITZ [*entering with bottles*]: Well, here's something to drink with it.

THEODOR: Where are the roses that are supposed to fall from the ceiling?

MITZI: That's right, we forgot the roses! [*Standing on a chair, letting flowers fall onto the table*] There.

CHRISTINE: Good heavens! The girl is getting carried away!

THEODOR: Well, not on the plates! . . .

FRITZ: Where do you want to sit, Christine?

THEODOR: Where's the corkscrew?

FRITZ [*takes one from the sideboard*]: Here's one. [*As* MITZI *tries to open the bottle*] Here, give it to me . . .

THEODOR: I'll do it—[*taking bottle and corkscrew from him*] Meanwhile you might give us a little . . .

[*He mimes playing the piano.*]

MITZI: Of course, how chic!

[*She runs to the piano, pulling things off onto a chair.*]

FRITZ [*to* CHRISTINE]: Shall I?

CHRISTINE: Oh, yes, please do. I've been longing to hear you play for quite a while.

FRITZ [*at piano*]: You can play a little bit too, can't you?

CHRISTINE [*turning away*]: Oh, Lord . . .

MITZI: Christine does play beautifully. And she can sing, too.

FRITZ: Really? But you never told me that! . . .

CHRISTINE: Did you ever ask?

FRITZ: Where did you learn how to sing?

CHRISTINE: I didn't actually learn how. My father gave me some lessons—but I don't really have much of a voice. And you know, since my aunt died, it's much quieter around the house now.

FRITZ: What do you actually do all day long?

CHRISTINE: Oh Lord, I've got plenty to do.

FRITZ: Around the house, you mean?

CHRISTINE: Well, yes. I do quite a lot of music copying.

THEODOR: Music?

CHRISTINE: Of course.

THEODOR: Well, that must pay enormously.

[*The others laugh.*]

Well, for that I'd pay enormously. I imagine copying all those notes is a frightful job.

MITZI: It really is absurd for her to go to such trouble. [*To* CHRISTINE] If I had a voice as good as yours, I'd have gone on the stage a long time ago.

THEODOR: You don't even need a voice. . . . And I suppose you do nothing at all all day long, right?

MITZI: Would you be so kind? I've got two little brothers who go to school.—I get them dressed in the morning, and then I do their homework with them.

THEODOR: But there's no truth to that.

MITZI: Well, if you don't believe me!—And up until last fall I had a job in a store from eight in the morning until eight at night—.

THEODOR [*gently mocking*]: And where was this?

MITZI: In a women's clothing store. My mother wants me to go back to that.

THEODOR [*same tone*]: And why did you leave then?

FRITZ [*to* CHRISTINE]: Well, now you must sing something for us.

THEODOR: All right, children, we'd better eat now and then you'll play. All right? . . .

FRITZ [*rising; to* CHRISTINE]: Come, darling.

[*He leads her to the table.*]

MITZI: Oh, the coffee!—Now it's boiling over, and we haven't even eaten yet.

THEODOR: None of that matters now!

MITZI: But it's really boiling over!

[*She puts out the flame; they all sit down at the table.*]

THEODOR: What'll you have, Mitzi? But I'll tell you right now, the dessert comes last. You're going to have to eat everything else first. [*As* FRITZ *starts to pour*] No, not like that! It's done differently now. Don't you know the latest fashions? [*Standing, he says solemnly, with affected gravity, first to* CHRISTINE, *then to each in turn . . .*] Choice Voeslauer, eighteen . . . [*pronouncing the year unintelligibly*] Choice Voeslauer, eighteen . . . Choice Voeslauer, eighteen . . . Choice Voeslauer, eighteen . . .

[*He sits.*]

MITZI [*laughing*]: He's always doing something foolish.

THEODOR: Prosit!

[*He raises his glass; they all clink glasses.*]

MITZI: Long life, Theodor!

THEODOR [*rising*]: Ladies and gentlemen—

FRITZ: No, not yet!

THEODOR [*sitting*]: Well, I can wait.

[*They eat.*]

MITZI: I love speeches at the dinner table. So, I have a cousin who always speaks in verse.

THEODOR: And what kind of regiment is he in . . . ?

MITZI: Now, stop that! . . . Honestly, he does all his speeches by heart, and in verse. But I tell you, Christine, it's really magnificent. And he's quite an elderly gentleman, too.

THEODOR: Oh, one still finds elderly gentlemen who speak in verse.

FRITZ: But you're not drinking at all, Christine.

[*He clinks glasses with her.*]

THEODOR [*clinking glasses with* MITZI]: To old gentlemen who speak in verse!

MITZI [*merrily*]: To young gentlemen—even if they don't speak at all. . . . For instance, Herr Fritz . . . Herr Fritz, we can drink to a less formal relationship now, if you wish—and Christine and Theodor must as well.

THEODOR: But not with this wine. It's not the right kind for that. [*Rising, goes through same act as before*] Xeres de la Frontera *mille huit cent cinquante*—Xeres de la Frontera—Xeres de la Frontera—Xeres de la Frontera.

MITZI [*sipping*]: Ah—

THEODOR: Can't you wait until we all drink? . . . All right, children . . . Before we officially begin our less formal relationship, let us drink to the happy coincidence which . . . and so forth and so on.

MITZI: Yes, all right.

[*They drink.* FRITZ *and* MITZI *link arms, as do* THEODOR *and* CHRISTINE, *glasses in hand as is the custom.* FRITZ *kisses* MITZI, THEODOR *tries to kiss* CHRISTINE.]

CHRISTINE [*smiling*]: Is that necessary?

THEODOR: Absolutely, otherwise it doesn't count.

[*He kisses her.*]

Well now, everyone. Take your places, *s'il vous plaît.*

MITZI: It's getting awfully hot in here.

FRITZ: That's from all those candles Theodor lit.

MITZI: And from that wine.

[*She leans back in her chair.*]

THEODOR: Just come over here. Now at last you'll get the best part. [*Cutting a piece of the pastry and putting it in her mouth*] There you are, you little pussycat, you. Good, huh?

MITZI: Very! . . .

[*He gives her one more piece.*]

THEODOR: All right, Fritz, now's the time! You could play something for us now.

FRITZ: Shall I, Christine?

CHRISTINE: Please do.

MITZI: But make it something chic.

[THEODOR *fills the glasses.*]

I can't drink any more.

[*She drinks.*]

CHRISTINE [*sipping*]: This wine is so heavy.
THEODOR [*pointing to the wine*]: Fritz!

[FRITZ *empties his glass and crosses to piano.* CHRISTINE *sits by him.*]

MITZI: Herr Fritz, play "The Imperial Eagle."
FRITZ: "The Imperial Eagle"? How does it go?
MITZI: Ted, can't you play "The Imperial Eagle"?
THEODOR: I can't play the piano at all.
FRITZ: I do know it. I just can't remember it.
MITZI: I'll sing it for you . . . La . . . la . . . la . . . la, la, la, la . . . la . . .
FRITZ: Aha! I do know it after all.

[*He plays, but not quite correctly.*]

MITZI [*going to the piano*]: No, it's like this—

[*She picks out the tune with one finger.*]

FRITZ: Oh, yes.

[*He plays and* MITZI *sings.*]

THEODOR: This brings back more sweet memories doesn't it?
FRITZ [*making more mistakes, stops playing*]: That doesn't work. I have absolutely no ear for that.

[*He improvises;* MITZI *speaks right after the first measure.*]

MITZI: That's no good.
FRITZ [*laughing*]: Now don't get nasty. That's my music.
MITZI: But it's not good for dancing.
FRITZ: Just try it once.
THEODOR [*to* MITZI]: Come on, let's try it . . .

[*He takes her by the waist. They dance.* CHRISTINE *stands by the piano, watching him play. The doorbell rings. He suddenly stops, but* MITZI *and* THEODOR *continue to dance.*]

THEODOR and MITZI [*together*]: What's that? Well!
FRITZ: The bell just rang. [*To* THEODOR] Did you invite anyone else?

THEODOR: Of course not. You don't need to answer it.
CHRISTINE [*to* FRITZ]: What's the matter?
FRITZ: Nothing . . .

[*Bell rings again.* FRITZ *stands up, but doesn't move.*]

THEODOR: You're simply not at home.
FRITZ: But anyone out in the hallway can hear the piano . . . and see the lights from out in the street.
THEODOR: Don't be so ridiculous! You're just not at home.
FRITZ: But it makes me nervous.
THEODOR: Well, what would it be then? A letter!—or a telegram—You certainly wouldn't be expecting a visit at . . . [*looking at his watch*] nine o'clock?

[*Bell rings again.*]

FRITZ: By no means, but still I must see.—

[*He exits.*]

MITZI: Well, the two of you are not being chic. . . .

[*She strikes a few keys on the piano.*]

THEODOR: Come on, stop that!—[*To* CHRISTINE] Well, what's wrong? Does the doorbell make you nervous too?

[FRITZ *returns with an air of artificial composure.*]

THEODOR and CHRISTINE [*together*]: Well, who was it? . . .
FRITZ [*with a forced smile*]: You must be so good as to excuse me. Meanwhile, go in there.
THEODOR: Well, what's going on?
CHRISTINE: Who is it?
FRITZ: It's nothing, my child. I just have to speak a few words to this gentleman. . . .

[*He holds the door to the next room open and accompanies the girls in. They exit.* THEODOR *hesitates at the exit with a questioning look to* FRITZ.]

FRITZ [*softly, with a look of fear*]: It's him! . . .
THEODOR: Ah . . . !
FRITZ: Go on in, go in—
THEODOR: Now listen, please don't do anything foolish. It could be a *trap* . . .
FRITZ: Go . . . ! Go . . . !

[THEODOR *exits into the next room.* FRITZ *goes quickly out into the corridor, so the stage is empty for a few moments. He reappears with an elegantly dressed man of about thirty-five. He wears a yellow overcoat, gloves, and carries his hat.*]

FRITZ [*as he enters*]: Sorry to keep you waiting.
GENTLEMAN [*in an extremely gentle tone*]: Oh, that's all right. I'm very sorry to have disturbed you.
FRITZ: Certainly not. Don't you want to—

[*He points out a chair.*]

GENTLEMAN: I see I have disturbed you . . . having a little party, eh?
FRITZ: Just a couple of friends.
GENTLEMAN [*sitting down, ever affable*]: Probably a masquerade?
FRITZ [*self-consciously*]: What do you mean?
GENTLEMAN: Well, your friends are wearing ladies' hats and cloaks.
FRITZ: Oh well . . . [*Smiling*] Perhaps there are some lady friends here too . . .

[*He is silent.*]

GENTLEMAN: Sometimes life is quite amusing—isn't it?

[*He looks fixedly at* FRITZ. FRITZ *endures his gaze a while, then looks away.*]

FRITZ: One may well ask to what one owes the honor of your visit?
GENTLEMAN: Certainly. . . . [*Calmly*] My wife forgot her veil here with you, it seems.
FRITZ: Your wife here with me? . . . Her . . . [*Smiling*] Such a peculiar sense of humor . . .

GENTLEMAN [*rising suddenly, vigorously, almost angrily, stands with hand on chair*]: She forgot it, I tell you.

[FRITZ *stands. They face each other.* GENTLEMAN *raises a fist as though to strike him.*]

[*With rage and loathing*] Oh!

[FRITZ *steps back in defense.* GENTLEMAN *continues after a long pause.*]

Here are your letters.

[*He takes out a packet of letters from his overcoat pocket and throws them on the desk.*]

I must ask for the ones which you have received.

[FRITZ *shakes his head.* GENTLEMAN *continues emphatically, with emotion*] I don't want them to be found here—later.

FRITZ [*intensely*]: No one will find them.

[GENTLEMAN *looks at him. Pause.*]

What else do you want from me? . . .
GENTLEMAN [*mockingly*]: What *else* do I want—?
FRITZ: I am at your disposal . . .
GENTLEMAN [*bows coldly*]: Good.—

[*He glances around the room; when he notices the table settings, the women's hats, etc., a violent expression passes over his face as if he is about to burst with rage.*]

FRITZ [*seeing this, says again*]: I am completely at your disposal.—I'll be home until twelve o'clock tomorrow.

[GENTLEMAN *bows, turns to leave.* FRITZ *starts to follow. He waves him away. After he leaves* FRITZ *goes to the desk, then rushes to the window, looks out through a crack in the blinds, and watches the* GENTLEMAN *walking down the sidewalk. He moves away from the window and stands for a moment looking at the floor. Then he opens the door to the adjoining room and calls.*]

Theodor . . . do you have a moment?

THEODOR [*entering excitedly—this scene should move quickly*]: Well . . .

FRITZ: He knows.

THEODOR: He knows nothing. Of course, you fell right into his trap. In the end, you did confess. You're such a fool, I tell you . . . you are—

FRITZ [*indicating the letters*]: He brought my letters back.

THEODOR [*disconcerted*]: Oh! . . .

[*Pause.*]

I always say, don't write any letters.

FRITZ: He was the one who was down there this afternoon.

THEODOR: Well, then what happened? Tell me.

FRITZ: You must do something for me now, Theodor.

THEODOR: I'll arrange things.

FRITZ: There's no longer any question of that.

THEODOR: Well, then . . .

FRITZ: Anyway, it's going to be fine . . . [*breaking off*]—After all, we shouldn't make the poor girls wait so long.

THEODOR: They can just wait. What did you want to say?

FRITZ: It would be a good idea for you to go and look for Lensky today.

THEODOR: Right away, if you want.

FRITZ: You won't catch him now . . . but between eleven and twelve o'clock tonight he's sure to be at the café . . . perhaps you could both come back here then. . . .

THEODOR: Go on now, don't make such a face. . . . Nine-nine percent of these cases turn out fine.

FRITZ: It's for sure that this case won't turn out fine.

THEODOR: Please remember last year—that affair between Dr. Billinger and Herz. That was exactly the same situation.

FRITZ: Oh, stop. You know it yourself—he might just as well have shot me dead right in this room—it would be the same in the end anyway.

THEODOR [*affectedly*]: Oh, that's splendid. That's a magnificent way of looking at it . . . And we, Lensky and I, we're nothing? Do you suppose we'd allow that—?

FRITZ: Oh, please, quit that! . . . You two'll just have to accept whatever is proposed.

THEODOR: Ah—

FRITZ: And what is it all about anyway, Theodor? As if you didn't know.

THEODOR: Nonsense. It's all a matter of luck after all. . . . You could just as well get him . . .

FRITZ [*without paying attention*]: She saw it coming. We both saw it coming. Suspected it would. We knew it . . .

THEODOR: Come now, Fritz . . .

FRITZ [*locking letters in desk*]: What is she doing right now? Does he . . . Theodor, tomorrow you must discover what's happened there.

THEODOR: I'll try . . .

FRITZ: . . . Make sure, too, there's no unnecessary delay . . .

THEODOR: It can hardly happen before day after tomorrow morning.

FRITZ [*almost alarmed*]: Theodor!

THEODOR: Come on, now . . . chin up.—After all, inner convictions also count for something, don't they?—And I'm firmly convinced that everything . . . is going to turn out all right. [*Attempting to cheer himself up*] I don't know why myself, but I'm just convinced of it.

FRITZ [*smiling*]: What a good fellow you are!—But just what'll we say to the girls?

THEODOR: That's really immaterial. We simply send them away.

FRITZ: Oh, no. We've got to appear to be as cheerful as possible. Christine mustn't suspect anything at all. I'll go sit at the piano again, and in the meantime you call them back in here.

[THEODOR *turns with a dissatisfied look.*]

And what will you say to them?

THEODOR: That it's none of their business.

FRITZ [*seated at piano, turning to him*]: No, no—
THEODOR: That it concerns a friend.—That will do.

[FRITZ *plays a few notes.*]

THEODOR: If you please, ladies.

[*He opens the door; they enter.*]

MITZI: Well, at last! Has that man already left?
CHRISTINE [*hurrying to* FRITZ]: Who was here with you, Fritz?
FRITZ [*continuing to play*]: There she goes again, being curious.
CHRISTINE: I beg you, Fritz, tell me.
FRITZ: Darling, I really can't tell you. Actually, it concerns people you don't even know.
CHRISTINE [*coaxingly*]: Come on, Fritz. Tell me the truth.
THEODOR: Of course, she's certainly not leaving you in peace . . . just don't you tell her anything! You promised him!
MITZI: Come on, Christine, don't be such a bore. Let them have their fun! They're just trying to put on airs!
THEODOR: I've got to finish this waltz with Fräulein Mitzi. [*Imitating a clown*] Maestro—a little music, please!

[FRITZ *plays;* THEODOR *and* MITZI *dance.*]

MITZI [*after a few bars*]: I can't!

[*She falls back into an armchair.* THEODOR *kisses her and sits down with her on an arm of the chair.* FRITZ, *seated at the piano, takes* CHRISTINE *by the hands, looks at her.*]

CHRISTINE [*as if awakening*]: Why don't you go on playing?
FRITZ [*smiling*]: That's enough for today. . . .
CHRISTINE: Oh, you know, I wish I could play like that. . . .
FRITZ: Do you play a lot? . . .
CHRISTINE: I don't get much chance, there's always something to do at home. And then of course, we have such a bad upright piano.
FRITZ: I'd like to try it sometime. Anyway I'd really like to see your room sometime.

CHRISTINE:[*smiling*]: It isn't nearly as nice as your place! . . .

FRITZ: And there's something else I'd like—sometime I'd like you to tell me a lot about yourself—quite a lot—I really don't know much about you.

CHRISTINE: There's not much to tell—I don't have any secrets either—unlike some people . . .

FRITZ: Haven't you loved someone else?

[*She just looks at him. He kisses her hands.*]

CHRISTINE: And I'll never love anyone else either . . .

FRITZ [*with an almost painful expression*]: Don't say it . . . Don't say it. Just what do you know? . . . Does your father really care for you, Christine?—

CHRISTINE: Oh, Lord! . . . There was a time when I told him everything too—

FRITZ: Well, you mustn't reproach yourself, my child. . . . Sometimes people simply have secrets.—That's just the way the world is.

CHRISTINE: . . . If I only knew that you cared for me.—Then everything would be all right.

FRITZ: Don't you know that?

CHRISTINE: If you always spoke to me the way you are now, then yes . . .

FRITZ: Christine! Come now, you must be rather uncomfortable sitting like that.

CHRISTINE: Just let me stay like this.—It's all right.

[*She lays her head against the piano.* FRITZ *gets up and strokes her hair.*]

Oh, that's nice.

[*Silence in the room.*]

THEODOR: Where are the cigars, Fritz?

[FRITZ *goes over to him at the sideboard where he has been searching.* MITZI *has dozed off.* FRITZ *hands* THEODOR *a little box of cigars.*]

FRITZ: And black coffee!

[*He pours two cups.*]

THEODOR: Don't you children want to have some coffee too?

FRITZ: Mitzi, shall I pour you a cup? . . .

THEODOR: We should let them sleep. . . . By the way, you shouldn't have any coffee now. You should go to bed as soon as possible and see to it that you get some proper rest.

[FRITZ *looks at him and laughs bitterly.*]

Oh well, with things as they are . . . It isn't really a matter of being grand or profound, but of being as sensible as possible. . . . That's the important thing . . . in matters of this sort.

FRITZ: Well, you're still coming by tonight with Lensky, aren't you?

THEODOR: That's nonsense. Tomorrow morning is time enough.

FRITZ: But I'm asking you.

THEODOR: Very well, then . . .

FRITZ: Are you escorting the girls home?

THEODOR: Yes, in fact right away . . . Mitzi! . . . Arise!—

MITZI: You two are having black coffee—! Give me some too!—

THEODOR: Here you are, my child . . .

[*He gives her his cup.*]

FRITZ [*to* CHRISTINE]: Tired, my darling? . . .

CHRISTINE: It's nice when you talk like that.

FRITZ: Very tired?—

CHRISTINE [*smiling*]: It's the wine—I've got a bit of a headache too . . .

FRITZ: Well, that'll certainly go away in the fresh air!

CHRISTINE: Are we going already?—Are you escorting us?

FRITZ: No, my child. I'm staying at home now. . . . I've still some things to do.

CHRISTINE [*suddenly remembering*]: Now . . . What have you got to do now?

FRITZ [*almost sternly*]: Now Christine, you've got to learn not to do that!—[*Gently*] You know, I'm simply worn out. . . . Theodor and I were running around for two hours out in the country today—

THEODOR: Oh, that was delightful! Sometime very soon we must all go out to the country together.

MITZI: Oh, that'll be chic! And you could both wear your uniforms, too.

THEODOR: Now there's some feeling for nature!

CHRISTINE: When will we see each other again?

FRITZ [*a bit nervously*]: I'll certainly write to you.

CHRISTINE [*sadly*]: Farewell.

[*She turns to leave.*]

FRITZ [*noticing her sadness*]: We'll see each other tomorrow, Christine.

CHRISTINE [*happily*]: Yes?

FRITZ: In the park . . . down by the old fort just like before . . . at, say, six o'clock . . . Yes? Is that all right with you?

[CHRISTINE *nods* yes!]

MITZI [*to* FRITZ]: Are you coming with us, Fritz?

THEODOR: She can put such affection into the word "you"—!

FRITZ: No, I'm staying home now.

MITZI: He's got it easy! We've got such a long trip home . . .

FRITZ: But, Mitzi, you're leaving almost all of this wonderful dessert behind. Wait, I'll wrap it up for you.—Well?

MITZI [*to* THEODOR]: Would that be all right?

[FRITZ *wraps up the dessert.*]

CHRISTINE: She's like a little child.

MITZI [*to* FRITZ]: Wait, in return I'll help you put out the candles.

[*She blows them all out, one by one, leaving the light on the desk.*]

CHRISTINE: Shouldn't I open the window for you?—It's so stuffy in here.

[*She opens the window facing the house across the street.*]

FRITZ: Well, children. Now I'll light the way for you.

MITZI: Are the lights already out on the stairs?

THEODOR: It goes without saying.

CHRISTINE: Ah, that breeze through the window is nice, coming in here like that! . . .

MITZI: A little May breeze . . .

[*They are at the door;* FRITZ *has the candlestick in his hand.*]

Well, we thank you for your hospitality!—

THEODOR [*impatiently*]: Come, come, come, come . . .

[FRITZ *accompanies them out. The door remains open. Their voices can be heard outside. We then hear the outer door opening.*]

MITZI: Oh, no!—

THEODOR: Careful of the steps there.

MITZI: Thanks very much for the dessert . . .

THEODOR: Shhh, you'll wake the neighbors!—

CHRISTINE: Good night!

THEODOR: Good night!

[FRITZ *is heard closing and locking the door to the apartment.—As he enters and puts the candle on the desk, we hear the downstairs door open and shut. He goes to the window and waves to his friends below.*]

CHRISTINE [*from the street*]: Good night!

MITZI [*playfully*]: Good night, my darling child! . . .

THEODOR [*scolding*]: Now, Mitzi! . . .

[*The words, the laughter, and the footsteps fade away.* FRITZ *is whistling the "Imperial Eagle" march, which fades away last. He continues to look out the window for a couple of seconds, then sinks into the armchair near the window.*]

[*Curtain*]

ACT TWO

[CHRISTINE*'s room: modest and tidy.* CHRISTINE *is just getting dressed to leave.* CATHERINE *appears, after knocking.*]

CATHERINE: Good evening, Fräulein Christine.

CHRISTINE [*standing before the mirror and turning around*]: Good evening.

CATHERINE: You're just about to leave?

CHRISTINE: I'm not in such a hurry.

CATHERINE: I'm just coming from my husband to ask if you want to have supper with us over in the park; they're playing music there today.

CHRISTINE: Thanks very much, Frau Binder. . . . I can't today . . . another time, all right?—But you're not angry, are you?

CATHERINE: Oh, not at all . . . why should I be? I'm sure you'll have a better time there than with us.

[CHRISTINE *gives her a look.*]

CATHERINE: Is your father already at the theater? . . .

CHRISTINE: Oh no, he's coming home earlier than usual. Why, it doesn't start until seven-thirty now!

CATHERINE: Right, I'm always forgetting that. Then I'll just wait for him—because I've been wanting to ask him for a long time now about some free passes to the new piece. . . . Can they be picked up already? . . .

CHRISTINE: Of course . . . why, nobody is going anymore, especially now when the evenings are getting so nice.

CATHERINE: Yes, well, otherwise our kind never get a chance . . . if we don't happen to know someone in the theater. . . . But don't stay on my account, Fräulein Christine, if you must leave. My husband will certainly be very sorry . . . and someone else too . . .

CHRISTINE: Who?

CATHERINE: Mr. Binder's cousin is staying with us, of course. . . . Do you know, Fräulein Christine, he has a steady job now?

CHRISTINE [*indifferently*]: Ah.

CATHERINE: And with a very nice salary. And such a decent young fellow. And he has such high regard for you—

CHRISTINE: Well, then—good-bye, Frau Binder.

CATHERINE: People could say whatever they want about you—but that young fellow wouldn't believe a word of it . . .

[CHRISTINE *gives her a look.*]

CHRISTINE: There certainly are men like that . . .

CATHERINE: Adieu, Frau Binder.

CATHERINE: Adieu . . . [*Not too malicious in tone*] Just don't be too late for your date, Fräulein Christine!

CHRISTINE: What do you really want from me?—

CATHERINE: Not a thing. You're right: after all, you're only young once!

CHRISTINE: Adieu.

CATHERINE: But I would really like to give you some advice, Fräulein Christine: you ought to be a bit more cautious!

CHRISTINE: Well, what does that mean?

CATHERINE: Look—Vienna is really such a large city. . . . Do you have to have your dates so close to home?

CHRISTINE: Well, that's of no concern to anyone else.

CATHERINE: I just didn't want to believe it when Mr. Binder told me. He's the one who saw you. Go on, I told him, you must have seen wrong. That Fräulein Christine, she's not the sort of person to go walking in the evening with elegant young gentlemen, and even if she did, she'd be smart enough not to go walking right here in our street! Well, he says, you can just ask her yourself! And, he says, it's just no wonder—she never comes over to see us anymore. But instead she's constantly running around with that Schlager girl, Mitzi—is that the company for a respectable young lady?—Men are really so vulgar, Fräulein Christine!—And naturally he had to go tell his cousin Franz and of course he got nice and mad—and for Fräulein Christine he'd walk on glowing coals, and whoever says anything about you will have to deal with him. And the way you do the housekeeping and the way you were so nice to your maiden aunt—God rest her soul—and the way you live so modestly and so secluded, and so . . . [*Pausing*] Maybe you'll come with us to the music after all?

CHRISTINE: No . . .

[WEIRING *appears, a lilac branch in his hand.*]

WEIRING: Good evening. . . . Ah, Frau Binder. Well, how are you doing?

CATHERINE: Fine, thanks.

WEIRING: And little Lina?—And your husband? . . .

CATHERINE: All healthy, thank God.

WEIRING: Well, that's fine.—[*To* CHRISTINE] Are you still at home in this nice weather—?

CHRISTINE: I was just about to go out.

WEIRING: That's smart!—There's a breeze outside today, eh, Frau Binder, it's something wonderful. Just now I was walking through the park down by the old fort—the lilac is blooming there—it's splendid! I also committed a transgression!

[*He gives* CHRISTINE *the lilac branch.*]

CHRISTINE: Thank you, Father.

CATHERINE: Be glad the caretaker didn't catch you.

WEIRING: Go over there sometime, Frau Binder—it still smells just as nice as if I hadn't plucked off this little branch.

CATHERINE: But if everyone thought like that—

WEIRING: That would, of course, be too bad!

CHRISTINE: Adieu, Father!

WEIRING: If you would like to wait a couple of minutes, you could accompany me over to the theater.

CHRISTINE: I . . . I promised Mitzi that I would go meet . . .

WEIRING: Ah yes.—That's also much smarter. Young people belong together. Adieu, Christine . . .

CHRISTINE [*kissing him—then*]: Adieu, Frau Binder!

[*She exits.* WEIRING *gazes affectionately after her.*]

CATHERINE: That's quite an intimate friendship she's got with Fräulein Mitzi.

WEIRING: Yes.—I'm really very glad that Tina has some stimulation and isn't sitting at home all the time. Just what does the girl actually get out of life! . . .

CATHERINE: Yes, of course.

WEIRING: I just can't tell you, Frau Binder, how much it hurts sometimes when I come home like this from a rehearsal—and there she sits and sews—and in the afternoon, we scarcely get up from the table, and she's sitting down again writing her music notes . . .

CATHERINE: Oh well, of course the millionaires have it better than our kind. But what about her singing?

WEIRING: It's not very promising. Her voice is adequate for the parlor, of course, and she sings well enough for her father—but one can't live off that.

CATHERINE: Well, that's too bad.

WEIRING: I'm glad that she realizes it herself. At least she'll be spared all the disappointment.—Of course, I could get her into the chorus at our theater—

CATHERINE: With *her* figure, of course!

WEIRING: But there really aren't any prospects in that.

CATHERINE: A daughter certainly does bring problems! When I think that in five or six years my little Lina will also be grown up—

WEIRING: Well, why don't you sit down, Frau Binder?

CATHERINE: Oh, thank you so much, but my husband is coming for me right away—really, I just came up to invite Christine . . .

WEIRING: Invite—?

CATHERINE: Yes, to hear the music over in the park. I was also thinking how that might cheer her up a bit—she certainly does need it after all.

WEIRING: That certainly couldn't hurt—especially after this dismal winter. Well, why isn't she going with you—?

CATHERINE: I don't know . . . Maybe because Binder's cousin is coming along.

WEIRING: Ah, that's quite possible. She simply can't stand him. She told me that herself.

CATHERINE: Well, just why not? Franz is a very respectable person—he's even got a steady job now; after all, that's a blessing nowadays . . .

WEIRING: For a . . . poor girl—

CATHERINE: It's a blessing for every girl.

WEIRING: Now tell me, Frau Binder, is such a blossoming young creature really meant for nothing but a respectable person who happens to have a steady job?

CATHERINE: Isn't that wisest, after all! A girl can't wait for a count, after all, and if one ever does come along, he usually leaves without getting married . . .

[WEIRING *is at the window.*]

[*Pausing*] Oh well . . . That's why I always say that one can't be too cautious with a young girl—especially as far as social life—

WEIRING: Is she expected to just throw her youthful years out the window like that?—And what does such a poor creature finally get for all her good behavior, even if—after all those years of waiting—sure enough, the garment worker does come along!

CATHERINE: Herr Weiring, even if my husband is a garment worker, he's a decent and good husband, and I've never had to complain about . . .

WEIRING: [*soothingly*]: But Frau Binder—that's not directed at you! . . . Why, you certainly didn't throw your youth out the window.

CATHERINE: I don't remember anything about that anymore.

WEIRING: Don't say that—now you can tell me anything you want—after all, memories are the best thing you have from life.

CATHERINE: I don't have any memories at all.

WEIRING: Now, now . . .

CATHERINE: And what's left over, then, when a woman does have the sort of memories you imagine . . . ? Regrets.

WEIRING: Well, and what's left over, then—if she—doesn't even have something to remember—? When all of life has just gone by like that—[*very simply, without pathos*]—one day like the other, without happiness and without love—is that better perhaps?

CATHERINE: But Herr Weiring, just think after all about the old lady—your maiden sister! . . . But it still hurts you, when people talk about her, Herr Weiring . . .

WEIRING: It still does hurt me, yes . . .

CATHERINE: Of course . . . when two people have clung to each other like that. . . . I've always said one doesn't very often find a brother like you.

[WEIRING *makes a parrying gesture.*]

CATHERINE: Yes, it's true. After all, at quite a young age you had to take the place of her father and mother.

WEIRING: Yes, yes—

CATHERINE: Yes, that must certainly be another kind of consolation. When you know you were the benefactor and protector of such a poor creature—

WEIRING: Yes, at one time I, too, imagined that—when she was still a beautiful young girl—and I fancied myself God knows how wise and noble. But then later, when the gray hairs came on so slowly, and the wrinkles, and when one day followed the other—and her whole youth—and the young girl so gradually became the old lady—indeed such a thing is hardly noticeable—only then did I begin to sense what I'd actually done!

CATHERINE: But Herr Weiring—

WEIRING: Yes, I can still see her before me, as she so often sat across from me in the evening by the lamp, in that room over there, looking at me like that with her quiet smile, with that certain expression, accepting God's will—as if she still wanted to thank me for something—and I—I would have most liked to fling myself down on my knees before her, to beg her pardon for having guarded her so well against all dangers—and against all happiness!

[*Pause.*]

CATHERINE: And yet many a woman would be glad if she had always had such a brother at her side . . . and nothing to regret . . .

[MITZI *enters.*]

MITZI: Good evening! . . . My, but it's already quite dark in here . . . you simply can't see a thing anymore—Ah, Frau Binder. Your husband is downstairs, Frau Binder, waiting for you . . . Isn't Christine at home? . . .

WEIRING: She left a quarter of an hour ago.

CATHERINE: Well, didn't you meet her? She did have a date with you, didn't she?

MITZI: No . . . in any case we missed each other. . . . You are going to hear the music with your husband, as he told me—?

CATHERINE: Yes, he's so very enthusiastic about that sort of thing. Say, Fräulein Mitzi, you've got a charming little hat on. New, isn't it?

MITZI: But not at all.—Well, don't you know the latest fashion? It's from last spring, just newly trimmed.

CATHERINE: Did you do the new trimming on it yourself?

MITZI: Well of course.

WEIRING: So skillful!

CATHERINE: Certainly—I always forget that you worked for a year in a women's clothing store.

MITZI: I'll probably go back into another one. My mother wants it that way—so there's nothing I can do about it.

CATHERINE: So how's your mother doing?

MITZI: All right—she has a bit of a toothache—but the doctor says it's only rheumatism . . .

WEIRING: Yes, but now it's high time for me . . .

CATHERINE: I'll go down with you right now, Herr Weiring . . .

MITZI: I'll go along too. . . . But take your topcoat along, Herr Weiring; it'll get rather cool later on.

WEIRING: Do you think so?

CATHERINE: Yes, of course. . . . Just how can anyone be so careless?

[CHRISTINE *appears.*]

MITZI: Well, here she is . . .

CATHERINE: Back from your walk already?

CHRISTINE: Yes. Greetings, Mitzi. . . . I've got such a headache . . .

[*She sits down.*]

WEIRING: How's that? . . .

CATHERINE: That's probably from the breeze . . .

WEIRING: Well then, what's wrong, Christine! . . . Please light the lamp, Fräulein Mitzi.

[MITZI *gets it ready.*]

CHRISTINE: But I can do that myself.

WEIRING: I'd like to see your face, Christine! . . .

CHRISTINE: But Father, it's really nothing at all, it's certainly from the breeze outside.

CATHERINE: Some people just can't take the spring.

WEIRING: Fräulein Mitzi, you really are staying with Christine, aren't you?

MITZI: Of course I'm staying here . . .

CHRISTINE: But it's really nothing at all, Father.

MITZI: My mother doesn't make so much of a fuss with me when I have a headache . . .

WEIRING [*to* CHRISTINE, *who is still sitting*]: Are you that tired? . . .

CHRISTINE [*getting up from the chair, smiling*]: I'm already getting up again.

WEIRING: Well—now you look quite different again.—[*To* CATHERINE] She looks quite different when she laughs, doesn't she . . . ? So adieu, Christine . . .

[*He kisses her.*]

[*At the door*] Just don't let that little head hurt any more when I come home! . . .

CATHERINE [*softly to* CHRISTINE]: Did you two have a quarrel?

[CHRISTINE *makes an indignant gesture.*]

WEIRING [*at the door*]: Frau Binder . . . !

MITZI: Adieu! . . .

[WEIRING *and* CATHERINE *exit.*]

MITZI: You know what your headache comes from? From that sweet wine yesterday. I'm so surprised that I haven't felt anything at all from it. . . . But it was fun, wasn't it . . . ?

[CHRISTINE *nods.*]

MITZI: They're very chic people, both of them—can't say anything at all against that, can you?—And Fritz's place is beautifully furnished, really, splendid! At Ted's . . . [*Breaking off*] Ah nothing . . . —Come now, do you still have such a bad headache? Then why don't you say *something*? . . . Well, what's *wrong*?

CHRISTINE: Just think—he didn't come.

MITZI: He stood you up? That serves you right!

CHRISTINE: Well, what does that mean? Just what did I do?—

MITZI: You're spoiling him, you're too nice to him. That way a man really can't help getting arrogant.

CHRISTINE: But you really don't know what you're saying.

MITZI: I know exactly what I'm talking about.—All this time I've been upset about you. He arrives too late for your date, doesn't escort you home, goes into the loge and sits down with strangers, simply stands you up—and you calmly put up with all that, and on top of that you look at him—[*parodying her*]—with such lovesick eyes.

CHRISTINE: Come on, don't talk like that, don't make yourself look bad. You're really fond of Theodor, too.

MITZI: Fond—of course I'm fond of him. But Ted doesn't get to see that and no other man in the world does either, that I should fret about him—men are just not worth it, none of them.

CHRISTINE: I've never heard you speak like that, never!—

MITZI: Well really, my dear Tina—we've just never talked with each other like this before. I just didn't dare. You wouldn't believe the kind of respect I've had for you! . . . But you know, I've always thought to myself: once it happens to you, it'll get you but good!—The first time really knocks you off your feet!—But you can also be glad of the fact that the first time you fall in love you'll have such a good friend right there to support you.

CHRISTINE: Mitzi!

MITZI: Don't you believe I'm your good friend? God knows what kind of things you'll get in your head if I'm not here to tell you: child, he's a man just like the others, and none of them are worth a single bad hour. That's what I always say! You can't believe a word they tell you.

CHRISTINE: Just what are you saying?—Men, men—so what do I care about men!—I'm really not interested in any others.—I'll never be interested in any other man my whole life!

MITZI: . . . Well, what do you really think . . . So did he . . . ? Of course—it's all happened before, but then you should have done it differently . . .

CHRISTINE: Just be quiet!

MITZI: Well, what do you want from me then? I can't do anything about that—a person should think about such things sooner and simply wait until someone comes along whose serious intentions you can see right away in his face. . . .

CHRISTINE: Mitzi, I can't take such talk today, it hurts me.—

MITZI [*good-naturedly*]: Oh, come on—

CHRISTINE: You'd better leave me . . . don't be angry . . . you'd better leave me alone!

MITZI: Well, why should I be angry? I'm just leaving. I didn't want to upset you, Christine, really . . . [*As she turns to leave*] Ah, Herr Fritz.

[FRITZ *has entered.*]

FRITZ: Good evening!

CHRISTINE [*shouting for joy*]: Fritz, Fritz!

[*She rushes toward him, into his arms.* MITZI *steals away, with an expression of "I'm not needed here."*]

FRITZ [*extricating himself*]: But—

CHRISTINE: They all say that you'll leave me! You're not leaving, right?—Not just yet—not just yet . . .

FRITZ: Come, who's saying that? . . . Now what's wrong then . . . ? [*Caressing her*] But darling! . . . I just really thought you'd be pretty alarmed if I suddenly came on in here.—

CHRISTINE: Oh—just as long as you're here!

FRITZ: Come on, now, just calm down—were you waiting for me a long time?

CHRISTINE: Well, why didn't you come?

FRITZ: I was delayed and got there too late. I was in the park just now and didn't find you—and was about to go home again. But suddenly I was seized by such a longing, a longing for this sweet, dear little face . . .

CHRISTINE [*happily*]: Is that true?

FRITZ: And then suddenly I got an indescribable desire to see just where you live—yes, seriously—I had to see it sometime—and then I couldn't stand it and came on up here . . . so you don't mind?

CHRISTINE: Oh Lord!

FRITZ: No one saw me—and anyway I knew your father was at the theater.

CHRISTINE: What do I care about other people!

FRITZ: So here's—? [*Looking around the room*] So this is your room? Very nice . . .

CHRISTINE: But you can't see anything at all.

[*She starts to take the shade off the lamp.*]

FRITZ: No, just leave it, that's blinding me, it's better like this. . . . So here's . . . ? This is the window you told me about, where you always do your work, eh?—and the beautiful view here! [*Smiling*] How many roofs to look over . . . And over there—yes, just what's that, that black thing that can be seen over there?

CHRISTINE: That's the mountain behind the Vienna Woods!

FRITZ: Right! You really do have a more beautiful view than I do.

CHRISTINE: Oh!

FRITZ: I'd like to live this high up. I find it very beautiful to look over all these roofs. And it must be quiet on this street too—?

CHRISTINE: Ah, there's enough noise during the daytime.

FRITZ: So do wagons ever go past here?

CHRISTINE: Rarely, but there's a blacksmith's shop right over there in that house.

FRITZ [*sitting down*]: Oh, that's not very pleasant.

CHRISTINE: One gets used to it and just doesn't hear it at all anymore!

FRITZ [*quickly getting up again*]: Am I really here for the first time—? It all seems so familiar to me! . . . It's exactly the way I imagined it.

CHRISTINE [*when he makes a move to take a closer look around the room*]: No, you mustn't look at anything in here.—

FRITZ: Now what sort of pictures are those? . . .

CHRISTINE: Come on! . . .

FRITZ: Ah, I'd like to take a look at these.

[*He moves the lamp up to the pictures.*]

CHRISTINE: . . . *Farewell* and *Return Home.*

FRITZ: Right—*Farewell* and *Return Home*!

CHRISTINE: Well, I know those pictures aren't beautiful.—There's one hanging in my father's room that's much better.

FRITZ: What sort of picture is that?

CHRISTINE: It's a girl looking out the window and outside it's winter, you know—and it's called *Forsaken.*—

FRITZ: Well . . . [*Putting the lamp down*] Ah, and there is your library.

[*He sits down beside the small bookrack.*]

CHRISTINE: You'd better not have a look at them—

FRITZ: Why not then? Ah!—Schiller . . . Hauff . . . an encyclopedia . . . Good grief!—

CHRISTINE: It goes only to *G* . . .

FRITZ [*smiling*]: Ah yes . . . that annual: *The Book for Everyone* . . . You look at the pictures in it, don't you?

CHRISTINE: Of course I've looked at the pictures.

FRITZ [*still seated*]: So who is the gentleman up there above the stove?

CHRISTINE [*didactically*]: That's Schubert, of course.

FRITZ [*getting up*]: Correct—

CHRISTINE: Since Father is so fond of him. Father also used to compose songs, very beautiful songs.

FRITZ: But he doesn't do it anymore?

CHRISTINE: Not anymore.

[*Pause.*]

FRITZ [*sitting down*]: It's so cozy here!—

CHRISTINE: Do you really like it?

FRITZ: Very much . . . well, what's this?

[*He picks up a vase with artificial flowers standing on the table.*]

CHRISTINE: So now he's found something else! . . .

FRITZ: No, my child, this doesn't belong in here with these other things. . . . It looks like it's covered with dust.

CHRISTINE: Well, these things aren't really covered with dust.

FRITZ: Artificial flowers always look like they're covered with dust. . . . There should be real flowers in your room. Flowers that are fresh and smell sweet. From now on I'll . . .

[*He breaks off; turns away to hide his agitation.*]

CHRISTINE: What? . . . What were you going to say?

FRITZ: Nothing, nothing . . .

CHRISTINE [*getting up; affectionately*]: What?—

FRITZ: I was going to say I'll send you fresh flowers tomorrow . . .

CHRISTINE: And now you're already regretting it?—Of course you are! Tomorrow you won't be thinking of me anymore.

[FRITZ *makes a parrying gesture.*]

CHRISTINE: Certainly—you don't think of me when you don't see me.

FRITZ: But what are you saying?

CHRISTINE: Oh, I know it. I just feel it.

FRITZ: Now how can you think that?

CHRISTINE: You're the one to blame for it. Because you're always keeping secrets from me! . . . Because you won't tell me anything about yourself at all.—Just what do you do all day long?

FRITZ: But darling, it's really very simple. I go to lectures—occasionally—then I go to the café . . . then I read . . . sometimes I play the piano too—then I chat with this person or that—then I go visiting—but all that's quite unimportant. It's really boring to talk about that.—Incidentally, I must leave now, my child . . .

CHRISTINE: Just now—

FRITZ: Well, your father will be here soon.

CHRISTINE: Not for a good while yet, Fritz.—Stay a while—a minute—stay a while—

FRITZ: And then I have something else . . . Theodor is expecting me . . . I have something else to discuss with him.

CHRISTINE: Today?

FRITZ: Today, of course.

CHRISTINE: You'll see him tomorrow too.

FRITZ: I may not even be in Vienna tomorrow.

CHRISTINE: Not in Vienna?—

FRITZ [*calmly and cheerfully, noticing her anxiety*]: Well, yes. Doesn't that happen? I'm going away for the day—or perhaps even for two, my child.—

CHRISTINE: Where to?

FRITZ: Where to! . . . Oh, anywhere—Good Lord, now don't make such a face. . . . I'm going out to the estate, to see my parents. . . . Well . . . is that sinister too?

CHRISTINE: Look, you never tell me about them either!

FRITZ: No, what a child you are . . . You just don't understand how wonderful it is to be so completely alone with each other. Tell me now, don't you feel it?

CHRISTINE: No, it's not wonderful at all that you never tell me anything about yourself. . . . Look, I'm interested in everything that concerns you. I really am . . . everything—I would like more from you than the one hour in the evening that we sometimes spend together. And then you're gone again, and I don't know anything at all . . . and then a whole night goes by and a whole day, with so many hours—and I know nothing. It often makes me so sad.

FRITZ: So why are you sad about that?

CHRISTINE: Well, because then I have such a longing for you, as if you weren't even in the same city, as if you were somewhere completely different! For me, you've disappeared then, you're so far away . . .

FRITZ [*somewhat impatiently*]: But . . .

CHRISTINE: Now look, it's really true! . . .

FRITZ: Come over here to me!

[*She is at his side.*]

Now after all, you know as well as I do just this one thing—That you love me at this moment. . . . [*As she tries to speak*] Don't talk about eternity. [*More to himself*] Perhaps there really are moments which spread an aura of eternity about themselves.— . . . That's all that we can understand, that's all that belongs to us . . .

[*He kisses her.—Pause.—He gets up.—*]

[*Bursting out*] Oh how wonderful it is, here with you, how wonderful! . . .

[*He stands at the window.*]

How far away the world is, in the midst of the many houses down there . . . I feel so solitary here, so alone with you . . . [*Softly*] So safe . . .

CHRISTINE: If you would always talk like that . . . then I could almost believe . . .

FRITZ: Well what, my child?

CHRISTINE: That you love me as much as I dreamed you did—the day you gave me that first kiss . . . do you remember?

FRITZ [*passionately*]: I do love you!—

[*He embraces her, then tears himself away.*]

But let me go now—

CHRISTINE: Are you already sorry you said it to me? You certainly are free, you certainly are free—you can just go and leave me, whenever you want . . . You didn't promise me anything—and I haven't demanded anything from you . . . Whatever becomes of me now is really all the same—after all I was happy once. I really don't want any more out of life. I would just like for you to know that and for you to believe that I didn't love anyone else before you and that I won't love anyone—if someday you won't want me anymore—

FRITZ [*more to himself*]: Don't say it, don't say it—the doorbell is ringing . . . too wonderful . . .

[*A knock at the door.*]

FRITZ [*startled*]: It's probably Theodor . . .

CHRISTINE [*disconcerted*]: He knows you're here with me—?

[THEODOR *enters.*]

THEODOR: Good evening.—Impudent, aren't I?

CHRISTINE: Do you have such important things to discuss with him?

THEODOR: Certainly—and I've been looking for him just about everywhere.

FRITZ [*softly*]: Why didn't you wait downstairs?

CHRISTINE: What is it you're whispering to him?

THEODOR [*intentionally loudly*]: Why didn't I wait downstairs? . . . Well, had I known for sure that you were up here . . . But I couldn't risk walking back and forth downstairs for two hours . . .

FRITZ [*pointedly*]: So . . . You're going with *me* tomorrow?

THEODOR [*comprehending*]: Right . . .

FRITZ: That's wise . . .

THEODOR: But I've been running around so much I must ask permission to sit down for ten seconds.

CHRISTINE: Please do.

[*She busies herself at the window.*]

FRITZ [*softly*]: Anything new? Have you found out something about her?

THEODOR [*softly, to* FRITZ]: No, I just came up here to get you because you are being reckless. Why get worked up unnecessarily, like this? You should get some sleep. . . . You need rest! . . .

[CHRISTINE *is again with them.*]

FRITZ: Say, don't you find this room simply lovely?

THEODOR: Yes, it's very nice . . . [*To* CHRISTINE] Do you stay at home here all day?—By the way, it really is quite livable. A bit high up for my taste.

FRITZ: That's exactly what I find so pretty.

THEODOR: But now I'm going to take Fritz away from you; we've got to get up early tomorrow.

CHRISTINE: So you're really going away?

THEODOR: He's coming back, Fräulein Christine!

CHRISTINE: Will you write me?

THEODOR: But if he's back again tomorrow—

CHRISTINE: Ah, I know, he's going away for longer than that . . .

[FRITZ *winces.*]

THEODOR [*noticing that*]: Well then, does a person have to write immediately? I would never have thought that you were so sentimental, Fräulein Christine . . . *Christine,* I meant to say—we're such good friends, after all. . . . So . . . now just give each other a farewell kiss, since you won't . . .

[*He breaks off.*]

Well, just act as if I'm not here.

[FRITZ *and* CHRISTINE *kiss.* THEODOR *takes out a cigarette case, puts a cigarette in his mouth, and looks for a match in the pocket of his topcoat. When he can't find any*—]

THEODOR: Say, Christine, dear, don't you have any matches?
CHRISTINE: Oh yes, there are some in there.

[*She points to a matchbox on the chest of drawers.*]

THEODOR: There aren't any more in here.—
CHRISTINE: I'll bring you one.

[*She quickly runs into the adjoining room.*]

FRITZ [*gazing after her; to* THEODOR]: Oh Lord, how *deceptive* times like this can be.
THEODOR: Well, just what sort of times?
FRITZ: Now I'm on the verge of believing my happiness would be here, that this sweet girl—[*breaking off*]—but a time like this is so very deceptive . . .
THEODOR: Insipid nonsense . . . How you'll laugh about that.
FRITZ: I'll probably have no more time for that.
CHRISTINE [*comes back with the matches*]: Here you are, Herr Theodor!
THEODOR: Thanks very much . . . So adieu.—[*To* FRITZ] Well, what else do you want, now?—
FRITZ [*looking up and down in the room, as if he wanted to take in everything one more time*]: One can scarcely part from here.
CHRISTINE: Come on, you're just making fun.
THEODOR [*vigorously*]: Come.—Adieu, Christine.
FRITZ: Farewell . . .
CHRISTINE: Auf Wiedersehn!—

[THEODOR *and* FRITZ *leave.*]

CHRISTINE [*stands still uneasily, then going to the door, which stands open; in an undertone*]: Fritz . . .

FRITZ [*coming back in once more and pressing her to his heart*]: Farewell! . . .

[*Curtain*]

ACT THREE

[*The same room as in the previous act. Noontime.* CHRISTINE *alone, seated at the window, sewing, puts her work down again.* LINA, *the nine-year-old daughter of* CATHERINE, *enters.*]

LINA: Good day, Fräulein Christine!

CHRISTINE [*very preoccupied*]: Greetings, child. Well, what do you want?

LINA: Mother sent me to see if I could get the theater tickets right away.—

CHRISTINE: Father isn't home yet, child; do you want to wait?

LINA: No, Fräulein Christine, I'll come back after dinner.

CHRISTINE: Fine.—

LINA [*already leaving, turns around again*]: And Mother sends Fräulein Christine her greetings and wants to know if Fräulein Christine still has a headache?

CHRISTINE: No, child.

LINA: Adieu, Fräulein Christine!

CHRISTINE: Adieu!—

[MITZI *is at the door, just as* LINA *goes out.*]

LINA: Good day, Fräulein Mitzi.

MITZI: Hi there, you little brat!

[LINA *exits.*]

CHRISTINE [*getting up and goes to* MITZI as she comes in]: So are they back?

MITZI: Well, how should I know?

CHRISTINE: And you don't have a letter, nothing—

MITZI: No.

CHRISTINE: Then you don't have a letter either?

MITZI: Well, why should we write to each other?

CHRISTINE: They've been gone since the day before yesterday!

MITZI: Oh well, that's really not so long! That's why a person really shouldn't make such a fuss. I don't understand you at all. . . . Now just look at you. Why, you're all weepy. Your father is bound to notice something when he comes home.

CHRISTINE [*simply*]: My father knows everything.—

MITZI [*almost alarmed*]: What?—

CHRISTINE: I told him.

MITZI: That was another smart thing to do. But naturally, one can see everything right away, just from your face.—Does he know *who* it is, after all?

CHRISTINE: Yes.

MITZI: And did he get nasty?

[CHRISTINE *shakes her head.*]

MITZI: Well, what did he say?—

CHRISTINE: Nothing . . . He walked away rather quietly, as usual.—

MITZI: And still it was stupid of you to say anything at all. . . . You'll soon see . . . Do you know why your father didn't say anything—? Because he thinks Fritz will marry you.

CHRISTINE: So, what are you talking about?

MITZI: Know what I think?

CHRISTINE: What then?

MITZI: That the whole story about a trip is phony.

CHRISTINE: What?

MITZI: Maybe they're not gone at all.

CHRISTINE: They're gone—I know.—Last night I went past his house, the Venetian blinds are down, he's not there.—

MITZI: All right, I believe that. They probably are gone.—But they're simply not coming back—not to us at least.—

CHRISTINE [*anxiously*]: Hey—

MITZI: Well, it's certainly possible!—

CHRISTINE: You say that so calmly—

MITZI: Oh well—whether it's today or tomorrow—or in six months, it will work out the same after all.

CHRISTINE: You really don't realize what you're saying . . . You don't know Fritz—he's really not like that, the way you think.—I really did see that the other day, when he was here, in this room. He just tries to pretend to be indifferent sometimes—but he loves me . . . [*As if she can guess* MITZI*'s reaction*]—Yes, yes—not forever, of course, I know that—but that sort of thing doesn't just come to an end all at once—!

MITZI: I really don't know Fritz all that well.

CHRISTINE: He's coming back, and Theodor is certainly coming back too.

[MITZI *makes a gesture signifying indifference.*]

CHRISTINE: Mitzi . . . Do something for my sake.

MITZI: Just don't get so stirred up—well, what do you want?

CHRISTINE: You go over to Theodor's place, it's quite close by, just take a look . . . in the building, if he's there, and if he's not, maybe they'll know when he's coming.

MITZI: I'm certainly not going to run after any man.

CHRISTINE: He really doesn't need to find out at all. Perhaps you'll run into him. It'll soon be one o'clock,—right now he's going out to eat—

MITZI: So why don't you go ask them about Fritz?

CHRISTINE: I don't dare—He just can't stand that sort of thing. . . . And he's surely not there yet. But perhaps Theodor is already there and he knows when Fritz is coming. I'm begging you, Mitzi!

MITZI: Sometimes you're so childish—

CHRISTINE: Do it for my sake! Go there! There's certainly no harm in it, after all.—

MITZI: Well, if it's so very important for you, then I'll just go. But it won't do much good. They're surely not there yet.

CHRISTINE: And you'll come back right away . . . won't you . . .

MITZI: Oh well, my mother will just have to wait a bit for her meal.

CHRISTINE: Thank you, Mitzi, you're so kind.

MITZI: Of course I'm kind—but just be reasonable now . . . won't you? . . . So, greetings!

CHRISTINE: Thank you!—

[MITZI *leaves.* CHRISTINE *alone, straightens up the room, gathers the sewing things together, and so forth. Then she goes to the window and looks out. A minute later* WEIRING *comes in; at first she does not see him. He is profoundly agitated, anxiously viewing his daughter as she stands at the window.*]

WEIRING: She still doesn't know, she still doesn't know . . .

[*He stands still at the door not venturing a step farther.* CHRISTINE *turns around, notices him, is startled.*]

WEIRING [*trying to smile, steps farther into the room*]: Well, Christine . . . [*As if calling her to him*]

[CHRISTINE *goes to him, as if to drop down before him; he doesn't allow her to.*]

WEIRING: So . . . what do you think, Christine? We—[*with resolve*]—we'll just forget it, don't you think?

[CHRISTINE *lifts her head.*]

WEIRING: Well now . . . I—and you!

CHRISTINE: Father, didn't you understand me this morning? . . .

WEIRING: Yes, well, what do you want then, Christine? . . . I must tell you what I think about it! Right? Well, then . . .

CHRISTINE: What's that supposed to mean, Father?

WEIRING: Come here, my child . . . Listen to me calmly. After all I listened calmly to you, when you told me.—We really must—

CHRISTINE: Don't talk to me like that, Father, I beg you . . . If you've thought about it now and realize you can't forgive me, then drive me away—but don't talk like that . . .

WEIRING: Just listen to me calmly, Christine! Then you can do whatever you want . . . Look, Christine, you're so young.—Haven't you ever thought . . . [*very hesitantly*] . . . how the whole thing could be a mistake—?

CHRISTINE: Why are you telling me that, Father?—I know what I've done—and I'm not demanding anything either—not from you nor from anyone else in the world, if it was a mistake . . . I told you, drive me away, but . . .

WEIRING [*interrupting her*]: Just how can you talk like that . . . ? Even if it was a mistake, is that any cause for despair in such a young creature as you—Just think, after all, how beautiful, just beautiful life is. Just think how many things are there to delight in, how much youth, how much happiness still lies before you . . . Look, I don't get that much out of the world anymore, and yet even for me life is beautiful—and I can still look forward to so many things. Like how you and I will be together—and what we want to do with our lives—you and I . . . how you will start—to sing again, when the lovely season is here, and how when it's vacation time, we'll go to the country, to the world of nature, for the whole day—really—oh, there are so many beautiful things . . . so much. It really is absurd to give up everything right away, because of having to sacrifice that first bit of happiness or what seemed like it—

CHRISTINE [*anxiously*]: Why . . . do I have to sacrifice it then . . . ?

WEIRING: Was it ever that? Do you really believe, Christine, that you didn't have to tell your father until now? I knew it long ago!—And I also knew you'd tell me. No, it was never happiness for you! . . . Well, don't I know those eyes? They wouldn't have had tears in them so often, and those cheeks wouldn't have turned so pale, if you had loved a man who deserved it.

CHRISTINE: How can you . . . What do you know . . . What have you found out?

WEIRING: Nothing, nothing at all . . . but you did tell me yourself, what he is, after all . . . Such a young fellow—well, what does he know?—Does he have any idea what's falling into his lap—well, does he know the difference between what's real and what isn't—

and all your absurd love—well, does he understand anything about that?

CHRISTINE [*more and more anxiously*]: You and he . . . —You were at his place?

WEIRING: Just what do you mean by that! He did go away, didn't he? But Christine, I'm still in my right mind, I do have eyes in my head after all! Look my child, forget about it! Just forget about it! Your future certainly lies somewhere completely different! You can be, you'll again be as happy as you deserve. One day you'll also find someone who knows what he has found in you—

[CHRISTINE *has hurried to the chest of drawers, to get her hat.*]

WEIRING: Well, what are you going to do?

CHRISTINE: Leave me alone, I'm going to . . .

WEIRING [*very quickly*]: Where are you going?

CHRISTINE: To him . . . to him . . .

WEIRING: But just what are you thinking . . . ?

CHRISTINE: You're keeping something secret from me—let me go.—

WEIRING [*firmly holding her back*]: Now just come to your senses, my child. He's really not there at all . . . Perhaps he really has gone away, and for a very long time . . . Just stay here with me, what do you want over there . . . Tomorrow, or even this evening, I'll go over there with you. You really can't go into the street looking like this . . . Now, do you know what you look like . . . ?

CHRISTINE: You want to go over there with me—?

WEIRING: I promise you.—Now really, just stay here, sit down and come to yourself again. It's really almost enough to make a person laugh seeing you like this . . . all that for nothing, nothing at all. Well, can't you stand being here with your father anymore?

CHRISTINE: What do you *know*?

WEIRING [*increasingly at a loss*]: Just what am I supposed to know . . . ? I know that I love you, that you are my only child, that you should stay here with me—that you should have always stayed here with me—

CHRISTINE: Enough—let me—

[CHRISTINE *tears herself away from him and opens up the door, in which* MITZI *appears, then* THEODOR.]

MITZI [*crying out faintly when* CHRISTINE *rushes toward her*]: Just why are you scaring me like that . . . ?

[CHRISTINE *shrinks back when she sees* THEODOR, *standing still in the door, dressed in black.*]

CHRISTINE: What . . . just what is . . . ?

[*Not receiving any answer, she looks into* THEODOR*'s face; he tries to avoid her gaze.*]

Where is he, where is he? . . . [*In deepest anguish—not receiving any answer, she looks at their sad and embarrassed faces*] Where is he? [*To* THEODOR] Well, say something!

[THEODOR *tries to speak.*]

CHRISTINE [*gives him a hard stare, looks around, comprehends their facial expressions, and after her face gradually shows an understanding of the truth, she lets out a dreadful scream*]: Theodor! . . . He is . . .

[THEODOR *nods.*]

CHRISTINE [*clutching her forehead, not comprehending; goes up to* THEODOR, *takes him by the arm—as if insane*]: . . . He is . . . [*As if asking herself*] dead . . . ? . . .

WEIRING: My child—

CHRISTINE [*parrying him*]: Well, say something, Theodor.

THEODOR: You know everything.

CHRISTINE: I know nothing . . . I don't know what happened . . . believe me . . . I can't hear all that now . . . how it came about . . . Father . . . Theodor . . . [*To* MITZI] You know too . . .

THEODOR: An unfortunate accident—

CHRISTINE: Just what, just what?

THEODOR: He fell.

CHRISTINE: What does that mean? He . . .

THEODOR: He fell in a duel.

CHRISTINE [*crying out*]: Ah! . . .

[*She is in danger of collapsing;* WEIRING *holds her up, gives* THEODOR *a signal he should leave now. She notices that and grasps* THEODOR.]

Stay . . . I have to know everything. Do you think you can keep anything else secret from me now . . .

THEODOR: What else do you want to know?

CHRISTINE: Why—why did he fight a duel?

THEODOR: I don't know the reason.

CHRISTINE: With whom, with whom—? Who killed him, you'll know that, won't you? . . . Well, well—

THEODOR: Nobody you know . . .

CHRISTINE: Who, who?

MITZI: Christine!

CHRISTINE [*to* MITZI]: Who? Tell me— . . . Father!

[*No answer; she tries to leave.* WEIRING *holds her back.*]

I should at least be allowed to find out who killed him and for what—!

THEODOR: It was . . . a trivial reason . . .

CHRISTINE: You're not telling the truth . . . Why, why . . .

THEODOR: My dear Christine . . .

CHRISTINE [*goes up to him as if wanting to interrupt; at first she doesn't speak, looks at him and then suddenly screams*]: Because of a woman?

THEODOR: No—

CHRISTINE: Yes—for a woman . . . [*turning to* MITZI]—for *that* woman, whom he loved—And her husband—yes, yes, her husband killed him . . . And I . . . just what did I mean to him, Theodor . . . well, don't you have anything at all for me . . . didn't he write anything down . . . ? Didn't he tell you anything for me . . . ? Didn't you find anything . . . a letter . . . a note—

[THEODOR *shakes his head.*]

CHRISTINE: And that evening . . . when he was here, when you came up to get him . . . he knew it then, he already knew that perhaps he would never see me again . . . And from here he went off and let himself be killed for another woman—No, no—it's really not possible . . . well, didn't he know what he means to me . . . did he . . .

THEODOR: He knew it.—On that last morning, when we went out . . . he spoke about you as well.

CHRISTINE: He spoke about me as well! About me *as well*! And about what else then? About how many other people, about how many other things which meant just as much to him as I did?—About me as well! Oh God! . . . And about his father and about his mother, about his friends and about his room and about everything, about everything like that which was part of his life and which he had to leave just like me . . . he spoke with you about everything . . . and about me *as well* . . .

THEODOR [*moved*]: He surely did love you.

CHRISTINE: Love!—Him?—I meant no more to him than a pastime—and he died for another woman—! And I—adored him!—Didn't he know that? . . . That I gave him everything I could give him, that I would have died for him, that he was my god and lord and my bliss—didn't he notice that at all? He was able to go away from me with a smile, to go away from this room and let himself be gunned down for another woman . . . Father, Father—do you understand that?

WEIRING [*standing by her*]: Christine!

THEODOR [*to* MITZI]: Look, my child, you could have spared me that.

[MITZI *looks at him angrily.*]

THEODOR: I've had enough excitement . . . these past few days . . .

CHRISTINE [*with a sudden resolve*]: Theodor, take me there . . . I want to see him—I want to see him once more—that face—Theodor, take me there.

THEODOR [*parries, hesitantly*]: No . . .

CHRISTINE: Why not, then?—You can't deny me that, can you?—Well, shouldn't I be allowed to see him once more—shouldn't I—?

THEODOR: It's too late.

CHRISTINE: Too late?—To see his corpse . . . is it too late?

[*She doesn't understand.*]

Well . . . well—Is it—

THEODOR: He was buried this morning.

CHRISTINE [*with the utmost expression of horror*]: Buried . . . and I didn't know it? They shot him . . . and they laid him in a coffin and carried him out and buried him in the ground—and I wasn't allowed to see him once more?—For two days he's been dead—and you didn't come and tell me—?

THEODOR [*very moved*]: These two days I've . . . You can't have any idea of all the things these two days . . . Bear in mind that I also had the responsibility of informing his parents—I had to think about so many things—and then my own frame of mind . . .

CHRISTINE: Your . . .

THEODOR: And then it took . . . it took place very quietly and privately . . . Only the very closest relatives and friends . . .

CHRISTINE: Only the closest—! And I—? . . . What am I, then? . . .

MITZI: And that's just what they would have asked.

CHRISTINE: And what am I, then—? Less than all the others—? Less than his relatives, less than . . . you?

WEIRING: My child, my child. Come to me, come . . . [*Embracing her; to* THEODOR] Go now . . . leave me alone with her!

THEODOR: I'm very . . . [*with tears in his voice*] I had no idea . . .

CHRISTINE: No idea of what?—That I loved him?

[WEIRING *pulls her to him;* THEODOR *stares into space;* MITZI *stands by* CHRISTINE.]

CHRISTINE [*extricating herself from* WEIRING]: Take me to his grave!

WEIRING: No, no—

MITZI: Don't go there, Christine—

THEODOR: Christine . . . later . . . tomorrow . . . when you're calmer—

CHRISTINE: Tomorrow?—When I'm calmer?!—And in a month I'll be completely recovered, right?—And in half a year I can laugh again, eh—? [*Bursts out laughing*] And when does the next lover come along, then? . . .

WEIRING: Christine . . .

CHRISTINE: Just stay here . . . I'll find the way, even by myself . . .

WEIRING: Don't go.

MITZI: Don't go.

CHRISTINE: It would even be better . . . if I . . . Let me go, let me.

WEIRING: Christine, stay here . . .

MITZI: Don't go there!—You might even meet the other woman there—praying.

CHRISTINE [*to herself, with fixed gaze*]: I don't want to go there to pray . . . no . . .

[CHRISTINE *rushes offstage; the others are left speechless at first.*]

WEIRING: Hurry after her.

[THEODOR *and* MITZI *exit after her.*]

WEIRING: I can't, I can't . . .

[*He moves with difficulty from the door to the window.*]

What does she want . . . what does she want? . . . [*Looking through the window into the void*] She's not coming back—she's not coming back!

[*He sinks to the floor, sobbing loudly.*]

[*Curtain*]

Roundelay

TEN DIALOGUES

Characters

The Prostitute

The Soldier

The Chambermaid

The Young Gentleman

The Young Wife

The Husband

The Sweet Young Thing

The Poet

The Actress

The Count

Another Chambermaid

~

Vienna, 1890s

I. THE PROSTITUTE AND THE SOLDIER

[*Late in the evening, at a bridge over the Danube.* SOLDIER *enters, whistling, on his way back to the barracks.*]

PROSTITUTE: Hey, come here handsome!

[SOLDIER *turns around and then continues on his way again.*]

PROSTITUTE: Don't you want to come with me?

SOLDIER: So I'm the handsome one.

PROSTITUTE: Sure, who else? Go on, come with me. I live nearby.

SOLDIER: I don't have time. I've got to get back to the barracks!

PROSTITUTE: You'll get back to the barracks in plenty of time. It's nicer here with me.

SOLDIER [*up close to her*]: That's sure possible.

PROSTITUTE: Shhh! A policeman might come any moment.

SOLDIER: A policeman! That's ridiculous! I've got my pistol, don't I?

PROSTITUTE: Go on, come with me.

SOLDIER: Leave me alone. Anyway, I'm broke.

PROSTITUTE: I don't want your money.

SOLDIER [*stops; they are standing at a street lamp*]: You don't want any money? Just who do you think you are, anyway?

PROSTITUTE: Sure, I take money from civilians, but a guy like you can get it for free.

SOLDIER: So maybe you're the one my buddy Huber was telling me about.

PROSTITUTE: I don't know anybody named Huber.

SOLDIER: Sure, you're the one, all right. You know, he picked you up over there—at that café down by the river—and went home with you.

PROSTITUTE: Look, I've taken lots of guys home with me from that café . . . eh! eh!

SOLDIER: All right then, let's go, let's go.

PROSTITUTE: Hey! What's your hurry?

SOLDIER: Well, what are we waiting for? I've got to get back to the barracks by ten.

PROSTITUTE: Just how long have you been in the service?

SOLDIER: Just what's that to you? Do you live far?

PROSTITUTE: Ten minutes' walk.

SOLDIER: That's too far. Give me a little kiss.

PROSTITUTE [*kissing him*]: That's the best part for me anyhow—when I like a guy!

SOLDIER: Not for me. Naw, I'm not goin' with you. It's too far.

PROSTITUTE: You know something, come over tomorrow—in the afternoon.

SOLDIER: Sure. Give me your address.

PROSTITUTE: But maybe you won't show up.

SOLDIER: Hey, I told you I would, didn't I?

PROSTITUTE: Say, you know what?—If you don't want to go all the way to my place tonight, how about—there . . . down there . . .

[*She points to the Danube.*]

SOLDIER: What's down there?

PROSTITUTE: It's nice and quiet there . . . and there's nobody around.

SOLDIER: Aw, that's no good!

PROSTITUTE: With me, it's always good. Go on, stay with me for a while. Who knows if we'll even be alive tomorrow?

SOLDIER: Well come on—but let's make it quick!

PROSTITUTE: Be careful, it's so dark here. One slip, and you'll wind up in the Danube.

SOLDIER: That might be best anyhow.

PROSTITUTE: Shhh—just take it easy. There's a bench along here somewhere.

SOLDIER: You really know your way around here.

PROSTITUTE: I'd like to have a guy like you for a lover.

SOLDIER: I'd just keep you jealous all the time.

PROSTITUTE: I'd sure cure you of that.

SOLDIER: Oh yeah—

PROSTITUTE: Not so loud. You know sometimes a cop loses his way down here. You wouldn't think we were right in the middle of Vienna, would you?

SOLDIER: Hey, come over here, come on.

PROSTITUTE: What do you think you're doing? If we slip, we'll wind up down in the water.

SOLDIER [*grabbing her*]: Ah, you—

PROSTITUTE: Just hold on tight.

SOLDIER: Don't worry about that . . .

* * * * *

PROSTITUTE: Sure would have been better on the bench.

SOLDIER: On or off . . . Come on up.

SOLDIER: Hey, what's your rush?

SOLDIER: I've got to get back to the barracks, I'm already late.

PROSTITUTE: Come on, just what's your name?

SOLDIER: What do you care what my name is?

PROSTITUTE: My name's Léocadia.

SOLDIER: Ha! I've never heard that one before.

PROSTITUTE: Hey!

SOLDIER: Now what do you want?

PROSTITUTE: Come on, at least give me something for the janitor, so he'll open the door this late!—

SOLDIER: Ha! . . . What do you take me for? So long! Léocadia . . .

PROSTITUTE: Why you good-for-nothing cheapskate!

[*He has disappeared.*]

II. THE SOLDIER AND THE CHAMBERMAID

[*Sunday evening in the Prater Gardens. A path leading from the amusement park to dark, tree-lined walks. The wild music of the amusement park is audible, as well as the sounds of a cheap dance, a clumsy polka played on wind instruments.*]

CHAMBERMAID: Hey, how come you kept wantin' to get out of there so soon?

[*The* SOLDIER *responds with an embarrassed, stupid laugh.*]

CHAMBERMAID: It's been so wonderful. I just love to dance.

[*The* SOLDIER *grasps her around the waist; she lets him.*]

CHAMBERMAID: But we're not dancing anymore. Why are you holding me so tight?

SOLDIER: What's your name? Kathy?

CHAMBERMAID: You've always got some Kathy on your brain.

SOLDIER: Wait, I know . . . I know . . . It's Marie.

CHAMBERMAID: Say, it's getting so dark here! I'm getting scared.

SOLDIER: You don't need to worry with me around. I can handle it!

CHAMBERMAID: Thank God you're with me! Where are we going anyway? There's nobody around. Come on, let's go back—it's so dark!

SOLDIER [*puffing on his cigar of Virginia tobacco so that it lights up in a red glow*]: There, now it's getting lighter! Ha, ha, ha! You beautiful thing.

CHAMBERMAID: Say, what are you doing? If I had known this, I'd . . .

SOLDIER: Devil take me, if anyone at the dance hall was as nice and soft as you, Fräulein Marie.

CHAMBERMAID: Have you tried 'em all out like that?

SOLDIER: Oh well, when you're dancing, you notice things. All sorts of things! Ha!

CHAMBERMAID: But you danced more with that sour-faced blond than you did with me.

SOLDIER: She's just an old friend of somebody I know.

CHAMBERMAID: You mean the corporal with the turned-up mustache?

SOLDIER: Nah, the civilian who was sitting at the table before. You know, the one with the funny voice.

CHAMBERMAID: Oh, yeah, now I know. He's pretty fresh.

SOLDIER: Did he try and do something with you? I'll show him! . . . What'd he do?

CHAMBERMAID: Oh, nothing.—I just saw how he was with the other girls.

SOLDIER: Now tell me, Fräulein Marie . . .

CHAMBERMAID: Look out, you'll burn me with your cigar.

SOLDIER: Excuse me!—Fräulein Marie! Can't I just call you Marie?

CHAMBERMAID: I don't know you that well yet.

SOLDIER: Lots of people can't even stand each other and still use first names.

CHAMBERMAID: Maybe next time, when we . . . Oh, but, Herr Franz—

SOLDIER: So you know my name?

CHAMBERMAID: But, Herr Franz . . .

SOLDIER: Just call me Franz, Fräulein Marie.

CHAMBERMAID: Don't get so fresh—but shhh! If somebody was to come this way . . .

SOLDIER: Even if somebody comes, they can't see two steps ahead of them.

CHAMBERMAID: For heaven's sake, where are we going?

SOLDIER: Look, there's a couple just like us.

CHAMBERMAID: Where? I don't see anything.

SOLDIER: There . . . in front of us.

CHAMBERMAID: What did you mean—just like us?

SOLDIER: Well, I just meant they like each other too.

CHAMBERMAID: Hey, be careful! What's this? I almost fell down.

SOLDIER: Oh, that's only the park railing.

CHAMBERMAID: Well just don't push me like that, or I'll fall.

SOLDIER: Shhh, not so loud!

CHAMBERMAID: Say, look out, or I really will scream.—Hey, what are you doing? . . . Hey—

SOLDIER: There's not a soul around for miles.

CHAMBERMAID: So let's go back with the others.

SOLDIER: We don't need the others, do we, Marie . . . ? For this . . . Ha, ha!

CHAMBERMAID: But Herr Franz, please, for heaven's sake, look, if I had . . . known what . . . oh . . . oh . . . come!

* * * * *

SOLDIER [*blissfully*]: Jesus Christ, don't stop . . . ah . . .

CHAMBERMAID: . . . I can't even see your face.

SOLDIER: What do you mean—my face . . .

* * * * *

SOLDIER: Hey look, Fräulein Marie, are you just going to lay there in the grass like that?

CHAMBERMAID: Come on, help me up, Franz.

SOLDIER: Well hurry up.

CHAMBERMAID: Oh Jesus, Franz.

SOLDIER: So, now it's just Franz.

CHAMBERMAID: You're awful, Franz.

SOLDIER: Yeah, sure. Wait a minute.

CHAMBERMAID: Why are you letting go of me?

SOLDIER: Just let me light my cigar.

CHAMBERMAID: It sure is dark.

SOLDIER: It'll be light again by morning.

CHAMBERMAID: Can't you at least say you like me?

SOLDIER: Well, you must have noticed that, Fräulein Marie.

[*He laughs.*]

CHAMBERMAID: Where are we going now?

SOLDIER: Back, of course.

CHAMBERMAID: Come on, not so fast, please!

SOLDIER: Now what? You think I like walking around in the dark?

CHAMBERMAID: Tell me Franz, do you like me?

SOLDIER: But I just told you I like you, didn't I?

CHAMBERMAID: Then can't you give me a little kiss?

SOLDIER [*condescendingly*]: There now . . . You can hear the music again—can't you?

CHAMBERMAID: So maybe you'd like to go dancing again?

SOLDIER: Sure, why not?

CHAMBERMAID: Listen Franz, I've got to go home. I'm already in trouble. The mistress is such a . . . If she had her way, I wouldn't get to go out at all.

SOLDIER: Sure, go on home then—

CHAMBERMAID: I just thought, Herr Franz, that you'd walk me home.

SOLDIER: Walk you home? Ah!

CHAMBERMAID: Look, I get so depressed going home by myself.

SOLDIER: Where do you live anyway?

CHAMBERMAID: It's not that far—just to Porzellan Street.

SOLDIER: Oh yeah? That's on my way, anyhow. . . . But now's too early for me . . . They're still dancing and I've got a late pass . . . don't have to be back to the barracks till twelve. I'm going dancing some more.

CHAMBERMAID: Sure, I know. Now it's that sour-faced blond's turn!

SOLDIER: Ha!—She doesn't have such a sour face.

CHAMBERMAID: Oh God, men are awful! I bet you do this to all the girls.

SOLDIER: Even I couldn't do that!

CHAMBERMAID: Franz, please. For now—just stay with me for now—

SOLDIER: Okay, okay. All well and good. But I do get to dance.

CHAMBERMAID: I'm not dancing with anyone but you tonight!

SOLDIER: Well, here it is . . .

CHAMBERMAID: What?

SOLDIER: The dance hall, of course! Now that didn't take long, did it? They're still playing that same thing . . . Ta dah rada, Ta dah rada . . . [*Singing along*] So, if you want to wait here for me, I'll walk you home . . . If not . . . See you around.—

CHAMBERMAID: Okay, I'll wait.

[*They enter the dance hall.*]

SOLDIER: Say, how about a glass of beer, Fräulein Marie? [*Turning to a blond who dances by with an orderly; very formally*] May I have this dance, Fräulein?—

III. THE CHAMBERMAID AND THE YOUNG GENTLEMAN

[*Hot summer afternoon.—The parents are away in the country.—The cook has the day off.—The* CHAMBERMAID *is in the kitchen, writing a letter to the* SOLDIER, *who is her boyfriend. The bell rings from the room of the* YOUNG GENTLEMAN. *She gets up and goes to the room of the* YOUNG GENTLEMAN. *The* YOUNG GENTLEMAN *is lying on a sofa, smoking and reading a French novel.*]

CHAMBERMAID: You rang, sir?

YOUNG GENTLEMAN: Ah yes, Marie, ah yes, I rang, yes . . . Now what did I . . . yes, that's right, let down the blinds, Marie . . . It's cooler when the blinds are down . . . yes . . .

[*The* CHAMBERMAID *goes to the window and lets down the blinds.*]

YOUNG GENTLEMAN [*continuing to read*]: What are you doing, Marie? Ah yes. But now it's simply too dark to read, isn't it?

CHAMBERMAID: The young gentleman is always working so hard.

YOUNG GENTLEMAN [*affectedly ignoring her comment*]: Well, that's fine.

[*The* CHAMBERMAID *leaves. The* YOUNG GENTLEMAN *tries to go on reading, soon drops the book and rings again. The* CHAMBERMAID *reappears.*]

YOUNG GENTLEMAN: Oh, Marie . . . yes, what did I want to say . . . Oh, yes . . . is there perhaps some cognac in the house?

CHAMBERMAID: Yes, but it has probably been locked up.

YOUNG GENTLEMAN: Well, who has the keys?

CHAMBERMAID: Lini has the keys.

YOUNG GENTLEMAN: Who is Lini?

CHAMBERMAID: Lini is the cook, Herr Alfred.

YOUNG GENTLEMAN: Well, go say something to Lini.

CHAMBERMAID: But Lini has the day off today.

YOUNG GENTLEMAN: Is that so . . . ?

CHAMBERMAID: Perhaps I should get something from the café for the young gentleman . . . ?

YOUNG GENTLEMAN: Oh no . . . it's hot enough as it is. I don't need any cognac. But Marie, would you bring me a glass of water? Wait, Marie—let it run till it's nice and cool—.

[*The* CHAMBERMAID *exits. The* YOUNG GENTLEMAN *gazes after her; she turns around toward him at the door; the* YOUNG GENTLEMAN *looks into space.—The* CHAMBERMAID *turns on the water faucet and lets the water run. In the meantime she goes into her little room, washes her hands, and arranges her curls in front of the mirror. Then she brings the* YOUNG GENTLEMAN *the glass of water. She walks over to the sofa. The* YOUNG GENTLEMAN *sits up halfway; the* CHAMBERMAID *hands him the glass, and their fingers touch.*]

YOUNG GENTLEMAN: Thanks.—Well, what is it—? Now be careful, just put the glass on the tray there . . .

[*He lies back down and stretches out.*]

Say, what time is it?—

CHAMBERMAID: Five o'clock, sir.

YOUNG GENTLEMAN: Well, five o'clock.—That's good.—

[*The* CHAMBERMAID *leaves, but turns around at the door. The* YOUNG GENTLEMAN *follows her with his eyes, she notices that and smiles. The* YOUNG GENTLEMAN *remains lying on the sofa for a while, then suddenly gets up. He goes to the door, comes back again and lies down on the sofa. He tries to read again. After a few minutes, he rings again. The* CHAMBERMAID *appears again with a smile she does not try to hide.*]

YOUNG GENTLEMAN: Oh, by the way, Marie, I meant to ask you—didn't Dr. Schueller come by this morning?

CHAMBERMAID: No, no one came by this morning.

YOUNG GENTLEMAN: Well, that's strange. So, Dr. Schueller didn't come by? You do know Dr. Schueller, I suppose?

CHAMBERMAID: Certainly. He's the tall gentleman with the black beard.

YOUNG GENTLEMAN: That's right. Then maybe he did come by?

CHAMBERMAID: No, nobody came, Herr Alfred.

YOUNG GENTLEMAN [*resolutely*]: Come here, Marie.

CHAMBERMAID [*stepping somewhat closer*]: Of course.

YOUNG GENTLEMAN: Closer . . . well . . . ah . . . I only thought . . .

CHAMBERMAID: Thought what, sir?

YOUNG GENTLEMAN: I thought . . . thought—about your blouse . . . What kind of . . . Well, just come closer. I'm not going to bite you after all.

CHAMBERMAID [*coming to him*]: What about my blouse? Don't you like it, sir?

YOUNG GENTLEMAN [*takes hold of her blouse and pulls the* CHAMBERMAID *down to him*]: It's blue, isn't it? Such a pretty blue. [*Simply*] You dress very nicely, Marie.

CHAMBERMAID: But, Herr Alfred . . .

YOUNG GENTLEMAN: Well, what is it? . . .

[*He opens her blouse; matter-of-factly.*]

And you have such beautiful, white skin, Marie.

CHAMBERMAID: You're flattering me, sir.

YOUNG GENTLEMAN [*kissing her on the breast*]: That can't hurt you, can it?

CHAMBERMAID: Oh, no.

YOUNG GENTLEMAN: Well, you're sighing! Why are you sighing, Marie?

CHAMBERMAID: Oh, Herr Alfred . . .

YOUNG GENTLEMAN: And what pretty little slippers you have on, Marie . . .

CHAMBERMAID: . . . But . . . sir . . . what if the doorbell rings?—

YOUNG GENTLEMAN: Who'd be ringing now?

CHAMBERMAID: But, sir . . . look—it's so light in here . . .

YOUNG GENTLEMAN: You don't need to be bashful in front of me. You don't need to be bashful in front of anybody . . . as pretty as you are. Yes, upon my soul, Marie, you're so . . . Do you know, even your hair smells nice.

CHAMBERMAID: Herr Alfred . . .

YOUNG GENTLEMAN: Don't make such a fuss, Marie . . . I've seen you look different. The other night, when I came home late, I went to the kitchen for a glass of water, the door to your room was open and . . . well . . .

CHAMBERMAID [*hiding her face*]: Oh God, I had no idea you could be so naughty, Herr Alfred.

YOUNG GENTLEMAN: I saw a lot then . . . I saw this . . . and this . . . and this . . . and—

CHAMBERMAID: But, Herr Alfred!

YOUNG GENTLEMAN: Come on, come . . . right here . . . like that, yes, like that . . .

CHAMBERMAID: But if somebody rings the doorbell now—

YOUNG GENTLEMAN: Now just stop . . . we simply won't answer it . . .

* * * * *

[*Doorbell rings.*]

YOUNG GENTLEMAN: Good grief! He's making enough noise, isn't he?—He probably rang before, and we just didn't notice it.

CHAMBERMAID: Oh, no. I was listening the whole time.

YOUNG GENTLEMAN: Well, go see who it is—look through the peephole.

CHAMBERMAID: Oh, Herr Alfred . . . but you are . . . no . . . so naughty!

YOUNG GENTLEMAN: Please go see . . .

[*The* CHAMBERMAID *goes out. The* YOUNG GENTLEMAN *quickly opens the blinds. The* CHAMBERMAID *comes in again.*]

CHAMBERMAID: Anyway he must have left. Nobody's there now. Maybe it was Dr. Schueller.

YOUNG GENTLEMAN [*unpleasantly*]: That's fine.

[*She moves in closer, he pulls away from her.*]

YOUNG GENTLEMAN: Look—I'm going to the café now, Marie.

CHAMBERMAID [*affectionately*]: So soon . . . Herr Alfred?

YOUNG GENTLEMAN [*sternly*]: I'm going to the café now. If Dr. Schueller should come by . . .

CHAMBERMAID: He won't be coming anymore today.

YOUNG GENTLEMAN [*more sternly*]: If Dr. Schueller should come by today . . . I, I . . . I'll be—at the café.—

[*He goes into the other room. She takes a cigar from the smoking stand, puts it in her pocket, and leaves.*]

IV. THE YOUNG GENTLEMAN AND THE YOUNG WIFE

[*Evening. A salon of a house on Schwind Street, furnished in trite elegance. The* YOUNG GENTLEMAN *has just entered, lights the candles while still wearing his hat and topcoat. Then he opens the door to the adjoining room and glances into it. The glow of the candles extends from the salon over the parquet floor to a canopied bed by the outside wall. A reddish glow spreads from the fireplace in one corner of the bedroom onto the curtains of the bed.—The* YOUNG GENTLEMAN *inspects the bedroom as well. He takes an atomizer from the dressing table and spreads a fine spray of violet perfume onto the pillows of the bed. He walks through both rooms with the atomizer and continuously squeezes the little bulb, so that the smell of violets soon is everywhere.*

Then he takes off his hat and topcoat. He sits down on the blue velvet armchair, lights up a cigarette and smokes. After a little while, he arises again and makes certain that the green Venetian blinds are closed. Suddenly he goes into the bedroom again and opens the drawer of a night table. He gropes around in it and finds a tortoise hairpin. He looks for a place to hide it and finally puts it in the pocket of his topcoat.

Then he opens a cuphoard in the salon, takes out a silver tray with a bottle of cognac and two small liqueur glasses and sets everything on the table. He goes over to his topcoat again, from which he takes out a small white package. He opens it and puts it with the cognac, goes to the cupboard again, and takes out two little plates and silverware. He takes a glazed chestnut out of the little packet and eats it.

Then he pours out a glass of cognac and drinks all of it quickly. He looks at his watch. He walks up and down the room.—He stops a while in front of the large full-length mirror, arranges his hair and little mustache with his pocket comb.—Now he walks to the door to the entryway and listens intently. Nothing is stirring. The doorbell rings. The YOUNG GENTLEMAN *is slightly startled. He sits down on the armchair and doesn't arise until the door opens and the* YOUNG WIFE *enters.—*

The YOUNG WIFE *enters, thickly veiled; closes the door behind her; then stops a moment, laying her hand on her heart, as if she had to overcome intense agitation.*

The YOUNG GENTLEMAN *goes up to her, takes her left hand and presses a kiss on her black-embroidered white glove.*]

YOUNG GENTLEMAN [*softly*]: Thank you.

YOUNG WIFE: Oh, Alfred—Alfred!

YOUNG GENTLEMAN: Come, my lady . . . Come, Frau Emma . . .

YOUNG WIFE: Just leave me alone for a moment—please . . . oh, if you please, Alfred!

[*She is still standing at the door. The* YOUNG GENTLEMAN *stands in front of her, holding her hand.*]

YOUNG WIFE: Just where am I?

YOUNG GENTLEMAN: At my place.

YOUNG WIFE: This house is dreadful, Alfred.

YOUNG GENTLEMAN: How can you say that? It's a very respectable house.

YOUNG WIFE: I just met two men on the stairs.

YOUNG GENTLEMAN: Anyone you know?

YOUNG WIFE: It's possible. I'm not sure.

YOUNG GENTLEMAN: Pardon me, my lady—but surely you know who your friends are.

YOUNG WIFE: Yes, but I couldn't see a thing.

YOUNG GENTLEMAN: Well, even if they were your best friends—they couldn't have recognized you. Even I . . . if I didn't know it was you . . . with this veil on—

YOUNG WIFE: There are two of them.

YOUNG GENTLEMAN: Don't you want to come a bit closer . . . ? At least you can take off your hat!

YOUNG WIFE: What do you think you're doing, Alfred? I told you: five minutes . . . No, not a minute longer . . . I swear it—

YOUNG GENTLEMAN: All right, your veil.

YOUNG WIFE: There are two of them.

YOUNG GENTLEMAN: Oh well, both veils—at least let me see you.

YOUNG WIFE: Do you really love me, Alfred?

YOUNG GENTLEMAN [*deeply hurt*]: Emma—you are asking me that? . . .

YOUNG WIFE: It's so hot in here.

YOUNG GENTLEMAN: But you have your fur cape on—surely you'll catch cold.

YOUNG WIFE [*finally entering the room, throws herself into the armchair*]: I'm dead tired.

YOUNG GENTLEMAN: Allow me.

[*He takes off her veils; removes her hat pin; puts hat, pin, and veils aside. The* YOUNG WIFE *lets him do it. The* YOUNG GENTLEMAN *stands in front of her, shaking his head.*]

YOUNG WIFE: What's the matter?

YOUNG GENTLEMAN: You've never looked so beautiful.

YOUNG WIFE: How's that?

YOUNG GENTLEMAN: Alone . . . to be alone with you—Emma—

[*He sinks down onto one knee beside the armchair, takes both her hands, and covers them with kisses.*]

YOUNG WIFE: And now . . . just let me go. I've done what you asked of me.

[*The* YOUNG GENTLEMAN *lets his head sink into her lap.*]

YOUNG WIFE: You promised me you'd be good.

YOUNG GENTLEMAN: Yes.

YOUNG WIFE: It's suffocating in this room.

YOUNG GENTLEMAN [*getting up*]: You still have your cape on.

YOUNG WIFE: Here, put it with my hat.

[*The* YOUNG GENTLEMAN *takes off her cape and puts it on the sofa too.*]

YOUNG WIFE: And now—adieu—

YOUNG GENTLEMAN: Emma!—Emma!—

YOUNG WIFE: The five minutes were up long ago.

YOUNG GENTLEMAN: It hasn't even been one minute!—

YOUNG WIFE: Alfred, tell me exactly what time it is.

YOUNG GENTLEMAN: It's a quarter past six, on the dot.

YOUNG WIFE: I should've been at my sister's long ago.

YOUNG GENTLEMAN: You can see your sister anytime . . .

YOUNG WIFE: Oh God, Alfred, how did you get me into this?

YOUNG GENTLEMAN: Because . . . I adore you, Emma.

YOUNG WIFE: How many others have you said that to?

YOUNG GENTLEMAN: Since I set eyes on you, no one.

YOUNG WIFE: What a frivolous woman I am! If anyone had told me . . . even a week ago . . . even yesterday . . .

YOUNG GENTLEMAN: It was the day before yesterday that you promised me you'd . . .

YOUNG WIFE: You were tormenting me so. But I didn't want to do it. God knows—I didn't want to . . . Yesterday I finally made up my mind . . . Do you know, yesterday evening I even wrote you a long letter?

YOUNG GENTLEMAN: I didn't get any letter.

YOUNG WIFE: I tore it up. Oh, I should have sent you that letter.

YOUNG GENTLEMAN: No doubt it's better this way.

YOUNG WIFE: Oh no, it's disgraceful . . . of me. I just don't understand myself. Adieu, Alfred, let me go.

[*The* YOUNG GENTLEMAN *embraces her and covers her face with ardent kisses.*]

YOUNG WIFE: So that's how . . . you keep your word . . .

YOUNG GENTLEMAN: One more kiss—just one.

YOUNG WIFE: The last one.

[*He kisses her. She returns the kiss; their lips remain joined together for a long time.*]

YOUNG GENTLEMAN: Shall I tell you something, Emma? Now I know for the first time what happiness is.

[*The* YOUNG WIFE *sinks back into an armchair.*]

YOUNG GENTLEMAN [*sitting down on the arm of the chair, gently puts one arm around the back of her neck*]: . . . or at least what it could be.

[*The* YOUNG WIFE *gives a deep sigh. The* YOUNG GENTLEMAN *kisses her again.*]

YOUNG WIFE: Alfred, Alfred, what are you doing to me!

YOUNG GENTLEMAN: It isn't so uncomfortable here—is it? . . . And we are so completely safe here! It's so much nicer than those rendezvous out-of-doors . . .

YOUNG WIFE: Oh, just don't remind me of that.

YOUNG GENTLEMAN: But I shall always recall those meetings with infinite delight. Every minute at your side is a sweet memory.

YOUNG WIFE: Do you still remember the Industrial Ball?

YOUNG GENTLEMAN: Do I remember . . . ? Yes, I sat next to you during supper, quite close. Your husband had champagne . . .

[*The* YOUNG WIFE *gives him an accusing look.*]

YOUNG GENTLEMAN: I was just going to talk about the champagne. Tell me, Emma, don't you want a glass of cognac?

YOUNG WIFE: Just a drop, but first give me a glass of water.

YOUNG GENTLEMAN: Of course . . . Now, let's see, where—ah yes . . .

[*He throws back the portieres and goes into the bedroom. The* YOUNG WIFE *gazes after him. The* YOUNG GENTLEMAN *comes back with a carafe of water and two drinking glasses.*]

YOUNG WIFE: Where were you?

YOUNG GENTLEMAN: In the . . . next room.

[*He pours out a glass of water.*]

YOUNG WIFE: Now I am going to ask you something, Alfred—and you've got to swear to tell me the truth.

YOUNG GENTLEMAN: I swear.

YOUNG WIFE: Has another woman ever been in these rooms?

YOUNG GENTLEMAN: After all, Emma—this house has been here for twenty years!

YOUNG WIFE: You know what I mean, Alfred . . . with you! Close to you!

YOUNG GENTLEMAN: With me—here—Emma!—How could you think such a thing?

YOUNG WIFE: Well then, have you . . . how shall I say . . . But no, I'd rather not ask. It's better I didn't. It's my fault anyway. One pays for everything . . .

YOUNG GENTLEMAN: Just what's the matter with you? Just what's bothering you? Pays for what?

YOUNG WIFE: No, no, no, I mustn't think about it . . . Otherwise I'll die of shame.

YOUNG GENTLEMAN [*with the carafe of water in his hand, sadly shakes his head*]: If you only knew how you are hurting me, Emma.

[*The* YOUNG WIFE *pours out a glass of cognac.*]

YOUNG GENTLEMAN: I want to tell you something, Emma. If you're ashamed to be here—if this is the way you feel about me—if you don't feel that you mean all the happiness in the world to me—then maybe you should go.

YOUNG WIFE: Yes, I'll do just that.

YOUNG GENTLEMAN [*grasping her hand*]: But if you only knew that I can't live without you, that kissing your hand means more to me than the affection of all the other women in the world . . . Emma, I'm not like those other young people who know how to play the game—perhaps I'm too naive . . . I . . .

YOUNG WIFE: But what if you really are like those other young people?

YOUNG GENTLEMAN: Then you wouldn't be here today—you're not like other women.

YOUNG WIFE: How do you know that?

YOUNG GENTLEMAN [*pulling her onto the sofa and sitting down close be-*

side her]: I've been thinking a great deal about you. I know that you're unhappy.

[*The* YOUNG WIFE *is pleased.*]

YOUNG GENTLEMAN: Life is so empty, so futile—and then—so short—so horribly short! There's only one happiness . . . to find someone who loves you—

[*The* YOUNG WIFE *has taken a candied pear from the table; she puts it into her mouth.*]

YOUNG GENTLEMAN: Half for me!

[*She gives it to him with her lips.*]

YOUNG WIFE [*grasping the hands of the* YOUNG GENTLEMAN, *which threaten to go astray*]: What are you doing, then, Alfred . . . Is this the way you keep your promise?

YOUNG GENTLEMAN [*swallowing the pear, then more daringly*]: Life is so short.

YOUNG WIFE [*weakly*]: But that's no reason to—

YOUNG GENTLEMAN [*mechanically*]: Oh, yes it is.

YOUNG WIFE [*more weakly*]: Now look, Alfred, you did promise to be good . . . And it's so bright . . .

YOUNG GENTLEMAN: Come, come, my one, my only . . .

[*He lifts her up from the sofa.*]

YOUNG WIFE: Then what are you doing?

YOUNG GENTLEMAN: It's not so bright in there.

YOUNG WIFE: Is there another room here?

YOUNG GENTLEMAN [*drawing her along*]: A beautiful room . . . and quite dark.

YOUNG WIFE: We should just stay in here.

[*The* YOUNG GENTLEMAN, *already behind the portiere with her in the bedroom, undoes her bodice.*]

You're so . . . oh God, what are you doing to me!—Alfred!

YOUNG GENTLEMAN: I adore you, Emma!

YOUNG WIFE: Well just wait then, just wait, at least . . . [*Weakly*] Go . . . I'll call you.

YOUNG GENTLEMAN: Just let you h—let me—[*his speech is becoming confused*] . . . let . . . me—help—you.

YOUNG WIFE: Why, you're tearing all my—

YOUNG GENTLEMAN: You aren't wearing a corset?

YOUNG WIFE: I never wear a corset. And neither does the actress Odilon. But you can unbutton my shoes.

[*The* YOUNG GENTLEMAN *unbuttons her shoes, kisses her feet.*]

YOUNG WIFE [*slipping into bed*]: Oh, I'm cold.

YOUNG GENTLEMAN: It will get warm right away.

YOUNG WIFE [*laughing softly*]: Do you think so?

YOUNG GENTLEMAN [*to himself, unpleasantly moved*]: She shouldn't have said that.

[*He undresses in the dark.*]

YOUNG WIFE [*affectionately*]: Come, come, come!

YOUNG GENTLEMAN [*thus in a better mood again*]: Right away—

YOUNG WIFE: It smells like violets here.

YOUNG GENTLEMAN: It's you that smells that way . . . Yes— [*To her*] It's you.

YOUNG WIFE: Alfred . . . Alfred!!!!

YOUNG GENTLEMAN: Emma . . .

* * * * *

YOUNG GENTLEMAN: I obviously love you too much . . . it's as if I were out of my mind.

YOUNG WIFE: . . .

YOUNG GENTLEMAN: These past few days I've been crazy. I felt it coming.

YOUNG WIFE: Don't think anything of it.

YOUNG GENTLEMAN: Oh certainly not. After all, it's perfectly natural for a man to . . .

YOUNG WIFE: Don't . . . don't . . . You're nervous. Just calm yourself . . .

YOUNG GENTLEMAN: Are you acquainted with Stendhal?

YOUNG WIFE: Stendhal?

YOUNG GENTLEMAN: The *Psychologie de l'amour*?

YOUNG WIFE: No, why do you ask?

YOUNG GENTLEMAN: It contains a story which is very significant.

YOUNG WIFE: What kind of story is it?

YOUNG GENTLEMAN: A whole company of cavalry officers has gathered—

YOUNG WIFE: Oh.

YOUNG GENTLEMAN: And they tell each other about their love affairs. And each one reports that with the woman he loved the most, that is, the most passionately . . . that with this woman he—well, in short, with her the same thing happened to each of them that happened to me just now.

YOUNG WIFE: I see.

YOUNG GENTLEMAN: I find that very significant.

YOUNG WIFE: I see.

YOUNG GENTLEMAN: But that's not all. Only one of the officers declares that . . . it had never happened to him in his whole life, but then, Stendhal adds—he was a notorious braggart.

YOUNG WIFE: Well.

YOUNG GENTLEMAN: But still it is upsetting, that's the stupid part, as unimportant as it actually is.

YOUNG WIFE: Of course. And, after all you know . . . you did promise me you'd be good.

YOUNG GENTLEMAN: Come on, don't laugh, that doesn't help matters any.

YOUNG WIFE: But I'm not laughing. That Stendhal story is really very interesting. I always thought that it was only older . . . or very . . . you know, people who have lived a lot . . .

YOUNG GENTLEMAN: What's gotten into you? That doesn't have anything to do with it at all. Anyway, I completely forgot the nicest story in Stendhal. One of the cavalry officers there tells that he spent no less than three nights, or was it six? . . . I can't remember, with a woman he had wanted for weeks and weeks—*désirée*—you understand—and they did nothing all those nights on end, they did nothing but weep for happiness . . . both of them . . .

YOUNG WIFE: Both of them?

YOUNG GENTLEMAN: Yes. Does that surprise you? I find it so understandable . . . especially when two people love each other.

YOUNG WIFE: But of course there are lots of people who don't weep.

YOUNG GENTLEMAN [*nervously*]: Well, of course . . . that was an exceptional case, too.

YOUNG WIFE: Oh—but I thought Stendhal was saying that all cavalry officers weep on such occasions.

YOUNG GENTLEMAN: You see, now you're making fun of me.

YOUNG WIFE: But what has gotten into you! Just don't be so childish, Alfred!

YOUNG GENTLEMAN: Well, it makes me nervous, that's all . . . And not only that, but I have the feeling that you're constantly thinking about it. And that embarrasses me all the more.

YOUNG WIFE: I'm not thinking about it at all.

YOUNG GENTLEMAN: Oh yes you are. If I were only convinced that you loved me.

YOUNG WIFE: Do you need any more proof?

YOUNG GENTLEMAN: See . . . you're always making fun.

YOUNG WIFE: How is that? Come on, give me your sweet little head.

YOUNG GENTLEMAN: Oh, that feels good.

YOUNG WIFE: Do you love me?

YOUNG GENTLEMAN: Oh, I'm just so happy.

YOUNG WIFE: But you don't need to weep as well.

YOUNG GENTLEMAN [*extremely irritated, drawing away from her*]: Again, again. And after I just asked you . . .

YOUNG WIFE: Because I say you don't have to weep? . . .

YOUNG GENTLEMAN: You said: not to weep as well.

YOUNG WIFE: You're nervous, my darling.

YOUNG GENTLEMAN: I know that.

YOUNG WIFE: But you shouldn't be. I'm even glad that it . . . that we, that we can be, so to speak, good companions.

YOUNG GENTLEMAN: You're starting all over again.

YOUNG WIFE: Don't you remember! It was one of our first conversations. We wanted to be good friends, nothing more. Oh, that was so nice . . . it was at my sister's, during the quadrille at the grand ball in January . . . Oh my God, I should have left here a long time ago . . . my sister has been waiting for me—what am I going to tell her . . . Adieu, Alfred—

YOUNG GENTLEMAN: Emma—! Do you want to leave me like this!

YOUNG WIFE: Yes—like this!—

YOUNG GENTLEMAN: Five more minutes . . .

YOUNG WIFE: Fine. Five more minutes. But you must promise me . . . not to move? . . . All right? . . . I want to give you one more kiss as a farewell . . . Shhh . . . quiet . . . don't move, I said, or else I'll get right up, you, my sweet . . . sweet . . .

YOUNG GENTLEMAN: Emma . . . my ador— . . .

* * * * *

YOUNG WIFE: My Alfred—

YOUNG GENTLEMAN: Ah, it's heaven with you.

YOUNG WIFE: But now I really must go.

YOUNG GENTLEMAN: Oh let your sister wait.

YOUNG WIFE: I've got to go home now. It's much too late for my sister. Exactly what time is it, then?

YOUNG GENTLEMAN: Well how should I find that out?

YOUNG WIFE: Just look at your watch.

YOUNG GENTLEMAN: My watch is in my vest.

YOUNG WIFE: Then get it.

YOUNG GENTLEMAN [*getting up with a powerful jolt*]: Eight o'clock.

YOUNG WIFE [*arising quickly*]: Oh my God . . . Quick, Alfred, give me my stockings. Just what am I going to say, then? They'll surely be waiting for me at home . . . eight o'clock . . .

YOUNG GENTLEMAN: Then when will I see you again?

YOUNG WIFE: Never.

YOUNG GENTLEMAN: Emma! Don't you love me anymore?

YOUNG WIFE: It's precisely for that reason. Give me my shoes.

YOUNG GENTLEMAN: Never again? Here are your shoes.

YOUNG WIFE: There's a buttonhook in my bag. Please, quickly . . .

YOUNG GENTLEMAN: Here's the buttonhook.

YOUNG WIFE: Alfred, this can cost us both our necks.

YOUNG GENTLEMAN [*extremely unpleasantly moved*]: How is that?

YOUNG WIFE: Well, what am I supposed to say if he asks me, "Where have you been?"

YOUNG GENTLEMAN: "I was at my sister's."

YOUNG WIFE: Yes, if I could only lie.

YOUNG GENTLEMAN: Well, you've simply got to.

YOUNG WIFE: All this for someone like you. Oh, come here . . . let me kiss you once more.

[*She embraces him.*]

—And now—leave me alone, go into the other room. I can't get dressed with you around.

[*The* YOUNG GENTLEMAN *goes into the salon, where he gets dressed. He eats some of the pastry, and drinks a glass of cognac.*]

YOUNG WIFE [*calls out after a while*]: Alfred!

YOUNG GENTLEMAN: My darling.

YOUNG WIFE: It is better after all that we didn't weep.

YOUNG GENTLEMAN [*smiling, not without pride*]: How can you speak so flippantly—

YOUNG WIFE: How would it be . . . if one day we should accidentally meet socially?

YOUNG GENTLEMAN: Accidentally—one day . . . But surely you're also going to be at the Lobheimers' tomorrow?

YOUNG WIFE: Yes. Will you be there too?

YOUNG GENTLEMAN: Of course. May I ask you for the cotillion?

YOUNG WIFE: Oh, I won't go. What are you thinking of?—I would certainly . . . [*entering the salon fully dressed, she takes a chocolate pastry*] . . . die of shame.

YOUNG GENTLEMAN: So, tomorrow at the Lobheimers', that's good.

YOUNG WIFE: No, no . . . I'll decline; definitely—

YOUNG GENTLEMAN: All right, the day after tomorrow . . . here.

YOUNG WIFE: What's gotten into you?

YOUNG GENTLEMAN: At six . . .

YOUNG WIFE: There are coaches at the corner, aren't there?—

YOUNG GENTLEMAN: Yes, as many as you want. All right, here at six, the day after tomorrow. Just say yes, my dearest darling.

YOUNG WIFE: . . . We'll discuss it at the cotillion tomorrow.

YOUNG GENTLEMAN [*embracing her*]: My darling.

YOUNG WIFE: Don't mess up my hair again.

YOUNG GENTLEMAN: All right, tomorrow at the Lobheimers', and the day after tomorrow here in my arms.

YOUNG WIFE: Farewell . . .

YOUNG GENTLEMAN [*suddenly uneasy again*]: And what will you—tell him tonight?—

YOUNG WIFE: Don't ask . . . don't ask . . . it's all too dreadful.—Why do I love you so much!—Adieu.—If I meet people on the stairs again, I'll have a stroke.—Ah!—

[*The* YOUNG GENTLEMAN *kisses her hand once more. The* YOUNG WIFE *leaves. The* YOUNG GENTLEMAN *stays behind, alone. Then he sits down on the sofa and smiles.*]

YOUNG GENTLEMAN [*to himself*]: So, at last, an affair with a respectable woman.

V. THE YOUNG WIFE AND THE HUSBAND

[*A comfortable bedchamber. Ten-thirty in the evening. The* YOUNG WIFE *is lying in bed, reading. The* HUSBAND, *in his dressing gown, is just entering the room.*]

YOUNG WIFE [*without looking up*]: You've stopped working?

HUSBAND: Yes. I'm too tired. And besides . . .

YOUNG WIFE: Well?—

HUSBAND: I suddenly felt so lonesome at my desk. I had a longing for you.

YOUNG WIFE: [*looking up*] Really?

HUSBAND [*sitting down on the bed with her*]: Don't read any more today. You'll ruin your eyes.

YOUNG WIFE [*shutting the book*]: What is it, then?

HUSBAND: Nothing, my child. I'm in love with you! You surely know that!

YOUNG WIFE: One could almost forget it sometimes.

HUSBAND: One should forget it sometimes.

YOUNG WIFE: Why?

HUSBAND: Because otherwise marriage would be imperfect. It would . . . how should I say it . . . it would lose its sanctity.

YOUNG WIFE: Oh . . .

HUSBAND: Believe me—it is true. . . . If we hadn't sometimes forgotten that we were in love with each other during the five years we've been married, we would probably no longer be in love.

YOUNG WIFE: That's too deep for me.

HUSBAND: The point is simply this: we've already had perhaps ten or twelve love affairs with each other. . . . Doesn't it seem that way to you too?

YOUNG WIFE: I haven't been counting!—

HUSBAND: If we had completely savored our first love affair, if I had involuntarily yielded to my passion for you from the very beginning, the same thing would have happened to us that happens to millions of other lovers. We would be finished with each other.

YOUNG WIFE: Oh . . . is that what you mean?

HUSBAND: Believe me—Emma—I was worried in the first days of our marriage that it would end like that.

YOUNG WIFE: So was I.

HUSBAND: There, you see? Wasn't I right? That's why it's sometimes good to live together just as good friends for a while.

YOUNG WIFE: Is that so?

HUSBAND: And that way we can continue to experience new honeymoons together, since I never let our honeymoons . . .

YOUNG WIFE: Extend into months.

HUSBAND: Exactly.

YOUNG WIFE: And now . . . it seems that another period of friendship has run out then—?

HUSBAND [*pressing her tenderly to him*]: That just might be.

YOUNG WIFE: But what if it . . . were different for me?

HUSBAND: But it's not different for you. After all, you are the wisest and most charming being there is. I am very happy and fortunate that I found you.

YOUNG WIFE: It's rather nice that you are able to come courting—from time to time.

HUSBAND [*has also come to bed*]: Actually marriage seems much more mysterious for a man who has seen a bit of the world—go on, lay your head on my shoulder—for a man who has seen the world—than for you young ladies from good families. You come to us pure and . . . at least to a certain extent, ignorant, and thus you actually have a much clearer understanding of the nature of love than we do.

YOUNG WIFE: Oh!

HUSBAND: Certainly. Because we've become quite bewildered and insecure through the various experiences which we perforce have had to pass through before marriage. You young ladies hear a lot and know too much and probably read too much as well. But, for all that, you still don't really understand what we men in fact go through. That which we commonly call love is made completely disgusting for us, because, after all, what kind of creature are we finally forced to resort to?

YOUNG WIFE: Yes, what kind of creatures are they?

HUSBAND [*kissing her on the brow*]: Be glad, my child, that you have no knowledge of such affairs. By the way, they are usually quite pitiful beings . . . let us cast no stones against them.

YOUNG WIFE: But what I want to know is—this compassion.—It really doesn't seem justified here.

HUSBAND [*with splendid charitableness*]: They deserve it. You young ladies from good families, who can quietly wait in the safekeeping of your parents until an honorable man asks for your hand in marriage—you don't realize the misery which drives most of those poor creatures into the arms of sin.

YOUNG WIFE: Well, do they all sell themselves that way?

HUSBAND: I wouldn't go so far as to say that. And I'm not referring just to material misery. But there is also—what one might call—a misery of morals, a defective concept of what is permitted and more importantly of what is noble.

YOUNG WIFE: But why are they to be pitied—? They're doing quite well, aren't they?

HUSBAND: You have strange notions, my child. You mustn't forget that such beings are destined by their very nature to fall ever deeper and deeper. There is no stopping them.

YOUNG WIFE [*nestling against him*]: Falling is evidently rather pleasant.

HUSBAND [*painfully moved*]: Why how can you talk like that, Emma? I should think that to a respectable woman such as you there can be nothing more disgusting than all those women who are not respectable.

YOUNG WIFE: Of course, Karl, of course. I was just putting it that way. Go on, tell me some more. It's so nice when you talk to me like this. Tell me something.

HUSBAND: About what?—

YOUNG WIFE: Well—about those creatures.

HUSBAND: What's gotten into you?

YOUNG WIFE: But I've asked you over and over, since we were first married, you know, to tell me something about your youth.

HUSBAND: Well, why does that interest you?

YOUNG WIFE: Well, aren't you my husband? And it's really unfair that I don't know anything at all about your past, isn't it—?

HUSBAND: But you surely don't expect me to be so tactless as to—But enough, Emma . . . that would certainly be a desecration.

YOUNG WIFE: And yet . . . you have held who knows how many other women in your arms, just as you are holding me now.

HUSBAND: Those were women. You are my wife.

YOUNG WIFE: But you must answer one question for me . . . or else . . . or else . . . there will be no honeymoons.

HUSBAND: You have such a manner of speaking . . . just bear in mind that you are a mother . . . that our little girl is lying asleep right in there. . . .

YOUNG WIFE [*nestling up to him*]: But I would also like a boy.

HUSBAND: Emma!

YOUNG WIFE: Go on, don't be like that . . . of course I'm your wife . . . but sometimes I'd like to be . . . your mistress too.

HUSBAND: Would you? . . .

YOUNG WIFE: Well—but first my question.

HUSBAND [*accommodatingly*]: Well?

YOUNG WIFE: Was there . . . a married woman—among them?

HUSBAND: Why?—What do you mean by that?

YOUNG WIFE: You know what I mean.

HUSBAND [*slightly upset*]: What makes you ask such a question?

YOUNG WIFE: I'd just like to know if . . . that is—there are such women . . . I know that. But I'd like to know if you? . . .

HUSBAND [*gravely*]: Are you acquainted with such a woman?

YOUNG WIFE: Well, I really don't know.

HUSBAND: Is there perhaps such a woman among your friends?

YOUNG WIFE: How can I know for certain whether there is—or not?

HUSBAND: Did perhaps one of your friends once . . . People talk about all sorts of things when they are—when women are by themselves—Did one of your friends confess to you—?

YOUNG WIFE [*uncertainly*]: No.

HUSBAND: Do you suspect that one of your friends, that she . . .

YOUNG WIFE: Suspect . . . oh . . . suspect.

HUSBAND: So it seems.

YOUNG WIFE: Of course not, Karl, certainly not. Now that I think about it . . . I don't believe that a single one of them is capable of that after all.

HUSBAND: Not a single one?

YOUNG WIFE: Not a single one of my friends.

HUSBAND: Promise me something, Emma.

YOUNG WIFE: Well, what?

HUSBAND: Promise me that you will never associate with a woman about whom you have even the slightest suspicion that she . . . doesn't lead a completely irreproachable life.

YOUNG WIFE: Must I promise you that?

HUSBAND: Of course I know that you wouldn't purposely associate with such women. But you might just accidentally—In fact it is quite frequently the case that those very women whose reputations are not the best seek the company of respectable women, partly as relief and partly out of a certain . . . how shall I say it . . . out of a certain homesickness for virtue.

YOUNG WIFE: Well.

HUSBAND: Yes. I think what I've said in this respect is quite correct. Homesickness for virtue. But one thing you can be sure of is that all those women are really very unhappy.

YOUNG WIFE: Why?

HUSBAND: Are you asking me that, Emma?—But how can you?—Just imagine what kind of existence those women lead! Full of lies, malice, vulgarity, and full of dangers.

YOUNG WIFE: Yes, of course. You're certainly right about that.

HUSBAND: Definitely—but they pay for that bit of happiness . . . that bit . . .

YOUNG WIFE: Of pleasure.

HUSBAND: Why pleasure? What makes you call it pleasure?

YOUNG WIFE: Well—it has to be something, after all—! Otherwise they wouldn't do it, would they?

HUSBAND: It's nothing . . . just intoxication.

YOUNG WIFE [*reflectively*]: Just intoxication.

HUSBAND: No, it isn't even intoxication. Like everything else—it's paid for at great price!

YOUNG WIFE: Well . . . you were once involved in something like that yourself—right?

HUSBAND: Yes, Emma.—It is my saddest memory.

YOUNG WIFE: Well, who was it? Tell me! Do I know her?

HUSBAND: What's gotten into you?

YOUNG WIFE: Was it long ago? Was it a long time before you married me?

HUSBAND: Don't ask. I beg of you, please don't ask.

YOUNG WIFE: But Karl!

HUSBAND: She is dead.

YOUNG WIFE: Seriously?

HUSBAND: Yes . . . I know it sounds ridiculous, but I have the feeling that all those women die young.

YOUNG WIFE: Did you love her very much?

HUSBAND: A man does not love a woman who lies.

YOUNG WIFE: But why . . .

HUSBAND: Intoxication . . .

YOUNG WIFE: Then it's really . . . ?

HUSBAND: Don't talk about it anymore, I beg of you. All that is long past. I have loved only one woman . . . and that's you. A man can love only where there is purity and truth.

YOUNG WIFE: Karl!

HUSBAND: Oh, how safe, how good a man feels in such arms. Why didn't I know you as a child? I'm sure I would never have looked at another woman then.

YOUNG WIFE: Karl!

HUSBAND: And you are beautiful! . . . beautiful! . . . Oh come . . .

[*He puts out the light.*]

* * * * *

YOUNG WIFE: Do you know what I can't help thinking about tonight?

HUSBAND: About what, my darling?

YOUNG WIFE: About . . . about . . . about Venice.

HUSBAND: That first night . . .

YOUNG WIFE: Yes . . . that's right . . .

HUSBAND: What is it?—Tell me!

YOUNG WIFE: You do love me as much tonight.

HUSBAND: Yes, just as much.

YOUNG WIFE: Ah . . . If you could always . . .

HUSBAND [*in her arms*]: What?

YOUNG WIFE: My Karl!

HUSBAND: What do you mean? If I could always . . .

YOUNG WIFE: Oh well.

HUSBAND: What would happen, if I could always? . . .

YOUNG WIFE: Then I would always be sure that you loved me.

HUSBAND: Yes. But you can be sure of that anyway. A man cannot always be the loving husband, he must also go out into the hostile world, he must struggle and strive! Don't ever forget that, my child! There's a time for everything in marriage—that's just the beauty of it. There aren't many couples who, five years later, can still remember—their Venice.

YOUNG WIFE: Of course!

HUSBAND: And now . . . good night, my child.

YOUNG WIFE: Good night!

VI. THE HUSBAND AND THE SWEET YOUNG THING

[*A private dining room in the Riedhof Restaurant. Comfortable, moderate elegance. The gas stove is burning.—The* HUSBAND, *the* SWEET YOUNG THING.

The remains of a meal are to be seen on the table, meringues with whipped cream, fruit, cheese. A Hungarian white wine is in the wineglasses.

The HUSBAND *is smoking a Havana cigar and is leaning back in the corner of a sofa. The* SWEET YOUNG THING *is sitting beside him on a chair and is eating the whipped cream out of a meringue with her spoon, noisily and with gusto.*]

HUSBAND: Taste good?
SWEET YOUNG THING [*not letting herself be disturbed*]: Mmm . . .
HUSBAND: Do you want another one?
SWEET YOUNG THING: No, I've eaten too many as it is.
HUSBAND: You don't have any more wine.

[*He pours out a glass for her.*]

SWEET YOUNG THING: No . . . Listen, I just won't drink it, sir.
HUSBAND: There you go again, being so formal.
SWEET YOUNG THING: Was I?—Well, you know, sir, it's just so hard to get used to things.
HUSBAND: Sir?
SWEET YOUNG THING: What?
HUSBAND: You said "sir" again. Come, sit by me.
SWEET YOUNG THING: Just a minute . . . I'm not finished yet.

[*The* HUSBAND *gets up, goes and stands behind the chair and embraces the* SWEET YOUNG THING, *turning her head toward him.*]

Well, what is it?

HUSBAND: I'd like a kiss.

SWEET YOUNG THING [*giving him a kiss*]: You are, sir . . . oh, pardon me, you are so fresh.

HUSBAND: Did that just now occur to you?

SWEET YOUNG THING: Well, no. It occurred to me earlier . . . on the street, when . . . oh, sir—

HUSBAND: Sir?

SWEET YOUNG THING: I'm sorry.—What you must think of me.

HUSBAND: What do you mean?

SWEET YOUNG THING: My coming to a private dining room with you right away.

HUSBAND: Well, now actually it wasn't right away.

SWEET YOUNG THING: But you do have a nice way of asking.

HUSBAND: Do you think so?

SWEET YOUNG THING: And, after all, what's wrong with that?

HUSBAND: Of course.

SWEET YOUNG THING: Whether we go for a walk or—

HUSBAND: It's really much too cold to go walking.

SWEET YOUNG THING: Yes, of course, it was too cold.

HUSBAND: But here it's nice and warm, isn't it?

[*He sits down again, embraces the* SWEET YOUNG THING, *and draws her to his side.*]

SWEET YOUNG THING [*weakly*]: Well.

HUSBAND: Now tell me . . . You had noticed me before, hadn't you?

SWEET YOUNG THING: Oh sure. As far back as Singer Street.

HUSBAND: I don't mean just today. But also the day before yesterday, and the day before that, when I was following you.

SWEET YOUNG THING: Lots of people follow me.

HUSBAND: I can imagine. But did you notice me?

SWEET YOUNG THING: You know, sir . . . ah, I'm sorry . . . do you know what happened to me the other day? My cousin's husband was following me in the dark and didn't even recognize me.

HUSBAND: Did he speak to you?

SWEET YOUNG THING: What do you think! Do you suppose every fellow is as fresh as you are?

HUSBAND: But those things do happen, after all.

SWEET YOUNG THING: Of course they happen.

HUSBAND: Well, what do you do then?

SWEET YOUNG THING: Do!—Nothing.—I just don't answer them.

HUSBAND: Hmm . . . but you answered me.

SWEET YOUNG THING: Well, are you angry with me?

HUSBAND [*kissing her vehemently*]: Your lips taste like that whipped cream.

SWEET YOUNG THING: Oh, they're just naturally sweet.

HUSBAND: I suppose many men have told you that?

SWEET YOUNG THING: Many men! There you go, imagining things again!

HUSBAND: Now, be honest . . . How many men have kissed these lips?

SWEET YOUNG THING: Why do you ask? You probably wouldn't believe me if I told you!

HUSBAND: Well, why wouldn't I?

SWEET YOUNG THING: Just guess!

HUSBAND: So, let's say—now you mustn't be angry?

SWEET YOUNG THING: Why should I be angry?

HUSBAND: All right, I suppose . . . twenty.

SWEET YOUNG THING [*extricating herself from him*]: Well—why not say at least a hundred?

HUSBAND: But I was just guessing.

SWEET YOUNG THING: Well, you didn't guess very well.

HUSBAND: All right, ten.

SWEET YOUNG THING [*offended*]: Certainly. A girl who lets a stranger talk to her on the street and then goes right along with him to a private dining room!

HUSBAND: Don't be so childish. Whether we're walking together on the street or sitting in a room . . . after all, we are here at a restaurant. The waiter can come in at any moment . . . there really isn't anything wrong about that . . .

SWEET YOUNG THING: That's just what I thought too.

HUSBAND: Have you ever been in a private dining room before?

SWEET YOUNG THING: All right, to tell the truth: yes.

HUSBAND: See, I like it that you are at least being candid with me.

SWEET YOUNG THING: But it wasn't the way that . . . that you're thinking. I was in a private dining room with a girlfriend and her fiancé once, at Mardi Gras, earlier this year.

HUSBAND: Actually it wouldn't be so terrible if one time you were with . . . your lover—

SWEET YOUNG THING: Of course it wouldn't be so terrible. But I don't have a lover.

HUSBAND: Oh, go on.

SWEET YOUNG THING: I don't have one, cross my heart.

HUSBAND: Now you aren't going to try and make me believe that I . . .

SWEET YOUNG THING: That you what . . . I really don't have one . . . for more than half a year now.

HUSBAND: Ah yes . . . But before that? Who was it then?

SWEET YOUNG THING: Say, why are you so curious?

HUSBAND: I'm curious because I love you.

SWEET YOUNG THING: You mean it?

HUSBAND: Of course. Surely you must be aware of that. So tell me something.

[*He presses her firmly to him.*]

SWEET YOUNG THING: What do you want me to tell you?

HUSBAND: Now don't make me beg you. I'd just like to know who it was.

SWEET YOUNG THING [*laughing*]: Well, just a man.

HUSBAND: All right . . . all right—Who was it?

SWEET YOUNG THING: He looked a little bit like you.

HUSBAND: I see.

SWEET YOUNG THING: If you didn't look so much like him—

HUSBAND: Well, what then?

SWEET YOUNG THING: So why ask, if you already know . . .

HUSBAND [*understanding*]: All right then, so that's why you let me talk to you.

SWEET YOUNG THING: Well, yes it was.

HUSBAND: Now I really don't know whether to be delighted or upset.

SWEET YOUNG THING: Well, if I were you, I'd be delighted.

HUSBAND: Of course.

SWEET YOUNG THING: And the way you talk reminds me a lot of him too . . . and the way you look at a person . . .

HUSBAND: What was he, then?

SWEET YOUNG THING: No, the eyes—

HUSBAND: What was his name, then?

SWEET YOUNG THING: No, don't look at me like that, I beg you.

[*The* HUSBAND *embraces her. Long, ardent kiss. The* SWEET YOUNG THING *shakes herself, starts to get up.*]

HUSBAND: Why are you moving away?

SWEET YOUNG THING: It's about time for me to go home.

HUSBAND: Later.

SWEET YOUNG THING: No, I really do have to go home. What do you think my mother will say?

HUSBAND: You live with your mother?

SWEET YOUNG THING: Of course I live with my mother! What did you think?

HUSBAND: I see—with your mother. Do you live alone with her?

SWEET YOUNG THING: Oh sure, alone! There are five of us! Two boys and two more girls.

HUSBAND: Now you don't have to sit so far away. Are you the oldest girl?

SWEET YOUNG THING: No, I'm the second. Kathy is first, she works at a flower shop—then comes me.

HUSBAND: Where do you work?

SWEET YOUNG THING: Oh, I'm at home.

HUSBAND: All the time?

SWEET YOUNG THING: Well, after all, someone has to be at home.

HUSBAND: Yes, of course.—And then what do you actually tell your mother when you . . . come home so late?

SWEET YOUNG THING: That really doesn't happen very often.

HUSBAND: All right, today for example. Your mother will ask you, won't she?

SWEET YOUNG THING: Why, sure, she'll ask me.—No matter how careful I am, she always wakes up when I come in.

HUSBAND: All right then, what do you tell her then?

SWEET YOUNG THING: Well, I just say I was at the theater.

HUSBAND: And will she believe that?

SWEET YOUNG THING: Well, why shouldn't she believe it? I often do go to the theater. Just last Sunday I was at the opera with my girlfriend and her fiancé and my older brother.

HUSBAND: And where did you get the tickets?

SWEET YOUNG THING: Well, you see, my brother is a hairstylist!

HUSBAND: Of course, a hairstylist . . . ah, I suppose he's a hairstylist for the theater.

SWEET YOUNG THING: Why are you asking so many questions?

HUSBAND: I'm just interested. And what does your other brother do?

SWEET YOUNG THING: He's still going to school. He wants to be a teacher. Well . . . can you imagine!

HUSBAND: And then you have another, younger sister?

SWEET YOUNG THING: Yes, she's still just a brat, but lately you've got to keep your eye on her all the time. You just have no idea how spoiled these little girls get in school! Would you believe it! The other day I caught her out on a rendezvous!

HUSBAND: What?!

SWEET YOUNG THING: Really! She went for a walk at seven-thirty the other evening on Strozzi Street with a boy from the school across the street. Such a little brat!

HUSBAND: And what did you do then?

SWEET YOUNG THING: How she got spanked!

HUSBAND: Are you that strict?

SWEET YOUNG THING: Well, who would do it if I didn't? My older sister is working, my mother does nothing but complain,—everything always lands on me.

HUSBAND: My God! But you're sweet!

[*He kisses her and becomes more affectionate.*]

You also remind me of someone.

SWEET YOUNG THING: Do I—who's that?

HUSBAND: No one in particular . . . it was a time . . . well, in my youth. Go on, drink, my dear!

SWEET YOUNG THING: How old are you anyway? You . . . well . . . I don't even know your name.

HUSBAND: Karl.

SWEET YOUNG THING: No kidding? Is your name Karl?

HUSBAND: Was his name Karl too?

SWEET YOUNG THING: No, listen, this is fantastic . . . it's just—no, it's the eyes . . . the look . . .

[*She shakes her head.*]

HUSBAND: But who was he?—You still haven't told me.

SWEET YOUNG THING: He was rotten—that's for sure, otherwise he wouldn't have jilted me.

HUSBAND: Were you very fond of him?

SWEET YOUNG THING: Of course I was fond of him.

HUSBAND: I know what he was—a lieutenant.

SWEET YOUNG THING: No, he wasn't in the military. They wouldn't take him. His father had a house on . . . but what do you need to know that for?

HUSBAND [*kisses her*]: Your eyes are actually gray. At first I thought their color was black.

SWEET YOUNG THING: Well, aren't they pretty enough for you?

[*The* HUSBAND *kisses her eyes.*]

SWEET YOUNG THING: No, no—I just can't stand that . . . oh, please—oh God . . . no, let me up . . . just for a moment—please.

HUSBAND [*more and more affectionate*]: Oh, no.

SWEET YOUNG THING: But Karl, please . . .

HUSBAND: How old are you?—Eighteen, right?

SWEET YOUNG THING: Just past nineteen.

HUSBAND: Nineteen . . . and I'm—

SWEET YOUNG THING: You're thirty . . .

HUSBAND: And a little more.—Let's not talk about that.

SWEET YOUNG THING: He was also thirty-two, when I first met him.

HUSBAND: And how long ago was that?

SWEET YOUNG THING: I can't remember . . . Hey, Karl, there must have been something in the wine.

HUSBAND: Why do you say that?

SWEET YOUNG THING: I'm all . . . you know—everything is going around.

HUSBAND: Then just hold on tight to me. Like this . . .

[*He presses her to him and becomes more and more affectionate; she scarcely wards him off.*]

You know what, my dear? Now we might really go places.

SWEET YOUNG THING: Yes . . . home.

HUSBAND: Not home exactly . . .

SWEET YOUNG THING: Then what do you mean? . . . Oh no, oh no . . . I'm not going anywhere, why what's gotten into you—

HUSBAND: All right, now listen to me, my child, the next time we meet, you understand we'll arrange it in such a way that . . .

[*He has sunk to the floor, his head in her lap.*]

That's nice, oh, that is nice.

SWEET YOUNG THING: Oh, what are you doing?

[*She kisses his hair.*]

Hey, Karl, there must have been something in the wine—so sleepy . . . hey, what would happen if I couldn't get up anymore? But, but, look, but, Karl . . . if someone should come in . . . please . . . if the waiter—

HUSBAND: There'll be . . . no waiter . . . coming in here . . . that's for sure . . .

* * * * *

[*The* SWEET YOUNG THING *is leaning with closed eyes in the corner of the sofa. The* HUSBAND *is walking up and down, after having lit a cigarette. A prolonged silence.*]

HUSBAND [*gazing at the* SWEET YOUNG THING *for a long time; to himself*]: Who knows what kind of person she really is—Good grief . . . so quickly too . . . It wasn't very cautious of me . . . Hmm . . .

SWEET YOUNG THING [*without opening her eyes*]: There must have been something in the wine.

HUSBAND: Why do you say that?

SWEET YOUNG THING: Otherwise . . .

HUSBAND: Why do you blame everything on the wine?

SWEET YOUNG THING: Where are you? Why are you so far away? Come over here by me.

[*The* HUSBAND *goes over to her and sits down.*]

SWEET YOUNG THING: Now tell me, are you really fond of me?

HUSBAND: Surely you know that . . .

[*He interrupts himself quickly.*]

Of course.

SWEET YOUNG THING: You know . . . I still think . . . Come on, tell me the truth, what was in the wine?

HUSBAND: Well, do you think I . . . I would poison you?

SWEET YOUNG THING: Look, I just don't understand it. I'm really not like that . . . And we've only known each other for . . . Say, I'm not like that . . . I swear to God—if you were to think that of me—

HUSBAND: Well—what are you worrying about then? I don't think badly of you at all. I just think that you love me.

SWEET YOUNG THING: Yes . . .

HUSBAND: After all, when two young people are alone in a room together, having supper and drinking wine . . . There doesn't have to be anything at all in the wine . . .

SWEET YOUNG THING: Well, I was just saying that.

HUSBAND: But why?

SWEET YOUNG THING [*rather defiantly*]: Because I was ashamed.

HUSBAND: But, that's ridiculous. There's simply no reason for that. Especially since I remind you of your first lover.

SWEET YOUNG THING: Yes.

HUSBAND: The first one.

SWEET YOUNG THING: Sure . . .

HUSBAND: Now it would interest me to know who the others were.

SWEET YOUNG THING: There weren't any.

HUSBAND: That's simply not true. It just can't be.

SWEET YOUNG THING: Come on, please don't torment me.—

HUSBAND: You want a cigarette?

SWEET YOUNG THING: No, thank you very much.

HUSBAND: Are you aware of how late it is?

SWEET YOUNG THING: Well?

HUSBAND: It's eleven-thirty.

SWEET YOUNG THING: Is that so!

HUSBAND: Well, . . . how about your mother? She's used to it, isn't she?

SWEET YOUNG THING: Do you really want to send me home so soon?

HUSBAND: Well, you did say earlier that—

SWEET YOUNG THING: My, you certainly have changed. What did I ever do to you?

HUSBAND: Why, what's the matter, child? What's gotten into you?

SWEET YOUNG THING: I swear, it was just the way you looked, otherwise you would have had to . . . lots of men have asked me to go to private dining rooms with them.

HUSBAND: Well, do you want . . . to come here again with me sometime soon? . . . Or we could go somewhere else—

SWEET YOUNG THING: I don't know.

HUSBAND: Now, what do you mean, you don't know?

SWEET YOUNG THING: Well, if you'd just ask me.

HUSBAND: All right, when? First of all, I think I should make it clear to you that I don't live in Vienna. I just come here for a few days now and then.

SWEET YOUNG THING: Ah, go on, you're not Viennese?

HUSBAND: Actually I am Viennese. But now I live nearby . . .

SWEET YOUNG THING: Well, where?

HUSBAND: Good lord, what difference does it make?

SWEET YOUNG THING: Don't worry, I won't show up there.

HUSBAND: Oh lord, if it'll make you happy, go ahead. I live in Graz.

SWEET YOUNG THING: Are you serious?

HUSBAND: Well now, why should that surprise you?

SWEET YOUNG THING: You're married, aren't you?

HUSBAND [*extremely astonished*]: Yes, but how do you know that?

SWEET YOUNG THING: It just seemed that way.

HUSBAND: And wouldn't that bother you at all?

SWEET YOUNG THING: Of course I'd prefer it if you were single.—But, after all, you're married.

HUSBAND: So just tell me, how do you know that?

SWEET YOUNG THING: Well, when a man says he doesn't live in Vienna and doesn't always have time—

HUSBAND: That isn't so improbable.

SWEET YOUNG THING: I just don't believe it.

HUSBAND: And it doesn't trouble your conscience to tempt a married man to infidelity?

SWEET YOUNG THING: Look, I bet your wife is out doing the same thing you are.

HUSBAND [*very indignantly*]: Now see here, that's enough. Such remarks—

SWEET YOUNG THING: But I thought you weren't married.

HUSBAND: Whether I am or not—one shouldn't make such remarks.

[*He has gotten up.*]

SWEET YOUNG THING: Karl, now look, Karl, what's the matter? Are you angry? Hey, I really didn't know you were married. I was just saying that. Come on over here, and be nice to me again.

HUSBAND [*going to her after a few seconds*]: You really are strange creatures, you . . . women.

[*He becomes affectionate again at her side.*]

SWEET YOUNG THING: Come on . . . don't . . . anyway, it's so late now—

HUSBAND: All right, but just listen. Let's talk seriously, all right? I'd like to see you again, often.

SWEET YOUNG THING: Honest?

HUSBAND: But if that's to happen . . . in that case I'll need to rely on you. I can't always take care of you.

SWEET YOUNG THING: But I'm taking care of myself now.

HUSBAND: But you're . . . well, I suppose one can't say inexperienced—but you're young—and—men are in general an unprincipled lot.

SWEET YOUNG THING: Oh Jeez!

HUSBAND: And I don't mean that just in the moral sense.—Well, surely you understand me.

SWEET YOUNG THING: Hey, just what do you think I am?

HUSBAND: All right then—if you want to love me—me alone—then we'll work it out so that—even if I do generally live in Graz. A place like this, where someone could walk in on us at any moment, is certainly no good.

[*The* SWEET YOUNG THING *nestles against him.*]

HUSBAND: The next time . . . we'll be together somewhere else, all right?

SWEET YOUNG THING: All right.

HUSBAND: Where we won't be disturbed at all.

SWEET YOUNG THING: All right.

HUSBAND [*embracing her ardently*]: We'll talk about the rest of it on the way home.

[*He gets up, opens the door.*]

Waiter . . . the check!

VII. THE SWEET YOUNG THING AND THE POET

[*A small room, furnished in comfortable good taste. Drapes keeping the room in semidarkness; the net curtains on the windows are red. A large desk, cluttered with books and papers. An upright piano against the wall. The* SWEET YOUNG THING *and the* POET *enter together. The* POET *locks the door.*]

POET: Ah, my darling.

[*He kisses her.*]

SWEET YOUNG THING [*with hat and cape*]: Hey! This is beautiful! Except that you can't see anything!

POET: Your eyes just have to get used to the twilight.—Those sweet eyes—

[*He kisses her on the eyes.*]

SWEET YOUNG THING: But these sweet eyes don't have time for that.

POET: Why not?

SWEET YOUNG THING: Because I am only going to be here for one minute.

POET: You can take off your hat, can't you?

SWEET YOUNG THING: For just the one minute?

POET [*taking the pin out of her hat and laying the hat aside*]: And your cape too—

SWEET YOUNG THING: What are you doing?—I really do have to leave right away.

POET: But you must get some rest! After all, we did walk for three hours.

SWEET YOUNG THING: We drove.

POET: Sure, we drove home—but we ran around for three full hours in the forest at Weidling-on-the-Brook. So just come sit down, my child . . . wherever you wish—here at the desk—but no, that's not comfortable. Sit down on the sofa.—Like this.

[*He pushes her down.*]

If you're very tired, you can even lie down. Like this.

[*He lays her out on the sofa.*]

There, just put your little head on the pillow.

SWEET YOUNG THING [*laughing*]: But I'm really not that tired!

POET: You just don't realize it. So—and if you're sleepy, you can just go to sleep. I'll be very quiet. By the way, I can play a lullaby for you . . . one of my own . . .

[*He goes to the upright piano.*]

SWEET YOUNG THING: One of your own?

POET: Yes.

SWEET YOUNG THING: But Robert, I thought you were a doctor.

POET: What do you mean? I told you I was a writer.

SWEET YOUNG THING: Well, aren't writers all doctors?

POET: No, not all of them. Take me, for instance. But what makes you think of that now?

SWEET YOUNG THING: Well, because you said just now that the piece you're playing is one of your own.

POET: Yes, but . . . maybe it isn't one of mine after all. It doesn't matter who wrote it, as long as it's beautiful—right?

SWEET YOUNG THING: Of course . . . it's got to be beautiful—that's the main thing—!

POET: Do you know what I mean by that?

SWEET YOUNG THING: By what?

POET: Well, what I said just now.

SWEET YOUNG THING [*sleepily*]: Well of course.

POET [*gets up, goes to her; stroking her hair*]: You didn't understand a word.

SWEET YOUNG THING: Hey, I'm not *that* stupid, you know.

POET: Of course you are. But that's just why I love you. Ah, it's beautiful, when women are stupid. I mean, the way you are.

SWEET YOUNG THING: Go on, why are you being so mean?

POET: You sweet little angel. It's nice to lie there on that soft Persian rug, isn't it?

SWEET YOUNG THING: Oh yes. Don't you want to go on and play the piano some more?

POET: No, I'd rather stay here with you.

[*He strokes her.*]

SWEET YOUNG THING: Come on, don't you want to have some light?

POET: Oh no . . . why, this twilight is so relaxing. It's as if we were bathing in sunbeams all day. Now we've gotten out of the bath, so to speak, and are putting on . . . the twilight like a bathrobe—[*laughs*]—oh no—that needs to be put differently . . . Don't you think?

SWEET YOUNG THING: I don't know.

POET [*gently withdrawing from her*]: Such divine stupidity!

[*He takes a notebook and writes a few words in it.*]

SWEET YOUNG THING: Say, what are you doing? [*Turning toward him*] What are you writing down there?

POET [*softly*]: Sun, bath, twilight, robe . . . [*Pocketing the notebook; aloud*] Nothing . . . Now just tell me, my darling, wouldn't you like something to eat or drink?

SWEET YOUNG THING: Actually I'm not thirsty, but I am hungry.

POET: Hmm . . . I'd prefer it if you were thirsty. You see, I've got some cognac here, but I'd have to go out for food.

SWEET YOUNG THING: Can't you send out for something?

POET: That would be difficult, the maid is no longer around—never mind—I'll just go myself—well, what do you like?

SWEET YOUNG THING: It seems hardly worth it now. I've really got to get home anyway.

POET: No more talk of that, my child. I'll tell you what: when we leave here, we'll go out for supper somewhere.

SWEET YOUNG THING: Oh, no. I don't have any time for that. And besides where would we go? Suppose we were seen by someone I know?

POET: Do you know so many people?

SWEET YOUNG THING: But it would be terrible if only one of them saw us.

POET: Why would that be so terrible?

SWEET YOUNG THING: Well, what do you think? If Mother ever found out . . .

POET: Maybe we could go some place where nobody would see us; after all, there are restaurants with individual dining rooms.

SWEET YOUNG THING [*singing*]: Yes, "at supper in a private dining room with you!"

POET: Have you ever been in a private dining room before?

SWEET YOUNG THING: To tell the truth—yes.

POET: Who was the lucky man?

SWEET YOUNG THING: It wasn't what you're thinking . . . I was with my girlfriend and her fiancé. They took me along.

POET: I see. And you expect me to believe that?

SWEET YOUNG THING: Well, you don't have to believe me!

POET [*close to her*]: Are you blushing? It's gotten too dark to see anything! I can't even make out your features.

[*He runs his hand over her cheeks.*]

But I can recognize you this way too.

SWEET YOUNG THING: Well, just be careful that you don't confuse me with some other girl.

POET: It's strange . . . I can't remember what you look like.

SWEET YOUNG THING: Thanks a lot!

POET [*seriously*]: Say, it's almost uncanny, but I can't even picture you.—In a way, it's as if I've already forgotten you.—If I couldn't remember the sound of your voice either . . . what would you really be then?—Both near and far at the same time . . . uncanny.

SWEET YOUNG THING: Come on, what are you talking about—?
POET: Nothing, my angel, nothing. Where are your lips . . . ?

[*He kisses them.*]

SWEET YOUNG THING: Wouldn't you rather have some light?
POET: No . . .

[*He becomes very affectionate.*]

Tell me, do you love me?
SWEET YOUNG THING: Very much . . . oh, very much!
POET: Did you ever love anyone else as much as me?
SWEET YOUNG THING: Well I already told you—no.
POET: But . . .

[*He sighs.*]

SWEET YOUNG THING: Well, he was my fiancé.
POET: I'd rather you didn't think about him now.
SWEET YOUNG THING: Come on . . . What are you doing . . . look . . .
POET: We can just picture ourselves in a palace in India.
SWEET YOUNG THING: I'm sure they're not as naughty there as you are.
POET: Don't be an idiot! Ah, divine—if you only knew what you mean to me.
SWEET YOUNG THING: Well?
POET: Don't keep pushing me away. I'm not doing anything to you—for the time being.
SWEET YOUNG THING: Say, my corset hurts.
POET [*simply*]: Take it off.
SWEET YOUNG THING: All right. But you mustn't be naughty.
POET: I won't.

[*The* SWEET YOUNG THING *having gotten up, takes off her corset in the dark.*]

POET [*meanwhile, sitting on the sofa*]: Tell me, aren't you at all interested in knowing my last name?

SWEET YOUNG THING: Sure, what's your name?

POET: I'd rather not tell you my real name, but what I call myself.

SWEET YOUNG THING: So what's the difference?

POET: Well, I mean my pen name.

SWEET YOUNG THING: Hey, don't you write under your real name?

[*The* POET *is close to her.*]

SWEET YOUNG THING: Hey . . . come on! . . . Don't do that.

POET: What a wonderful fragrance rises from you. How sweet.

[*He kisses her bosom.*]

SWEET YOUNG THING: Why, you're tearing my chemise.

POET: Take it off . . . take it off . . . all that is superfluous.

SWEET YOUNG THING: But Robert!

POET: And now let's enter our Indian palace.

SWEET YOUNG THING: Tell me first, do you really love me?

POET: But I adore you.

[*He kisses her ardently.*]

I just adore you, my darling, my springtime . . . my . . .

SWEET YOUNG THING: Robert . . . Robert . . .

* * * * *

POET: That was blissful, sheer heavenly . . . I call myself . . .

SWEET YOUNG THING: Robert, oh my Robert!

POET: I call myself Biebitz.

SWEET YOUNG THING: Why do you call yourself Biebitz?

POET: That's not my name—I just call myself that . . . but perhaps you don't know the name?

SWEET YOUNG THING: No.

POET: Don't you know the name: Biebitz? Ah—that's divine! Really? You're not just saying you don't know it, are you?

SWEET YOUNG THING: I never heard of it, cross my heart.

POET: Well, don't you ever go to the theater?

SWEET YOUNG THING: Oh sure—I was there just the other day with a—you know, with my girlfriend and her uncle; we went to the opera to see *Cavalleria Rusticana.*

POET: Hmm, so you never go to the Royal Theatre?

SWEET YOUNG THING: No one ever gives me tickets.

POET: I'll send you a ticket right away.

SWEET YOUNG THING: Oh yes, do! But don't forget! Make it for something that's fun.

POET: Of course . . . fun . . . you wouldn't want to see something sad?

SWEET YOUNG THING: Not really.

POET: Even if it were a play by me?

SWEET YOUNG THING: Go on—a play by you? You write for the theater?

POET: Excuse me, I just want to have some light. I haven't seen you since you became mine—my sweetheart!

[*He lights a candle.*]

SWEET YOUNG THING: No, don't, I'm so ashamed! At least give me some covers.

POET: Later!

[*He comes to her with the candle and gazes at her for a long time.*]

SWEET YOUNG THING [*covering her face with her hands*]: Oh, no, Robert!

POET: You are beautiful, you are beauty personified, perhaps even nature herself, you are holy simplicity.

SWEET YOUNG THING: Ouch, you're dripping wax on me! Hey, why don't you be more careful!

POET [*putting the candle aside*]: You are what I've searched for all along. You love me alone; you would also love me if I were a clerk in a dry goods store. That's a comfort. I must confess to you that until this moment I had a certain suspicion. Tell me honestly, didn't you sense that I was Biebitz?

SWEET YOUNG THING: Look, I don't know what you want from me. I really don't know anyone named Biebitz.

POET: Such is fame! No, forget what I said, just forget the name I told you. I'm Robert and I'll leave it at that. I was only joking. [*Lightly*] I'm not really a writer, I'm a clerk and at night I play the piano for folksingers.

SWEET YOUNG THING: Sure, but now you've got me all mixed up . . . no, and the way you look at a person. Just what's going on—just what is it with you, anyway?

POET: It's very strange—it's hardly ever happened to me before, my darling, I'm practically crying. You move me deeply. Stay with me, will you; we'll be very much in love.

SWEET YOUNG THING: Hey, is that true, about the folksingers?

POET: Yes, but don't ask me anymore. If you love me, don't ask me anything at all. Say, can you take off for a few weeks?

SWEET YOUNG THING: What do you mean, take off?

POET: I mean, away from home?

SWEET YOUNG THING: Oh sure!! How could I?! What would my mother say? And besides, they couldn't get along at home without me.

POET: I had pictured how beautiful it would be, together with you, alone somewhere for a few weeks in the solitude of the forest, in nature. Nature . . . in nature . . . And then, one day, adieu—to part from each other, without knowing whither.

SWEET YOUNG THING: So now you're talking about saying good-bye! And I thought you liked me so much.

POET: It's just for that very reason—

[*He bends down to her and kisses her on the brow.*]

You sweet creature!

SWEET YOUNG THING: Come on, hold me tight, I'm so cold.

POET: It's about time for you to get dressed. Wait, I'll light a few more candles for you.

SWEET YOUNG THING [*arising*]: Now don't look.

POET: I won't. [*At the window*] Tell me, my child, are you happy?

SWEET YOUNG THING: How do you mean?

POET: I mean, in general, are you happy?

SWEET YOUNG THING: Well, things could be better.

POET: You don't understand. You've already told me enough about how things are at home. I know you're not a princess. But I mean, if you could just disregard all that and feel alive. Don't you feel alive at all?

SWEET YOUNG THING: Hey, don't you have a comb?

POET [*goes to the dressing table, gives her the comb; gazing at her*]: My God, you look enchanting!

SWEET YOUNG THING: Hey . . . don't!

POET: Come on, stay here a while. Stay here, I'll get something for supper, and . . .

SWEET YOUNG THING: But it's already much too late.

POET: It isn't even nine yet.

SWEET YOUNG THING: Hey, would you be so kind, I've really got to get going now.

POET: So, when will we see each other again?

SWEET YOUNG THING: Well, when do you want to see me again?

POET: Tomorrow.

SWEET YOUNG THING: What day is tomorrow?

POET: Saturday.

SWEET YOUNG THING: Oh, I can't. I've got to take my little sister to see her guardian.

POET: All right, Sunday . . . hmm . . . Sunday . . . on Sunday . . . let me explain something to you.—I'm not Biebitz, but Biebitz is a friend of mine. Someday I'll introduce you to him. But his play is being performed on Sunday. I'll send you a ticket and then meet you at the theater. Then you can tell me how you like the play, all right?

SWEET YOUNG THING: Really, all this stuff about Biebitz—it just makes me all confused.

POET: I'll really know you when I hear how you felt about this play.

SWEET YOUNG THING: Well . . . I'm ready.

POET: Then come, my darling!

[*They leave.*]

VIII. THE POET AND THE ACTRESS

[*A room in a country inn. It is an evening in spring, the moon hangs over the meadows and hills, the windows are open. Vast silence. The* POET *and the* ACTRESS *enter: as they enter, the candle in the* POET*'s hand goes out.*]

POET: Oh . . .

ACTRESS: What's wrong?

POET: The candle.—But we don't need it. See, there's plenty of light. Wonderful!

[*The* ACTRESS *suddenly sinks down, with hands folded, at the window.*]

POET: Now what's wrong with you?

[*The* ACTRESS *is silent.*]

POET [*going over to her*]: Now what are you doing?

ACTRESS [*indignantly*]: Can't you see I'm praying—?

POET: Do you believe in God?

ACTRESS: Why, I'm certainly not some pallid scoundrel.

POET: I see!

ACTRESS: Just come here and kneel down. You can pray for once, too. You won't lose any pearls from your crown.

[*The* POET *kneels down beside her and embraces her.*]

ACTRESS: You libertine!—[*Arising*] And don't you know to whom I was praying?

POET: To God, I assume.

ACTRESS [*with great mockery*]: Yes, of course! I was praying to you.

POET: Then why were you looking out the window?

ACTRESS: You tell me instead just where you've dragged me off to, you seducer!

POET: But my child, that was really your idea. You wanted to go to the country—and particularly to this place.

ACTRESS: Well, wasn't I right?

POET: You certainly were. It's so charming here. Especially when you consider that it's only two hours from Vienna—complete solitude. And what a landscape!

ACTRESS: Isn't it? You could probably write all sorts of things here, if, by chance, you had any talent.

POET: Have you been here before?

ACTRESS: Have I been here before? Ha! I lived here for years.

POET: With whom?

ACTRESS: Well, with Fritz, of course.

POET: Oh, I see!

ACTRESS: I just adored that man!—

POET: You've already told me that.

ACTRESS: Oh please—I'll just leave, if I'm boring you!

POET: You—bore me? . . . You obviously don't realize what you mean to me . . . You're a world in yourself . . . You're the divine essence, you are creative genius . . . You are . . . Actually you're holy simplicity . . . Yes, you . . . But you shouldn't be talking about Fritz now.

ACTRESS: That just slipped out! Well!—

POET: I'm glad you understand about that.

ACTRESS: Come here and give me a kiss!

[*The* POET *kisses her.*]

ACTRESS: But now let's say good night. Farewell, my darling!

POET: What do you mean by that?

ACTRESS: Just that I'm going to lie down and go to sleep!

POET: Yes—that may be, but as far as saying good night is . . . Just where am I to stay, then?

ACTRESS: There must be lots of other rooms in this building.

POET: But those other rooms hold no attraction for me. By the way, don't you think I should light the candle now?

ACTRESS: Yes.

POET [*lighting the candle on the night table*]: What a pretty room . . . and the folks here are so pious. Nothing but pictures of saints . . . It would be interesting to spend some time among these people . . . certainly a different world. How little we know about other people.

ACTRESS: Stop talking rubbish and go hand me my purse from the table over there.

POET: Here you are, my one and only!

[*The* ACTRESS *takes a small framed miniature from her little purse and places it on the night table.*]

POET: What's that?

ACTRESS: That's the Madonna.

POET: Do you always have it with you?

ACTRESS: That's my talisman. And now go, Robert!

POET: But what sort of joke is that? Can't I help you?

ACTRESS: No, you must go now.

POET: And when should I come back?

ACTRESS: In ten minutes.

POET [*kissing her*]: Au revoir!

ACTRESS: Well, where will you go?

POET: I'll walk up and down in front of the window. I love to walk outdoors at night. My best ideas come to me that way. And especially when I'm near you, with the breath of your longing surrounding me, so to speak . . . borne aloft by your art.

ACTRESS: You're talking like an imbecile . . .

POET [*painfully*]: Some women might say . . . like a poet.

ACTRESS: Just go now. But don't start up an affair with the waitress—

[*The* POET *exits. The* ACTRESS *undresses. She listens as the* POET *goes down the wooden stairs and she hears his steps beneath the window. As soon as she is undressed, she goes to the window and looks down; he is standing there, she calls down to him in a whisper.*]

Come!

[*The* POET *comes quickly up the steps and rushes toward her. Meanwhile she has lain down in bed and put out the light. He locks up.*]

ACTRESS: Well, now you can sit down beside me and tell me something.

POET [*sitting down beside her on the bed*]: Shouldn't I close the window? Aren't you cold?

ACTRESS: Oh no!

POET: What shall I tell you?

ACTRESS: Tell me, to whom are you being unfaithful at this moment?

POET: Unfortunately I'm not being unfaithful to anyone, yet.

ACTRESS: Well, if it's any satisfaction to you, I'm deceiving someone too.

POET: I can imagine that.

ACTRESS: And whom do you think it is?

POET: Why my dear child, I haven't the slightest idea.

ACTRESS: Then guess.

POET: Wait a minute . . . It's your manager.

ACTRESS: My dear, I'm not a chorus girl.

POET: Well, it was just a thought.

ACTRESS: Guess again.

POET: All right, you're deceiving that actor . . . Benno—

ACTRESS: Ha! The man doesn't even like women . . . don't you know that? He's actually having an affair with the mailman!

POET: I can't believe it—!

ACTRESS: So come give me a kiss!

[*The* POET *embraces her.*]

ACTRESS: Just what are you doing?

POET: So don't torture me like this.

ACTRESS: Listen Robert, let me make a suggestion. Lie down on the bed with me.

POET: Accepted!

ACTRESS: Come quickly. Come quickly!

POET: Yes . . . if I'd had my way, I'd have already . . . Do you hear that . . .

ACTRESS: Hear what?

POET: The crickets are chirping outside.

ACTRESS: You must be mad, my child, there aren't any crickets around here.

POET: But you do hear them, don't you?

ACTRESS: Just hurry up!

POET: Here I am.

[*He moves toward her.*]

ACTRESS: Well, just lie there nice and quiet . . . Shhh . . . don't move.

POET: Just what's gotten into you?

ACTRESS: You'd like to have an affair with me, wouldn't you?

POET: That must surely be obvious at this point.

ACTRESS: Well, of course, lots of men would like to . . .

POET: But there can be little doubt that at this moment I have the best chance.

ACTRESS: Then come, my cricket! From now on, I'll call you cricket.

POET: That's fine . . .

ACTRESS: Well, whom am I deceiving?

POET: Whom? . . . Me, perhaps . . .

ACTRESS: My child, you've gone terribly soft in the head.

POET: Or someone . . . whom you've never even seen . . . someone you don't know, someone—who is destined for you and whom you can never find . . .

ACTRESS: Please, don't talk such fantastic nonsense.

POET: . . . Isn't it strange . . . even you—and yet one would suppose that—But no, it would deprive you of your best, if one were to . . . come, come—come—

* * * * *

ACTRESS: After all, that's nicer than acting in idiotic plays . . . don't you think?

POET: Well, I do think it's good that sometimes you get to act in decent plays, after all.

ACTRESS: You conceited dog, you're certainly not thinking of your own play again, are you?

POET: Indeed I am!

ACTRESS [*seriously*]: It is a splendid play indeed!

POET: Well of course!

ACTRESS: You are a great genius, Robert!

POET: By the way, *now* you could tell me why you cancelled your performance the day before yesterday. Surely there was nothing at all wrong with you.

ACTRESS: Well, I did it to annoy you.

POET: Oh? But why? What have I done to you?

ACTRESS: You were conceited.

POET: In what way?

ACTRESS: Everyone at the theater thinks so.

POET: I see.

ACTRESS: But I told them: the man may have a right to be conceited.

POET: And what did they say to that?

ACTRESS: What could they say? Anyway, I don't talk to any of those people.

POET: I see.

ACTRESS: They'd all like nothing better than to poison me. But they won't succeed.

POET: Don't think about other people now. Just be happy that we're here together and tell me you love me.

ACTRESS: Do you need even more proof?

POET: That's not something that can be proved.

ACTRESS: But that's magnificent! What more do you want?

POET: How many others have you proved it to this way? . . . Did you love them all?

ACTRESS: Oh no. I only loved one man.

POET [*embracing her*]: My . . .

ACTRESS: Fritz.

POET: My name is Robert. What can I mean to you, if you're thinking about Fritz now?

ACTRESS: You are a whim.

POET: That's nice to know.

ACTRESS: Now tell me, aren't you proud?

POET: Well, what should I be proud of?

ACTRESS: I think you certainly have reason to be.

POET: Oh, because of that.

ACTRESS: Well, certainly, because of that, my pale cricket!—Well, what about the chirping? Are they still chirping?

POET: Incessantly. Can't you hear them?

ACTRESS: Of course I can. But those are frogs, my child.

POET: You're mistaken, frogs croak.

ACTRESS: Certainly they croak.

POET: But not here, my child; this is chirping.

ACTRESS: You are by far the most stubborn person I've ever encountered. Now kiss me, my frog!

POET: Please don't call me that. It simply makes me nervous.

ACTRESS: Well, what shall I call you?

POET: I do have a name, after all: Robert.

ACTRESS: Oh, but it's so stupid.

POET: Even so, I'm asking you to call me by my name.

ACTRESS: All right, Robert, give me a kiss . . . Ah!

[*She kisses him.*]

Are you satisfied now, frog? Hahahaha.

POET: Mind if I light a cigarette?

ACTRESS: Give me one, too.

[*He takes a cigarette case from the night table, takes out two cigarettes, lights both and gives her one.*]

ACTRESS: By the way, you haven't said a word yet about my performance last night.

POET: What performance?

ACTRESS: Well.

POET: Ah yes. I wasn't at the theater.

ACTRESS: You do like to make jokes.

POET: Absolutely not. After you'd cancelled the day before yesterday,

I assumed that you still wouldn't be in full possession of your powers last night, so I decided not to go.

ACTRESS: Well, you certainly missed a lot.

POET: I did?

ACTRESS: It was sensational!! The people turned pale.

POET: I suppose you actually saw them?

ACTRESS: Benno said: My child, you performed divinely.

POET: Hmm! . . . And yet you were so sick just the day before.

ACTRESS: Of course—and I was, too. Do you know why? Out of longing for you.

POET: A while ago you said that you cancelled the performance just to annoy me.

ACTRESS: But what do you know about my love for you? Of course, all that leaves you cold. And I've been lying in bed for nights on end with a high fever. One hundred and four degrees!

POET: That is rather high, for a whim.

ACTRESS: You call that a whim? I'm dying of love for you, and you call it a whim—?!

POET: And Fritz? . . .

ACTRESS: Fritz! . . . Don't talk to me about that galley slave!—

IX. THE ACTRESS AND THE COUNT

[*The bedroom of the* ACTRESS. *Very luxuriously furnished. It is twelve noon. The blinds are still down; a candle is burning on the night table; the* ACTRESS *is still lying in her canopied bed, numerous newspapers strewn on the covers. The* COUNT *enters, in the uniform of a captain of the mounted dragoons. He stops at the door.*]

ACTRESS: Ah, Herr Count.

COUNT: Her ladyship your mother has given me permission; otherwise I would not have—

ACTRESS: Please, come closer.

COUNT: I kiss your hand. Pardon me—having just come in off the street . . . I can't see a thing yet. Well . . . here we are—[*at her bed*]—I kiss your hand.

ACTRESS: Won't you sit down, Herr Count.

COUNT: Her ladyship your mother said that you were indisposed . . . I hope it is nothing serious, Fräulein.

ACTRESS: Nothing serious? I was near death!

COUNT: Good heavens, why how can that be possible?

ACTRESS: In any case, it's very nice of you to take the trouble to come over.

COUNT: Near death! And yet you performed so divinely last night.

ACTRESS: It was a great triumph, wasn't it?

COUNT: Magnificent! . . . The entire audience was swept away. As for my own feelings . . .

ACTRESS: Thank you for the beautiful flowers.

COUNT: You're quite welcome, Fräulein.

ACTRESS [*directing her eyes toward a large basket of flowers on a small table at the window*]: There they are.

COUNT: You were literally showered with garlands and flowers last night.

ACTRESS: They're all still lying in my dressing room. I brought just yours home with me.

COUNT [*kissing her hand*]: That is very kind of you.

[*The* ACTRESS *suddenly takes his hand and kisses it.*]

COUNT: But Fräulein.

ACTRESS: Don't be alarmed, Herr Count, that doesn't put you under any obligation at all.

COUNT: You are a strange creature . . . one might even say an enigma.—

[*Pause.*]

ACTRESS: I'm sure Fräulein Birken is easier to figure out.

COUNT: Yes, little Birken is no problem, but of course, I know her only slightly.

ACTRESS: Ha!

COUNT: Believe me. But you are a problem. The kind I've always longed for. I just didn't realize the great pleasure I missed until yesterday, when I saw you act . . . for the first time.

ACTRESS: How can that be?

COUNT: Well, you see, Fräulein, it is difficult for me to get to the theater. I am accustomed to dining late . . . Then, by the time I arrive, the best part is past. Isn't that true?

ACTRESS: Then you must eat earlier from now on.

COUNT: Yes, I already thought about that. Or about not even dining at all, perhaps. Actually, I don't really enjoy dining anymore.

ACTRESS: Just what sort of pleasure does a young old man like you enjoy now?

COUNT: I sometimes ask myself the same question! But I'm not an old man. There must be another reason.

ACTRESS: Do you think so?

COUNT: Yes. For instance, Louie says I'm a philosopher. What he means, Fräulein, is that I think too much.

ACTRESS: Yes . . . thinking, that can cause problems.

COUNT: I have too much time on my hands—that's why I do so much thinking. You see, Fräulein, I thought, if they would transfer me to Vienna, then things would get better. There's amusement here, stimulation. But basically it's really no different here than it was up there.

ACTRESS: Where is "up there"?

COUNT: You know, Fräulein, down there in Hungary, in the small towns, where I was generally stationed.

ACTRESS: Whatever were you doing in Hungary?

COUNT: Well, as I say, Fräulein, the military service.

ACTRESS: But why did you stay so long in Hungary?

COUNT: Well, that's just the way it happens.

ACTRESS: It must be enough to drive a person insane.

COUNT: But why? Actually, there's more for a person to do there than here. You know, Fräulein, there are recruits to be trained, cavalry horses to be broken in . . . and of course the countryside isn't as bad as they say. Some of it is quite beautiful, the lowlands—and such a sunset. It's too bad I'm not a painter. I sometimes thought if I were a painter, I'd paint it. There was one in the regiment, a young fellow, named Splany, who could have done it.—But here I'm telling you dull stories, Fräulein.

ACTRESS: Oh please, I'm enjoying myself royally.

COUNT: You know, Fräulein, you're easy to talk to; Louie told me that. And that's something one seldom finds.

ACTRESS: Well of course, in Hungary.

COUNT: But it's like that in Vienna too! People are the same all over. It's just that there are more people here, that's the only difference. Tell me, Fräulein, do you really like people?

ACTRESS: Like—?? I hate them! I can't even look at them! I never even see people. I'm always alone, no one ever sets foot in this house.

COUNT: You see, I thought you were really a misanthrope. That must occur often with artists. When one's up there in higher realms like that . . . well, you're better off. Anyway, at least you know what you're living for!

ACTRESS: Who told you that? I haven't the slightest idea what I'm living for!

COUNT: If you please, Fräulein—famous—celebrated—

ACTRESS: Do you think that's happiness!

COUNT: Happiness! Please, Fräulein, happiness doesn't exist. None of those things that people talk about most really exist . . . love, for instance. It's the same sort of thing.

ACTRESS: You may be right about that.

COUNT: Pleasure . . . intoxication . . . all well and good. I've nothing to say against them . . . they are safe. I'm experiencing pleasure right now . . . good, I know it. Or I'm intoxicated, that's nice too. That's also safe. And when it's over, it's simply over.

ACTRESS [*grandly*]: It's over.

COUNT: But if one doesn't, how shall I say, yield to the moment, and starts thinking about the future or the past . . . then it's just finished. The future . . . is sad . . . the past is uncertain . . . In short, it only gets confusing. Am I right?

ACTRESS [*nodding, her eyes wide open*]: You seem to have grasped the essence of it, Count.

COUNT: And you see, Fräulein, once one understands that, then it's all the same, whether one lives in Vienna or on the plains of Hungary or even in the small town of Steinamanger. For example . . . where may I put my cap? Oh, thank you . . . what were we talking about just now?

ACTRESS: The small town of Steinamanger.

COUNT: Right. So, as I say, there's not much difference. Whether I spend the evening at the officers' mess or at the club, it really doesn't matter.

ACTRESS: And how does all this relate to love?

COUNT: Well, if a man believes in it, there will always be someone there who loves him.

ACTRESS: Fräulein Birken, for instance.

COUNT: I really don't understand why you keep bringing up poor little Birken, Fräulein.

ACTRESS: She is your mistress, after all.

COUNT: So who told you that?

ACTRESS: Everyone knows that.

COUNT: Everyone except me—that's remarkable.

ACTRESS: Well, you did fight a duel because of her!

COUNT: Perhaps I was shot dead and didn't even notice it.

ACTRESS: You are a man of honor, my dear Count. Come sit closer.

COUNT: With your permission.

ACTRESS: Over here.

[*She draws him to her and runs her hand through his hair.*]

I knew you would come today!

COUNT: Oh, and why?

ACTRESS: I knew it last night at the theater.

COUNT: Could you see me from the stage?

ACTRESS: But my dear man! Couldn't you tell that I was acting just for you?

COUNT: Can it be possible?

ACTRESS: My heart took wing when I saw you sitting in the front row!

COUNT: Took wing? Because of me? I had no idea that you even noticed me!

ACTRESS: You can drive a woman to desperation with that lofty manner of yours.

COUNT: Certainly, Fräulein . . .

ACTRESS: "Certainly, Fräulein"?! . . . Well, at least unbuckle your saber!

COUNT: With your permission.

[*He unbuckles his saber, leans it against the bed.*]

ACTRESS: And now just give me a kiss.

[*The* COUNT *kisses her; she does not let go of him.*]

ACTRESS: If only I'd never set eyes on you.

COUNT: It's better this way, after all!—

ACTRESS: Sir, you are a poseur!

COUNT: I—Why do you say that?

ACTRESS: Can you imagine how happy most men would be if they could be in your situation right now!

COUNT: I'm very happy.

ACTRESS: Well, I thought there was no such thing as happiness. Why are you looking at me that way? Why Count, I do believe you are afraid of me!

COUNT: As I say, Fräulein, you are a problem.

ACTRESS: Oh, don't bother me with your philosophy . . . come to me. And now ask me for anything at all . . . you can have everything you want. You're far too handsome.

COUNT: All right, with your permission then—[*kissing her hand*]—I shall return this evening.

ACTRESS: This evening . . . but I am performing.

COUNT: After the performance.

ACTRESS: You ask for nothing else?

COUNT: I will ask for everything else after the performance.

ACTRESS [*injured*]: Then ask all you want, you miserable poseur.

COUNT: You see, Fräulein . . . my dear, we've been so open with each other up until now. . . . To me it would be so much nicer tonight, after the theater . . . more comfortable than now, when . . . Right now I keep feeling as if the door could open at any moment . . .

ACTRESS: It doesn't open from the outside.

COUNT: I just think it would be foolish to spoil something at the beginning which might possibly turn out to be quite beautiful.

ACTRESS: Might possibly! . . .

COUNT: To tell the truth, I think love in the morning is horrible.

ACTRESS: Well—you are the most insane man I have ever run across!

COUNT: I'm not talking about just any female . . . of course, in the end, it is generally the same. But women like you . . . no, Fräulein, you can call me a fool as much as you wish. But women like you . . . are not to be had . . . before breakfast. And therefore . . . you see . . . therefore . . .

ACTRESS: God, but you're sweet!

COUNT: You do understand what I said, don't you? The way I picture it—

ACTRESS: Well, how do you picture it?

COUNT: I imagine . . . I'm waiting for you in a coach after the theater, then we drive together somewhere for supper—

ACTRESS: I'm not Fräulein Birken.

COUNT: I certainly didn't say you were. I just feel that the mood of the thing is important. It's only after supper that I get into the right mood. That's the nicest part, driving home together after supper, and then . . .

ACTRESS: And then what?

COUNT: Then . . . that depends on how things develop.

ACTRESS: Come sit closer. Closer.

COUNT [*sitting down on the bed*]: There seems to be a wonderful aroma . . . coming from the pillows—jasmine, isn't it?

ACTRESS: It's very hot in here, don't you think?

[*The* COUNT *bends down and kisses her neck.*]

ACTRESS: But my dear Count, that certainly goes against your plans.

COUNT: What are you talking about? I have no plans.

[*The* ACTRESS *draws him to her.*]

COUNT: It really is hot.

ACTRESS: Do you think so? And so dark, as if it were evening . . . [*Seizing him*] It is evening . . . it is night . . . Close your eyes, if it's too bright for you. Come! . . . Come! . . .

[*The* COUNT *no longer resists.*]

* * * * *

ACTRESS: Now what was that about being in the mood, you poseur?

COUNT: You're a little devil.

ACTRESS: Why Count! What a thing to say.

COUNT: Well then, an angel.

ACTRESS: And you really should have been an actor! Honestly! You certainly understand women! And do you know what I'm going to do now?

COUNT: Well?

ACTRESS: I'm going to tell you that I never want to see you again.

COUNT: But why?

ACTRESS: No, no. You're too dangerous for me! You could drive a woman crazy. You stand there now, as if nothing had happened.

COUNT: But . . .

ACTRESS: I ask you to remember, my dear Count, that I was your lover just now.

COUNT: How could I ever forget!

ACTRESS: Then what about tonight?

COUNT: And what do you mean by that?

ACTRESS: Well—you did want to wait for me after the theater, didn't you?

COUNT: Very well, then what about the day after tomorrow?

ACTRESS: What's that about the day after tomorrow? We were talking about tonight.

COUNT: There really wouldn't be much sense in that.

ACTRESS: You old man!

COUNT: You just don't understand. I mean it more—how shall I say—from the standpoint of the soul.

ACTRESS: What does your soul have to do with it?

COUNT: Well, believe me, that's an important part of it. It's a fallacy to try to separate the two.

ACTRESS: Don't bother me with your philosophy. If I want that, I'll read a book.

COUNT: One never really learns from books.

ACTRESS: That's probably true! And that's why you should wait for me tonight. We'll agree about your soul then, you rogue!

COUNT: All right then, with your permission, I'll send my coach . . .

ACTRESS: You'll wait for me here, at my place—

COUNT: . . . After the performance.

ACTRESS: Of course.

[*He buckles on his saber.*]

ACTRESS: Whatever are you doing?

COUNT: I think it's time for me to go. Actually, I'm sure I've stayed too long already for a formal call.

ACTRESS: Well, tonight won't be a formal call.

COUNT: Do you think so?

ACTRESS: Let me attend to that. And now give me one more kiss, my little philosopher. Oh, you seducer, you . . . sweet child, you kidnapper, you polecat . . . you . . .

[*After she has vehemently kissed him several times, she vehemently shoves him away from her.*]

My dear Count, it was a great honor for me!

COUNT: I kiss your hand, Fräulein! [*At the door*] Au revoir.

ACTRESS: Adieu, small town of Steinamanger!

X. THE COUNT AND THE PROSTITUTE

[*Morning, toward six. A shabby room with one window; the dirty yellowish blinds are down. Threadbare green curtains. A bureau with a few photographs on it and a cheap, strikingly tasteless woman's hat. Cheap Japanese fans behind the mirror. A table covered by a reddish protective cloth and a kerosene lamp, burning with a dim, smelly flame beneath a yellow paper lampshade. Beside the lamp, a jug with leftover beer and a half-empty glass. On the floor beside the bed, women's clothes are lying in disarray, as if they had been quickly pulled off. The* PROSTITUTE *is lying asleep in bed, breathing quietly. The* COUNT *is lying on the sofa, fully dressed, in a topcoat of artificial leather; his hat is lying on the floor at the head of the sofa.*]

COUNT [*moves, rubs his eyes, arises quickly, remains sitting up, looks around*]: Well, how did I get . . . Ah yes. . . . Then I did go home with that woman after all . . .

[*He gets up quickly, sees her in bed.*]

Well there she is . . . The things that can still happen to a man my age. I have no idea; did they carry me up here, I wonder? No . . . well, I did see—I came into the room . . . well . . . I was still awake then or had waked up . . . or . . . or maybe it's just that this room reminds me of something? . . . Good lord, oh well . . . yes . . . I did see it yesterday . . . [*Looking at his watch*] Just what! Yesterday, a few hours ago—But I knew something had to happen . . . I felt it . . . Yesterday when I started drinking, I felt it . . . But what did happen? . . . so, nothing . . . or did it? . . . Good lord . . . nothing like this has happened to me . . . for . . . at least ten years now, where I didn't know . . . Well, the fact is, I was simply soused. If only I could remember just when . . . Anyway, I know exactly when I went with Louie into that whores' café and . . . no, no . . . We were still together when we left Sacher's Hotel . . . and then, on the way, he was already . . . Yes, that's it, I rode in my coach with Louie . . . Why am I racking my brain then? It doesn't make any difference anyway. Let's just get out of here.

[*He gets up. The lamp rocks.*]

Oh! [*Looking at the sleeping girl*] At least she's sound asleep. I just don't know what happened.—I'll put some money for her on the nightstand . . . and then so long . . .

[*He stands in front of her, looks at her for a long time.*]

If only one didn't know what she is!

[*He gazes at her for a long time.*]

I've known many women who didn't look so virtuous even in their sleep. Good lord . . . Of course, Louie would say I'm philosophizing again, but it's true, it seems to me, sleep makes us all equal, just like its brother, death . . . Hmm, if only I knew whether . . . No, I'm sure I would remember . . . No, no, I passed out on the couch here before . . . nothing happened . . . It's unbelievable how women tend to look alike when . . . Well, let's go.

[*He is about to leave.*]

Oh, that's right.

[*He takes his wallet and is all set to take out a bill.*]

PROSTITUTE [*waking up*]: Well . . . who's this, up so early?—[*Recognizing him*] Hi, baby.

COUNT: Good morning. Sleep well?

PROSTITUTE [*stretching herself*]: Ah, come here. Give me a little kiss.

COUNT [*bending down toward her, reflects, pulling back away*]: I was just leaving . . .

PROSTITUTE: Leaving?

COUNT: It's high time, after all.

PROSTITUTE: You want to leave like this?

COUNT [*almost embarrassed*]: Like this . . .

PROSTITUTE: So long, then; come again some other time.

COUNT: Yes, God be with you. Well, won't you offer me your little hand?

[*The* PROSTITUTE *gives him her hand from beneath the covers.*]

COUNT [*takes her hand and kisses it mechanically; notices that and laughs*]: Like the hand of a princess. You know, when one sees only . . .

PROSTITUTE: Why are you looking at me like that?

COUNT: When one sees only your little head, like this . . . every woman does indeed look innocent when she first wakes up . . . Good lord, a man might imagine anything and everything were possible, if it weren't for that stench of kerosene . . .

PROSTITUTE: Yeah, that lamp's always been a problem.

COUNT: Just how old are you, anyway?

PROSTITUTE: Well, what do you think?

COUNT: Twenty-four.

PROSTITUTE: Oh sure!

COUNT: Are you older than that?

PROSTITUTE: I'm going on twenty.

COUNT: And how long have you been . . .

PROSTITUTE: How long I have been in the business? A year!

COUNT: Well, you sure did start early.

PROSTITUTE: Better too early than too late.

COUNT [*sitting down on the bed*]: But tell me, are you really happy?

PROSTITUTE: Am I what?

COUNT: All right, I mean, are you doing well?

PROSTITUTE: Oh, I'm always doing well.

COUNT: I see . . . Listen, hasn't it ever occurred to you that you might be something else?

PROSTITUTE: What should I be, then?

COUNT: All right . . . You really are, after all, a beautiful girl. Perhaps you could have a lover, for example.

PROSTITUTE: What makes you think I don't?

COUNT: Yes, I know—but I mean one, you know, one who supports you, so that you don't have to go with just anyone.

PROSTITUTE: I don't go with just anyone. Thank God, I don't need that, I just pick them out.

[*The* COUNT *looks around the room.*]

PROSTITUTE [*noticing that*]: Next month we're moving downtown, to Spiegel Street.

COUNT: We? Who's we?

PROSTITUTE: Well, the madam and the couple of other girls who live here too.

COUNT: There are others living here too?—

PROSTITUTE: Next door here . . . don't you hear it . . . that's Millie, she was in the café too.

COUNT: Somebody's snoring in there.

PROSTITUTE: That's Millie, all right, she'll go on snoring all day now, until ten o'clock tonight. Then she'll get up and go down to the café.

COUNT: But that's a dreadful life.

PROSTITUTE: It sure is. And it makes the madam sore too. But I'm always out on the streets by twelve noon.

COUNT: What are you doing on the streets by noon?

PROSTITUTE: What am I doing? I just make my rounds.

COUNT: Ah yes . . . of course . . .

[*He gets up, takes out his wallet, and lays a bill for her on the nightstand.*]

Adieu!

PROSTITUTE: Are you going then . . . ? Well, so long . . . Come again soon.

[*She lies down on her side.*]

COUNT [*stopping again*]: Listen, tell me. Does all this really matter to you anymore?—Does it?

PROSTITUTE: Does what matter?

COUNT: I mean, don't you enjoy it anymore?

PROSTITUTE [*yawning*]: I just want to sleep.

COUNT: It doesn't really matter to you, whether a man is young or old, or whether a man . . .

PROSTITUTE: What are you asking me?

COUNT: . . . Well, it's just—[*suddenly coming to something*]—good lord, now I know who you remind me of, it's . . .

PROSTITUTE: Do I look like somebody?

COUNT: Unbelievable, unbelievable—but now I ask you, please, don't say anything at all, at least for a minute . . .

[*He looks at her.*]

The very same face, the very same face.

[*He suddenly kisses her on the eyes.*]

PROSTITUTE: Well . . .

COUNT: Good lord, it's too bad that you . . . aren't something else. . . . You could be a real success!

PROSTITUTE: You're just like Franz.

COUNT: Who is Franz?

PROSTITUTE: He's a waiter at the café we girls go to.

COUNT: How am I just like Franz?

PROSTITUTE: He's always saying I could be a success too, and that I should marry him.

COUNT: Why don't you?

PROSTITUTE: Thanks a lot . . . I don't want to get married. No, not for any price. Maybe later.

COUNT: Those eyes . . . those very same eyes . . . Louie would say for sure I'm a fool—but I want to kiss you on the eyes once more . . . like this . . . and now God be with you, I'm going now.

PROSTITUTE: So long . . .

COUNT [*at the door*]: Say . . . tell me . . . doesn't it surprise you at all that . . . ?

PROSTITUTE: That what?

COUNT: That I don't want anything from you?

PROSTITUTE: There's lots of men who aren't up to it early in the morning.

COUNT: Oh well . . . [*To himself*] It's stupid of me to want her to be surprised. . . . All right, so long.

[*He is at the door.*]

I'm actually annoyed. I know, of course, it's only the money that such women . . . it's nice that . . . but why say "such women" . . . at least she doesn't pretend . . . say—I'll tell you what, I'll come back very soon.

PROSTITUTE [*with eyes closed*]: Good.

COUNT: When are you at home?

PROSTITUTE: I'm always at home. Just ask for Léocadia.

COUNT: Léocadia . . . Fine—Well, God be with you. [*At the door*] My head's still foggy from that wine. This is absurd . . . Here I am with a woman like this and I do nothing but kiss her on the eyes, because she reminds me of someone . . . [*Turning to her*] Say, Léocadia, does it happen very often that people leave you like this?

PROSTITUTE: Like what?

COUNT: Like I am.

PROSTITUTE: You mean early in the morning?

COUNT: No . . . does it happen often that a man comes to you, and doesn't ask for anything?

PROSTITUTE: No, that's never happened to me before.

COUNT: Well then, what are you thinking? Do you suppose I don't like you?

PROSTITUTE: Why shouldn't you like me? You certainly liked me last night.

COUNT: I like you now, too.

PROSTITUTE: But you liked me better last night.

COUNT: What makes you believe that?

PROSTITUTE: Well, why are you asking these stupid questions?

COUNT: Last night . . . I see. Well, tell me, didn't I pass out on the couch before . . . ?

PROSTITUTE: But of course you did . . . along with me.

COUNT: With you?

PROSTITUTE: Yes, well, don't you remember?

COUNT: I've . . . we've both . . . of course . . .

PROSTITUTE: But you fell asleep right away.

COUNT: I did, right away . . . I see . . . So, that's the way it was! . . .

PROSTITUTE: Yes, baby. But you sure must have been good and drunk, if you still don't remember that.

COUNT: Well . . . —And yet . . . there is a certain similarity . . . So long . . . [*Listening intently*] Well, what's that?

PROSTITUTE: The chambermaid's up already. Just give her something on your way out. The outside door's open, you won't have to tip the janitor.

COUNT: Yes. [*In the entryway*] All right . . . It certainly would have been nice, if I had only kissed her on the eyes. That would have come close to being an adventure . . . But it simply wasn't my destiny.

[*The* CHAMBERMAID *stands at the door; opens it.*]

Ah—there you are . . . Good night.—

CHAMBERMAID: Good morning.

COUNT: Yes, of course . . . good morning . . . good morning.

[*Curtain*]

The Green Cockatoo

Characters

Prospère, *proprietor and bartender of the Green Cockatoo, formerly managing director of a theater*

Grasset, *an intellectual*

Lebrêt, *a tailor*

Police Inspector

Grain, *a tramp*

Scaevola

Jules

Henri Baston

Léocadia, *an actress, Henri's wife*

Viscount François de Nogeant

Chevalier Albin de la Tremouille

Michette

Flipotte

Duke Émile de Cadignan

Guillaume

The Marquis de Lansac

Séverine, *his wife*

Rollin, *a poet*

Georgette

Balthasar

Maurice

Étienne

Aristocrats, actors and actresses, citizens and their wives

~

Prospère's tavern, in Paris, the evening of July 14, 1789

[*The Green Cockatoo barroom. A rather small basement room. In the distant background, right, seven steps lead to the street entrance, closed off by a door. A second door, left, barely visible backstage. A number of small wooden tables take up almost the entire room. The bar is left center; behind it a number of small barrels and wine casks. The room is illuminated by oil lamps hanging from the ceiling. The bartender,* PROSPÈRE, *is onstage. Enter citizens* LEBRÊT *and* GRASSET.]

GRASSET [*still on the stairs*]: In here, Lebrêt, I know this place. My old friend the director will still have a barrel of wine hidden somewhere, even though all Paris is dying of thirst.

PROSPÈRE: Good evening, Grasset. So, are you back here again? All done with theorizing? Do you want an acting job with me again?

GRASSET: Yes, of course! Bring some wine. I'm a guest here—and you're the bartender.

PROSPÈRE: Wine? Where should I get some wine? Tonight they plundered all the wine cellars in Paris. And I'll bet you were in on that.

GRASSET: Out with the wine—for the mob that will be here an hour from now . . . [*Listening intently*] Do you hear something, Lebrêt?

LEBRÊT: It's like a soft rolling of thunder.

GRASSET: Good—citizens of Paris . . .[*To* PROSPÈRE] You've surely got one more barrel on hand for the mob. Bring it out. My friend and admirer Citizen Lebrêt, a tailor from the Rue St. Honoré, is paying for everything.

LEBRÊT: Sure, sure, I'm paying.

[PROSPÈRE *hesitates.*]

GRASSET: Show him you've got money, Lebrêt.

[LEBRÊT *pulls out his purse.*]

PROSPÈRE: Well, I'll see if I . . .

[*He opens the tap of a barrel and fills two glasses.*]

Where did you come from, Grasset? From the Palais Royal?

GRASSET: I certainly did . . . I gave a speech there. So you see, my dear sir, it's my turn now. Do you know who spoke just ahead of me?

PROSPÈRE: Well?

GRASSET: Camille Desmoulins! Of course, I took a risk. And tell me, Lebrêt, who got more applause, Desmoulins or I?

LEBRÊT: You . . . no doubt.

GRASSET: And how did I do?

LEBRÊT: Magnificently.

GRASSET: Do you hear that, Prospère? I stood up there on the table . . . I looked monumental . . . I certainly did—and a thousand, five thousand, ten thousand people all gathered around me—just like they did earlier around Camille Desmoulins . . . and cheered me on.

LEBRÊT: They cheered louder for you.

GRASSET: They certainly did . . . not by much, but louder. And now they're all marching over to the Bastille . . . and, if I may say so, they obeyed my call. By nightfall it'll be ours, I swear to you.

PROSPÈRE: Yes, of course, if the walls would only collapse from your speeches!

GRASSET: How's that . . . ? Speeches!—Are you deaf?—Now there's shooting going on. Our good soldiers are in on that. They've got that same diabolically passionate hatred for that accursed prison as we do. They know that their fathers and brothers are locked up behind those walls. . . . But they wouldn't be shooting if we hadn't spoken. My dear Prospère, the power of the spirit is enormous. There— [*To* LEBRÊT] Where do you have the documents?

LEBRÊT [*pulling pamphlets out of his pocket*]: Here . . .

GRASSET: Here are the most recent pamphlets that were just distributed at the Palais Royal. Here's one by my friend Cerutti, "A Statement for the French People," here's one by Desmoulins, who, to be sure, speaks better than he writes . . . "France, the Free Country."

PROSPÈRE: Well, when will we finally get to see yours, the one you're always telling us about?

GRASSET: We don't need any more. The time for action has come. Whoever sits behind his four walls today is a scoundrel. Anyone who's a man must be out in the streets!

LEBRÊT: Bravo, bravo!

GRASSET: In Toulon they killed the mayor, in Brignolles they plundered a dozen residences . . . but here in Paris we are still bored, and we put up with everything.

PROSPÈRE: But that can't be said any longer.

LEBRÊT [*who has been drinking all along*]: Arise, you citizens, arise!

GRASSET: Arise! . . . Close your store, and join us now!

PROSPÈRE: Well, I'll join you when the time is right.

GRASSET: Yes, of course, when there's no more danger.

PROSPÈRE: My dear sir, I love freedom just as much as you—but above all I have to think about my job.

GRASSET: For the citizens of Paris, there's only one job now: to free their brothers.

PROSPÈRE: Yes, for those who don't have anything else to do!

LEBRÊT: What's he saying there! . . . He's mocking us!

PROSPÈRE: That didn't occur to me in the least.—It's best that you leave now . . . my performance starts soon. I can't use you here.

LEBRÊT: What kind of performance? . . . Is there a theater here?

PROSPÈRE: Certainly it's a theater. Your friend played a part here just two weeks ago.

LEBRÊT: You had a part here, Grasset? . . . Why did you let that fellow get away with mocking you!

GRASSET: Calm down . . . it's true, I had a part here, because this isn't your ordinary bar . . . it's a hangout for criminals . . . come on . . .

PROSPÈRE: Pay up first.

LEBRÊT: If this is a hangout for criminals then I'll not pay a sou.

PROSPÈRE: Well after all, just explain to your friend where he is.

GRASSET: It's a strange place! People come here and play the part of criminals—and then there are others who are criminals without realizing it.

LEBRÊT: Well—?

GRASSET: Let me call your attention to the fact that what I said just now was very witty and could mean the success of an entire performance.

LEBRÊT: I don't understand anything you're saying.

GRASSET: Why, I told you that Prospère was my director. And he's still putting on plays with his people, only of a different kind than before. My former colleagues sit around here and act as if they were criminals. Do you understand? They tell hair-raising stories they've never experienced—they speak of outrages they haven't committed . . . and the audience that comes here has the thrilling sensation of sitting among the most dangerous rabble of Paris—among rogues, burglars, murderers—and—

LEBRÊT: What kind of audience?

PROSPÈRE: The most elegant people of Paris.

GRASSET: Aristocrats . . .

PROSPÈRE: Gentlemen from the royal court—

LEBRÊT: Down with them!

GRASSET: For them it's something that wakes up their wearied senses. This is where I started out, Lebrêt; this is where I gave my first speech, as if it were a joke . . . and here I began to hate those filthy dogs who sat among us in their pretty clothes, smelling of perfume, corroded . . . And it's quite all right with me, my good friend Lebrêt, that you also get to see the location of where your distinguished friend got his start. [*In a different tone*] Say, Prospère, if the thing were to go wrong . . .

PROSPÈRE: What thing?

GRASSET: Well, the thing with my political career . . . Would you give me an acting job again?

PROSPÈRE: Not for the world.

GRASSET [*lightly*]: Why not?—Perhaps someone else could have a chance besides your Henri.

PROSPÈRE: Apart from that . . . I'd be afraid that you might forget yourself at some point—and fall upon one of my paying customers in all seriousness.

GRASSET [*flattered*]: Well, that might just be possible.

PROSPÈRE: I . . . I still have myself under control after all—

GRASSET: Now really, Prospère, I must say that I could admire you and your self-control if I didn't happen to know that you're a coward.

PROSPÈRE: Ah, my dear sir, what I accomplish in my line of work is enough for me. It gives me pleasure enough when I can tell those fellows to their faces what I think and can insult them to my heart's content—while they regard it as fun. That's also a way of giving vent to one's rage—

[*He pulls out a dagger and admires its sparkle.*]

LEBRÊT: Citizen Prospère, what's that supposed to mean?

GRASSET: Don't be afraid. I'll wager the dagger isn't even sharpened.

PROSPÈRE: But you could be wrong about that, my friend. Someday the time will come when the joke definitely will turn serious—and I'm prepared for that in any and all events.

GRASSET: That time is near. We are living in an eminent era! Come, Citizen. Lebrêt, let us go to our people. Farewell, Prospère, either you'll see me again as a distinguished figure or never again.

LEBRÊT [*staggering*]: As a distinguished figure . . . or . . . never again—

[*They exit.* PROSPÈRE *remains onstage, sits down on a table, opens up a pamphlet, and reads aloud.*]

PROSPÈRE: "Now the beast is caught in the trap: strangle it!"—He doesn't write badly, that little Desmoulins. "Never have the victorious been offered greater booty. Forty thousand palaces and castles, two-fifths of all the estates shall be the reward for bravery—they who believe themselves conquerors will be enslaved, the nation shall be purified."

[*The* POLICE INSPECTOR *enters.*]

PROSPÈRE [*eyeing him*]: Well, is the rabble reporting in early today?

POLICE INSPECTOR: Don't joke with me, my dear Prospère—I'm the police inspector for your district.

PROSPÈRE: And how can I be of service?

POLICE INSPECTOR: I'm directed to be present in your establishment this very evening.

PROSPÈRE: That will be a special honor for me.

POLICE INSPECTOR: That's not what it's about, my good man. The authorities want clarification as to what is actually going on at your place. For some weeks now—

PROSPÈRE: This is a place of amusement, Inspector, nothing more.

POLICE INSPECTOR: Let me finish. For some weeks now this establishment is said to be the scene of dissolute orgies.

PROSPÈRE: You've been badly informed, Inspector. They're having fun here, nothing more.

POLICE INSPECTOR: That's how it starts out. I know. But my report says it ends up differently. Weren't you an actor?

PROSPÈRE: Managing director, Inspector, managing director of a distinguished troupe which last performed in the Rue St. Denis.

POLICE INSPECTOR: That's immaterial. Didn't you acquire a small inheritance?

PROSPÈRE: Not worth talking about, Inspector.

POLICE INSPECTOR: Didn't your troupe dissolve?

PROSPÈRE: So did my inheritance.

POLICE INSPECTOR [*smiling*]: Very good. [*Both smile.—Suddenly serious*] And then you set up a tavern?

PROSPÈRE: Which did wretchedly.

POLICE INSPECTOR: —Whereupon you hit on an idea which, it cannot be denied, was a bit ingenious.

PROSPÈRE: You flatter me, Inspector.

POLICE INSPECTOR: You have assembled your troupe again to perform a type of peculiarly offensive comedy.

PROSPÈRE: If it were offensive, Inspector, I wouldn't have my audience—which, I may say, is the most genteel audience in Paris. The Viscount de Nogeant is my daily customer. The Marquis de

Lansac comes frequently, and the Duke de Cadignan, Inspector, is a most zealous admirer of my number-one actor, the illustrious Henri Baston.

POLICE INSPECTOR: And probably an admirer of the art, or arts, of your female artists as well.

PROSPÈRE: If you knew those little female artists of mine, Inspector, you wouldn't blame anyone in the whole world for that.

POLICE INSPECTOR: Enough. It has been reported to the authorities that the entertainments offered by your—how shall I say it—

PROSPÈRE: The word "artists" would suffice.

POLICE INSPECTOR: I'll settle for the word "personnel"—that the entertainments offered by your personnel exceed the permissible in every sense. Speeches are said to have been delivered here by your—how shall I say it—by your artistic criminals . . . now, just how does my report put it . . . [*continues to look up in a notebook*]—that are not only immoral, which wouldn't bother us very much, but that are also quite capable of inciting rebellion.—In such an volatile period as the one in which we live, this can in no way be an immaterial matter to the authorities.

PROSPÈRE: Inspector, I can only counter this accusation by politely inviting you to observe it for yourself sometime. You will see that nothing at all rebellious happens here, simply because my audience wouldn't rebel. Only theatrical performances go on here—that's all.

POLICE INSPECTOR: I will not, of course, accept your invitation; however I will remain here on the authority of my official position.

PROSPÈRE: I believe I can promise you the best of entertainment, Inspector, but I would take the liberty of advising you to remove your official garb and to appear here in civilian dress. The spontaneity of my artists would suffer, as would the mood of my audience, if a police inspector were to be seen here—particularly in uniform.

POLICE INSPECTOR: You're right, Monsieur Prospère, I will withdraw and return as an elegant young man.

PROSPÈRE: That'll be easy for you, Inspector. Or you are even welcome as a rogue—but not as a police inspector—that would attract attention.

POLICE INSPECTOR [*exiting*]: Adieu.

PROSPÈRE [*bowing*]: Wait until that blessed day when I see you and all your kind . . .

[*The* INSPECTOR *encounters* GRAIN *at the door, who is in utter rags and who is alarmed to see the* POLICE INSPECTOR. *The latter first eyes him, smiles, and then turns obligingly to* PROSPÈRE.]

POLICE INSPECTOR: One of your artists is already here? . . .

[*He exits.*]

GRAIN [*speaking whiningly, in a voice full of pathos*]: Good evening.

PROSPÈRE [*after looking at him for a long time*]: If you are one of my troupe, you definitely have my approval, because I just don't recognize you.

GRAIN: What do you mean by that?

PROSPÈRE: Stop joking and take off the wig—I really would like to know who you are.

[*He seizes him by the hair.*]

GRAIN: Ouch!

PROSPÈRE: It's real after all—good grief—who are you? . . . You seem to be a genuine tramp after all.

GRAIN: Of course I am.

PROSPÈRE: Well, what do you want from me?

GRAIN: I have the honor of speaking with Citizen Prospère . . . the proprietor of the Green Cockatoo?

PROSPÈRE: That I am.

GRAIN: My name is Grain . . . at times Carniche . . . in some instances Blazing Brimstone—but I was imprisoned under the name of Grain, Citizen Prospère—and that's what matters.

PROSPÈRE: Ah—I understand. You want an acting job with me, and right now you're performing something for me. Fine and good. Continue.

GRAIN: Don't take me for a con man, Citizen Prospère. I am an honorable man. When I say that I was imprisoned, that's the whole truth.

[PROSPÈRE *looks at him askance.*]

GRAIN [*pulling a piece of paper out of his coat*]: Here, Citizen Prospère. You can see from this that I was released yesterday afternoon at four o'clock.

PROSPÈRE: "After two years' confinement"—good grief! This is real, after all!—

GRAIN: Did you still doubt that, Citizen Prospère?

PROSPÈRE: Just what were you up to, that they gave you two years—

GRAIN: They would've hanged me, but to my good fortune I was no more than a child when I killed my poor aunt.

PROSPÈRE: My good fellow, what's this about killing your aunt?

GRAIN: I wouldn't have done it, Citizen Prospère, if my aunt hadn't gone and deceived me with my best friend.

PROSPÈRE: Your aunt?

GRAIN: She certainly did—she was closer to me than aunts generally are with nephews. Relationships in our family were peculiar . . . I was embittered, extremely embittered. May I tell you about that?

PROSPÈRE: Tell it all the same, perhaps we'll be able to work out some arrangement.

GRAIN: My sister was no more than a child when she ran away from home—and what do you think—with whom?

PROSPÈRE: I can't guess.

GRAIN: With her uncle. And that man abandoned her—with a child.

PROSPÈRE: A real child, I should hope.

GRAIN: That's tactless of you, Citizen Prospère, to joke about such things.

PROSPÈRE: Let me tell you something, you Blazing Brimstone. The stories about your family bore me. Do you think I'm just here for every vagabond scoundrel to tell me stories about whom he's killed? What's all this got to do with me? I take it you want something or other from me—

GRAIN: Of course I do, Citizen Prospère. I am coming to ask you for work.

PROSPÈRE [*mockingly*]: May I call your attention to the fact that I don't have any aunts for you to murder here? This is a place of amusement.

GRAIN: Oh, that one time was enough for me. I want to become a respectable person—they referred me to you.

PROSPÈRE: Who, if I may ask?

GRAIN: An amiable young man who was locked up in my cell three days ago. Now he is alone. He's called Gaston . . . and you know him.—

PROSPÈRE: Gaston! Now I know why he's been absent for three nights now. One of my best pickpocket performers.—The stories he told—ah, that shook them.

GRAIN: It certainly did. And now they've caught him!

PROSPÈRE: How did they catch him? After all, he didn't really steal.

GRAIN: Yes he did. But it must have been the first time, for he seems to have been incredibly clumsy about it. Just think—[*confidingly*]—to reach into a lady's pocket on the Boulevard des Capucines—and simply pull out her purse—a complete amateur.—You inspire me with confidence, Citizen Prospère—and so I want to confess to you—there was a time when I, too, carried out little tricks of that kind, but never without my dear father. When I was still a child, when we were all still living together, when my poor aunt was still alive—

PROSPÈRE: Just what are you whining about? I find that tasteless! You'd killed her, didn't you?

GRAIN: Too late. But what I was going to say—hire me on here. I want to do just the reverse from Gaston. He played a criminal and became one—I . . .

PROSPÈRE: I'll try it out with you. Your outfit alone will be effective. And at a given moment you'll simply tell the thing about your aunt. How it was. Someone or other will just ask you.

GRAIN: I thank you, Citizen Prospère. And as far as my salary is concerned—

PROSPÈRE: Tonight you're making a guest appearance, since I can't pay you any salary for that yet.—You'll get enough to eat and drink . . . and I'll not haggle about a few francs for a night's lodging.

GRAIN: I thank you. And you can simply introduce me to your other colleagues as a guest performer from the provinces.

PROSPÈRE: Oh no . . . we'll tell them right away that you're a real murderer. They'll like that far better.

GRAIN: Excuse me, I certainly don't want to incriminate myself—but I don't understand you.

PROSPÈRE: When you've been with our theater longer, you'll start to understand.

[SCAEVOLA *and* JULES *enter.*]

SCAEVOLA: Good evening, Director!

PROSPÈRE: Proprietor . . . Just how many times do I need to tell you that it will spoil the whole joke if you call me "Director."

SCAEVOLA: Whatever you are, I don't think we'll be performing tonight.

PROSPÈRE: Well, why not?

SCAEVOLA: People won't be inclined.—There's a hellish uproar out in the streets, and people are screaming like madmen, especially in front of the Bastille.

PROSPÈRE: What concern is that to us? That clamor has been going on for months, and our audience hasn't stayed away. They're having a good time, just as before.

SCAEVOLA: Yes, like the gaiety of people who are about to be hanged.

PROSPÈRE: I just hope I live to see it!

SCAEVOLA: For the time being, give us something to drink to put me in the mood. I'm just not in the mood today.

PROSPÈRE: That frequently happens to you, my dear sir. I must tell you that I was thoroughly dissatisfied with you yesterday.

SCAEVOLA: In what way, may I ask?

PROSPÈRE: The story you gave us about the burglary was simply silly.

SCAEVOLA: Silly?

PROSPÈRE: It certainly was. Completely unbelievable. Bellowing alone just won't do it.

SCAEVOLA: I didn't bellow.

PROSPÈRE: But you're always bellowing. I'll just have to rehearse the pieces with you. One cannot rely on an inspiration like yours. That only works for Henri.

SCAEVOLA: Henri, it's always Henri. Henri is a ham. My burglary scene yesterday was a masterpiece. Henri will never produce anything like that in a lifetime.—If I'm not enough for you, my dear sir, I'll simply go to a decent theater. This really is a sleazy outfit anyway . . . Ah . . . [*Noticing* GRAIN] Now who is this? . . . This one certainly doesn't belong to our group! Perhaps you've hired someone new? What sort of getup does this fellow have on?

PROSPÈRE: Calm down, he's not a professional actor. He's a real murderer.

SCAEVOLA: Ah yes. . . . [*Going up to him*] Very pleased to get to know you. Scaevola is my name.

GRAIN: They call me Grain.

[*The whole time* JULES *has been walking around the tavern, sometimes stopping, like someone who is inwardly tortured.*]

PROSPÈRE: Well, what's wrong with you, Jules?

JULES: I'm learning my part.

PROSPÈRE: What sort of part?

JULES: Pangs of conscience. Today I'm playing a man who has pangs of conscience. Look at me. What do you think of the wrinkle here on my brow? Don't I look as if all the furies of hell . . . ?

[*He walks up and down.*]

SCAEVOLA [*bellowing*]: Wine—wine! Over here!

PROSPÈRE: Calm down . . . there's not even an audience here yet.

[HENRI *and* LÉOCADIA *come in.*]

HENRI: Good evening!

[*He greets the people seated behind him with a slight movement of his hand.*]

Good evening, gentlemen!

PROSPÈRE: Good evening, Henri! What's this I see? You—with Léocadia!

GRAIN [*has been attentively gazing at* LÉOCADIA; *to* SCAEVOLA]: I'm sure I know that woman . . .

[*He goes on speaking quietly to the others.*]

LÉOCADIA: Yes, my dear Prospère, here I am!

PROSPÈRE: I haven't seen you for a year. Let me welcome you!

[*He tries to kiss her.*]

HENRI: Stop that!—

[*His gaze frequently rests on* LÉOCADIA *with pride, passion, and also with a certain anxiety.*]

PROSPÈRE: But Henri . . . Old colleagues! . . . Your former director, Léocadia!

LÉOCADIA: Prospère, where did those good old days . . . !

PROSPÈRE: What are you sighing for! If anyone has ever been a success it's you! Of course, a beautiful young woman always has it easier than we do.

HENRI [*furiously*]: Stop that!

PROSPÈRE: Why do you keep screaming at me like that? Because you're back together with her again?

HENRI: Be quiet!—She became my wife yesterday.

PROSPÈRE: Your . . . ? [*To* LÉOCADIA] Is he joking?

LÉOCADIA: He really married me. Yes.—

PROSPÈRE: Then I congratulate you. So . . . Scaevola, Jules—Henri has gotten married.

SCAEVOLA [*coming forward*]: My best wishes!

[*He winks at* LÉOCADIA. JULES *likewise squeezes both their hands.*]

GRAIN [*to* PROSPÈRE]: Ah, how peculiar—I saw that woman . . . a couple of minutes after I got out, again.

PROSPÈRE: How's that?

GRAIN: That was the first beautiful woman I'd seen in two years. I was very moved. But it was a different gentleman with whom—

[*He goes on speaking to* PROSPÈRE.]

HENRI [*in a high-pitched tone, enthusiastic, but not declamatory*]: My beloved Léocadia, my wife! . . . Everything that happened before is now past. In a moment like this so much is blotted out.

[SCAEVOLA *and* JULES *have moved to the rear.* PROSPÈRE *moves forward again.*]

PROSPÈRE: What kind of moment?

HENRI: Now we are united by a holy sacrament. That is more than human vows. Now God is over us, everything that happened before can be forgotten. Léocadia, a new era is dawning. Everything will be holy, our kisses, Léocadia, as wild as they may be, are holy from now on. My beloved Léocadia, my wife! . . . [*Gazing at her with a glowing expression*] . . . Doesn't she have a different look about her from the one you knew before? Isn't her brow pure? What once was, is now blotted out. Isn't that true, Léocadia?

LÉOCADIA: Certainly, Henri.

HENRI: And everything is good. Tomorrow we leave Paris. Today Léocadia appears for the last time at the Porte de St. Martin, and today I perform for the last time with you.

PROSPÈRE [*disconcerted*]: Are you in your right mind, Henri?—You want to leave me? And the director of the Porte de St. Martin certainly won't consider releasing Léocadia. She is, after all, the success of his establishment. They say the young men, especially, flock there.

HENRI: Be quiet. Léocadia will go with me. She will never leave me. Tell me that you'll never leave me, Léocadia. [*Brutally*] Tell me!

LÉOCADIA: I'll never leave you!

HENRI: If you did, I'd . . . [*Pausing*] I've had enough of this life. I want some quiet. Quiet is what I want.

PROSPÈRE: But just what do you intend to do, Henri? Really, it's ridiculous. I'll make you a suggestion. Take Léocadia away from the Porte de St. Martin—but let her stay here, with me. I'll hire her. I'm short on talented actresses anyway.

HENRI: My decision is made, Prospère. We are leaving the city. We're going out into the country.

PROSPÈRE: Into the country? Where to?

HENRI: To my aged father, who lives alone in our poor village—whom I haven't seen in seven years. He scarcely hoped to see his prodigal son again. He'll be glad to take me in.

PROSPÈRE: What can you do in the country? They're starving in the country. Life's more than a thousand times worse for those people than in the city. Just what are you intending to do? You're not the sort of man to till the fields. Don't get that idea.

HENRI: People will see I'm that sort of man after all.

PROSPÈRE: Soon there'll be no more grain growing in all of France. You're heading for certain misery.

HENRI: Heading for happiness, Prospère. Aren't we, Léocadia? We often dreamed of that. I long for the peace and quiet of the broad landscape. Yes, Prospère, in my dreams I see myself walking across the fields with her in the evening, amid endless tranquillity, surrounded by the wonderful, comforting sky. Yes, we are fleeing this terrible and dangerous city. A magnificent peace will surround us. We've often dreamed of that, haven't we, Léocadia?

LÉOCADIA: Yes, we often have.

PROSPÈRE: Listen, Henri, you should think it over. I'll be glad to raise your salary, and I'll give Léocadia just as much as you.

LÉOCADIA: Are you listening, Henri?

PROSPÈRE: I really don't know who'll take your place here. None of my people has such priceless inspiration as you, none is as popular with my audience as you . . . Don't leave us!

HENRI: I certainly think nobody'll take my place.

PROSPÈRE: Then stay here with me, Henri!

[*He casts a glance at* LÉOCADIA; *she indicates that she'll take care of things.*]

HENRI: And I promise you, my departure will be hard for the audience—for *them,* not for me. Today—for my last appearance—I've arranged something that'll make all of them shudder . . . an inkling of the end of their world will come over them . . . for the end of their world is near. But I'll experience that only from afar . . . we'll be told about it out there, Léocadia, many days after it has happened. . . . But they'll shudder, I tell you. And you yourself will say: Henri never acted so well.

PROSPÈRE: What will you play? What? Do you know, Léocadia?

LÉOCADIA: I never do know anything.

HENRI: Well, doesn't anybody realize what kind of artist is hidden within me?

PROSPÈRE: Of course we realize it. And that's exactly why I'm saying that such talent shouldn't be buried out in the country. What an injustice to you! And to art!

HENRI: I couldn't care less for art. I want quiet. You don't understand that, Prospère. You've never been in love.

PROSPÈRE: Oh!—

HENRI: *I'm* so in love.—I want to be alone with her—that's it . . . Léocadia, that's the only way we can forget everything. But then we'll be so happy, as people have never been before. We'll have children—you'll make a fine mother, Léocadia, and a good wife. Everything, everything will be blotted out.

[*Long pause.*]

LÉOCADIA: It's getting late, Henri—I've got to go to the theater. Farewell, Prospère. I'm glad I finally got to see your famous place, where Henri celebrates such triumphs.

PROSPÈRE: Well, why didn't you ever come here before?

LÉOCADIA: Henri didn't want me to—well, you know, because of the young people I'd be sitting with here.

HENRI [*has moved toward the back*]: Give me a drink, Scaevola.

[*He drinks.*]

PROSPÈRE [*to* LÉOCADIA, *while* HENRI *can't hear*]: A real fool, that Henri—if only you had been *just* sitting with them here.

LÉOCADIA: Listen, I'll not stand for such remarks.

PROSPÈRE: I'll give you some advice, so pay attention, you stupid trash. He'll kill you someday.

LÉOCADIA: Just what's going on?

PROSPÈRE: You were seen only yesterday with one of your boyfriends again.

LÉOCADIA: That wasn't any boyfriend, you fool, that was . . .

HENRI [*turning hastily*]: What's wrong with you? No joking, if you please. Cut out that whispering. There are no more secrets. She's my wife.

PROSPÈRE: Well, what have you done about a wedding present for her?

LÉOCADIA: Oh Lord, he doesn't think about such things.

HENRI: Well, you'll still get it today.

LÉOCADIA: What is it then?

SCAEVOLA and JULES: What are you giving her?

HENRI [*quite seriously*]: When you've finished your scene, you can come over here and watch me act.

[*They laugh.*]

HENRI: A wife has never received a more magnificent wedding present. Come, Léocadia. Good-bye, Prospère, I'll be back soon.

[HENRI *and* LÉOCADIA *exit, as* VISCOUNT FRANÇOIS DE NOGEANT *and* CHEVALIER ALBIN DE LA TREMOUILLE *enter.*]

SCAEVOLA: What a pathetic braggart.

PROSPÈRE: Good evening, you filthy swine.

[ALBIN *recoils in fear.*]

FRANÇOIS [*ignoring that*]: Wasn't that little Léocadia of the Porte de St. Martin leaving here with Henri?

PROSPÈRE: Of course it was. What of it?—After all, if she went to a lot of trouble, she might even remind you that you're still something of a man.

FRANÇOIS [*laughing*]: That might not be impossible. It seems to me we're here somewhat early today?

PROSPÈRE: Well, meanwhile you can just kill time with your pansy pal here.

[ALBIN *is about to rise up in anger.*]

FRANÇOIS: Now just stop that. [*To* ALBIN] See, I told you how it is here. Bring us some wine.

PROSPÈRE: I'll do just that. The time is about to come when you'll be quite satisfied with water from the Seine.

FRANÇOIS: Of course, of course . . . but for today I would ask for some wine, and no less than the best.

[PROSPÈRE *goes to the bar.*]

ALBIN: That's really a horrible fellow.

FRANÇOIS: Just remember, it's all a joke. But there are other places, too, where quite similar things are said seriously.

ALBIN: But—isn't that prohibited?

FRANÇOIS [*laughs*]: One can tell that you're from the provinces.

ALBIN: Recently we've had a rather nice state of affairs out there, too. The peasants are getting insolent in such a way . . . one no longer knows what to do.

FRANÇOIS: What do you expect? The secret is that the poor devils are hungry.

ALBIN: Well, what can I do about that? Or what can my granduncle do about it?

FRANÇOIS: How does your granduncle come into this?

ALBIN: He comes into this because they just had a meeting in our village—quite openly—and at it they called him quite simply a grain profiteer.

FRANÇOIS: Is that all . . . ?

ALBIN: Well, I ask you!

FRANÇOIS: Tomorrow let's go over to the Palais Royal, and you'll hear what kind of vicious speeches those fellows are making there. But we're letting them speak, that's the best one can do. They're basically good people—one must allow them to let off steam that way.

ALBIN [*pointing to* SCAEVOLA *and the others*]: What kind of suspicious characters are they? Just look how they're staring.

[*He reaches for his sword.*]

FRANÇOIS [*pulling his hand away*]: Don't be ridiculous! [*To the three others*] You don't need to start yet. Wait until more of the audience is here. [*To* ALBIN] They're the most respectable people in the world, these actors. I guarantee you've no doubt sat at a table with worse rogues.

ALBIN: But they were better dressed.

[PROSPÈRE *brings wine;* MICHETTE *and* FLIPOTTE *come in.*]

FRANÇOIS: Greetings, children, come over and sit with us.

MICHETTE: Well—here we are. Come along, Flipotte. She's still a bit shy.

FLIPOTTE: Good evening, young gentleman!

ALBIN: Good evening, my ladies!

MICHETTE: The little one is sweet.

[*She sits down on* ALBIN*'s lap.*]

ALBIN: So please tell me, François, are these respectable women?

MICHETTE: What's he saying?

FRANÇOIS: No, that's not quite the case. The ladies who come in here—Lord, you are stupid, Albin!

PROSPÈRE: What may I bring the duchesses?

MICHETTE: Bring me a really sweet wine.

FRANÇOIS [*pointing to* FLIPOTTE]: A friend of yours?

MICHETTE: We live together. In fact, we have only one bed between us.

FLIPOTTE [*blushing*]: Will that be so unpleasant when you come to visit her?

[*She sits down on* FRANÇOIS*'s lap.*]

ALBIN: That one's certainly not at all shy.

SCAEVOLA [*gets up, moving sullenly to the young people's table*]: I've finally got you again! [*To* ALBIN] And you, you wretched seducer, you'll see that you . . . She's mine!

[PROSPÈRE *looks on.*]

FRANÇOIS [*to* ALBIN]: It's a joke, a joke . . .

ALBIN: She's not his—?

MICHETTE: Come on, just let me sit where I please.

[SCAEVOLA *stands by with clenched fists.*]

PROSPÈRE [*behind him*]: Well, well!

SCAEVOLA: Ha ha!

PROSPÈRE [*seizing him by the collar*]: Ha ha! [*Aside, to him*] That's all you can think about. You don't have a sou's worth of talent. Bellowing. That's the only thing you can do.

MICHETTE [*to* FRANÇOIS]: He did it better the other day—

SCAEVOLA [*to* PROSPÈRE]: I'm still not in the mood. I'll do it again later, when there're more people; you'll see, Prospère—I need an audience.

[DUKE ÉMILE DE CADIGNAN *enters.*]

CADIGNAN: Everything's already in full swing!

[MICHETTE *and* FLIPOTTE *go up to him.*]

MICHETTE: My dear sweet duke!

FRANÇOIS: Good evening, Émile! . . . [*Introducing them*] My young friend Chevalier Albin de la Tremouille—the Duke de Cadignan.

CADIGNAN: I'm very pleased to make your acquaintance. [*To the girls who are clinging to him*] Let go of me, my pets!—[*To* ALBIN] Are you also taking a look at this strange bar?

ALBIN: It totally perplexes me.

FRANÇOIS: The chevalier arrived in Paris just a couple of days ago.

CADIGNAN [*laughing*]: You picked yourself a fine time for that.

ALBIN: How's that?

MICHETTE: Such perfume he keeps using! There's no other man in all Paris who has such a pleasant smell. [*To* ALBIN] . . . You wouldn't notice that, except like this.

CADIGNAN: She's just talking about the seven or eight hundred men she knows as well as she knows me.

FLIPOTTE: Will you allow me to play with your sword?

[*She pulls his sword out of its scabbard and makes it sparkle as she moves it back and forth.*]

GRAIN [*to* PROSPÈRE]: That's the one! . . . That's the one I saw her with!

[PROSPÈRE *seems astonished; lets him go on talking.*]

CADIGNAN: Henri isn't here yet? [*To* ALBIN] When you see that fellow, you'll not regret having come here.

PROSPÈRE [*to* CADIGNAN]: Well, so you're here again too? That's delightful. We'll certainly not have that pleasure much longer.

CADIGNAN: Why? I feel very comfortable here with you.

PROSPÈRE: I believe that. But, in any event, since you'll be one of the first . . .

ALBIN: What does that mean?

PROSPÈRE: You surely understand me—Those who are most fortunate will be the first to . . . !

[*He goes to the back.*]

CADIGNAN [*after some thought*]: If I were the king, I'd make him my court jester; that is, I would have many court jesters, but he would be one of them.

ALBIN: What did he mean, that you are one of the more fortunate ones?

CADIGNAN: He means, Chevalier . . .

ALBIN: Please don't use "Chevalier" with me. Everyone calls me Albin, just Albin, simply because I look so young.

CADIGNAN [*smiling*]: Fine . . . but then you must call me Émile, all right?

ALBIN: I'll be glad to, if you'll allow me, Émile.

CADIGNAN: Those people, they're getting uncannily witty.

FRANÇOIS: What's uncanny about it? I find it very reassuring. After all, as long as the rabble feels like joking, it won't turn into anything serious.

CADIGNAN: It's just that those jokes are much too peculiar. Today I encountered something else which gives one pause for thought.

FRANÇOIS: Tell us.

FLIPOTTE and MICHETTE: Yes, tell us, our dear sweet duke!

CADIGNAN: Do you know Lelange?

FRANÇOIS: Of course—that village . . . one of the Marquis de Montferrat's finest hunting grounds is located there.

CADIGNAN: Quite right. My brother is staying with him now at his château, and he writes me the thing I'll tell you now. At Lelange they have a mayor who is very unpopular.

FRANÇOIS: If you can name me one who is popular—

CADIGNAN: Just listen—The women of that village went and marched in front of the mayor's house—with a coffin . . .

FLIPOTTE: How's that? . . . They were carrying what? Carrying a coffin? I wouldn't want to carry a coffin for all the world.

FRANÇOIS: Do be quiet—after all, nobody's asking you to carry a coffin. [*To* CADIGNAN] Well?

CADIGNAN: And then a few of the women went into the mayor's residence and declared that he must die—but he would be given the honor of being buried.—

FRANÇOIS: Well, was he killed?

CADIGNAN: No—at least my brother didn't write me anything about that.

FRANÇOIS: Well then! . . . Ranters, gossip mongers, clowns—that's what they are. Today they're in Paris for a change, bellowing at the Bastille—as they've done half a dozen times already . . .

CADIGNAN: Well—if I were the king, I'd have put an end to it . . . long ago . . .

ALBIN: Is it true that the king is so softhearted?

CADIGNAN: You haven't been presented to His Majesty yet?

FRANÇOIS: The chevalier is in Paris for the very first time.

CADIGNAN: Yes, you are incredibly young. How old are you, if one may ask?

ALBIN: I just look so young—I'm already seventeen . . .

CADIGNAN: Seventeen—how much you still have ahead of you! I'm twenty-four . . . and already starting to regret how much of my youth I've wasted.

FRANÇOIS [*laughing*]: That's good! For you, Duke . . . for you every day is lost, if you haven't made a conquest of a woman or slain a man.

CADIGNAN: The unfortunate thing is that one almost never conquers the right woman—and always slays the wrong man. And thus one's youth is wasted. It's just as Rollin says.

FRANÇOIS: What does Rollin say?

CADIGNAN: I was thinking about his new play, which they're doing at the National Theatre—it contains such a pretty comparison. Don't you recall?

FRANÇOIS: I don't have any memory at all for verses—

CADIGNAN: Neither do I, unfortunately . . . I just recall the meaning. . . . He says that youth which isn't enjoyed is like a shuttlecock left lying in the sand, instead of being cast into the breeze.

ALBIN [*precociously*]: I find that very true.

CADIGNAN: Isn't it?—After all, the feathers gradually lose their color and fall out. Far better for it to fall into the bushes, where it won't be found again.

ALBIN: How's that to be understood?

CADIGNAN: It's more a matter of feeling. If I just knew the verses, you'd understand it right away.

ALBIN: It occurs to me, Émile, that you too could write poetry, if you only wanted.

CADIGNAN: Why?

ALBIN: It seems to me that since you've been here, life has been bursting into flames—

CADIGNAN [*smiling*]: Indeed? Is it bursting into flames?

FRANÇOIS: Won't you sit down with us, then?

[*Two* ARISTOCRATS *enter meanwhile and sit down at one of the tables, somewhat removed in the background.* PROSPÈRE *appears to be saying rude things to them.*]

CADIGNAN: I can't stay. But I'll come back here one more time anyway.

MICHETTE: Stay here with me!

FLIPOTTE: Take me along!

[*They try to hold on to him.*]

PROSPÈRE [*coming forward*]: Just let him go! You're not nearly depraved enough for him. He's got to run off to a streetwalker—that's where he's happiest.

CADIGNAN: I'm very definitely coming back, so as not to miss Henri.

FRANÇOIS: Imagine, Henri was just leaving with Léocadia, when we came.

CADIGNAN: Well—He married her. Did you know that?

FRANÇOIS: Is it true?—What will the others say about that?

ALBIN: What others?

FRANÇOIS: After all, she's popular with everyone.

CADIGNAN: And he wants to go away with her . . . what do I know? . . . That's what I was told.

PROSPÈRE: Well? That's what you were told?—

[*He looks at* CADIGNAN.]

CADIGNAN [*looks at* PROSPÈRE; *then*]: It's too stupid for words. Léocadia was created to be the world's greatest and most splendid whore.

FRANÇOIS: Who doesn't know that?

CADIGNAN: What could be more foolish than to deprive a person of their true calling? [*Since* FRANÇOIS *laughs*] I don't mean that in jest. Like a conqueror or poet—one must also be born a whore.

FRANÇOIS: You're being paradoxical.

CADIGNAN: I'm sorry for her—and for Henri. He should stay here—not here—I'd like to put him in the National Theatre—although there too—I always feel that nobody would understand him as fully as I do. However, that can be deceptive—for I feel that way about most artists. But I must say, were I not the Duke de Cadignan, I would really like to be such an actor—such an . . .

ALBIN: Like Alexander the Great . . .

CADIGNAN [*smiling*]: Yes—like Alexander the Great. [*To* FLIPOTTE] Give me my sword. [*Putting it into its scabbard*] That is, after all, the most beautiful way to poke fun at the world; a person who can perform for us whatever he wants is certainly greater than the rest of us.

[ALBIN *gazes at him in astonishment.*]

Don't think too much about what I say. It's all true only for the moment.—Good-bye!

MICHETTE: Give me a kiss, before you go!

FLIPOTTE: Me too!

[*They cling to him;* CADIGNAN *kisses them both at the same time and exits.*]

ALBIN [*meanwhile*]: A wonderful human being! . . .

FRANÇOIS: That's certainly true . . . but the fact that such human beings exist is almost reason enough not to get married.

ALBIN: By the way, set me straight, could you explain for me what kind of women they are?

FRANÇOIS: Actresses. They're from Prospère's troupe too—he's now the proprietor of this bar. But in the past they weren't much different from what they are today.

[GUILLAUME *plunges onto the stage, as if out of breath.*]

GUILLAUME [*going over to the table where the* ACTORS *are sitting, hand on his heart, laboriously steadying himself*]: Saved, yes, saved!

SCAEVOLA: What's going on, what's wrong with you?

ALBIN: What's happened to that man?

FRANÇOIS: This is playacting now. Pay attention!

ALBIN: Ah—?

MICHETTE and FLIPOTTE [*moving quickly over to* GUILLAUME]: What's going on? What's wrong with you?

SCAEVOLA: Sit down, have a drink!

GUILLAUME: More! More! . . . Prospère, more wine!—I've been running! My tongue is stuck to the roof of my mouth. They were right on my heels.

JULES [*startled*]: Ah, pay heed, they're right on our heels everywhere.

PROSPÈRE: Well, just go ahead and tell us exactly what happened. . . . [*To the* ACTORS] Agitation! More agitation!

GUILLAUME: Women, over here . . . women!—Ah—

[*He embraces* FLIPOTTE.]

This also restores a man to life. [*To* ALBIN, *who is extremely disconcerted*] Devil take me, my young sir, if I thought I'd see you alive again . . . [*As if listening intently*] They're coming, they're coming!—[*Going over to the door*] No, it's nothing.—They . . .

ALBIN: How peculiar! . . . There's a real uproar outside, as if people are sweeping by in great haste. Is that also being directed from in here?

SCAEVOLA [*to* JULES]: He strikes that tone every time . . . just too stupid for words!—

PROSPÈRE: Well, go on and explain why they're right on your heels again.

GUILLAUME: Nothing special. But if they get me, it would certainly cost me my head—I set a house on fire.

[*The young* ARISTOCRATS *return during this scene and take their seats at the tables.*]

PROSPÈRE [*softly*]: Go on, go on!

GUILLAUME [*likewise*]: Go on with what? Isn't it enough that I set a house on fire?

FRANÇOIS: Now just tell me, my dear sir, why you set the house on fire.

GUILLAUME: Because the head of the highest court lives in it. We wanted to start with that man. We wanted to spoil the pleasure of the good Parisian landlords who open their houses to the people who send us poor devils to the penitentiary.

GRAIN: This is good! This is good!

GUILLAUME [*gazes at* GRAIN *in astonishment, then goes on speaking*]: All the houses are in for it. Just three more fellows like me and there'll be no judges left in Paris!

GRAIN: Death to the judges!

JULES: Certainly . . . but perhaps there's one we can't destroy.

GUILLAUME: I'd like to know which one.

JULES: The judge within us.

PROSPÈRE [*softly*]: That's in bad taste—stop it. Scaevola! Go ahead and bellow! Now's the moment!

SCAEVOLA: Some wine over here, Prospère—we want to drink to the death of all judges in France!

[*The* MARQUIS DE LANSAC, *his wife* SÉVERINE, *and the poet* ROLLIN *enter during his last few words.*]

SCAEVOLA: Death to all who have power in their hands today! Death!

MARQUIS: Do you see, Séverine, this is the way we are received.

ROLLIN: I warned you, Marquis.

SÉVERINE: Why?

FRANÇOIS [*standing up*]: What do I see! The Marquise! Permit me to kiss your hand. Good evening, Marquis! Greetings, Rollin! So you're venturing into this establishment, Marquise?

SÉVERINE: I've been told so much about it. And besides, we're certainly in the midst of adventure today—isn't that right, Rollin?

MARQUIS: Yes, just imagine, Viscount—where do you think we're coming from?—From the Bastille.

FRANÇOIS: Are they still making such an uproar over there?

SÉVERINE: Well of course!—It looks as if they wanted to storm it.

ROLLIN [*declaiming*]: Just like a deluge surging at the shore,
And deeply ired that the child she bore,
Should earth withstand—

SÉVERINE: No more, Rollin!—We had our coach halt near there. It's a magnificent sight—crowds always do have something splendid about them.

FRANÇOIS: Indeed, indeed, if only they didn't have such a foul smell.

MARQUIS: And my wife wouldn't give me any peace. . . . Now I had to bring her over here.

SÉVERINE: Then just what is so special about this place?

PROSPÈRE [*to the* MARQUIS]: Well, are you here too, you dried-up rogue? Did you bring your wife along because she's not safe enough for you at home?

MARQUIS [*with forced laughter*]: He is one of a kind!

PROSPÈRE: Now take heed she doesn't get snatched away from you here. Such elegant ladies sometimes get a hell of an urge to try it with a genuine tramp.

ROLLIN: I'm suffering unspeakably, Séverine.

MARQUIS: My dear child, I prepared you for this—there's still time for us to go.

SÉVERINE: Well, what are you trying to say? I find it delightful. Let's just go sit down!

FRANÇOIS: Permit me, Marquise, to introduce Chevalier de la Tremouille. He is also here for the first time. The Marquis de Lansac; Rollin, our illustrious poet.

ALBIN: Very pleased.

[*They bow and sit down.*]

Is she one of those who performs here or . . . I simply don't know what's what.

FRANÇOIS: Now don't be so dense!—She's the genuine wife of the Marquis de Lansac . . . an extremely respectable lady.

ROLLIN [*to* SÉVERINE]: Tell me that you love me.

SÉVERINE: Yes, yes, but don't ask me every minute.

MARQUIS: Have we already missed any of the scenes?

FRANÇOIS: Not many. It appears that one over there is playing an arsonist.

SÉVERINE: Chevalier, are you indeed the cousin of little Lydia de la Tremouille, who got married today?

ALBIN: Yes, of course. That was one reason, among others, that I came to Paris.

SÉVERINE: I remember seeing you in the church.

ALBIN [*embarrassed*]: I'm extremely flattered, Marquise.

SÉVERINE [*to* ROLLIN]: What a sweet young man.

ROLLIN: Ah, Séverine, you've never come across a man that you didn't like.

SÉVERINE: Oh yes, I have—and right away I married him.

ROLLIN: Oh, Séverine, I'm always afraid—there are moments when you are in danger of your own husband.

PROSPÈRE [*bringing wine*]: There you are! I wish it were poison, but for the time being I'm not permitted to serve that to you riffraff.

FRANÇOIS: You're bound to get your chance, Prospère.

SÉVERINE [*to* ROLLIN]: What's the matter with those two pretty girls? Why don't they come any closer? After all, now that we're here, I want to be part of everything. I find this to be an extremely civilized place, in every respect.

MARQUIS: Just have patience, Séverine.

SÉVERINE: Recently I find the best entertainment to be out in the street.—Do you know what occurred to us yesterday, when we went for a drive on the Promenade de Longchamps?

MARQUIS: Ah please, my dear Séverine, why . . .

SÉVERINE: A fellow out there jumped up onto the running board of our carriage and screamed: "Next year you'll be standing behind your coachman and we'll be sitting inside the carriage!"

FRANÇOIS: Ah, that is rather severe.

MARQUIS: Oh Lord, I find one shouldn't talk about those things at all. Paris is running a sort of fever now, which will pass soon enough.

GUILLAUME [*suddenly*]: I see flames, flames, everywhere I look, tall, red flames.

PROSPÈRE [*aside, to him*]: Now you're playing a madman, not a criminal.

SÉVERINE: He sees flames?

FRANÇOIS: But they haven't gotten to their real specialty yet.

ALBIN [*to* ROLLIN]: I can't begin to tell you how confused I am already by all this.

MICHETTE [*goes to the* MARQUIS]: I haven't greeted you at all yet, my sweet filthy old swine.

MARQUIS [*embarrassed*]: She's only joking, dear Séverine.

SÉVERINE: I don't think so. Just tell me, my little one, how many love affairs have you had already?

MARQUIS [*to* FRANÇOIS]: It's wonderful how the Marquise, my consort, immediately feels at home in every sort of circumstance.

ROLLIN: Yes, it is wonderful.

MICHETTE: Have you ever counted your love affairs?

SÉVERINE: When I was just your age . . . certainly.—

ALBIN [*to* ROLLIN]: Tell me, Monsieur Rollin, is the Marquise acting or is she really like that?—I absolutely don't know what is what.

ROLLIN: Reality . . . acting . . . can you tell the difference so precisely, Chevalier?

ALBIN: After all.

ROLLIN: I can't. And what I find so characteristically special here is the way all apparent differences are suspended, so to speak. Reality turns into performance—performance into reality. Just look at the Marquise, for one. The way she is chatting with those creatures, as if they were her equals. At the same time she is . . .

ALBIN: Something quite different.

ROLLIN: I thank you for that, Chevalier.

PROSPÈRE [*to* GRAIN]: Now, how did that story go?

GRAIN: What?

PROSPÈRE: The story about your aunt, the one that got you two years in prison?

GRAIN: Well I told you, I strangled her.

FRANÇOIS: That one is weak. He's an amateur. I've never seen him before.

GEORGETTE [*coming in hastily, dressed like a whore of the lowest kind*]: Good evening, my children! Isn't my Balthasar here yet?

SCAEVOLA: Georgette! Sit over here with me! Your Balthasar will come in good time.

GEORGETTE: If he isn't here in ten minutes, he won't be coming on time anymore—he won't be coming back at all.

FRANÇOIS: Watch out for this one, Marquise. This one is, in reality, the wife of that Balthasar, about whom she was speaking just now and who will be coming very soon.—She's playing the part of an extremely common streetwalker; Balthasar does her pimp. Nonetheless she's the most loyal wife one can find in all Paris.

[BALTHASAR *enters.*]

GEORGETTE: My Balthasar!

[*She runs toward him and embraces him.*]

Well, here you are!

BALTHASAR: Everything is all set.

[*Quiet on all sides.*]

It wasn't worth the trouble. I almost felt sorry for him. You should size up your people better, Georgette—I'm tired of killing such promising young fellows for only a few francs.

FRANÇOIS: Fabulous . . .

ALBIN: How's that?—

FRANÇOIS: He does the punch lines so well.

[*The* POLICE INSPECTOR *enters in disguise and sits down at a table.*]

PROSPÈRE [*to him*]: You're arriving at a good moment, Inspector. That's one of my most distinguished performers.

BALTHASAR: There's got to be another way of earning our daily bread. Upon my soul, I'm no coward, but one pays a bitter price for this kind of earning.

SCAEVOLA: I can believe that.

GEORGETTE: Just what's wrong with you today?

BALTHASAR: I'll tell you, Georgette!—I think you're just a bit too affectionate with the young gentlemen.

GEORGETTE: Look what a child he is. Now be sensible, Balthasar! After all, I have to be affectionate to inspire them with confidence.

ROLLIN: What she's saying there is downright profound.

BALTHASAR: If I should ever think that you felt something for another . . .

GEORGETTE: What does one say to that! This stupid jealousy will send him to his grave yet.

BALTHASAR: I heard you sigh today, Georgette, and that was at a moment when the young man's confidence was already inspired enough!

GEORGETTE: A woman just can't stop pretending to be in love all that suddenly.

BALTHASAR: Watch your step, Georgette, the Seine is deep. [*Impetuously*] If you were to betray me—

GEORGETTE: Never, never!

ALBIN: I just don't understand this at all.

SÉVERINE: Rollin, that's the right idea!

ROLLIN: Do you think so?

MARQUIS [*to* SÉVERINE]: We can still go, Séverine.

SÉVERINE: Why? I'm starting to feel very comfortable here.

GEORGETTE: My Balthasar, I adore you.

[*They embrace.*]

FRANÇOIS: Bravo! Bravo!

BALTHASAR: What kind of idiot is that?

POLICE INSPECTOR: This is going too far!—This is—

[MAURICE *and* ÉTIENNE *appear. They are dressed like young aristocrats, but it is apparent that they are merely in threadbare costumes.*]

ACTORS [*speaking from the actors' table*]: Who are those people?

SCAEVOLA: Devil take me, if it isn't Maurice and Étienne.

GEORGETTE: Of course that's who it is.

BALTHASAR: Georgette!

SÉVERINE: Lord, those young people look so attractive!

ROLLIN: It is distressing, Séverine, that every attractive face excites you so violently.

SÉVERINE: Well, what did I come here for?

ROLLIN: Then at least tell me that you love me.

SÉVERINE [*with a look*]: You have a short memory.

ÉTIENNE: Now, where do you think we've just come from?

FRANÇOIS: Listen, Marquis, these are two witty young men.

MAURICE: We've come from a wedding.

ÉTIENNE: You do have to dress up a bit for that. Otherwise those damned secret police come after you.

SCAEVOLA: Did you at least get a decent haul?

PROSPÈRE: Let's see.

MAURICE [*taking watches out of his doublet*]: What'll you give me for these?

PROSPÈRE: For that one there? A *louis d'or.*

MAURICE: Really!

SCAEVOLA: It isn't worth any more than that!

MICHETTE: That's definitely a lady's watch. Give it to me, Maurice.

MAURICE: What'll you give me for it?

MICHETTE: Look at me! . . . Now, isn't that enough?—

FLIPOTTE: No, give it to me—look at me—

MAURICE: My dears, I can get that without risking my head.

MICHETTE: You're a conceited monkey.

SÉVERINE: I swear that's not just comedy.

ROLLIN: Of course not. Everywhere there is something genuine that keeps flashing through. That's what's really delightful about it.

SCAEVOLA: Just what wedding was that?

MAURICE: The wedding of Mademoiselle de la Tremouille—she married the Count de Banville.

ALBIN: Do you hear, François?—I assure you, they're genuine thieves.

FRANÇOIS: Calm down, Albin. I know those two. I've seen them perform a dozen times before. Playing pickpockets is their specialty.

[MAURICE *pulls some purses out of his doublet.*]

SCAEVOLA: Well, you could be generous today.

ÉTIENNE: It was quite a magnificent wedding. All the aristocracy of France was there. Even the king was represented.

ALBIN [*agitated*]: That's all true!

MAURICE [*rolling money across the table*]: This is for you, my friends, so that you see we are sticking together.

FRANÇOIS: Stage props, my dear Albin.

[*He gets up and takes a couple of coins.*]

There's certainly something for us, too.

PROSPÈRE: Go ahead and take some . . . you never earned anything in your life as honestly as this.

MAURICE [*holding up a garter studded with diamonds*]: And to whom shall I present this?

[GEORGETTE, MICHETTE, *and* FLIPOTTE *snatch at it.*]

MAURICE: Patience, my sweet little pets, we'll talk about that later. I'll give it to the one who invents a new sign of affection.

SÉVERINE: Don't you want to let me compete in that?

ROLLIN: You're driving me insane, Séverine.

MARQUIS: Séverine, don't we want to leave now? I think . . .

SÉVERINE: Oh no. I'm doing splendidly. [*To* ROLLIN] Ah, I'm getting into such a mood—

MICHETTE: Just how did you get to that garter?

MAURICE: There was such a throng in the church . . . and when a woman thinks she's being courted . . .

[*They all laugh. In the meanwhile* GRAIN *has removed* FRANÇOIS*'s purse.*]

FRANÇOIS [*holding the money; to* ALBIN]: Fake money, pure and simple. Are you reassured now?

[GRAIN *tries to withdraw.*]

PROSPÈRE [*follows him, speaking softly*]: Give me the purse you lifted from that gentleman right now.

GRAIN: I—

PROSPÈRE: Immediately . . . or it'll go hard with you.

GRAIN: You don't need to be rude about it.

[*He gives it to him.*]

PROSPÈRE: Just stay here. I don't have time to search you now. Who knows what else you've pocketed. Go on back to your place.

FLIPOTTE: I'm going to win that garter!

PROSPÈRE [*to* FRANÇOIS, *tossing the purse at him*]: There's your purse. You lost it out of your pocket.

FRANÇOIS: Thank you, Prospère. [*To* ALBIN] You see, we are actually among the most respectable people in the world.

[HENRI, *who has been present for a prolonged time now, seated behind the others, gets up suddenly.*]

ROLLIN: Henri, here's Henri.—

SÉVERINE: Is he the one you've been telling me so much about?

MARQUIS: Of course. He's the one people really come here to see.

[HENRI *steps forward, very theatrically, remaining silent.*]

ACTORS: Henri, what's the matter?

ROLLIN: Notice that gaze. A world of passion. He's surely playing the role of someone who's committed a crime of passion.

SÉVERINE: That's magificent!

ALBIN: Well, why doesn't he speak?

ROLLIN: It's as if he were entranced. Just look at that. Now watch . . . he has committed some kind of terrible deed.

FRANÇOIS: He's a bit theatrical. It's as if he were preparing for a monologue.

PROSPÈRE: Henri, Henri, where are you coming from?

HENRI: I killed a man.

ROLLIN: What did I tell you?

SCAEVOLA: Who?

HENRI: My wife's lover.

[PROSPÈRE *watches him, obviously with the feeling that, at this moment, it could be true.*]

HENRI [*looks up*]: Well yes, I did it. Why are you looking at me like that? That's just the way it is. Is it so very astonishing? After all, you know what kind of creature my wife is; it had to end like that.

PROSPÈRE: And what about her—where is she?

FRANÇOIS: See, the proprietor is getting into the spirit of it. Look how that makes it seem so real.

[*Uproar outside, not too intense.*]

JULES: What's that uproar outside?

MARQUIS: Do you hear it, Séverine?

ROLLIN: It sounds like troops marching past.

FRANÇOIS: Oh no, that's our beloved people of Paris, just listen to them clamoring.

[*Uneasiness in the basement room; it gets quiet outside.*]

Go on, Henri, go on.

PROSPÈRE: Well then tell us, Henri!—Where is your wife? Where did you leave her?

HENRI: Oh, I'm not worried about her. She won't die from that. Whether it's this man or some other, what does it matter to women? There are a thousand other attractive men running around Paris—whether it's this man or some other—

BALTHASAR: May that happen to all who take our wives from us.

SCAEVOLA: And to all who take what belongs to us.

POLICE INSPECTOR [*to* PROSPÈRE]: Those are provocative lines.

ALBIN: It's alarming . . . the people are serious about it.

SCAEVOLA: Down with the profiteers of France! Let's bet that the fellow he caught with his wife was also one of those dirty dogs who rob us of our daily bread.

ALBIN: I suggest we go.

SÉVERINE: Henri! Henri!

MARQUIS: But Marquise!

SÉVERINE: Please, my dear Marquis, ask that man how he got hold of his wife . . . or I'll ask him myself.

MARQUIS [*hesitating*]: Tell me, Henri, just how did you succeed in catching the two of them?

HENRI [*lost in thought for a long time*]: Well, do you know my wife?— She's the prettiest and yet the lowest sort of creature under the sun.—And I loved her.—We've known each other seven years . . . but she's only been my wife since yesterday. In those seven years there wasn't a day, not a single day, that she didn't deceive me, for everything about her is a lie. Her eyes, as well as her lips, her kisses and her smile. And I knew it!

FRANÇOIS: He's declaiming a little.

HENRI: Every man, young and old, every man who appealed to her—and every man who paid her—every man, I think, who wanted her, had her—And I knew it!

SÉVERINE: Not every man can admit that about himself.

HENRI: And at the same time she loved me. . . . Can any of you understand that, my friends? She came back to me again and again—back to me from all of them—from the handsome and the ugly, the wise and the stupid, the scoundrels and the cavaliers—back to me again and again.—

SÉVERINE [*to* ROLLIN]: If only all of you would just realize that coming back like that is precisely what love is about.

HENRI: What I've suffered . . . agonies, agonies!

ROLLIN: That's shattering!

HENRI: And yesterday I married her. We had a dream. No—I had a dream. I wanted to get away from here with her. To solitude, the country, to that magnificent peace and quiet. We wanted to live like other happy couples—we also dreamed of a child.

ROLLIN [*softly*]: Séverine!

SÉVERINE: Oh yes, that's all right.

ALBIN: François, this person is speaking the truth.

FRANÇOIS: Of course, the story about love is true, but he's also telling a story about murder.

HENRI: I arrived a day too late . . . there was someone she hadn't forgotten, otherwise—I think—there wouldn't have been any more men . . . but I caught them together . . . and now he is gone.

ACTORS: Who? . . . Who? How did it happen? . . . Where is his body?—Are you being pursued? . . . How did it happen? . . . Where is she?

HENRI [*more and more agitated*]: I accompanied her . . . to the theater . . . It was to have been her last performance today . . . I kissed her . . . at the door—and she went up to her dressing room and I left like a man with nothing to fear.—But I wasn't even a hundred steps away when it began . . . inside me . . . do you understand . . . a tremendous uneasiness. . . . and it was as if something were forcing me to turn around . . . so I turned around and went back up. But then I was ashamed and left again . . . again I was a hundred steps from the theater . . . when it seized me . . . so I went back again. Her scene was over . . . she doesn't have much to do, she just stands on the stage for a while, half naked—and then she's finished. . . . I stand in front of her dressing room, I lean with my ear to the door and hear whispering. I can't distinguish any words . . . the whispering ceases . . . I kick open the door . . . [*bellowing like a fierce animal*]—it was the Duke of Cadignan and I've murdered him.—

PROSPÈRE [*after a long time he regards it as true*]: Madman!

[HENRI *looks up, gazes at* PROSPÈRE *fixedly.*]

SÉVERINE: Bravo! Bravo!

ROLLIN: What are you doing, Marquise? The moment you call out "Bravo!" you're making it all into playacting again—and there are no more pleasurable thrills.

MARQUIS: I don't find those thrills so pleasurable. My friends, let us applaud, that's the only way we can free ourselves from this spell.

PROSPÈRE [*to* HENRI, *during the uproar*]: Save yourself, flee, Henri!

HENRI: What's that? What's that?

PROSPÈRE: Let that be enough for now, see to it that you get away from here!

FRANÇOIS: Quiet! . . . Let's hear what the proprietor is saying!

PROSPÈRE [*after brief reflection*]: I'm telling him he should leave before the sentries at the city gates are informed. That handsome duke was a favorite of the king—they'll put you on the rack! You should have used the knife on your wife instead, that riffraff!

FRANÇOIS: Such teamwork . . . Splendid!

HENRI: Prospère, which of us is insane, you or I?

[*He stands there, trying to read* PROSPÈRE*'s eyes.*]

ROLLIN: It's wonderful—we all know he's acting, and yet, if the Duke de Cadignan were to enter here, he would be taken for a ghost.

[*Uproar outside, more and more intense. People come in; screaming is heard.* GRASSET *in the lead, others, among them* LEBRÊT, *push their way over the stairs. Shouts are heard offstage: "Freedom! Freedom!"*]

GRASSET: Here we are, my children, come in here!
ALBIN: What's that? Is that part of it?
FRANÇOIS: No.
MARQUIS: What's that supposed to mean?
SÉVERINE: What kind of people are they?
GRASSET: Come on in here! I tell you, my friend Prospère always has one more barrel left.

[*Uproar from the street.*]

GRASSET: And we've earned it! Friend! Brother! It's ours, it's ours!

[*Shouts offstage: "Freedom! Freedom!"*]

SÉVERINE: What's going on?
MARQUIS: Let us depart, let us depart, the scum is approaching.
ROLLIN: How do you propose to depart?
GRASSET: It has fallen, the Bastille has fallen!
PROSPÈRE: What are you saying?—Is he speaking the truth?
GRASSET: Don't you hear?

[ALBIN *starts to draw his sword.*]

FRANÇOIS: Now don't do that—otherwise we're all lost.
GRASSET [*staggering in over the stairs*]: And if you hurry, you can still see something funny outside . . . up on a very long pike the head of our esteemed Delaunay, governor of the Bastille.
MARQUIS: Is that fellow crazy?

[*Shouts offstage: "Freedom! Freedom!"*]

GRASSET: We've cut off the heads of a dozen of them, the Bastille belongs to us, the prisoners are free! Paris belongs to the people!

PROSPÈRE: Listen! Listen! Paris belongs to us!

GRASSET: Look, now he's getting his courage. Go on and scream, Prospère, nothing else can happen to you now.

PROSPÈRE [*to the* ARISTOCRATS]: What do you say to that? You rabble! The joke is over.

ALBIN: Didn't I say that?

PROSPÈRE: The people of Paris have won.

POLICE INSPECTOR: Quiet!—[*They laugh*] Quiet! . . . I forbid the continuation of this performance!

GRASSET: Who is that simpleton?

POLICE INSPECTOR: Prospère, I am making you responsible for all the provocative speeches which—

GRASSET: Is that fellow crazy?

PROSPÈRE: The joke is over, don't you understand? Well just tell them, Henri, now you may tell them! We'll protect you . . . the people of Paris will protect you.

GRASSET: Yes, the people of Paris.

[HENRI *stands there with a vacant stare.*]

PROSPÈRE: Henri really did murder the Duke de Cadignan.

ALBIN, FRANÇOIS, AND MAURICE: What's he saying there?

ALBIN and others: What does all that mean, Henri?

FRANÇOIS: Henri, say something!

PROSPÈRE: He found him with his wife—and he killed him.

HENRI: It's not true!

PROSPÈRE: Now you needn't fear anymore, now you can scream it to the world. I could've told you an hour ago she was the Duke's mistress. By God, I was about to tell you that . . . You, Blazing Brimstone—we knew it didn't we?

HENRI: Who saw her? Where was she seen?

PROSPÈRE: What does that concern you now! Yes, he is crazy . . . you killed him, you certainly can't do any more.

FRANÇOIS: For heaven's sake, is it really true or not?

PROSPÈRE: Yes, it is true!

GRASSET: Henri—from now on you shall be my friend. Long live freedom! Long live freedom!

FRANÇOIS: Henri, speak!

HENRI: She was his mistress? She was the Duke's mistress? I didn't know that . . . he's alive . . . he's alive—

[*Tremendous agitation.*]

SÉVERINE [*to the others*]: Well, what is the truth now?

ALBIN: For God's sake!

[CADIGNAN *pushes his way through the crowd on the stairs.*]

SÉVERINE [*spotting him first*]: The Duke!

[*Several others also cry out: "The Duke!"*]

CADIGNAN: Yes indeed—well, what's going on?

PROSPÈRE: Is it a ghost?

CADIGNAN: Not that I'm aware of! Let me in over here!

ROLLIN: What do you want to bet that everything is set up? Those fellows belong to Prospère's troupe. Bravo, Prospère, you brought that one off, didn't you?

CADIGNAN: What's going on? Are you still playacting in here, while outside . . . Don't you know what kind of things are going on outside? I saw Delaunay's head carried past on a pike. Well, why are you looking at me like that?—[*Stepping down the stairs*] Henri—

FRANÇOIS: Be on your guard against Henri.

[HENRI *plunges across the stage like a madman and thrusts his dagger into* CADIGNAN*'s neck.*]

POLICE INSPECTOR [*standing up*]: That's going too far!

ALBIN: He's bleeding!

ROLLIN: There's been a murder here!

SÉVERINE: The Duke is dying!

MARQUIS: I'm overcome, dear Séverine, that I should have brought you to this establishment today, of all days.

SÉVERINE: Why? [*With difficulty*] It turned out so wonderfully. It's not every day that one gets to see a real duke really murdered.

ROLLIN: I still don't understand it.

POLICE INSPECTOR: Quiet!—Nobody leave the establishment!—

GRASSET: What does he want?

POLICE INSPECTOR: I arrest this man in the name of the law.

GRASSET [*laughing*]: We're making the law now, you fools! Out with the rabble! Whoever kills a duke is a friend of the people. Long live freedom!

ALBIN [*drawing his sword*]: Make way! Follow me, my friends!

[LÉOCADIA *plunges in over the stairs. Some cry out: "Léocadia!"; others: "His wife!"*]

LÉOCADIA: Let me in here! I want to get to my husband! [*Moving forward, sees it all, cries out*] Who did that? Henri!

[HENRI *looks at her.*]

LÉOCADIA: Why did you do this?

HENRI: Why?

LÉOCADIA: Yes, yes, I know why. For my sake. No, no, don't say for my sake. I've never been worth that much in my lifetime.

GRASSET [*beginning a speech*]: Citizens of Paris, we want to celebrate our victory. Chance led us on our way through the streets of Paris to this agreeable proprietor. It couldn't have turned out more beautifully. Nowhere can the shout "Long live freedom!" ring more beautifully than by the corpse of a duke.

CITIZENS AND ACTORS: Long live freedom! Long live freedom!

FRANÇOIS: I think we'd better go—the people have gone insane. Let's go.

ALBIN: Shall we leave the corpse here with them?

SÉVERINE: Long live freedom! Long live freedom!

MARQUIS: Are you crazy?

CITIZENS AND ACTORS: Long live freedom! Long live freedom!

SÉVERINE [*leading the* ARISTOCRATS *toward the exit*]: Rollin, wait below my window tonight. I'll throw down the key, like the other night—we'll have a lovely time—I feel pleasantly excited.

[*Shouts offstage: "Long live freedom!" "Love live Henri!" "Long live Henri!"*]

LEBRÊT: Look at those people—they're running away from us.
GRASSET: Let them, for now—let them.—They'll not escape us.

[*Curtain*]

The Last Masks

A PLAY IN ONE ACT

Characters

Florian Jackwerth, *an actor*

Juliana Paschanda, *an attendant at Vienna's General Hospital*

Karl Rademacher, *a journalist*

Dr. Halmschlöger, *a resident physician at the hospital*

Dr. Tann, *another resident physician*

Alexander Weihgast, *a poet*

~

Vienna, turn of the twentieth century

[*A small room—so-called special anteroom—at the General Hospital, connected to a large ward: a movable linen curtain instead of a door. A bed at the left, an oblong table in the middle, with papers, vials, and so forth. Two chairs. An armchair beside the bed. A burning candle on the table. Onstage:* KARL RADEMACHER, *over fifty, very down-and-out, quite gray, seated in the armchair, with eyes closed.* FLORIAN JACKWERTH, *roughly twenty-eight, eyes very sparkling, as if feverish, smoothly shaven, thin, wearing a linen dressing gown, which he occasionally folds weightily. A hospital attendant,* JULIANA PASCHANDA, *is busy writing at the table—fat, good-natured, not yet old.*]

FLORIAN [*shoving back the curtain, just coming out of the ward, which is weakly illuminated by a hanging lamp, steps toward* JULIANA]: That Fräulein Paschanda is always working so hard.

JULIANA: Why, what are you doing now, getting up again? What'll that Herr Resident say then? Go back to sleep!

FLORIAN: Of course. I'm even thinking of taking a long sleep, as they say in Schiller's *Wallenstein.* Can I be of assistance to you, beautiful lady? And I don't mean with sleeping.

[JULIANA *isn't bothered by his remark.*]

FLORIAN [*sneaking over to* RADEMACHER]: Look, Fräulein Paschanda—just look over here!

JULIANA: What do you want, then?

FLORIAN [*going back to her*]: Good lord, I thought he was already dead.

JULIANA: That'll be a while yet.

FLORIAN: You think so, you think so?—Then good night, Fräulein Juliana Paschanda.

JULIANA: I'm not Fräulein, I'm Frau.

FLORIAN: Ah so! I've not yet had the honor of meeting your spouse, the Herr Paschanda.

JULIANA: I'd not wish that on you either. He works in the morgue.

FLORIAN: Thank you, thank you very much. I certainly have no need for that. Say, Frau Paschanda, [*confidentially*] did you see the Fräulein who honored me with a visit this afternoon?

JULIANA: Yes, the one in the red hat.

FLORIAN [*irritated*]: Red hat—red hat . . . She was a colleague of mine—yes indeed! We were acting together last year—in Olmütz. That Fräulein was the leading lady, your most humble servant was the romantic lead. Look at me, please—I don't need to say anything further. Yes indeed, I wrote her a postcard . . . simply a card—and she came right away. There's still loyalty in the theater. And she promised me she'll look around, she'll speak with an agent—so I can get a summer engagement when I am released from this place. That's why a Fräulein can have a very good heart, even when she's wearing a red hat, Frau von Paschanda. [*Increasingly provoked, later coughing*] Perhaps she'll come by again—I'll just write her, the next time she should put on a blue hat—because that Frau Paschanda can't stand the color red.

JULIANA: Shh! Shh! People are trying to sleep.

[*She listens intently.*]

FLORIAN: What is it, then?

JULIANA: I thought the Herr Resident—

[*Hospital clock strikes.*]

FLORIAN: So how late is it?

JULIANA: Nine.

FLORIAN: Who's got night rounds today, then?

JULIANA: That Dr. Halmschlöger.

FLORIAN: Ah, that Dr. Halmschlöger. A fine gentleman, only somewhat conceited. [*Seeing that* RADEMACHER *has awakened*] My pleasure, Herr von Rademacher.

[RADEMACHER *nods.*]

FLORIAN [*imitating* DR. HALMSCHLÖGER]: Well, my dear Rademacher, how are you today? [*Acting as if he's taking off his overcoat and handing it to* JULIANA] Ah, dear Frau Paschanda, won't you be so kind . . . ? Thank you so much.

JULIANA [*laughing against her will*]: How you can imitate people.

FLORIAN [*in a different tone, as if going from one bed to another*]: Nothing new? Nothing new? Good—good—good . . .

JULIANA: Why, that's the Chief of Staff. If he knew that!

FLORIAN: Well, just wait, that's nothing at all yet.

[*He suddenly drops down onto a chair; his face seems wracked by pain, and he rolls his eyes.*]

JULIANA: Why, for God's sake, why, that's—

FLORIAN [*interrupting his imitation for a moment*]: Well, who?

JULIANA: That one in bed seventeen, that Engstl—the roofer, who died a day before yesterday. Well, won't you stop? Why, you're committing a sin.

FLORIAN: Why, my dear Frau Paschanda, do you think people like us are here in the hospital for nothing? One can learn something from it.

JULIANA: The Herr Resident is coming.

[*She exits into the ward. As she shoves aside the curtain,* DR. HALMSCHLÖGER *and* DR. TANN *are seen at the back of the stage.*]

FLORIAN: Yes indeed, Herr Rademacher, I'm doing character studies here, you understand.

RADEMACHER: Really?

FLORIAN: Yes, lying in the hospital is worthwhile for people like us. You think I can't make use of that because I'm a comedian? Mistaken! To be specific, it's a discovery I've made, Herr Rademacher. [*Seriously*] Every sad individual countenance, even those benumbed by pain, can provide the inspiration for a funny routine in the theater. Once I've seen a person die, I know exactly how he looks when he's been told a joke.—But what's the matter with that, Herr Rademacher? Courage! Don't lose your sense of humor. Look at me—ha! A week ago—I was given up for—

not only by the learned doctors, that wouldn't have been so dangerous, but I gave myself up! And now I'm in fine fettle. And in one week—most obedient servant! "Farewell, then, you sweet house," as they say in Raimond's play! Whereby I take the liberty of most humbly inviting your Right Honorable Majesty to my first performance.

[*He coughs.*]

RADEMACHER: No doubt that'll hardly be possible.

FLORIAN: Isn't it odd? If we'd both stayed healthy, then perhaps we'd be mortal enemies.

RADEMACHER: But why, then?

FLORIAN: Well, I'd have played a comedy, and you'd have written a critique tearing me to pieces, and I've never been able to stand people who tear me to pieces. And this way we've become the best of friends.—Why tell me, Herr Rademacher, didn't I look just like you a week ago?

RADEMACHER: Perhaps there's a difference after all.

FLORIAN: Ridiculous! One just has to have a firm will. Do you know how I've gotten healthy?

[RADEMACHER *looks at him.*]

FLORIAN: You needn't look at me like that—there's not much more. I've simply not let any sad thoughts arise!

RADEMACHER: How did you do that, then?

FLORIAN: I simply imagined telling the most horribly coarse things to the people I was furious at. Oh what a relief that is, what a relief, I tell you! I even worked out to whom I'd appear as a ghost, once I'd died.—So, above all there's that colleague of yours in Olmütz—a malicious so-and-so! Well, and then the Herr Director, who deducted half my salary for improvising. The fact is, it was my performance and not the script which got people laughing at all. He should've been glad, the Herr Director. But instead—well, wait, wait! Why, I had a talent for appearing—oh, even in heaven I could've made a decent living for myself. . . .

You understand, I would've even accepted an engagement with the Spiritualists.

[DR. HALMSCHLÖGER, DR. TANN, *and* JULIANA *come in.*]

TANN [*young, somewhat slovenly attired person, with a hat on his head and an unlit cigar in his mouth*]: But please, Dr. Halmschlöger, don't take so long here this time.

HALMSCHLÖGER [*a carefully dressed young man, with a pince-nez, a short, full blond beard, and an overcoat thrown over his shoulders*]: No, I'll be finished right away.

TANN: Or I'm going along to the café.

HALMSCHLÖGER: I'll be finished right away.

FLORIAN: My pleasure, Herr Doctor.

HALMSCHLÖGER: How come you aren't lying in bed, then? [*To* JULIANA] Paschanda!

FLORIAN: I've just had enough sleep, Herr Doctor—why, things are going splendidly for me. May I take the liberty of inviting the Herr Doctor to my new performance . . . ?

HALMSCHLÖGER [*amused for a moment, then turns aside*]: Yes, yes. Well, my dear Rademacher, how are you?

[FLORIAN *gives* JULIANA *a signal referring to his earlier imitation.*]

RADEMACHER: It's going badly for me, Herr Doctor.

HALMSCHLÖGER [*gazing at the chart at the head of the bed;* JULIANA *holds the light*]: One hundred and three—well! Yesterday we had one hundred and four, after all.

[JULIANA *nods.*]

It's certainly going better. Well, good night.

[*He starts to leave.*]

RADEMACHER: Herr Doctor!

HALMSCHLÖGER: Do you wish something?

RADEMACHER: Please, Herr Doctor, how much longer do I have to live?

HALMSCHLÖGER: Well, you need to have a little more patience.

RADEMACHER: I don't mean it that way, Herr Doctor. I mean, when is it over for me?

[TANN *has sat down at the table and absentmindedly leafs through the papers.*]

HALMSCHLÖGER: What are you saying, then? [*To* JULIANA] Did he take his drops?

JULIANA: At seven-thirty, Herr Doctor.

RADEMACHER: Herr Doctor, I ask you very sincerely not to treat me the same way as everyone else. Oh, Herr Doctor, excuse—

HALMSCHLÖGER [*somewhat impatiently, but kindly*]: Not so loud, not so loud.

RADEMACHER: If you please, just one more word, Herr Doctor. [*Resolutely*] You've got to understand, I have to know the truth—I have to—for a very particular reason!—

HALMSCHLÖGER: The truth . . . I have every confidence—Well, in a certain sense, the future is a closed book to all of us—But I can say—

RADEMACHER: Herr Doctor—if I were still planning something very important—something which determines the fate of other people—and my peace—the peace of my dying hour . . .

HALMSCHLÖGER: Now, now!—Won't you explain yourself more precisely? [*Still kindly*] But I must ask you to be as brief as possible. I've still got two more rooms ahead of me. Imagine, if everyone took so long.—So please.

RADEMACHER: Herr Doctor, I've still got to speak with someone.

HALMSCHLÖGER: Well, you can certainly write to the person in question, if that reassures you. Or tomorrow afternoon between four and five you may receive whomever you want. I've nothing at all against that.

RADEMACHER: Herr Doctor—that may be too late—that's too late—I feel it . . . By tomorrow morning everything might be over. Today I must speak with—the person in question today.

HALMSCHLÖGER: That's not possible. What's all this supposed to mean? If it matters so much to you, you certainly should have already . . .

RADEMACHER [*pressing*]: Herr Doctor! You've always been very good to me—and I know I'm a bit pushy—but look, Herr Doctor, once it's quite certain that tomorrow or the day after I'll be taken down to the morgue, then one might think that one can presume to ask for more than someone else.

TANN: So, Halmschlöger, what is it, then?

HALMSCHLÖGER: Just a moment.—[*Somewhat impatiently*] So, briefly, please, what do you wish?

RADEMACHER: I've absolutely got to speak with a friend of mine. A certain Herr Weihgast—Alexander Weihgast.

HALMSCHLÖGER: Weihgast? Do you mean the famous poet?

RADEMACHER: Yes!

HALMSCHLÖGER: He's a friend of yours?

RADEMACHER: Was—was—at an earlier time.

HALMSCHLÖGER: So, write him a card.

RADEMACHER: What good does that do me? He'll no longer find me here. I've got to speak with him this very day—right away . . .

HALMSCHLÖGER [*firmly*]: Herr Rademacher, it's impossible. And that's enough. [*Gently*] To reassure you, today I'll write Herr Weihgast, whom I by chance know personally. I'll write him a word this very day and leave it up to him to come to see you tomorrow at a suitable time.

RADEMACHER: You know that Herr Weihgast, Herr Doctor? [*Suddenly*] Then bring him here—bring him here!

HALMSCHLÖGER: Well listen, listen, Herr Rademacher, at this point one just doesn't know—

RADEMACHER [*greatly excited*]: Herr Doctor, why I know it's brazen of me—but you're certainly human, after all, Herr Doctor, and you look at things humanely. Not like some others who only judge by set patterns. And you know, Herr Doctor, here is someone who must die tomorrow and who has one last wish, for whom it's such an enormous concern, and I can grant his wish . . . I'm asking you, Herr Doctor, go over to him, bring him here to me!

HALMSCHLÖGER [*vacillating, looking at his watch*]: Yes—as far as I'm concerned, if I should decide to do that—if you please, Herr

Rademacher, how can I ask him—at this time of day . . . truly, it's such a peculiar imposition! Consider it yourself, after all.

RADEMACHER: Oh, Herr Doctor, I know my friend Weihgast. If you tell him his old friend Rademacher is dying at the General Hospital and wants to see him once more—oh, he'll not pass up the chance—I implore you, Herr Doctor—for you it's simply a walk—isn't it? But for me—for me . . .

HALMSCHLÖGER: Yes, that's just it! Of course, it means nothing to me. But for you—yes, indeed, the excitement could have grave consequences.

RADEMACHER: Herr Doctor—Herr Doctor! Why, we're men! After all, one hour earlier or later doesn't matter.

HALMSCHLÖGER [*calmingly*]: Well, well, well! [*After brief reflection*] All right, I'll ride over there.

[RADEMACHER *tries to thank him.*]

HALMSCHLÖGER [*warding him off*]: Naturally I can't assume any guarantee that I can bring him here. But since it seems to be of so much concern to you—[*Since* RADEMACHER *wants to thank him again*] Fine and good, fine and good.

[*He turns away.*]

TANN: Well finally!

HALMSCHLÖGER: Dear Tann, I must ask you to look into the other rooms—in the meantime, it's nothing special—two injections—the attendant will tell you, after all—

TANN: Why what is it, then, what is it, then?

HALMSCHLÖGER: An odd story. The poor devil's requesting me to bring in an old friend, to whom he evidently has something important to confide. Do you know who it is? That Weihgast, the poet.

TANN: Well, and are you going to go over there? Why tell me, are you his servant, then? Well listen, the people here are simply exploiting your good nature.

HALMSCHLÖGER: Dear friend, it's a matter of sensitivity. It's just such things that are the most interesting part of our profession, as I see it.

TANN: That's another perception.

HALMSCHLÖGER: So won't you be so kind, then?

TANN: Naturally. There's no more time for the café today?

HALMSCHLÖGER: Perhaps I'll come over later on.

[HALMSCHLÖGER, TANN, *and* JULIANA *exit.*]

FLORIAN [*coming back in*]: Why, what did you have to discuss with the Doctor for so long?

RADEMACHER [*worked up, almost cheerful*]: I'm getting one more visit—I'm getting one more visit.

FLORIAN [*interested*]: What's that? A visit? Now? In the middle of the night?

RADEMACHER: Yes, my dear Jackwerth—just pay attention, there's something to be learned here too . . . specifically, from this visit. You must look at the gentleman, when he comes in and then afterward, when he leaves. . . . Ah! [*Increasingly worked up*] If I just live to see it—if I just live to see it!—Give me a glass of water, Jackwerth—if you would, please.

[*This happens, he drinks greedily.*]

Thanks very much—thanks very much.—Yes, the machinery will hold out that long . . . [*Almost with anxiety*] If he just comes . . . if he just comes . . .

FLORIAN: Who are you talking about, then?

RADEMACHER [*to himself*]: Write to him? . . . No, I wouldn't get anything from that . . . No, I've got to have him here—here—facing me . . . eye to eye, head to head—ah!

FLORIAN [*as if concerned*]: Herr Rademacher . . .

RADEMACHER: Don't worry about me—it's quite unnecessary—good lord, I'm starting to feel quite well, I no longer even fear dying. . . . It won't be that bad, once he's been here. . . . Ah, Florian Jackwerth, what can I leave for you?

FLORIAN [*amazed*]: But why?

RADEMACHER: I'd like to show my gratitude. Specifically, you suggested this idea to me—yes indeed. I'll appoint you my heir. The key to my desk is under my pillow.—Don't you think that's something special?—Who knows? You could be mistaken . . . Perhaps there are some masterpieces there! I'm feeling better and better—good lord . . . At last I'm getting healthy again!

FLORIAN: Surely you are!

RADEMACHER: To fight—yes indeed, to fight! I'll try again. I'm not giving up yet—no. I'm certainly not so old—fifty-four . . . Why, after all, isn't that an age when one's still healthy? I'm somebody, Florian Jackwerth—I'm somebody, you can believe me. I've just been misfortunate. I'm just as good as anyone else who is highly successful, my dear sir—and I can take on all those who think themselves better than I am, just because they're luckier. [*Feverishly*] If only he comes . . . if only he comes . . . If you please, Lord God in Heaven, even if you've deserted me these fifty-four years, just give me strength for this last quarter of an hour, so that will even everything out, as well as it can. Let me live to see him sitting here in front of me—pale, totally destroyed—looking just as small now as he felt superior toward me all his life . . . Yes, my dear Jackwerth, the one I am expecting here is, to be specific, a friend of my youth. And twenty-five years ago—and even as recently as twenty—we were very good friends, for we both started from the same spot—just that we went a different way—he, increasingly higher, and I, increasingly lower. And today it's gone so far that he's a rich and famous poet and I'm a poor devil of a journalist and am dying miserably in the hospital.—But it doesn't matter, it doesn't matter—for now comes the moment when I can destroy him . . . and I'll do it! If only he comes—if only he comes! I know, Herr Jackwerth, your mistress was with you this afternoon—but what, then, is all the passion with which one awaits a loved one, compared to the longing for someone one hates, whom one has hated all one's life, and to whom one has neglected to say it.

FLORIAN: Why you're sure getting horribly excited, Herr Rademacher!—Why, you're losing your voice.

RADEMACHER: Don't worry—once he's here, I'll certainly be able to speak.

FLORIAN: Who knows? Who knows?—Listen, Herr Rademacher, let me make you a suggestion. Why not hold a rehearsal?—No, Herr Rademacher, I'm not joking. I know my way around, after all. You understand: it always depends on just how one *presents* it, doesn't it? Just what do you gain if you tell him: "You're a malicious person and I hate you,"—why, that won't work. Then he'll think: you can go on abusing me as long as you like, lying there in your little room with a one-hundred-and-two-degree fever, and I'll be walking around comfortably and smoking my little cigar.

RADEMACHER: I'll tell him something else, quite different. He'd soon get over someone being malicious. But he'll not recover from being ridiculous all his life to the people he may have loved most.

FLORIAN: So speak, speak. Imagine I'm the friend of your youth. I'm standing here, I've got a bag full of money, a head full of imagination—[*Acting the part*] "Here I am, old friend. You wished to speak to me. Please." Well, then.

RADEMACHER [*feverishly, increasingly talking himself into a fury*]: Yes indeed, I sent for you. But not to say good-bye to you, in memory of old friendship—no, to tell you something before it's too late.

FLORIAN [*acting*]: "You're putting me in a great suspense, old chum. What do you wish to inform me about?" So, go on—go on!

RADEMACHER: You think that you amount to more than I?—My dear friend, neither of us ever belonged to the ranks of the great, and, at times like this, here in the depths where we're at home, there's no difference between us. All your greatness is pure deception and fraud. Your fame—a heap of newspaper pages which will blow away in the wind the day after your death. Your friends?—Flatterers lying on their bellies before success, envious dwarves with clenched fists in their pockets, when your back is turned, fools, for whom you are just small enough for their admiration.—

But you're certainly smart enough to sense that yourself occasionally. I wouldn't have troubled you to come over here to inform you of that. It's possibly nasty for me to want to tell you something else. But it's unbelievable how little being nasty matters to a person, when one has no more days ahead to be ashamed about it.

[*He stands up.*]

Why, a hundred times now I just wanted to scream it in your face these last years when we happened to meet on the street and you favored me with a kind word. My dear friend, not only do I know you as do thousands of others—even your beloved wife knows you better than you think and saw through you as far back as twenty years ago—in the prime of your youth and success.—Yes, saw through you—and I know it better than anyone else. . . . For she was my mistress for two years and a hundred times she came running to me, disgusted by your vanity and emptiness, and she wanted to run away with me. But I was poor, and she was cowardly, and that's why she stayed with you and deceived you! It was more convenient for all of us.

FLORIAN: "Ha, you despicable man! You're lying!"

RADEMACHER: I? [*As if awakening*] Ah so . . . You. Jackwerth, you have the key. If he doesn't believe me—the letters are also in the desk. You're the executor of my will.—Various treasures of all kinds are there in my desk—who knows, perhaps nothing else is necessary to appreciate them than that I'm dead.—Why certainly, then the people will be concerned about me. Particularly when it's said I died in distress and poverty—for I am dying in distress and poverty—as I lived. Someone will certainly speak at my grave. Why just pay attention—devotion to duty—competency—victim of his profession . . . Yes, that's true, Florian Jackwerth, since I have a profession, I've been its victim—I've been a victim of my profession from the first moment on. And do you know what's destroyed me? Do you think it's the Latin letters on the chart there?—Oh no! It's my venom at having to bow and scrape to people I despised, just to get a position. From my disgust at having to write things I didn't believe in, just to keep from starving. From my fury at having to grind out lines for the most detestable people, who got their money through fraud and deception and that I was further helping them to do that with my talent. Of course, I can't complain: I always got my share of the contempt and hatred toward the rabble—only unfortunately not from anything else.

JULIANA [*entering*]: The Herr Resident.

RADEMACHER [*frightened*]: Alone?

JULIANA: No, a gentleman is with him.

[*Look of gratitude on* RADEMACHER'*s face.*]

FLORIAN: Pull yourself together now. Pity I can't be present.

[*He steals out.* HALMSCHLÖGER *and* WEIHGAST *enter.*]

HALMSCHLÖGER: So, here's the patient.

WEIHGAST [*elegantly clothed, very well-preserved gentleman of roughly fifty-five, with full gray beard, dark overcoat, and walking cane*]: I see—over here. [*Going over to* RADEMACHER; *cordially*] Rademacher—is it possible? Rademacher—so we see each other again! My dear friend!

HALMSCHLÖGER [*beckoning;* JULIANA *brings a chair for* WEIHGAST]: And now permit me, Herr Weihgast, that, as a physician, I request you not to extend the discussion any longer than a quarter hour. I'll make so bold as to come back myself after that time and accompany you down.

WEIHGAST: Thank you, Herr Doctor. You're very kind.

HALMSCHLÖGER: Oh, not at all, I should thank you. It's really no great difficulty . . .

WEIHGAST [*makes a parrying gesture*]: Fine, fine . . .

HALMSCHLÖGER: Well, Herr Rademacher, good-bye.

[*After threatening him in the kindly manner of a physician not to get excited, he exchanges some words with* JULIANA *and exits with her.*]

WEIHGAST [*having given his overcoat to* JULIANA, *he sits down; very cordially, almost genuinely*]: Well just tell me, my dear Rademacher, what kind of idea is it, to be lying in this place—in a hospital—!

RADEMACHER: Oh, I'm satisfied, I'm very well taken care of here.

WEIHGAST: Yes, you're surely in the best of hands. Dr. Halmschlöger is a very competent young physician and, what's more, a splendid person. As if the personal can ever be separated from the professional. But, in spite of that—you'll certainly excuse me—why didn't you turn to me?

RADEMACHER: How could I . . .

WEIHGAST: Even if you were no longer concerned with your old friend for all these years, you surely know that under the circumstances I'd be at your disposal in every way . . .

RADEMACHER: Just stop that, just stop that.

WEIHGAST: Oh well—please. Truly, it wasn't meant maliciously. All the same, it's not too late even now.—Dr. Halmschlöger tells me it's only a matter of time, of good care . . . you'll be leaving the hospital in a couple of weeks and, as far as convalescence in the country is concerned . . .

RADEMACHER: There's no longer any talk about those things.

WEIHGAST: Dr. Halmschlöger even informed me about this hypochondria—yes.

[*He finds it difficult to stand the look* RADEMACHER *is directing at him, but doesn't look away.*]

So, you sent for me, you wanted to speak with me. Well, I'm ready. Why are you smiling?—No, it's the glare from the light. The lighting here isn't the best.—Well, I'm waiting. I'll explain to Herr Dr. Halmschlöger that you didn't make use of the first five minutes. Well?—

[RADEMACHER *has already had his lips half open a few times, as if he wanted to speak; now again, but again he's silent.—Pause.*]

WEIHGAST: Just what became of you then? [*Slightly embarrassed*]

Hmm, right now that question is a bit awkward. I'm a little self-conscious, I must confess to you; for, externally considered, one might well believe I'm the one for whom life turned out better. And, after all—if one takes things the way they must really be taken after all—who experienced more disappointments? It's always the one who apparently attained more.—That sounds paradoxical, and so it is, after all.—Ah, if I could only tell you . . . nothing but controversy—nothing but cares—. I don't know if you've kept up with the recent agitation. Now they're crashing down on me . . . Who? The young people. When one reflects that ten years ago, one was young oneself. Now they're trying to dethrone me . . . When one reads those new reviews . . . Ah, it's enough to make one ill! They're treating me with scorn, with condescension. Why it's pitiable! When one has worked honestly and striven, given one's best—-and now . . . Ah, be glad you don't know anything about all those things. If I could choose today—begin my life over today . . .

RADEMACHER: Well?

WEIHGAST: I'd like to be a farmer in the country, a shepherd, an Arctic explorer—ah, whatever you want!—Only nothing about literature.—But the day isn't over yet.

RADEMACHER [*smiling oddly*]: Do you want to go to the Arctic?

WEIHGAST: Ah, no. But a new piece of mine is coming out at the beginning of next season. Then they shall see, then they shall see! And I'll not let them get me down! Just wait! Just wait!—Now, if all goes well, you shall be present then, my old friend. I promise to send you the tickets. Although your paper generally takes confounded little notice of me in general. Why my last two books were greeted by all of you with absolutely deadly silence. But of course, you don't have anything to do with that department. Well!—By the way, what kind of trivial, silly stuff . . . So, just go ahead and tell me. What do you have to say to me? If it's difficult for you to speak loudly . . . then I can move quite close.—Hmm . . . [*Pausing*] What will my wife say about it, when I tell her old Rademacher is lying in General Hospital . . . Your pride, my dear Rademacher, your damned pride . . . Well, we don't want to talk about that . . . By the way, my wife is temporarily not in Vienna—in Abbazia. Always suffering from something.

RADEMACHER: Nothing serious, I hope?

WEIHGAST [*pressing his hand*]: No, thank God. My dear sir, things would be bad for me then too. Truly I find myself when in her presence—the belief in myself again, when I'm almost to the point of losing the power to create, the desire to live. And the older one gets, the more one feels that this is, after all, the only true relationship there is. For the children . . . Oh God!

RADEMACHER: What's wrong, then? What are they doing?

WEIHGAST: My daughter is married. So, I'm a grandfather twice already now. You don't see it in me, I know. And my boy—boy!!—is doing his military service this year—running up debts—recently had a duel with a young Baron Wallerskirch—because of a *woman* . . . Yes, my dear sir, always the same stupidities. That's how one gets old, and life takes its course.

RADEMACHER: Yes, yes.

[*Pause.*]

WEIHGAST: Well, time's passing. I'm waiting. What do you have to say to me? I'm ready to do everything you wish . . . Shall I perhaps take steps with the Benevolent Association of Journalists? Or, in the event of your speedy recovery, can I perhaps contact the editor's office of *New Day* . . . Or—you'll excuse that I speak of such things—can I somehow help you with money problems . . .

RADEMACHER: Stop, stop. I don't need anything—anything . . . I just wanted to see you once more, my dear friend—that's all. Yes.

[*Extends him his hand.*]

WEIHGAST: So, I'm truly touched. Yes.—Well, when you're healthy again, I hope we'll see each other again more often . . . so there!

[*Painful pause.—The clock is heard ticking in the adjacent ward.*]

HALMSCHLÖGER [*entering*]: Well, here I am again. I hope I'm not too punctual?

WEIHGAST [*arising, visibly relieved*]: Yes, we're already finished.

HALMSCHLÖGER: Well, I'm glad about that. And I hope our patient is reassured—isn't he?

RADEMACHER [*nodding*]: I thank you.

WEIHGAST: So, good-bye, dear friend. If the Herr Doctor will permit, I'll just check back in a couple of days.

HALMSCHLÖGER: Surely. I'll leave instructions that you'll be allowed at any time . . .

WEIHGAST: Oh, I don't wish for you to make an exception on my account.

HALMSCHLÖGER: Paschanda!

[JULIANA *hands* WEIHGAST *his overcoat.*]

WEIHGAST: So, once more adieu—and a speedy recovery, and don't despair.

[*He walks toward the exit with* HALMSCHLÖGER.]

FLORIAN [*coming out from behind the curtain*]: Greetings, Herr Doctor, greetings!

HALMSCHLÖGER: Well listen, you're still not asleep!

WEIHGAST: What kind of person is this? He is staring at me in such an odd manner . . .

HALMSCHLÖGER: A poor devil of an actor.

WEIHGAST: I see, I see.

HALMSCHLÖGER: Has no inkling that in a week at the latest he'll be in his grave.

WEIHGAST: So, so.

[WEIHGAST*'s and* FLORIAN*'s gazes meet.*]

HALMSCHLÖGER: That's why I also regard any strictness as unnecessary, after all. Rules for dying patients—that just doesn't make any real sense.

WEIHGAST: Quite right.—Actually, I was very glad to make your closer acquaintance and to have the occasion to eavesdrop on you at work for once, so to speak. On the whole, it was very interesting for me in many ways.

HALMSCHLÖGER: Well, if I may ask, was it really something so important your friend had to inform you about?

WEIHGAST: No idea. We associated with each other in time long since past, he wanted to see me once more . . . that was all. [*In departing*] By the way, I believe my coming reassured him.

JULIANA: At your service.

WEIHGAST: Ah so.

[*He gives her a gratuity.* HALMSCHLÖGER *and* WEIHGAST *exit;* JULIANA *as well, behind them.*]

FLORIAN [*going quickly over to* RADEMACHER]: Well so, what was it, then? The man must have gigantic self-control. I know all about physiognomies, after all—but I didn't notice anything in him. How did he take it, then?

RADEMACHER [*without listening to him*]: How pathetic are the people who still have to go on living tomorrow.

FLORIAN: Herr Rademacher—so what's wrong, then? What about the key to the desk?

RADEMACHER [*as if awakening*]: Desk—?—Do what you want. Burn it up, for all I care!

FLORIAN: And the treasures? The masterpieces?

RADEMACHER: Masterpieces!—And even if . . . There's posterity even for the living. [*As if prophetic*] Now he's downstairs. Now he's going through the avenue—through the gate—now he's in the street—the lanterns are burning—the coaches are rolling—people are coming from above . . . and below . . .

[*He has slowly stood up.*]

FLORIAN [*giving him a serious look*]: Herr Rademacher!

RADEMACHER: What concern is he to me? What's his happiness, what are his cares to me? What did the two of us have to discuss with each other? Hey! Eh? . . .

[*He seizes* FLORIAN *by the hand.*]

What concern are those who will still be in the world tomorrow to people like us?

FLORIAN [*in anxiety*]: What do you want from me then?—Frau Paschanda!

[JULIANA *comes with the light.*]

RADEMACHER [*lets go of* FLORIAN*'s hand*]: Put it out, Frau Paschanda, I don't need a light anymore . . .

[*He sinks down onto the chair.*]

FLORIAN [*at the curtain, holding on to it with both hands*]: But now—isn't that . . . ?

[*Curtain*]

Countess Mitzi, or The Family Gathering

A COMEDY IN ONE ACT

Characters

Servant

Count Arpad Pazmandy

Mitzi (Maria), *his daughter*

Gardener

Prince Egon Ravenstein

Philipp

Lolo Langhuber

Wasner, *a coachman*

Professor Windhofer

[*Garden of the* COUNT*'s villa. Tall ornamental fence in background. A gate, roughly midstage, somewhat further to the right. The front of the one-story villa in left foreground, formerly a small hunting lodge, one hundred eighty years old, renovated thirty years ago. A terrace, not very deep, runs the length of the raised ground floor, with three wide steps leading into the garden. An open glass door from the terrace into the salon. The first floor has simple windows. A small balcony, decorated with flowers and belonging to a kind of attic, over the first floor. In front of the villa a lawn with flower beds. A garden bench, small tables and chairs beneath a tree in right foreground. The* COUNT, *an elderly gentleman with gray mustache, in riding clothes, still very good-looking, with the bearing and conduct of a former officer, enters from right, with riding whip in his hand. The* SERVANT *enters with him.*]

SERVANT: At what time does Your Lordship request dinner today?

COUNT [*speaking clipped jargon in the way of Hungarian-German officers, lighting a cigar*]: At two.

SERVANT: And at what time does Your Lordship request that the horses be harnessed?

MITZI [*appearing in the balcony, with palette and paintbrush in her hand; calls down*]: Good morning, Papa.

COUNT: Greetings, Mitzi.

MITZI: Once again you've gone and let me eat breakfast alone. Where have you been, then?

COUNT: Rather far away. Went out riding in the suburbs. It's simply beautiful today. What are you doing, then? Already at work? Will there soon be something else to see?

MITZI: Oh yes, Papa, just it's nothing but flowers again.

COUNT: Isn't the Professor coming to see you today?

MITZI: Yes, but not until around one.

COUNT: Well, don't let me disturb you.

[MITZI *throws him a kiss with her hand and disappears into the attic.*]

COUNT [*to the* SERVANT]: What do you want? Ah so, because of harnessing the horses? I'll not be going out riding any more today. Joseph can have himself a day off today. Or, wait a moment. [*Calling upstairs*] Say, Mitzi . . .

[MITZI *appears on the balcony.*]

COUNT: Excuse me for disturbing you once more. Do you perhaps need the coach today?

MITZI: No, thank you Papa. Not that I'm aware of . . . Thanks very much.

[*She disappears again.*]

COUNT: So, it's settled. Joseph can do whatever he wants this afternoon. As for you . . . see to it that Franz rubs down the old horse properly—we were a bit fiery today . . . both of us.

[*The* SERVANT *exits.*]

[*The* COUNT, *who has sat down on the bench, takes a newspaper lying on the table and reads.*]

GARDENER [*entering*]: Good morning, Your Lordship.

COUNT: Good morning, Peter. What's going on, then?

GARDENER: If Your Lordship will permit, I cut back the tea roses just now.

COUNT: But why so much?

GARDENER: The bush is quite full. It would hardly be advisable, Your Lordship, if we left them on there any longer. If Your Lordship would perhaps be able to use . . .

COUNT: Not able to use them. Well, what are you looking at, then? I'm not going into town today, I don't need any bouquet. Put the flowers individually into the vases and glasses standing around inside there, the way the fashion is now. [*Takes the flowers in his hand and smells them; seems to reflect*] Isn't that a coach stopping there?

GARDENER: It's His Highness's black horses. I recognize them by their hoofbeat.

COUNT: So, thank you very much.

[*He gives him back the roses. The* PRINCE *enters through the main gate. The* COUNT *goes over to him.*]

GARDENER: At your service, Your Highness.

PRINCE: Good morning, Peter.

[*The* GARDENER *exits right. The* PRINCE, *in a pale summer suit, slender, fifty-five but looking much younger, has the light diplomatic accent of a gentleman who speaks as much French as German.*]

COUNT: Greetings, old friend. How are things going, how do things stand?

PRINCE: Thank you. Splendid weather today.

[*The* COUNT *offers him a giant cigar.*]

PRINCE: Thank you, not before eating. One of my cigarettes, if you'll permit.

[*He takes a cigarette out of his cigarette case and lights it.*]

COUNT: So, a person gets to see you once again. Don't you have any idea how long you've not been here? Three weeks.

PRINCE [*glancing at attic*]: Has it really been that long now?

COUNT: Well, why do you make yourself so scarce, then?

PRINCE: Don't be angry. Why, it's true. And I'm really coming today just to tell you adieu.

COUNT: What, adieu?

PRINCE: To be specific, I'm leaving tomorrow.

COUNT: You're leaving? For where, then?

PRINCE: To the sea. And you . . . don't you have any plans yet?

COUNT: I still haven't thought about that at all . . . this year.

PRINCE: Oh well, you have it so simply beautiful out here . . . this giant park! But you'll certainly be traveling somewhere in the summer, after all.

COUNT: I still don't know. Why, it's all the same.

PRINCE: What's wrong, then?

COUNT: Dear old friend, it's going downhill.

PRINCE: How's that? What kind of strange expressions are those, Arpad? What does that mean, "downhill"?

COUNT: One's getting old, Egon.

PRINCE: Yes, but one gets used to it.

COUNT: What are you talking about? You're younger by five years.

PRINCE: By six. But fifty-five, that's no longer the springtime of life, either. Well—one accommodates oneself to it.

COUNT: Well, you always were a psychologist, old friend.

PRINCE: For the rest, I really don't know what you want. You look splendid.

[*He sits down. Glances up at the attic again, as he sometimes does. Pause.*]

COUNT [*with resolve*]: So, do you know the latest? She's getting married.

PRINCE: Who's getting married?

COUNT: Why do you ask, then . . . ? Why, you can imagine.

PRINCE: Ah so, I was thinking of Mitzi, to be specific. Oh well, it would be, after all . . . So, Lolo's getting married?

COUNT: Yes, Lolo.

PRINCE: But that's actually not the latest, is it?

COUNT: How's that?

PRINCE: After all, she's been promising you that, or threatening you, or, how shall one say it, for at least three years.

COUNT: For three? By all means, you can say for ten. Or for eighteen. Yes, really, ever since the business started between the two of us. Why, it was always a set idea of hers. "If a respectable person comes asking for my hand, I'll depart the stage immediately." That was her second word. After all, you've also heard it from her yourself a couple of times. And now he's simply come, the one she's been waiting for . . . and she's getting married.

PRINCE: Well, if only he's a respectable person.

COUNT: Well, jokes! So that's your involvement in such a serious moment!

PRINCE: Well.

[*He lays his hand on the* COUNT*'s arm.*]

COUNT: Why I assure you, it is a serious moment. No trifling matter, when one's more or less lived with a person almost twenty years, spent the best years with her, really shared joys and sorrows with her . . . one's no longer even thought it could ever end . . . and then she comes one fine day and says: "God bless my soul, dear friend, the wedding's very soon . . ." Now that's a hell of a business. [*Gets up, walking back and forth*] And, at the same time, I can't even blame her. Precisely because I understand it so well. What can you do!

PRINCE: You were always too much a good fellow, Arpad.

COUNT: What's good about that, then? Why shouldn't I understand it? She's hit thirty-eight. And she's said farewell to her profession. So everyone must sympathize with her, after all, that it's no fun for her to go on living as a retired ballerina and as the active mistress of Count Pazmandy, who, in time, is naturally becoming an old jackass too. Why, I was prepared for that. I can't blame her at all, good lord.

PRINCE: So, did you depart as good friends, then?

COUNT: Naturally. It was even a parting in good spirits, good lord. Why, at the start, I didn't realize just how hard it'd be for me. I've only gradually become conscious. It's just such a remarkable business . . .

PRINCE: What's so remarkable about it, then?

COUNT: Well, that I'm telling it to you. When I rode away from her then, for the last time, last week, at night, I suddenly felt, just how shall I say . . . very lighthearted. Now you're a free man, I thought to myself. You don't have to ride into town every evening God gave you and sit at the table with Lolo and chat or even just listen. Why, sometimes it was really dull—to the point of being unbearable. And to ride home again in the middle of the night and, in the end, to give an account as well . . . when you happened to have supper at the officers' club with an acquaintance, or go to the opera with your daughter, or to the Royal Theatre. So, what all should I tell you. I was downright prepared for riding home. Already had all kinds of plans in mind . . . oh, not what you're imagining . . . no, but to travel, what I've already been wanting to do for a very long time now, to Africa or India, as a free man . . . that is, I would've taken my girl along. Oh well, you're laughing because I still keep saying "girl."

PRINCE: Doesn't occur to me in the least. Mitzi really does still look like a young girl. Like a very young one. Especially lately, in her Florentine straw hat.

COUNT: Like a young girl? And at the same time she's exactly the age of Lolo. Well, you certainly know! We're getting old, Egon! All of us. Yes, yes . . . and lonely. But really, at the start I didn't notice it. It's only gradually come over me. The first days after the festive parting still weren't so bad. Not until yesterday, and the day before, as the hour came when formerly I was accustomed to riding into town . . . and now, when Peter brought me roses for Lolo, it goes without saying, it's become clear to me that I've become a widower for the second time in my life, in a way. Yes, dear friend. And now it's forever. Now comes loneliness. Now it's here.

PRINCE: But that's just ridiculous! Loneliness!

COUNT: Don't be angry, but you don't understand that. You've lived quite differently than I. After all, you've not gotten involved in anything else since your poor wife died ten years ago. In anything serious, I mean. And, moreover, you have a profession as well, as it were.

PRINCE: How's that, then?

COUNT: Well, member of the House of Lords.

PRINCE: Oh well.

COUNT: And, after all, twice you almost became a cabinet minister.

PRINCE: Almost . . .

COUNT: Who knows. Perhaps you'll really get caught someday. And now I'm quite finished. Three years ago I even let myself get pensioned off, jackass that I am.

PRINCE [*smiling*]: In return, you've become a full, free man now. Completely free. The world is open to you.

COUNT: But to no pleasure, old friend. That's the story. I've not even gone to the officers' club since then. Do you know what I've been doing these last evenings? I've sat under that tree there with Mitzi, and we've played dominoes.

PRINCE: Well, you see, that's not loneliness after all. When one has a daughter, besides one who is such an astute person, with whom you've always gotten along so well . . . By the way, what does she have to say about it then, now that you're spending all your evenings at home?

COUNT: Nothing. Why, that's sometimes occurred before, too. She doesn't say anything at all. What's she supposed to say, then? It seems to me she doesn't notice it at all. Do you think she knew something about Lolo?

PRINCE [*laughing*]: Now listen!

COUNT: Well, naturally! Why, I know. Naturally she knew it. After all, I was still almost a young man when her poor mother died. She couldn't have blamed me, in any case.

PRINCE: No, she couldn't. [*Gently*] But I can imagine she certainly must've sometimes felt she's alone a great deal.

COUNT: Did she complain about me? Now certainly you can tell me.

PRINCE: Why, I'm not Mitzi's confidant, after all. Naturally she never complained to me. Lord, perhaps she didn't feel that way at all. She's certainly been used to this secluded, quiet life for such a long time.

COUNT: Yes. And it's also to her liking, after all. And then she was quite heavily involved in the world, up until a few years ago. Between us, Egon, even as late as three years ago, even two, I firmly thought she'd decide after all.

PRINCE: Decide? Ah so . . .

COUNT: If you had any inkling what kind of people were still showing such lively interest in her quite recently . . .

PRINCE: That's very understandable.

COUNT: But she doesn't want to. She absolutely doesn't want to. So, from that I just think she couldn't have felt herself all that alone . . . otherwise she could've just decided, since she did have opportunities . . .

PRINCE: Goes without saying. Why, it's her free choice. And then Mitzi has this other resource as well, that she paints. That's exactly the way it was with my blessed Aunt Fanny Hohenstein, who wrote books up to an advanced age, and also wouldn't hear anything at all about marrying.

COUNT: It's just possible that's connected with artistic aspirations. Sometimes I just think those eccentricities might all be psychologically connected, in a way.

PRINCE: Eccentricities? But one can't say Mitzi's eccentric.

COUNT: Yes, now that's completely abated. One time earlier, however . . .

PRINCE: I've always found Mitzi very astute and very calm. After all, when someone paints roses and violets they have to be far from eccentric.

COUNT: Well, you won't regard me as so stupid for thinking that just because of the violets and roses. But, as a very young girl, if you can remember . . .

PRINCE: What, then?

COUNT: Well, that business of how Fedor Wangenheim asked for her hand.

PRINCE: Lord, are you still thinking about that? But that's not true at all. Why, that's already been a good eighteen or twenty years ago.

COUNT: How she wanted to go to the convent to become an Ursuline nun, rather than take the nice fellow as her husband, to whom she was already as good as engaged. And ran away from home. Can't that be called eccentric, after all?

PRINCE: But why bring up that ancient business today?

COUNT: Ancient? To me it seems as if it were last year. It was just at the time when my business with Lolo got started. When one thinks back like that! If someone had predicted to me at the time!

Do you know, it actually got started like some adventure. Quite thoughtless and crazy. Well, I don't want to commit any sins, but it was fortunate for all of us that my poor wife had already been dead for a couple of years by then. Lolo was my fate. Mistress and housewife at the same time. Because, you see, she could also cook so splendidly. And the comfort of being with her. And always in a good humor and never an angry word . . . Well, it's over. Let's not talk about that anymore. [*Pausing*] . . . But, tell me, aren't you staying with us for dinner? By the way, I'll call Mitzi.

PRINCE [*holding him back*]: Stop, I've got something else to tell you. [*Gently, as if humorously*] I have to prepare you for something.

COUNT: What? For what, then?

PRINCE: To be specific, I'll be presenting a young gentleman to you today.

COUNT: What, a young gentleman?

PRINCE: Yes, if you've nothing against that.

COUNT: What should I have against that? But who is it, then?

PRINCE: My son, dear Arpad.

COUNT [*extremely astonished*]: What?

PRINCE: Yes, my son. After all, before I travel away, I didn't want . . .

COUNT: Your son? You have a son?

PRINCE: Yes.

COUNT: Well, that sounds, after all, like . . . You have a young gentleman who is your son? Or rather, a son who is a young gentleman. How old is he, then?

PRINCE: Seventeen years.

COUNT: Seventeen! And he's telling me that only now! No, Egon . . . Egon! Why, tell me . . . Seventeen years . . . Say! Why, your wife must still have been alive, then . . .

PRINCE: Yes, my wife was still alive at the time. Sometimes one gets dragged into remarkable incidents, dear Arpad.

COUNT: Good lord, that certainly must be true!

PRINCE: And then one day one simply has a seventeen-year-old son, with whom one goes on trips.

COUNT: So, you're leaving with him?

PRINCE: I'm taking the liberty.

COUNT: No, I just can't tell you . . . so, he has a seventeen-year-old! . . .

[*He suddenly gives him his hand and embraces him.*]

And, if I may just ask . . . the mother of this gentleman, your son . . . how's that . . . because you were starting to tell me just now—

PRINCE: The mother's long since dead. Died a couple of weeks after the birth. A very young creature.

COUNT: A commoner?

PRINCE: Yes, of course. But a charming person. Well, sometime I'll tell you in more detail. As well as I myself can still remember. It was like a dream, the whole business. If the boy weren't still here . . .

COUNT: So, he's telling me that only now! Only today, before the fellow's coming for a visit.

PRINCE: One can never know how such a thing will be received.

COUNT: Come now. Received! Did you perhaps think . . . after all, I'm a bit of a psychologist too. Well, and that's a friend!

PRINCE: No one knew it, no one in the whole world.

COUNT: But you could've told me, after all. I really don't understand it, that you . . . Come on, it's really not very nice.

PRINCE: I wanted to see how the fellow developed. Why, one can never know . . .

COUNT: Oh well, with such a mixed parentage . . . But now you seem reassured?

PRINCE: Yes. He's a splendid chap.

COUNT [*embracing him again*]: So then, where's he been living up until now?

PRINCE: Rather far from Vienna his first years. In the Tyrol.

COUNT: With farmers?

PRINCE: With a small landowner. Then he attended his first schools in Innsbruck. And I've had him in the preparatory school in Krems these last years.

COUNT: So you've visited him sometimes?

PRINCE: Naturally.

COUNT: What does he actually think, then?

PRINCE: Until a few days ago he simply thought he no longer had his parents, no father either. And that I was a friend of his deceased father.

MITZI [*on the balcony*]: Good day, Prince Egon.

PRINCE: Good day, Mitzi.

COUNT: Well, don't you want to come downstairs a bit?

MITZI: If one's not disturbing . . .

[*She disappears.*]

COUNT: So, what do we tell Mitzi, then?

PRINCE: I'd like to leave that to you, naturally. But since I'm adopting the boy after all and, in just a few days, he'll probably bear my name, through an act of grace on the part of His Majesty . . .

COUNT [*astonished*]: What?

PRINCE: . . . it's probably best we tell Mitzi the truth right away.

COUNT: Naturally, naturally, why not, then? And even when you adopt him . . . It's funny, after all. A daughter always remains just a little girl for her father, however, even if she stays single.

[MITZI *appears—she is thirty-seven, still very good-looking, in a white dress and Florentine straw hat—and kisses the* COUNT, *then gives the* PRINCE *her hand.*]

MITZI: Well, how are things going, Prince Egon? One sees you so seldom.

PRINCE: Thank you, Mitzi. You're very busy?

MITZI: One paints one's little flowers.

COUNT: Don't be so modest, Mitzi. Professor Windhofer recently said she should by all means exhibit sometime. Doesn't need to hide behind our famous women painters.

MITZI: Yes, that's no doubt true, but I simply don't have any ambition.

PRINCE: Actually I'm not for exhibiting either. Then you're at the mercy of every newspaper hack.

MITZI: So are the members of the House of Lords as well. At least when they make a speech.

COUNT: And perhaps our kind isn't? They poke their noses into everything.

PRINCE: Well, the way the tendency is today, there are people who'd like to grumble about your pictures, Mitzi, just because you're a countess.

COUNT: He's right about that.

SERVANT [*entering*]: Your Lordship is requested to come to the telephone.

COUNT: Who is it, then? What is it, then?

SERVANT: Would Your Lordship please proceed to the extension in person?

COUNT: You'll excuse me a moment. [*Softly to him*] Tell her now, while I'm not present. I'd prefer it.

[*He exits.*]

MITZI: There's a telephone call . . . might Papa be already back in new shackles again after all?

[*She sits down.*]

PRINCE: In new ones?

MITZI: Lolo usually telephoned at this time. But now it's over with Lolo. You know that?

PRINCE: I found it out just now.

MITZI: And what do you have to say to that, Prince Egon? Why, I'm very sorry. If he starts something now, he'll surely go falling again. And I fear he's starting something again. He's still too young for his years.

PRINCE: Yes, yes.

MITZI [*turning around toward him*]: By the way, you've not been here for a long time.

PRINCE: You probably don't miss me very much . . . I fear . . . Art . . . and Lord knows what else . . .

MITZI [*simply*]: Nevertheless . . .

PRINCE: Very kind.

[*Pause.*]

MITZI: Why are you so reserved today? Just tell me about something. Isn't there anything at all new in the world?

PRINCE [*as if thinking about it for the first time*]: Our son has graduated.

MITZI [*wincing very slightly*]: I hope you also have more interesting news in store.

PRINCE: More interesting . . .

MITZI: Or at least news that concerns me personally more than the résumé of a young gentleman whom I don't know.

PRINCE: I think I'm obligated, however, to inform you about the more important stages in the career of this young gentleman. Why, when he was confirmed, I permitted myself to communicate that to you as well. But we don't need to speak further about it now.

[*Pause.*]

MITZI: Did he at least pass?

PRINCE: With distinction.

MITZI: Why, so the breed seems to be improving.

PRINCE: We would both hope so.

MITZI: And now the grand moment's also drawing near . . .

PRINCE: What kind of moment?

MITZI: Then don't you remember? Why, after graduation you wanted to disclose to him that you're his father.

PRINCE: I've already done that.

MITZI: You—have already told him that?

PRINCE: Yes.

MITZI [*after a pause, without looking at him*]: And his mother—is dead . . .

PRINCE: Provisionally dead.

MITZI: Forever.

[*She stands up.*]

PRINCE: As you wish.

[*The* COUNT *and the* SERVANT *enter.*]

SERVANT: But after all, Your Lordship gave Joseph the afternoon off yourself.

COUNT: Yes, yes, it's all right.

[*The* SERVANT *exits.*]

MITZI: What's wrong then, Papa?

COUNT: Nothing, nothing, my child. I've got to take a quick ride somewhere, and that confounded Joseph . . . Don't be angry, Mitzi, but I'd just like a few words with Egon . . . [*To him*] So, imagine, she already called me earlier. Lolo, to be specific. She didn't get an answer, and now Laura telephones me, her personal servant, no less, telephones me that she rode over here to my place just now.

PRINCE: To your place, over here?

COUNT: Yes.

PRINCE: Why, then?

COUNT: I can just imagine why. You know she's never been in the villa before, that goes without saying, and I've always promised her that she can come out someday and take a look at the villa and the park, before she gets married. Why, that always hurt her, that I can't receive her out here. Oh well, because of Mitzi. Which she also realized. And to bring her out sometime in secret, while Mitzi's not at home, well, I never got involved in such things. Well, and then she has me telephoned, the wedding's already the day after tomorrow, and she rode out just now.

PRINCE: Well, what does it matter? She's not coming as your mistress, after all, and whom do you need to be embarrassed of, then?

COUNT: Today, of all days . . . and now, when your son, the gentleman, will be coming right away.

PRINCE: I'll accept responsibility for him.

COUNT: But me, it doesn't suit me. I'll go to meet the coach and delay them. It just makes me nervous. Excuse me to your son, the gentleman, for the time being. Adieu, Mitzi, I'll be back right away.

[*He exits.*]

PRINCE: Fräulein Lolo announced she's coming, and that doesn't suit your good papa.

MITZI: What? Lolo announced? She's coming over here?

PRINCE: Your Papa, Mitzi, promised her that someday before her marriage she could take a look at the villa. And now he's going to meet the coach, to intercept them.

MITZI: How childish. Actually, how touching. I would have liked to have gotten to know her. Isn't it simply stupid? Here one has a father who spends almost half his life with a creature who's certainly very appealing . . . and one doesn't get to—doesn't have the right—to shake her hand even once. Why doesn't it suit him, then? He can no doubt imagine that I know everything.

PRINCE: Lord, that's just the way it is. Perhaps it would have also embarrassed him less if he weren't expecting one other visit, precisely at this time . . .

MITZI: One other visit?

PRINCE: Which I took the liberty of announcing to him.

MITZI: What kind of visit is that?

PRINCE: Our son.

MITZI: Are you . . . Your son is coming over here?

PRINCE: He'll be here in half an hour at the latest.

MITZI: Tell me, Prince . . . You're no doubt permitting yourself some fun with me?

PRINCE: By no means. With someone deceased . . . what are you thinking . . .

MITZI: It's true? He's coming over here?

PRINCE: Yes.

MITZI: So, evidently you still think it's a whim of mine, that I want to know nothing about the boy?

PRINCE: Whim . . . ? No. You're certainly carrying the matter out too consistently for it to be described that way. When one considers that you've brought yourself throughout all these years to not even ask about him . . .

MITZI: That's not to be further admired. I've brought myself to do more difficult things. At that time, when I had to give him up, a week after he came into the world.

PRINCE: Why, at that time, you, we had no other choice, after all. What I arranged at that time, and with which you, after all, declared yourself in agreement in the end, was definitely the most astute thing we could do in our situation.

MITZI: Astute, I never doubted that.

PRINCE: And not only astute, Mitzi. You know it wasn't just a question of our fate alone. Others would've perhaps been ruined if the truth had come to light at that time. With her ailing heart, my wife would've scarcely survived it.

MITZI: That ailing heart . . .

PRINCE: And your father, Mitzi . . . your father!

MITZI: He would've learned to accept it, you can rely on that. Why, the business with Lolo got started at that very time. Otherwise the other matter wouldn't have gone so smoothly. Otherwise he would have concerned himself a bit more about me. I wouldn't have been able to stay away for months, if it hadn't been just so very opportune for him. There was only one danger in the whole matter: that Fedor Wangenheim might possibly have shot you dead, dear Prince.

PRINCE: He shoot me? It could also have happened differently. Or do you believe in divine judgment? Then the outcome would also have been still open to question, by the way. For we poor mortals certainly can never know how the one up there thinks about such a matter.

MITZI: You'd speak differently in the House of Lords, if you ever opened up your mouth there.

PRINCE: Possibly. But, after all, the essential thing is that all the honesty and boldness wouldn't have done us the slightest good at that time. It would have been a needless cruelty against the people close to us. A dispensation could hardly have been obtained—and, moreover, the Princess would never have consented to the divorce: you know that as well as I.

MITZI: As if I'd attached the slightest importance to marriage.

PRINCE: Oh . . .

MITZI: Nothing. So that's nothing new to you? After all, I told you that at that time as well. You've no idea how, at that time, I . . . [*With a glance*] What . . . what would've become of me at that time. I would have followed you in every direction, in every direction, even as your mistress. I, with our child. To Switzerland, to America. Why, after all, we could've lived wherever it suited us. And perhaps they might not even have noticed in the House of Lords that you were away.

PRINCE: Yes, of course we could have fled and settled somewhere abroad . . . But you yourself probably no longer believe today that such a condition would've been pleasant or even bearable for you in the long run.

MITZI: Today, no. To be specific, I know you today. But I loved you at that time. And perhaps I could—have loved you for a very long time, if you hadn't been too cowardly at the time to assume responsibility for what happened . . . Too cowardly, Prince Egon . . .

PRINCE: Whether that's just the right word . . .

MITZI: Yes, I've no other. It wasn't up to me. *I* was ready to take everything on myself, with pleasure, with pride. I was ready to be a mother and to confess to being the mother of our child. You knew it, Egon! Seventeen years ago, in the little house in the forest where you kept me hidden, I told you I was ready to do that. But I was never one for doing things by halves. I wanted either to be a mother completely or not at all. On the day I had to give up the boy, I was also determined not to be concerned about him in any way. Therefore I find it ridiculous that you suddenly want to bring him over here. If you'll permit me some good advice, go to him, while Papa is with Lolo, and go back home with him.

PRINCE: I wouldn't think of it. After all I've had to hear again from you just now, it may well be settled that his mother's dead. But I must look after him all the more. He's my son, before the world as well. I've adopted him.

MITZI: You've—

PRINCE: Perhaps he'll bear my name as early as tomorrow. I'll introduce him where I please. Above all, of course, to my old friend, the Count, your Papa. If it's unpleasant for you to see this young person, you'll have no other choice but to withdraw to your room for the duration of his visit.

MITZI: If you think I find this tone very appropriate . . .

PRINCE: As little as I find your ill will.

MITZI: Ill will? Do I seem ill-willed? Listen . . . I'm just permitting myself to find your brilliant idea tasteless. For the rest, I'm in as good a mood as ever.

PRINCE: I don't doubt your otherwise good mood. Only now . . . For the rest, I'm by no means unaware that you've long since known how to become reconciled to your fate. I've certainly figured out how to submit to mine as well. In its way, that fate was just as grievous as yours.

MITZI: What? What kind of fate did you have to . . . Not everyone can become a cabinet minister, after all. Ah, so . . . your remark refers to Your Highness having shown me the honor of asking me for my hand ten years ago, after the death of your spouse of blessed memory?

PRINCE: And seven years ago as well, if you'd most kindly remember—

MITZI: Oh, certainly I remember. I've never given you occasion to doubt my memory.

PRINCE: And I hope, Mitzi, you never expected me to have the intention of doing something such as atoning for an offense by my courtship. I asked you to be my wife precisely because I had the conviction that true happiness could only be granted me at your side.

MITZI: True happiness! . . . You would have been mistaken.

PRINCE: I myself certainly believe that I might have been mistaken at that time. Ten years ago it may still have been too early. Perhaps still too early seven years ago as well. Today, no longer.

MITZI: Today as well, dear Prince. It's your unfortunate destiny that you never knew me, never knew anything about me. Not when I loved you, not when I hated you, and not even through the long time during which I've been indifferent to you.

PRINCE: I always knew you, Mitzi. I know more about you than you probably suspect. For example, I'm by no means unaware that you've also used these seventeen years for something better than bewailing a man who, at that time, was perhaps not quite worthy of you. Yes, I even know that you were intent on gaining some other experiences, after the disappointment you had with me.

MITZI: Disappointments? Well, I can assure you, to your consolation, dear Prince, that I had rather pleasant experiences as well.

PRINCE: I know that too. Would I otherwise dare to claim that I really know the history of your life?

MITZI: And do you perhaps imagine I don't know yours? Do you wish me to enumerate the list of your mistresses? From the name of the wife of the Bulgarian attachée in 1887 to Fräulein Theresa Gredun, if that's really her name . . . who, at least this spring, still held high rank at your court? I probably know even more than you do, for I also know about nearly every one of them with whom she betrayed you.

PRINCE: But better not to tell me anything about that. One doesn't get any real fun out of it, when one doesn't discover such things oneself.

[*A coach is heard approaching and stopping.*]

PRINCE: There he is. Perhaps you'll wish to disappear, before he steps into the park. I'll delay him that long.

MITZI: Don't trouble yourself . . . It pleases me to stay here. But if perhaps you believe it stirs me in the very slightest . . . It's a young gentleman who is visiting my father. Why, there he is already . . . Call of blood? It must be a myth. I don't notice anything at all, dear Prince.

[PHILIPP *has quickly entered through the main gate; he is seventeen years old, slender, attractive, elegant but not foppish; charmingly, somewhat boyishly forward—not without embarrassment, however.*]

PHILIPP: Good day.

[*He bows before* MITZI.]

PRINCE: Good morning, Philipp. Permit me, Countess, to introduce my son to you. This is Countess Mitzi. The daughter of my old friend, in whose house you are a guest.

[PHILIPP *takes the hand* MITZI *offers him and kisses it. Brief pause.*]

MITZI: Please, don't you want to have a seat?
PHILIPP: Thank you, Countess.

[*All remain standing.*]

PRINCE: You rode out here in the coach? You could send it back, since I have mine here.
PHILIPP: Wouldn't you rather ride back with me, Papa? To be specific, I think Wasner drives better than your Franz with the old horses from the manor.
MITZI: You're riding with Wasner?
PHILIPP: Certainly.
MITZI: With the gentleman himself? Do you also know that's a great honor? Wasner doesn't drive with just everyone. Two years ago, he was still driving Papa.
PHILIPP: Ah . . .
PRINCE: By the way, you're a bit late, Philipp.
PHILIPP: Yes, I very much beg your pardon. Actually, I overslept. [*To* MITZI] A few of us classmates got together yesterday evening. Perhaps the Countess knows that I graduated two weeks ago, and then we danced a bit yesterday evening.
MITZI: You seem to have accommodated yourself rather quickly to Viennese life, Herr . . .
PRINCE: Call him simply "Philipp," dear Mitzi.

MITZI: Please, don't we want to sit down, Philipp—[*With a glance at the* PRINCE] Papa will surely be here any moment.

[MITZI *and the* PRINCE *sit down.*]

PHILIPP [*while still standing*]: So, if I may permit myself to remark, I find the park splendid. It's considerably more beautiful than ours.

MITZI: You're familiar with Ravenstein Park?

PHILIPP: Naturally, Countess. Why, I've been living in the castle for three days now.

MITZI: What?

PRINCE: Gardens simply can't develop in the city the way they do out here. A hundred years ago, ours was certainly more beautiful than it is today. But that's also when our castle was still situated outside the city.

PHILIPP: Pity that people were allowed to build their houses all around our castle like that.

MITZI: We're better off. We'll probably not live to see the city move out toward us.

PHILIPP [*kindly*]: But why not, then, Countess . . . ?

MITZI: A hundred years ago, this was all still hunting ground. It borders directly on the Zoological Gardens. Do you see the wall over there, Philipp? And earlier, our villa was once a little hunting lodge of Empress Maria Theresa. The sandstone figure still out there at the pond is from that time too.

PHILIPP: And exactly how old is our castle, then, Papa?

PRINCE [*smiling*]: Our castle, my son, has been standing since the seventeenth century. Why, I showed you the room in which Emperor Leopold slept one night.

PHILIPP: Emperor Leopold, 1643 to 1705.

[MITZI *laughs.*]

PHILIPP: That's still coming from graduation. If I just get to be that old . . . [*Interrupting himself*] Pardon me! . . . I just mean—all that'll be forgotten within the next year. Of course, when I learned the date, I didn't yet realize that he, the emperor Leopold, was such a close acquaintance of ours.

MITZI: Why, you seem to derive a tremendous amount of fun out of this discovery, Philipp.

PHILIPP: Discovery . . . Yes, to confess honestly, that wasn't actually a discovery.

[*He looks at the* PRINCE.]

PRINCE: Just go on talking, just go on talking.

PHILIPP: So you know, Countess, to be specific, I always had the feeling that I wasn't born Philipp Radeiner.

MITZI: Radeiner? [*To the* PRINCE] That's the name by which . . . ?

PRINCE: Yes indeed.

PHILIPP: Of course, it was very pleasant for me to find my suspicions were confirmed—but I always knew that. After all, one's not stupid. Some of them at school had a suspicion too . . . that I . . . That fiction about Prince Ravenstein always traveling to Krems to inquire about the progress of the son of a deceased friend, that was a bit fanciful, the stuff of cheap novels, isn't it, Countess . . . ? And it was rather clear to the shrewder ones that princely blood is pounding in my veins. And, since I was one of the shrewdest . . .

MITZI: Why, it really seems . . . What kind of plans, then, do you have for the future, Philipp?

PHILIPP: In October I'll be doing my year of voluntary enlistment in the Sixth Dragoons, where we Ravensteins always serve. What happens with me then, whether I stay with the military, or become an archbishop, is, of course, a question of time . . .

MITZI: That would be the right thing, perhaps. The Ravensteins were always strong in their faith.

PHILIPP: Yes, that's the way it's already been written in world history. At first they were Catholic, in the Thirty Years' War they became Protestant, then they turned Catholic again, but, at all times, they were strong in their faith. It's just that it was always a different one.

PRINCE: Philipp, Philipp!

MITZI: Why, that's simply the new age, Prince Egon.

PRINCE: And the blood of the mother.

MITZI: You've been very hardworking; your Papa tells me you graduated with distinction.

PHILIPP: That was easy enough, Countess. I simply caught on rather quickly. That's probably the bourgeois blood in me too. I still had time for all kinds of things that weren't prescribed at school. I learned to ride and . . .

MITZI: And?

PHILIPP: To play the clarinet.

MITZI [*laughs*]: Why did you hesitate to say that?

PHILIPP: Why . . . well, because people all laugh whenever I say that I learned to play the clarinet. The Countess herself laughed too, after all. Isn't that funny? Has anyone ever laughed before, when the Countess told them that you paint as a pastime?

MITZI: You already know that as well?

PHILIPP: Oh yes, Highness . . . Papa told me that. And then there's even a flower painting—a kind of Chinese vase with a flowering golden chain and something else violet-colored—hanging in my bedroom at the castle.

MITZI: It's no doubt lilacs, the violet.

PHILIPP: Lilacs, of course. I recognized them right away too. It's just the word didn't occur to me.

SERVANT [*entering*]: A lady is here, who would like to speak to the Count. I've led her into the salon.

MITZI: A lady? . . . The gentlemen will excuse me a moment.

[*She exits.*]

PHILIPP: So, Papa, if it just depends on me, I'm in agreement.

PRINCE: With what? What does that mean?

PHILIPP: I'm in agreement with your choice.

PRINCE: Are you crazy, boy?!

PHILIPP: But Papa, you surely don't believe that you can conceal something from me. The bourgeois blood . . .

PRINCE: Just what are you thinking of?

PHILIPP: Look, Papa, the way you told me you'd like to introduce me above all to your old friend, the Count, and the Count has a daughter—which, by the way, I've known for a very long time now—then I had just a bit of fear that she'd perhaps be too young.

PRINCE [*irritated, has to laugh*]: Too young . . .

PHILIPP: Well, after all, it was noticeable that you harbor a certain preference for this daughter, you know. Why, you became absolutely embarrassed whenever you spoke of her. And then you told me all kinds of things about her which you certainly wouldn't have told me about someone else. Why, for example, should the paintings of just any young countess interest me then? Even if the lilacs can be differentiated from the flowering golden chain by their color. So, I thought to myself right away, you're bringing me over here just to see what kind of impression she makes on me. And, as I said, my only fear was that she might be too young—for my mother, not for your wife. Why, you could still lay claim on the youngest and most beautiful woman. But now I can tell you, Papa, she suits me quite fine, just the way she is.

PRINCE: You're really the most forward rascal I've ever come across. Do you really think I'd ever ask you, if one day it occurred to me to . . .

PHILIPP: Just don't ask, Papa . . . but, after all, it's necessary in a good family life that all members are mutually appealing to each other . . . isn't it?

[MITZI *and* LOLO LANGHUBER *enter.*]

MITZI: Please, Fräulein, keep on going. My father would certainly be very sorry if he missed your visit. [*Starting to make introductions*] Permit me to . . .

LOLO: Oh, Your Highness.

PRINCE: Oh, Fräulein Pallestri . . .

LOLO: Langhuber, if you please. To be specific, I've just come to thank the Count—he sent me such a splendid bouquet for my farewell performance.

PRINCE [*introducing them*]: My son Philipp. And this is Fräulein . . .

LOLO: Charlotte Langhuber.

PRINCE: Known until recently [*to* PHILIPP] by the name Pallestri.

PHILIPP: Fräulein Pallestri! Why, then I had the pleasure long ago . . .

PRINCE: What?

PHILIPP: To be specific, the Fräulein can be found in my collection.

PRINCE: What . . . what kind of collection do you have, then?

LOLO: But now there must really be a mistake, Your Highness. I can't remember . . .

PHILIPP: It goes without saying you can't remember, Fräulein, for of course you couldn't have felt it way out here, when I cut your picture out of the newspaper in Krems.

LOLO: No, thank God.

PHILIPP: To be specific, that was a hobby of ours in prep school. We had one of us who cut out the murder and accident pictures for himself.

LOLO: But that must've been a horrible person.

PHILIPP: And one who cut out the historical personalities, Arctic explorers, composers, and such people; and I myself collected the ladies of the theater. They look much better. Two hundred and thirteen. I'll show them to you someday, Papa. Very interesting. An Australian operetta singer is among them as well.

LOLO: Why, I just didn't know that Your Highness has a son. And such a grown-up one besides.

PHILIPP: Yes, Fräulein, until now I've been blossoming out in secret.

PRINCE: But now you're taking care of that very strikingly, one must say.

LOLO: But let him, Your Highness. I like it when young people are a bit lively like that.

PHILIPP: So, now the Fräulein's withdrawing into private life? What a pity. Precisely when I could finally have had the pleasure of admiring you on the boards, which means the world . . .

LOLO: Very charming, Your Highness, but unfortunately one doesn't have the time to wait for youth until it grows up. And now I'm simply of somewhat too advanced a vintage for the more mature ones.

PRINCE: It's said you're getting married shortly, Fräulein?

LOLO: Yes, I'm entering into the holy state of matrimony.

PHILIPP: And who is the lucky man, then, Fräulein, if one may ask?

LOLO: Who? He's sitting out there on the coach box.

MITZI: What? The coachman?

LOLO: But Countess—coachman?!—At best, like your Papa—if you'll just pardon me—when he sometimes happens to drive his bay horses himself. My fiancé is a cab proprietor, landowner, and citizen of Vienna, who only climbs up on the coach box himself when he chooses and just when he has a special esteem for someone. Now he's driving a certain Baron Radeiner. Just now, Countess, he drove him out to your Papa. By the way, I've no idea who he is, this Baron Radeiner.

PHILIPP: Permit me to introduce myself: Baron Radeiner.

LOLO: Your Highness?

PHILIPP: Since I arrived in Vienna, if anyone drives me at all, it's Wasner.

LOLO: Under an assumed name, Your Highness. That'll lead you to some pretty stories.

COUNT [*coming in heatedly*]: Good day. [*Surveying the situation*] Ah!

LOLO: It's an honor for me, Herr Count. To be specific, I wanted to take the liberty . . . I wanted to express my gratitude for the splendid bouquet.

COUNT: But you're most welcome, quite delighted.

PRINCE: Dear old friend, so, here he is, my son Philipp.

PHILIPP: It's a great honor for me, Herr Count.

COUNT [*giving him his hand*]: Welcome to my house—regard it as yours, at all times. It seems I no longer need to make introductions.

MITZI: No, Papa.

COUNT [*not without embarrassment*]: It's very charming of you, Fräulein. Why, you know best yourself how much I've always admired you . . . But, tell me, how did you get out here, then? To be specific, I was just taking my walk out there on the highway, where all the coaches must pass by, and I didn't see you at all.

LOLO: But Count, what are you thinking! The era of cabs is now past for me. I simply rode out on the local train, as is proper for me.

COUNT: I see, I see . . . But, as I hear, your fiancé is himself, after all . . .

LOLO: Why, he simply has more elegant passengers than me.

PHILIPP: Actually, I had the pleasure of riding out here with the Fräulein's fiancé.

COUNT: You're riding with Wasner? But, really, that all sounds . . . well, well . . . psychological connections.—[*Offering him one*] Would you care for a cigar?

PHILIPP [*taking it*]: Thank you very much.

PRINCE: But Philipp! Such a giant cigar before breakfast!

COUNT: Excellent. That's the healthiest thing of all. They give me very great pleasure. Why don't we sit down?

[*The* PRINCE, *the* COUNT, *and* PHILIPP *sit down.* MITZI *and* LOLO *stand close by.*]

COUNT: So, tomorrow you're leaving on a journey with your Papa?

PHILIPP: Yes, Count. I'm already looking forward to it enormously.

COUNT: Will you be away for a long time?

PRINCE: That depends on various circumstances.

PHILIPP: On the first of October, I have to report for duty.

PRINCE: And then maybe I'll head further south.

COUNT: Oh, that's the latest? How far south?

PRINCE [*with a glance at* MITZI]: Egypt, then perhaps a bit of hunting in the Sudan too.

MITZI [*to* LOLO]: I'll show you the park, Fräulein.

LOLO: Why, it's splendid. Our kind can't compete with that, to be sure.

[*They move forward, to the left.*]

MITZI: You have a garden at your house, too?

LOLO: Of course. Why, we have an ancestral castle too . . . in Ottakring. Wasner's great-grandfather was already a coachman. Isn't that beautiful! How the flowers hang down there. I'll have to do something like that too.

COUNT [*upset*]: Why are the ladies withdrawing?

MITZI: Just stop, Papa. I'm explaining the facade of our little castle to the Fräulein.

PHILIPP: Do ladies from the theater often come to your house, Count?

COUNT: No, that's more a coincidence!

[MITZI *and* LOLO *walk chatting into the part of the garden that isn't visible.*]

MITZI [*to* LOLO]: How peculiar that today I finally have the opportunity to speak to you, Fräulein. I've really been looking forward to this.

LOLO [*with a thankful glance*]: And I even more, Countess. Why, I've known you by sight for a long time. I often looked up into the boxes.

MITZI: But not at me.

LOLO: Why, that's past.

MITZI: Do you know, Fräulein, I'm really a bit hurt . . . for him.

LOLO: Hurt?

MITZI: It'll be a hard blow for him. I know best how very much attached he was to you. Even if he never said anything.

LOLO: Well, don't you think I also find it difficult, Countess? But I ask you, what other choices does one have, after all? I'm no longer that young, right? And eventually one does need security. As long as I had a profession, I could permit myself—how does one say—to subscribe to more liberal views. It was part of my position, so to speak. But now, as I withdraw into private life, just how would that look?

MITZI: Why, I understand completely. But, what will he do now?

LOLO: Perhaps he'll also marry. I tell you, Countess, there are still many out there who'd do anything to . . . Don't you realize, Countess, it was a hard decision for me too?

MITZI: Do you know what I sometimes wondered? If perhaps he didn't have the idea of making you his wife.

LOLO: Why, he already tried to, Countess.

MITZI: What?

LOLO: Do you know when he asked me the last time, Countess? It was less than four weeks ago.

MITZI: And you said no?

LOLO: I said no. It wouldn't have done anyone any good. I as Countess? Can you imagine that? I as your stepmother . . . Then we wouldn't have been able to chat with each other as comfortably as we are now.

MITZI: If you knew how much I admire you . . .

LOLO: But I don't want to make myself better than I am. Who knows if I might not, after all . . .

MITZI: What?

LOLO: The story's simply this: I've simply fallen madly in love with Wasner. You won't think badly of me because of that, will you? In those eighteen years I had nothing at all to reproach your Papa for. But it's no wonder passion cools off a bit in time. And before I would say anything against your Papa . . . no, no, Countess . . . after all, I owe your Papa too much gratitude for that. Oh Lord . . .

MITZI: What is it?

LOLO: He's standing over there, looking in.

[MITZI *looks in his direction.* WASNER, *who has just appeared at the gate, raises his top hat.*]

LOLO: Isn't it simply ridiculous, Countess? Whenever I see him so suddenly, my heart always flutters. Why, it hits an older woman all the worse.

MITZI: Old? You call yourself old? Why, there's not that much difference between us.

LOLO: Oh well.

[*Glance.*]

MITZI: I'm thirty-seven. But don't look at me so pityingly. There's no reason for that. Absolutely none.

LOLO [*reassured*]: Why, one hears all kinds of things like this, Countess . . . Of course I didn't believe it. Well, thank God it's true!

[*They clasp hands.*]

MITZI: I'd just like to congratulate your fiancé right away, if it's all right with you.

LOLO: No, something so charming . . . but if the Count . . . . perhaps he won't appreciate that.

MITZI: Dear Fräulein, I've always done as I see fit.

[*Both cross to entrance.*]

WASNER: At your service, Countess . . .

[*Meantime they have moved toward the* COUNT, *the* PRINCE, *and* PHILIPP *again.*]

COUNT [*to the* PRINCE]: Look over there.

WASNER: At your service, Count; it's an honor, Your Highness.

PRINCE [*standing up*]: Listen, dear Wasner, you can just take your bride home in your nice little carriage. I'll take my son along in my coach.

WASNER: Your son . . .

PHILIPP: So why didn't you tell me you were engaged, Wasner?

WASNER: Well, Your Highness didn't say anything either! Herr von Radeiner!!

COUNT [*to* LOLO]: So again, thank you very much for your friendly visit. I wish you the very best.

LOLO: I wish you that too, Count. By the way, to have such a daughter . . .

MITZI: It's a pity we didn't get to know each other sooner.

LOLO: Countess, it is really . . .

MITZI: So, again, dear Fräulein Lolo, all the best!

[*She embraces her. The* COUNT *is affected, somewhat moved.*]

LOLO: So, Count, thank you for the friendly reception—and now, adieu!

[LOLO *climbs into the coach, which has driven up.* WASNER *on the coach box, top hat in hand. They drive off.* MITZI *waves after them. The* COUNT *stands lost in thought. The* PRINCE *and* PHILIPP *stand up front.*]

PHILIPP: Dear Papa, I can see through the whole business.

PRINCE: Well?

PHILIPP: Fräulein Lolo is the Count's natural daughter, thus a sister of the Countess, her foster sister.

PRINCE: That's called a stepsister. But just go on, you diplomat.

PHILIPP: And they both love you, that goes without saying. The Countess and the ballet dancer. And this marriage between the ballerina and Wasner is your doing.

PRINCE: Just go on.

PHILIPP: Say, Papa—why, it occurs to me just now!

PRINCE: What?

PHILIPP: I don't know if I may say it.

PRINCE: Well, you haven't been so timid until now.

PHILIPP: If my mother might not be alive after all.

PRINCE: Hmm . . .

PHILIPP: If, by this remarkable chain of circumstances, it were my mother going back to town just now in the same coach I came in? If it were my own mother, whose picture I cut out of the paper—?

PRINCE: My boy, you'll definitely become a cabinet minister, at least for Agriculture.—But come, we too must take our leave.

[*The* COUNT *and* MITZI *come back again from the entrance.*]

PRINCE: So now, dear friend, it's unfortunately time to bid farewell.

COUNT: But don't you want to stay here . . . after all, it would be simply beautiful . . . if you could possibly stay for breakfast . . .

PRINCE: Unfortunately, it's not possible. We've got an engagement at the Hotel Sacher.

COUNT: But that's really a pity. And now we'll not see each other all summer.

PRINCE: Well, we're not so far away, after all.

COUNT: And tomorrow you leave on your journey?

PRINCE: Yes.

COUNT: Where to?

PRINCE: To the ocean, to Ostende.

COUNT: So, to Ostende. Actually, I've always wanted to go there.

PRINCE: Why, it would be very nice—

COUNT: Well, what do you think, Mitzi? Let's be fashionable. Let's go to Ostende too.

MITZI: I just don't know. Why, you can go in any case, dear Papa.

PHILIPP: It would really be very charming, Countess, I'd look forward to it tremendously.

MITZI [*smiling*]: You're very kind, Philipp.

[*She gives him her hand;* PHILIPP *kisses it.*]

COUNT [*to the* PRINCE]: It appears the children like each other quite well.

PRINCE: Seems so to me too. So, adieu. Adieu, dear Mitzi; adieu, dear old friend. I surely hope to see you again in Ostende.

COUNT: No doubt she'll come along. Won't you, Mitzi? After all, one can rent an atelier at the seashore too. Isn't that true, Mitzi?

[MITZI *is silent.*]

PRINCE: So, once more, auf Wiedersehen.

[*He gives them both his hand.* PHILIPP *kisses* MITZI*'s hand once more.*]

COUNT [*gives* PHILIPP *his hand*]: I was really very glad to meet you.

[*The* PRINCE *and* PHILIPP *exit. The coach has driven up; they climb in and leave. The* COUNT *and* MITZI *come forward and sit down at the table beneath the tree. Pause.*]

COUNT: A day like this is remarkable.

MITZI: Why, life itself is remarkable. Sometimes one just forgets that.

COUNT: You're certainly right about that, Mitzi.

[*Pause.*]

MITZI: Do you know, Papa, really, you could've introduced us earlier.

COUNT: How's that? Ah, you and . . .

MITZI: Me and Lolo. Such a dear person.

COUNT: Did you like her? Oh well, if I had known before . . . What's a person to do? Now it's simply over.

[MITZI *takes his hand. The* COUNT *stands up and kisses her on the forehead.*]

COUNT [*taking a few steps back and forth*]: By the way, what do you say, Mitzi, to . . . how did you like the fellow?

MITZI: Philipp? A bit impudent.

COUNT: Yes, impudent, but fashionable. I hope he stays in the military. After all, that's a more sensible career than diplomacy. Slow, but secure. If one lives that long, one gets to be a general. But in a political career . . . look at Egon . . . three times he might almost have become a cabinet minister . . . And even if he'd become one? [*Pacing up and down*] Yes, yes . . . it's going to get a bit lonely here for us this summer.

MITZI: Don't you want to go to Ostende after all, Papa?

COUNT: Yes, tell me . . . wouldn't you really like to come along? After all, it would really . . . do you know, without you . . . you don't need to look at me like that—I do realize I didn't pay as much attention to you all those years as I really should have . . .

MITZI [*taking his hand*]: But Papa, won't you forgive yourself after all? I understand completely.

COUNT: Oh well! But, do you see, without you the whole trip won't give me any pleasure. And what would you do all alone out here, then? Paint all day long?

MITZI: Well, here's the story . . . the Prince has asked for my hand.

COUNT: What? Is it possible? No, come now . . . And . . . and you said no?

MITZI: More or less.

COUNT: I see . . . oh well . . . After all, I've never talked you into doing anything. As you wish . . . But actually, I don't quite know why. I've been noticing for a long time that he . . . As far as age, you wouldn't be badly suited. And, as far as the other circumstances . . . Sixty million isn't to be scoffed at either. But, as you wish.

[MITZI *is silent.*]

COUNT: Or is it, in the end, because of the boy? I beg you, that would be carrying it too far. Such a thing happens in the best of families . . . And especially when his wife was always concerned about her heart, after all . . . One gets suddenly dragged into an affair, I just don't know how.

MITZI: And then one deserts such a poor creature, this commoner, and she goes to ruin.

COUNT: But surely it only happens that way in books. What should he do about it, then? Why, most of those women die young, unfortunately. And, who knows, if she hadn't died, whether he might not . . . Actually, I find it quite delightful of him, after all, that business with the boy. It takes courage for such a thing, after all. I could name you many a man . . . Well, let's not talk about that. So, if that's the only thing one has against him . . . And, after all, such a get-together in Ostende doesn't obligate anyone in the least.

MITZI: That's no doubt true.

COUNT: So then. I'll tell you something. You simply accompany me there. If you like it, you stay. If not, perhaps you can go over to London, to Aunt Lori. I just think there's no sense in your letting me leave here alone.

MITZI: So, fine.

COUNT: How's that?

MITZI: I'll go with you, Papa. But without any obligation. Completely nonbinding.

COUNT: You're going with me?

MITZI: Yes, Papa.

COUNT: Then I'm really very pleased. Thank you, Mitzi.

MITZI: But you needn't thank me, Papa. I'm glad to do it.

COUNT: You can't imagine in the least . . . without you, Mitzi . . . the memories, just of this year. You know, after all, that I was with Lolo in Normandy last year?

MITZI: Of course I know . . .

COUNT: And, by the way, as far as Egon is concerned . . . without my wanting to talk you into anything further . . . sometimes people get to know each other better in a couple of days in such a strange place than in years at home.

MITZI: Then it's settled, Papa, I'm traveling with you. As far as the rest is concerned, let's not talk about that . . . for the time being.

COUNT: So, do you know, I'll phone the travel office right away for train reservations tomorrow or the day after tomorrow.

MITZI: In such a hurry?

COUNT: Well, what sense is there in sitting around here, since we've decided. So, I'll call . . . Is that all right with you?

MITZI: Yes.

[*The* COUNT *embraces her.* PROFESSOR WINDHOFER *appears in the garden gate.*]

COUNT: Ah, why here comes your professor. Do you have a lesson today, then?

MITZI: Why, I've completely forgotten.

[*The* PROFESSOR—*attractive, roughly thirty-five, very elegant in gray frock coat and a blond goatee—enters the park. He removes his hat and comes forward.*]

PROFESSOR: Good day, Countess. Good day, Count.

COUNT: Good day, dear Professor, how are things going? Excuse me, I must make a call right now because we're leaving on a journey, you see.

PROFESSOR: You're leaving on a journey? Please don't let me disturb you, Count.

COUNT: No doubt I'll see you again, dear Professor.

[*He exits into the house.*]

PROFESSOR: You're leaving on a journey, Countess?

MITZI: Yes, to Ostende.

PROFESSOR: But that's a rather sudden decision.

MITZI: Rather. That's just the way it is with me.

PROFESSOR: Why then the lessons are no doubt over for this year? Pity.

MITZI: Yes, I'll hardly be able to do anything today, either . . . I feel a bit exhausted.

PROFESSOR: So . . . you're also somewhat pale, Maria.
MITZI: Do you think so?
PROFESSOR: How long will you be gone, then?
MITZI: Perhaps until fall—perhaps very late into fall.
PROFESSOR: So, no doubt we'll take up our lessons again in November?
MITZI [*smiling*]: I don't think so . . .
PROFESSOR: You don't think so . . .

[*They look at each other.*]

MITZI: I don't think so . . .
PROFESSOR: Then . . . I'm dismissed, Maria.
MITZI: How can you say that, Rudolf? It really isn't very nice.
PROFESSOR: Pardon me. The end just came a bit quicker than I thought.
MITZI: Better than when it comes too slowly. Don't you think?
PROFESSOR: Far be it from me to reproach you, my dear.
MITZI: And you really don't have any reason to. But we had a good time, didn't we?

[*She gives him her hand.*]

PROFESSOR [*kissing her hand*]: No doubt you'll be so kind as to give the Count my regards.
MITZI: You're leaving right away . . . ?
PROFESSOR [*gently*]: Isn't it best?
MITZI [*after a pause, looking him in the eyes*]: I surely think so.

[*They press each other's hands.*]

PROFESSOR: Farewell, Maria.
MITZI: Farewell . . . And my greetings to your wife and children.
PROFESSOR: I'll do that, Countess.

[*He exits.* MITZI *remains standing a while, looks after him.*]

COUNT [*reentering on the terrace*]: All set and ready. Departure tomorrow evening at nine-thirty, West Station. So, where's the Professor?

MITZI: I've sent him away.

COUNT: So—And what do you think, who has the compartment between yours and mine . . . Egon and his son. That'll be a surprise.

MITZI: Well yes . . . tremendous.

[*She exits into the house.*]

[*Curtain*]

Professor Bernhardi, Act I

Characters

Hochroitzpointner, *medical student*

Ludmilla, *nurse*

Dr. Oskar Bernhardi, *intern under Professor Bernhardi*

Professor Bernhardi, *doctor and professor of internal medicine, director of the Royal Elizabeth Institute*

Dr. Kurt Pflugfelder, *intern under Professor Bernhardi*

Professor Ebenwald, *doctor and professor of surgery, vice director of the Royal Elizabeth Institute*

Professor Tugendvetter, *doctor and professor of dermatology*

Dr. Adler, *lecturer in anatomical pathology*

Professor Cyprian, *doctor and professor of dermatology*

(*All at the Royal Elizabeth Institute*)

Franz Reder, *parish priest at St. Florian's Church*

Sexton

~

Vienna, turn of the twentieth century

[*A modest anteroom leading to a patient's room at St. Elizabeth's Hospital. At the right is a door leading to the hall and ward; in the background, the door to the patient's room. To the left is a rather wide window. Further left center is a longish table on which a thick official record book is lying, as well as files with patients' records, official documents, and all kinds of papers. A coatrack is beside the entrance. An iron stove is in the far right corner. Beside the window is a wide étagère, on top of which is a test-tube rack with a few bottles of medicine to the right. Books and journals are on the lower shelves. Locked cupboards are on both sides of the door in the middle. A white laboratory jacket, coat, and hat are hanging on the rack. A rather old photograph of the faculty hangs above the étagère. Several armchairs, as needed. Nurse* LUDMILLA *is in the middle of work at the étagère; she is roughly twenty-eight, fairly attractive, pale with large eyes which occasionally tear over somewhat.* HOCHROITZPOINTNER *comes out the door leading to the hall and ward; he is a young-looking twenty-five, medium stature, fat with a small mustache, dueling scar, pince-nez, and highly pomaded hair.*]

HOCHROITZPOINTNER: The professor isn't here yet? They've needed a long time downstairs today. [*Opening some of the files*] That's the third autopsy in a week now. Anything's possible in a unit with twenty beds. And tomorrow we've got another one.

LUDMILLA: Does the Herr Doctor think so? Sepsis?

HOCHROITZPOINTNER: Yes. By the way, has this one been reported to the authorities?

LUDMILLA: Naturally, Herr Doctor.

HOCHROITZPOINTNER: Well, nothing could be proved. But of course it was a prohibited operation. Well, all kinds of things go on out there in the world, Nurse.

[*He notices an open package lying on the table.*]

Ah, so, there are the invitations to our ball. [*Reading*] Under the patronage of Princess Stixenstein. Well, are you coming to our ball too, Nurse?

LUDMILLA [*smilingly*]: Probably not, Herr Doctor.

HOCHROITZPOINTNER: Then are you prohibited from dancing?

LUDMILLA: No, Herr Doctor, we're certainly not a religious order. Nothing at all is prohibited us.

HOCHROITZPOINTNER [*giving her a sly look*]: Oh, nothing at all?

LUDMILLA: But it just might not seem proper. And besides, the notions people have about our profession.

HOCHROITZPOINTNER: But why? So why not talk about "us doctors," then? Look at that Dr. Adler, for example. Even though he's an anatomical pathologist, he has quite a social life. As for me, I too am never in a better mood than in the dissection room.

[DR. OSKAR BERNHARDI *enters from the right; he is twenty-five, rather elegant, with a charming but somewhat uncertain manner.*]

OSKAR: Good morning.

HOCHROITZPOINTNER and LUDMILLA: Good morning, Intern.

OSKAR: Papa will be here right away.

HOCHROITZPOINTNER: So then it's already over downstairs, Intern? What have they confirmed, if one may ask?

OSKAR: Tumor emanated from the kidney and was quite sharply defined.

HOCHROITZPOINTNER: So they really could've still operated?

OSKAR: Yes, *could've.*—

HOCHROITZPOINTNER: If Professor Ebenwald had also thought that—

OSKAR: —then we'd have had the autopsy a week ago. [*At the table*] Ah, here are the printed invitations for our ball. Why were they sent to us over here . . . ?

HOCHROITZPOINTNER: This year's St. Elizabeth's Ball promises to be one of the most elegant Mardi Gras festivals of the season. It's been in the newspaper already. Why we've even heard the Herr Intern has dedicated a waltz to the committee.—

OSKAR [*makes a parrying gesture*]: But—[*Toward the ward*] Anything new in there?

HOCHROITZPOINTNER: The sepsis case is almost over.

OSKAR: Oh well . . . [*Regretfully*] Nothing could be done there.

HOCHROITZPOINTNER: I gave her a shot of camphor.

OSKAR: Yes, the art of prolonging life is something we know inside out.

[PROFESSOR BERNHARDI *enters from the right; he is over fifty, with a full beard streaked with gray, sleek hair, not too long, more urbane than academic in his behavior.* DR. KURT PFLUGFELDER, PROFESSOR BERNHARDI*'s chief intern, also enters—twenty-seven, with mustache and pince-nez, lively and at the same time somewhat stern by nature. Exchange of greetings.*]

PROFESSOR BERNHARDI [*still at the door*]: But—

[LUDMILLA *takes off his overcoat, which he wears draped around him; hangs it on a hook.*]

KURT: So I just can't help it, Herr Professor; after all, Dr. Adler would've certainly preferred it, had Professor Ebenwald's diagnosis been correct.

PROFESSOR BERNHARDI [*smilingly*]: But dear Dr. Pflugfelder! You smell treason everywhere. Just where will you end up, with your mistrust?

HOCHROITZPOINTNER: Good morning, Herr Professor.

PROFESSOR BERNHARDI: Good morning.

HOCHROITZPOINTNER: Just heard from Herr Doctor Oskar that we were right.

PROFESSOR BERNHARDI: Yes, Herr Colleague. But, at the same time, weren't we wrong in the end, after all? Or aren't you sitting in on Professor Ebenwald's classes anymore?

OSKAR: Dr. Hochroitzpointner is sitting in on classes in almost every department.

PROFESSOR BERNHARDI: Then you must have many people in your corner.

[HOCHROITZPOINTNER *compresses his lips.*]

PROFESSOR BERNHARDI [*in a friendly manner, laying a hand on his shoulder*]: Well, then, so what's new?

HOCHROITZPOINTNER: The sepsis case is going quite badly.

PROFESSOR BERNHARDI: So the poor girl's still alive, then?

KURT: They could've just as well kept that one for themselves in the Gynecology Department.

OSKAR: They just didn't have a bed open the day before yesterday.

HOCHROITZPOINTNER: What will we actually give as cause of death, then?

OSKAR: Well, sepsis, naturally.

HOCHROITZPOINTNER: And the cause of the sepsis? Because it was probably a prohibited operation, after all—

PROFESSOR BERNHARDI [*at the table in the meantime, has signed a few documents laid before him by* LUDMILLA]: We couldn't prove that. A violation couldn't be established. The report has been rendered; with that, the case is settled for us. And for the poor person in there . . . that's the way she was before.

[*He gets up and starts to proceed into the ward.* PROFESSOR EBENWALD *enters; he is a very tall, slender person around forty, overcoat draped around him; has a short full beard, glasses; speaks in an unsophisticated manner and with an occasionally somewhat exaggerated Austrian accent.*]

PROFESSOR EBENWALD: Good morning. Is perhaps—Ah, well, there you are, after all, Herr Director.

PROFESSOR BERNHARDI: Good morning, Herr Colleague.

PROFESSOR EBENWALD: Might Herr Director have a minute's time for me?

PROFESSOR BERNHARDI: Now?

PROFESSOR EBENWALD [*moving closer to him*]: If it were possible. To be specific, it's because of the replacement in Tugendvetter's department.

PROFESSOR BERNHARDI: Is there such great urgency to that? If Herr Colleague would perhaps come to my office in half an hour—

PROFESSOR EBENWALD: Yes, if I didn't have my class just then, Herr Director.

PROFESSOR BERNHARDI [*after brief consideration*]: I'll soon be finished in there. If perhaps you would be so good as to wait here, Herr Colleague.

PROFESSOR EBENWALD: Please, please.

PROFESSOR BERNHARDI [*to* OSKAR]: Have you already given Dr. Hochroitzpointner the official autopsy record?

OSKAR: Yes, correct. [*Taking it out of his pocket*] If you'll perhaps be so good, Herr Colleague, as to enter it right away.

HOCHROITZPOINTNER: Please.

[PROFESSOR BERNHARDI, OSKAR, KURT, *and* LUDMILLA *exit to the ward.* HOCHROITZPOINTNER *sits down and gets ready to write.* PROFESSOR EBENWALD *has gone to the window, looks down, wipes his glasses.*]

HOCHROITZPOINTNER [*intently*]: Won't the Herr Professor have a seat?

PROFESSOR EBENWALD: Don't let me disturb you, Hochroitzpointner. Well, how's it progressing, then?

HOCHROITZPOINTNER [*standing up*]: As well as possible, thank you, Herr Professor. Just the way things do a couple of weeks before the final comprehensives.

PROFESSOR EBENWALD: Well, certainly nothing will happen to you—with your diligence.

HOCHROITZPOINTNER: Yes, I feel fairly confident on the practical level, but hoary theory, Herr Professor . . .

PROFESSOR EBENWALD: Ah so. Well, that was never my strong suit either. [*Moving closer to him*] If it'll reassure you, I even flunked physiology at the time. You see, it doesn't especially damage the career.

[HOCHROITZPOINTNER, *having sat down, laughs with delight.*]

PROFESSOR EBENWALD [*looking over* HOCHROITZPOINTNER*'s shoulder*]: The official autopsy record?

HOCHROITZPOINTNER: Yes indeed, Herr Professor.

PROFESSOR EBENWALD: Great joy in Israel—isn't there?

HOCHROITZPOINTNER [*uncertainly*]: What do you mean, Herr Professor?

PROFESSOR EBENWALD: Well, because Bernhardi's department has triumphed.

HOCHROITZPOINTNER: Ah, the Herr Professor means the tumor was delineated.

PROFESSOR EBENWALD: And actually did emanate from the kidney.

HOCHROITZPOINTNER: But, after all, that couldn't really be established with absolute certainty. After all, it was more, if I may say so, a guess.

PROFESSOR EBENWALD: But Hochroitzpointner, to guess—! Just how could you suggest—! That's called intuition! Diagnostic perspicacity!

HOCHROITZPOINTNER: And under no circumstances would there have been any reason to operate, in any case.

PROFESSOR EBENWALD: Out of the question. Over there in the hospital they can allow themselves such experiments, but we're a relatively young, so-called private institute—Do you know, dear colleague, there are such cases where only the internal medicine specialists are in favor of operating. And thus, as far as those places are concerned, we're always operating too much. But just go on writing.

[HOCHROITZPOINTNER *begins writing.*]

PROFESSOR EBENWALD: Well, yes; excuse me for disturbing you once more. Naturally you're also sitting in on classes in Tugendvetter's department, aren't you?

HOCHROITZPOINTNER: Yes indeed, Herr Professor.

PROFESSOR EBENWALD: To be specific, I'd just like to ask you something in confidence. Just how does Dr. Wenger lecture, then?

HOCHROITZPOINTNER: Dr. Wenger?

PROFESSOR EBENWALD: Ah, well, he's the one who substitutes for the old man when he suddenly has the urge to go hunting or when an ailing prince sends for him.

HOCHROITZPOINTNER: Yes, of course, Dr. Wenger lectures for him then.

PROFESSOR EBENWALD: So, then, how does he lecture?

HOCHROITZPOINTNER [*uncertainly*]: Quite well, actually.

PROFESSOR EBENWALD: I see.

HOCHROITZPOINTNER: Perhaps somewhat too—too academically. But quite lively. Of course—but perhaps I shouldn't permit myself to speak about a future chief—

PROFESSOR EBENWALD: But why a future chief? After all, that hasn't been decided yet. There are also others. And, for the rest . . . this is, after all, a private conversation. We could just as well be sitting together over there in the Riedhof Restaurant and chatting. Well, just continue. What do you have against that Dr. Wenger? *Vox populi, vox dei.*

HOCHROITZPOINTNER: Well, actually I've less against his lecturing than his overall nature. You know, Herr Professor, he's simply a bit overbearing in his ways.

PROFESSOR EBENWALD: Aha. Dear colleague, that which you allude to is probably identical to what my cousin in Parliament in a recent speech quite strikingly called the jargon of the soul.

HOCHROITZPOINTNER: Ah, very good. Jargon of the soul. [*Courageously*] But Dr. Wenger's also got this other thing.

PROFESSOR EBENWALD: But that shouldn't make any difference. We do live in an empire of many dialects, after all.

[PROFESSOR BERNHARDI, OSKAR, KURT, *and* LUDMILLA *come out of the patient's room.*]

PROFESSOR BERNHARDI: So, here I am, Herr Colleague.

[LUDMILLA *lays a paper before him for his signature.*]

PROFESSOR BERNHARDI: What's this, then? Something else? Ah well. So, excuse me one more moment, Herr Colleague. [*While signing*] It just works amazingly, again and again.—[*To* PROFESSOR EBENWALD] To be specific, we've got a case of sepsis lying in there. Eighteen-year-old girl. Completely conscious. She'd like to get up, walk around, regards herself as quite healthy. And she no longer has a pulse. It could be over in an hour.

PROFESSOR EBENWALD [*professionally*]: We see that now and then.

HOCHROITZPOINTNER [*intently*]: Shall I perhaps give her another shot of camphor?

PROFESSOR BERNHARDI [*looking at him calmly*]: You could've spared the earlier one as well. [*Calming him*] By the way, you may have provided her the happiest hour of her life, although I know that wasn't your intention either.

HOCHROITZPOINTNER [*irritated*]: But why shouldn't I, Herr Director? After all, we're just not butchers . . .

PROFESSOR BERNHARDI: I don't recall having reproached you so.

[HOCHROITZPOINTNER *and* PROFESSOR EBENWALD *exchange glances.*]

PROFESSOR BERNHARDI [*to* LUDMILLA]: Does she have relatives?

LUDMILLA: Nobody's been here these three days.

PROFESSOR BERNHARDI: Not even her lover?

KURT: He'll be careful.

OSKAR: She didn't give his name. Who knows if she even knows him by name.

PROFESSOR BERNHARDI: And once they even called such a thing love's bliss. [*To* PROFESSOR EBENWALD] So, I am at your disposal, Herr Colleague.

OSKAR: Pardon, Papa, aren't you coming up here one more time? She asked for you, after all.

[KURT *has gone to the étagère and is busy with two test tubes.* OSKAR *walks over to him, they speak with each other, then go back into the patient's room.*]

LUDMILLA [*to* HOCHROITZPOINTNER]: I'm going on over to get the priest now.

HOCHROITZPOINTNER: Yes, go ahead. If you come back too late, it's not the end of the world either.

[LUDMILLA *leaves.* HOCHROITZPOINTNER *takes a few case histories out of a file and proceeds into the patient's room.*]

PROFESSOR EBENWALD [*has grown very impatient*]: So, to be specific, Herr Director. I've received a letter from Professor Heller in Graz. He'd be inclined to accept an offer to succeed Tugendvetter.

PROFESSOR BERNHARDI: Ah, would he.

PROFESSOR EBENWALD: Yes indeed, Herr Director.

PROFESSOR BERNHARDI: Did somebody ask him?

PROFESSOR EBENWALD: I was so bold—as an old friend and medical school classmate.

PROFESSOR BERNHARDI: But you did write to him privately?

PROFESSOR EBENWALD: Goes without saying, Herr Director. Since no final decision is being considered at present. At any rate, I feel I was all the more authorized, knowing that Professor Tugendvetter also views Professor Heller's candidacy with some favor.

PROFESSOR BERNHARDI [*a little sharply*]: Professor Tugendvetter isn't taking up his new position at the hospital until the start of the summer semester. Our conversation about this matter—and, if I may allow myself a comment, your correspondence with Professor Heller as well, Herr Colleague—seems to me therefore a little premature. And there's even less need to rush into this affair, since Tugendvetter's present intern, Dr. Wenger, has already demonstrated his aptitude for the position in a superb manner several times, at least as a substitute.

PROFESSOR EBENWALD: As far as that goes, I make no secret of my aversion in principle to provisional arrangements.

[PROFESSOR TUGENDVETTER *enters from right, roughly fifty, gray muttonchops, something jovial in his manner—intentionally humorous but at the same time uncertain and seeking applause. On the whole, he seems less like an academic than a stock market speculator. He comes in with his hat on, which he removes only after a few seconds.*]

PROFESSOR TUGENDVETTER: Good morning. Hello, Bernhardi. Greetings, Ebenwald. I was just looking for you upstairs, Bernhardi.

PROFESSOR EBENWALD: Perhaps I'm disturbing—

PROFESSOR TUGENDVETTER: But not at all. We have no secrets.

PROFESSOR BERNHARDI: Well, what's going on then? You want to speak to me?

PROFESSOR TUGENDVETTER: The matter is specifically this: His Excellency, the minister of education, has asked me if I'd be in position to take over the clinic right away.

PROFESSOR BERNHARDI: Right away?

PROFESSOR TUGENDVETTER: As soon as possible.

PROFESSOR BERNHARDI: But after all, they said that Brunnleitner was to continue heading the clinic up to the start of the summer semester.

PROFESSOR TUGENDVETTER: He requested leave. Poor devil. Six percent blood sugar. As in Bulwer-Lytton's *Last Days of Pompeii,* don't you know? [*He has the habit of absentmindedly ending some sentences, especially quotations, with trailing questions such as "don't you know?"*]

PROFESSOR BERNHARDI: Where did you hear that from? Is it reliable?

PROFESSOR TUGENDVETTER: Reliable? Since Flint himself said it to me. To be specific, I was in the Ministry yesterday. They're supposed to build me a new pavilion, after all. And, I'm getting that. He sends you best wishes, by the way.

PROFESSOR BERNHARDI: Who sends me best wishes?

PROFESSOR TUGENDVETTER: Flint. We talked a lot about you. He has a high opinion of you. He still recalls with pleasure the time when the two of you were interns together under Rappenweiler. His words. *Ipissima verba.* Well, that is a career. The first case since time immemorial, at least in Austria, in which a clinical professor becomes minister of education!

PROFESSOR BERNHARDI: He always was a good politician, your newest friend Flint.

PROFESSOR TUGENDVETTER: He's very interested in our, in your, no, for the time being, our institute.

PROFESSOR BERNHARDI: I'm not unaware of that. After all, he once wanted to ruin it out of self-interest, pure and simple.

PROFESSOR TUGENDVETTER: That didn't come from him. That was the whole council. It was the fight of the old against the young.

But that's all way back in the past. I assure you, Bernhardi, he is most favorably inclined toward the Royal Elizabeth Institute.

PROFESSOR BERNHARDI: And we could manage without that even today, thank God.

PROFESSOR TUGENDVETTER: I love the Spaniard when he's proud, as in Schiller's *Don Carlos,* don't you know?

PROFESSOR BERNHARDI: As for the rest, I'm interested, just for the time being of course, in how you reacted to his inquiry.

PROFESSOR TUGENDVETTER: I didn't react to it at all. [*Humorously*] Herr Director has a decision to make about this. Only when you let me know privately that you agree, will I submit my letter to the administration. You're also demanding something in writing, you pedant, as in *Faust,* don't you know?

PROFESSOR BERNHARDI: Naturally we won't keep you one day longer than you want to stay. I promise you I'll settle the affair in short order. Fortunately, you certainly have a very capable intern, who, for the present, will continue leading your department in your style.

PROFESSOR TUGENDVETTER: That little Wenger, certainly. Capable boy. Certainly. But, after all, you won't keep him in that position for long, will you?

PROFESSOR EBENWALD: I allowed myself just now the comment that I regard provisional arrangements as an unhealthy matter generally, and I was so bold as to make a statement about a letter that had reached me from Professor Heller in Graz, who would be ready to—

PROFESSOR TUGENDVETTER: I see. He's already written to me, too.

PROFESSOR BERNHARDI: Well, he certainly seems to be quite an active gentleman.

PROFESSOR TUGENDVETTER [*with a brief look at* PROFESSOR EBENWALD]: Say, Bernhardi, Dr. Heller would be a splendid acquisition for your institute.

PROFESSOR BERNHARDI: Why then he must've developed brilliantly in Graz. While he was in Vienna, he wasn't regarded as very capable.

PROFESSOR TUGENDVETTER: Who regarded him that way?

PROFESSOR BERNHARDI: You, for one. And we all do know to whom he owed his call to Graz at the time. There were just certain influences from upstairs.

PROFESSOR EBENWALD: And, in the end, it's certainly no disgrace to heal a prince.

PROFESSOR BERNHARDI: And I don't hold it against him. But one's whole career shouldn't depend on one particular case. As for his scientific achievements—

PROFESSOR TUGENDVETTER: Excuse me. I would be in a better position to judge that, after all. He's published some superb pieces.

PROFESSOR BERNHARDI: That may be. In any case, I infer from all this that you'd rather propose Dr. Heller as your successor, over your intern and pupil Wenger.

PROFESSOR TUGENDVETTER: Wenger is too young. I'm convinced he's not even thinking about it.

PROFESSOR BERNHARDI: That would be a mistake. His last piece about serum is making quite a stir.

PROFESSOR EBENWALD: Sensationalism, Herr Director. That's not the same thing.

PROFESSOR TUGENDVETTER: He's got talent. He's certainly got talent. But, as far as the reliability of his experiments—

PROFESSOR EBENWALD [*plainly*]: There are people who regard him—let's say, as a strange person.

PROFESSOR TUGENDVETTER: That's going too far. By the way, I can't prevent anyone from announcing his candidacy. Neither Heller nor Wenger.

PROFESSOR BERNHARDI: But I'm drawing your attention to the fact you'll have to decide on one of the two.

PROFESSOR TUGENDVETTER: But it doesn't depend on me, does it? After all, I'm not appointing my successor.

PROFESSOR BERNHARDI: But you will participate in the voting. I should hope the fate of your former department and of our institute will still interest you that much.

PROFESSOR TUGENDVETTER: I'm sure of that. That wouldn't be so bad. After all, we did found it, the Royal Elizabeth Institute—[*to* PROFESSOR EBENWALD] Bernhardi, myself, and Cyprian. "Three riders went riding out the gate"—as in the old ballad, don't you know? How long ago was that now?

PROFESSOR BERNHARDI: It's been fifteen years, dear Tugendvetter.

PROFESSOR TUGENDVETTER: Fifteen years, a beautiful time. Good heavens, it won't be easy for me to go. Say, Bernhardi, couldn't it perhaps be arranged that I could be both here and at the general hospital—

PROFESSOR BERNHARDI [*definitely*]: Absolutely not. As soon as you move over there, I'll appoint your present intern as your substitute—that goes without saying.

PROFESSOR EBENWALD: But then I will request that a decision about a permanent replacement be made as soon as possible.

PROFESSOR BERNHARDI: May I ask for what purpose? That just might appear as if we simply wanted to keep Wenger from proving his teaching ability over a couple of months.

PROFESSOR EBENWALD: I question that the Royal Elizabeth Institute was founded as a training ground for young lecturers.

PROFESSOR BERNHARDI: If you would just trust everything else to me, Herr Colleague Ebenwald. You'll certainly admit that until now nothing in our institute has been unnecessarily put off, nor has it been thoughtlessly rushed.

PROFESSOR EBENWALD: I exercise my right to reject as incorrect any insinuation that I, on my part, am calling for rushing, especially thoughtless rushing.

PROFESSOR BERNHARDI [*smilingly*]: I take note of it.

PROFESSOR EBENWALD [*looking at his watch*]: Must go to my department. My pleasure, gentlemen.

PROFESSOR BERNHARDI: Well, I too have to go to my office, at last. [*Allowing* PROFESSOR EBENWALD *to precede him*] Please, Herr Colleague, your students are already waiting.

PROFESSOR TUGENDVETTER: Grant me the request that I may be—as in Schiller's poem, don't you know?

PROFESSOR EBENWALD [*meeting* DR. ADLER *in the doorway*]: My pleasure.

[*He exits.* DR. ADLER *enters; he is short, dark, vigorous, lively, with eyes glowing, dueling scar, roughly thirty, wearing a white lab coat.*]

DR. ADLER [*to* PROFESSOR BERNHARDI *and* PROFESSOR TUGENDVETTER]: My pleasure.

PROFESSOR BERNHARDI: What brings you into the realm of the living, Dr. Adler?

DR. ADLER: I wanted to check further about something in the case history of your patient, Herr Director.

PROFESSOR BERNHARDI: Everything is at your disposal.

DR. ADLER: By the way, Herr Director, too bad you weren't downstairs just now. A case from Cyprian's department. Imagine, apart from the advanced syphilis which they diagnosed, an incipient tumor in the cerebellum, which is said to have produced no symptoms whatsoever.

PROFESSOR BERNHARDI: No, when one thinks that some people don't even live long enough to see all their diseases, so to speak, one might lose faith in providence.

OSKAR [*comes out of the ward, speaking to* PROFESSOR TUGENDVETTER]: My pleasure, Herr Professor.

PROFESSOR TUGENDVETTER: Hello there, musician Oskar. I've already heard—"Rapid Pulse," your dedicatory waltz.

OSKAR: But don't mention it, Herr Professor—

PROFESSOR BERNHARDI: What's that? Have you gone composing again without my even knowing it? [*Playfully pulling his ear*] Well, are you coming along?

OSKAR: Yes, I'm going to the laboratory.

PROFESSOR TUGENDVETTER: "Fathers and Sons," so it goes—don't you know?

[PROFESSOR TUGENDVETTER, PROFESSOR BERNHARDI, *and* OSKAR exit; HOCHROITZPOINTNER *enters from the ward.*]

HOCHROITZPOINTNER: My pleasure, Herr Lecturer.

DR. ADLER: Hello there, Herr Colleague. I'd like to ask you if I couldn't take another look at the case history.

HOCHROITZPOINTNER: Quite welcome, Herr Lecturer.

[DR. ADLER *takes a sheet out of a file.*]

DR. ADLER: Thank you very much, dear Dr. Hochroitz—isn't it?

HOCHROITZPOINTNER: Hochroitzpointner.

DR. ADLER: What a name you have.

HOCHROITZPOINTNER: Perhaps not a very lovely one?

DR. ADLER [*looking at the case history*]: But a splendid one. Right away one thinks of mountaintops and of climbing up glaciers. You're certainly from the Tyrol, aren't you, Herr Doctor?

HOCHROITZPOINTNER: Yes indeed. From Imst.

DR. ADLER: Ah, from Imst. I did some absolutely wonderful climbing from there as a medical student. On the Wetterfern, the one with the dome shape.

HOCHROITZPOINTNER: Last year they went and built a chalet there.

DR. ADLER: They're just building chalets everywhere now. [*Looking at the case history again*] No albumin, the whole time?

HOCHROITZPOINTNER: Absolutely not. It's been examined daily.

KURT [*coming out of the patient's room*]: Albumin has cropped up the past few days. Even in considerable quantities.

HOCHROITZPOINTNER: Yes indeed, in the past three days, to be sure.

DR. ADLER: Ah, there it is—of course.

HOCHROITZPOINTNER: Naturally it's in there, of course.

DR. ADLER [*to* KURT]: Well, how's it going for our Papa? He just hasn't been with us downstairs. [*Looking at the case history*] So, this week he's just been staying up here with you?

HOCHROITZPOINTNER: Yes. He was with Professor Ebenwald before. But since it was an inoperable case—

DR. ADLER: As a diagnostician, he's really first rate, your chief is. You can say what you will.

KURT [*smiling*]: What do you want to say, then?

DR. ADLER: How's that?

KURT: Well, because the Herr Lecturer uses the expression "You can say what you will."

DR. ADLER [*somewhat ingratiatingly*]: Then why are you so stern with me, Dr. Pflugfelder? I simply meant your principal strength here lies in diagnosis, not so much in therapy. In that respect, you go around experimenting a hell of a lot, in my humble view.

KURT: Well, Herr Lecturer, what are we to do in internal matters, then? After all, the new ways must be tried, if the old no longer help.

DR. ADLER: And tomorrow the new is already the old again. It's not your fault, of course. At one time I, too, took part in that sort of thing. But sometimes it really is annoying to have to grope around in the dark like that. That's why I sought refuge in anatomical pathology. There you are the chief controller, so to speak.

KURT: Excuse me, Herr Lecturer, there's one more above you, after all.

DR. ADLER: But he doesn't have time to be concerned about us. He's too much involved with another faculty. [*Looking at the case history*] So, an X-ray too? Well, do you really believe, then, that in such cases—

KURT: We feel obligated to try everything, Herr Lecturer. Especially where there's nothing more to lose. That's by no means fantasy—or even self-promotion, as some would contend—and one shouldn't hold it against the Professor.

DR. ADLER: But who holds it against him? I certainly don't.

KURT: I know you don't, Herr Lecturer. But there are others who do.

DR. ADLER: Everyone simply has their adversaries.

KURT: And those who envy them.

DR. ADLER: Naturally. Anyone who does something and attains something. Many enemies, many honors. Bernhardi really can't complain. A practice in the highest circles and in certain others which, fortunately, are even more lucrative—he's professor, he's director of the Royal Elizabeth Institute—

KURT: Well, who should it be then, if not Bernhardi? He's fought for the institute all along.

DR. ADLER: But of course. And I'd be the last to belittle his contributions. And the fact that he's risen so high, especially given today's changing attitudes—I have a certain right to talk about that, since I myself have never made a secret of my Jewish origin, even if, on my mother's side, I'm descended from an old family of the Viennese bourgeoisie. I even had occasion, in my student days, to shed blood for the Jewish side.

KURT: As is well known, Herr Lecturer.

DR. ADLER: Actually, I'm glad, Herr Doctor, to hear you give our director due and proper justice.

KURT: Why are you glad about that, Herr Lecturer?

DR. ADLER: You did belong to a German nationalist student society.

KURT: And an anti-Semitic one. Yes indeed, Herr Lecturer. And in general I'm still a member. Only since then I've also become anti-Aryan. I find people in general are a rather inadequate lot, apart from a few exceptions here and there.

[PROFESSOR CYPRIAN *enters from right, a small, older gentleman with long hair which is still almost blond. He speaks with something of a lilting drawl, keeps falling suddenly into a lecturing style, as if speaking to an audience.*]

PROFESSOR CYPRIAN: My pleasure, gentlemen.

[*Mutual greetings.*]

Is this Dr. Adler perhaps? Ah certainly, there you are. I was looking for you downstairs. Dr. Adler, can I rely on it that the skull from today's procedure won't also disappear, like the one from the paralytic the other day?

DR. ADLER: The servant has been given the job, Herr Professor—

PROFESSOR CYPRIAN: The servant isn't to be found. Probably in the tavern again. You'll live to see what I did, in my time in Prague, when I was working with Heschel. We employed an alcoholic servant like that in the Anatomical Pathology Institute too. The fellow bit by bit swilled up all the spirits from our specimens.

DR. ADLER: Ours still prefers brandy—for the time being, Herr Professor.

PROFESSOR CYPRIAN: So I'd like to come downstairs this evening. When are you down there, then?

DR. ADLER: I usually work until around midnight.

PROFESSOR CYPRIAN: Really, so then, I'll come down after ten.

[PROFESSOR BERNHARDI *and* OSKAR *enter from right.*]

PROFESSOR BERNHARDI: Good day. Greetings, Cyprian. Are you looking for me perhaps?

PROFESSOR CYPRIAN: Actually I had something to discuss with Dr. Adler. But it's very pleasant to meet you here. To be specific, I wanted to ask when you might have time to come with me to the Ministry of Education?

PROFESSOR BERNHARDI: What's going on, then?

[*They stand together alone.* OSKAR *goes into the ward right away. The other men stand conversing off to the side.*]

PROFESSOR CYPRIAN: There's nothing that particular. But I think we should strike while the iron's hot.

PROFESSOR BERNHARDI: I really don't understand you.

PROFESSOR CYPRIAN: Now's the most favorable moment to gain something for our institute. When a physician, a professor at a clinic, is in a leading position, that's a constellation we must take full advantage of.

PROFESSOR BERNHARDI: You're remarkably full of hope with regard to Flint.

PROFESSOR CYPRIAN: With good reason. I prophesied his career for him, when we were working together nearly thirty years ago in the laboratory for Brücke. He's an administrative genius. I've already drafted a memorandum. What we demand above all is government support, so we're no longer entirely dependent on those somewhat disreputable fund-raisings. Futhermore . . .

PROFESSOR BERNHARDI: You are forgetful in one respect: Flint is our most bitter enemy.

PROFESSOR CYPRIAN: But if you please, that was certainly long ago. He views the Royal Elizabeth Institute with the greatest favor today. Counselor Winkler himself told me that again just yesterday. Quite spontaneously.

PROFESSOR BERNHARDI: Well—

OSKAR [*coming out of the patient's room; rapidly to* PROFESSOR BERNHARDI]: Say, Papa, I think, if you still want to speak to her—

PROFESSOR BERNHARDI: Excuse me, dear Cyprian. Perhaps you'll be so kind as to wait five minutes for me.

[*He exits.*]

OSKAR [*to* PROFESSOR CYPRIAN]: A woman's dying, Herr Professor.

[*He follows his father into the ward.*]

KURT [*casually*]: A case of sepsis. Young girl. Abortion.

HOCHROITZPOINTNER: Until tomorrow, Herr Lecturer.

PROFESSOR CYPRIAN [*in his monotone fashion*]: When I was still an intern for Skoda, the head physician in our hospital—better not to mention names—he asked us interns, I mean, to call him in every case of death, if at all possible. He wanted to write a psychology of people's dying moments—supposedly. Right away I said to Bernitzer, who was an intern together with me, something's not right there. He's not interested in psychology. So, imagine, one day the head physician suddenly disappeared. A married man with three children. The following night a fellow in rags was found stabbed to death in some out-of-the-way street. Well, no doubt you're already guessing the point, gentlemen. It turned out the head physician and the tramp who'd been stabbed to death were the same person. For those many years he'd been living a double existence. During the day, he was the busy physician, at night he was a regular customer at all kinds of suspicious dives, a pimp.—

[*The priest,* FRANZ REDER, *enters, a young man of twenty-eight, with energetic, shrewd features. The* SEXTON *stays at the entrance.*]

DR. ADLER [*zealously*]: My pleasure, Father.

REDER: Good day, gentlemen. I would hope I'm not coming too late.

KURT: No, Father. The Herr Professor is with the patient right now. [*Introducing himself*] Intern Pflugfelder.

REDER: So they haven't completely given up hope?

OSKAR [*coming out of patient's room*]: Good day, Father.

KURT: Yes they have, Father, it's a totally hopeless case.

OSKAR: Please, if the Father will—

REDER: Perhaps I'll go on waiting until the Herr Professor has left the patient.

[*The sexton steps back, the door closes;* HOCHROITZPOINTNER *pushes over an armchair for* REDER, *who doesn't sit down yet.*]

REDER: Thank you, thank you.

PROFESSOR CYPRIAN: Yes, Father, if we could only attend the sick while we can still help. Sometimes the best we can do is console.

KURT: And lie.

REDER [*sitting down*]: That's a rather harsh word you're using, Herr Doctor.

KURT: Pardon, Father, that was directed only toward us physicians, naturally. By the way, sometimes that's precisely the most difficult and most noble part of our profession.

[PROFESSOR BERNHARDI *becomes visible at the door;* REDER *stands up.* LUDMILLA *comes out of the patient's room after* PROFESSOR BERNHARDI.]

PROFESSOR BERNHARDI [*somewhat taken aback*]: Oh, Father.

REDER: So, we're relieving each other, Herr Professor.

[*He gives him his hand.*]

Will I find the patient still in a conscious state?

PROFESSOR BERNHARDI: Yes. One could even say in a state of heightened consciousness. [*More to the others*] Absolute euphoria has set in with her. [*As if explaining to* REDER] She feels well, so to speak.

REDER: Well, that's very nice indeed. Who knows!—Just recently I had the pleasure to run into a healthy young man on the street who'd received extreme unction from me a couple of weeks earlier, absolutely prepared for death.

DR. ADLER: And who knows, perhaps it was the Father himself who gave him back the strength, the courage to live.

PROFESSOR BERNHARDI [*to* DR. ADLER]: The Father must have misunderstood me, Herr Doctor. [*To* REDER] To be specific, what I meant was the patient is completely unaware. She's dying, but she believes herself recovered.

REDER: Truly.

PROFESSOR BERNHARDI: And one might fear that your appearance, Father—

REDER [*quite gently*]: Don't be afraid for your patient, Herr Professor. I'm not coming here to pronounce a death sentence.

PROFESSOR BERNHARDI: Naturally, but even so—

REDER: Perhaps the patient could be made ready.

[PROFESSOR BERNHARDI *doesn't notice* LUDMILLA *proceed into the patient's room in response to a scarcely perceptible signal from* REDER*'s eyes.*]

PROFESSOR BERNHARDI: That certainly wouldn't improve the matter. As I already mentioned, Father, the patient is completely unaware. And she's expecting something quite different from your visit. On the contrary, she is completely overcome with the happy delusion that someone closely connected to her will appear in the next hour, will come to get her and take her for himself again—into life and happiness. I believe, Father, it wouldn't be a good thing, I'd almost dare to claim a work pleasing to God, if we tried to awaken her out of this final dream.

REDER [*following a little hesitation, more definitely*]: Is it possible, Herr Professor, that my appearance could affect the course of her illness unfavorably—

PROFESSOR BERNHARDI [*rapidly joining in*]: It wouldn't be impossible for the end to be accelerated, by perhaps only a few minutes, but all the same—

REDER [*more spiritedly*]: Once again: can your patient still be saved? Would my appearance be a danger in that sense? Then I'd naturally be prepared to withdraw immediately.

[DR. ADLER *nods approvingly.*]

PROFESSOR BERNHARDI: She's irretrievably lost, there can be no doubt of that.

REDER: Then, Herr Professor, I see absolutely no reason—

PROFESSOR BERNHARDI: Excuse me, Father, for the time being I'm still here as her physician. And at least as far as possible, it's my duty to let my patients die pleasantly, when nothing more lies in my powers.

[PROFESSOR CYPRIAN *shows slight impatience and disapproval.*]

REDER: Die pleasantly.—We probably understand different things by that, Herr Professor. And according to what the nurse told me, your patient requires absolution more urgently than many others.

PROFESSOR BERNHARDI [*with his ironic smile*]: Aren't we sinners all?

REDER: That probably doesn't pertain, Herr Professor. You can't know if somewhere in the depths of her soul, which God alone sees, she doesn't long to unburden herself through a final confession of all her sins, precisely in these final moments she has been given.

PROFESSOR BERNHARDI: Must I repeat once more, Father? The patient doesn't know she is lost. She is serene, happy—and unrepentant.

REDER: I would be committing an even greater sin myself if I were to withdraw from this threshold without having administered to this dying woman the consolations of our holy religion.

PROFESSOR BERNHARDI: God and every earthly judge will acquit you of this sin, Father. [*In response to his agitation*] Yes indeed, Father. For as her physician, I cannot allow you to go to this patient's bedside.

REDER: I was called here. I must therefore ask—

PROFESSOR BERNHARDI: Not by me, Father. And I can only repeat that, as a physician entrusted with the well-being of his patients until their final hour, I must unfortunately forbid you to cross this threshold.

REDER [*stepping forward*]: You're forbidding me that?

PROFESSOR BERNHARDI [*softly touching his shoulder*]: Yes, Father.

LUDMILLA [*hurrying out of the patient's room*]: Father—

PROFESSOR BERNHARDI: You were in there?

LUDMILLA: It's almost too late, Father.

[KURT *goes quickly into the patient's room.*]

PROFESSOR BERNHARDI [*to* LUDMILLA]: You told the patient the Father is here?

LUDMILLA: Yes, Herr Director.

PROFESSOR BERNHARDI: I see. And answer me quite calmly—how did the patient react? Did she say anything? Tell me. Well?

LUDMILLA: She said—

PROFESSOR BERNHARDI: Well?

LUDMILLA: She's just a bit frightened.

PROFESSOR BERNHARDI [*not angrily*]: Well, just tell me, will you, what did she say?

LUDMILLA: "Must I really die then?"

KURT [*coming out of the patient's room*]: It's over.

[*Brief pause.*]

PROFESSOR BERNHARDI: Don't be frightened, Father. It's not your sin. You just wanted to fulfil your duty. I wanted to do mine as well. I'm just sorry I wasn't successful.

REDER: You're not the one, Herr Professor, to grant me absolution. The poor creature has passed away in there as a sinner and without the consolations of religion. And that's your sin.

PROFESSOR BERNHARDI: I take it upon myself.

REDER: It remains to be proved, Herr Professor, whether you are in a position to do that. I bid farewell, gentlemen.

[*He exits. The others stay behind, agitated and in some embarrassment.* PROFESSOR BERNHARDI *looks at them in succession.*]

PROFESSOR BERNHARDI: So, tomorrow morning, dear Dr. Adler, the dissection.

PROFESSOR CYPRIAN [*to* PROFESSOR BERNHARDI, *not heard by the others*]: That wasn't right.

PROFESSOR BERNHARDI: But why not?

PROFESSOR CYPRIAN: And besides, it'll remain an isolated case. You won't change anything in principle.

PROFESSOR BERNHARDI: *In principle?* That wasn't my intention anyway.

DR. ADLER: I'd regard it as dishonest, Herr Director, if I didn't say at this very moment—that I cannot loyally stand by you in this matter.

PROFESSOR BERNHARDI: And it would be disloyal, Herr Doctor, if I didn't assure you right away I would have thought as much.

[PROFESSOR CYPRIAN *and* DR. ADLER *exit.* OSKAR *bites his lips.*]

PROFESSOR BERNHARDI: Well, my son, I would hope it won't damage your career.

OSKAR: But Papa.

PROFESSOR BERNHARDI [*putting an arm around his shoulder, tenderly*]: Well, I didn't want to offend you.

LUDMILLA: Herr Professor, I thought—

PROFESSOR BERNHARDI: What did you think? For what purpose anyway—well, now it's over.

LUDMILLA: After all, it's always been that way, Herr Director, and—[*Pointing to* HOCHROITZPOINTNER] the Herr Doctor—

HOCHROITZPOINTNER: Yes, of course I didn't forbid her, Herr Director.

PROFESSOR BERNHARDI: That goes without saying, Herr Doctor Hochroitzpointner. You're probably sitting in on lectures at the church too, aren't you?

HOCHROITZPOINTNER: Herr Director, we live in a Christian state.

PROFESSOR BERNHARDI: Yes. [*Looking at him steadily for a long time*] May the Lord pardon you—they know damned well what they're doing.

[*He exits with* KURT *and* OSKAR.]

HOCHROITZPOINTNER: But my child, what's gotten into you that you apologize? After all, you were just doing your duty. But what's wrong, then—Now you're even starting to cry—Just don't throw a fit on me again.

LUDMILLA [*sobbing*]: But Herr Director was so angry.

HOCHROITZPOINTNER: And even if he was angry—Herr Director. Well, he won't stay that way much longer. They'll break him!

[*Curtain*]

Hour of Realizing

A PLAY IN ONE ACT

Characters

Servant at Dr. Eckold's house

Dr. Karl Eckold, *physician*

Klara, *his wife*

Anna, *their housemaid*

Professor Rudolf Ormin

~

Dr. Eckold's residence in Vienna, early decades of the twentieth century

[DR. ECKOLD's *dining room, door in background to anteroom, door on right to waiting room, door on left to the other rooms of the house. Comfortable furnishings, without the appearance of being modern.* DR. KARL ECKOLD, *forty-five, turning bald, with dark brown full beard, uses a pince-nez for reading; and* KLARA, *his wife, forty, still beautiful, eating dessert at their dining-room table.*]

SERVANT [*bringing a visitor's card*]: The lady requests to be received quite soon, if possible.

ECKOLD [*calmly holding the card*]: As is well known, my office hour begins at three. It's barely two-thirty. Would the lady be so kind as to wait. Is anyone else there?

SERVANT: Three people have come by already.

ECKOLD: I can receive them only in due succession, that goes without saying.

[*The* SERVANT *exits;* ANNA, *the housemaid, brings the coffee;* KLARA *pours.*]

ECKOLD: Why, you set places for three, Anna. Evidently you completely forgot that Fräulein Bettina, or rather, Frau Doktor Bettina Wörmann, is dining in Salzburg today, or in Zurich, or God knows where.

KLARA: The place was set for Ormin, anyway.

ECKOLD: Ah yes. Did he call that he couldn't come?

[ANNA *exits.*]

KLARA: No. He wasn't at all sure about accepting our invitation. But he'll surely come back to say good-bye.

ECKOLD: He'll have all kinds of things to do before such a long trip. You'll call me then, won't you? I'd also like to bid him farewell.

[*He has gotten up and moves right, half turning around.*]

In any case, you'll be staying home, won't you?

KLARA: I've nothing planned. Why do you ask? Is there something we have to discuss?

ECKOLD: Nothing special. There's no hurry in the least. Well—

[*He looks at the clock and starts to exit to the right. The* SERVANT *enters with a telegram and a newspaper.* ECKOLD *goes toward him. The* SERVANT *lays the newspaper on the table.*]

ECKOLD [*opening the telegram*]: From Bettina.

KLARA [*going over to him*]: Already?

ECKOLD: From Bettina and Hugo, naturally.

[KLARA *stands beside him, reading along.*]

ECKOLD: From Innsbruck.

KLARA: Right! So, they went directly from the wedding banquet yesterday evening to the train.

ECKOLD: Quite logical.

KLARA [*reading*]: "Zurich tomorrow. We'll ask for news the day after tomorrow in Zurich, at the Palace Hotel."

ECKOLD [*reading*]: "A thousand greetings."

KLARA: Exactly the same route we took twenty-two years ago. It's just we weren't in such a hurry to go to Innsbruck.

ECKOLD [*without moving a muscle*]: Modern pace. We didn't exactly stay at the Palace Hotel in Lucerne either.

KLARA: That wasn't there yet in those days.

ECKOLD: Even if—

KLARA: It was quite nice—even without the Palace.

ECKOLD: All the same, Bettina landed better than you.

KLARA: But—

[*She softly touches his arm.* ECKOLD *moves away from her, toward the table, which he was already nearby. He remains standing, opens up and leafs through the newspaper.*]

ECKOLD: By that, I don't mean to reproach myself for anything in the least. But a million from your father simply isn't anything to be sniffed at, especially when it all works out so nicely, as with our Herr son-in-law. [*Glancing into the newspaper*] By the way, there's a notice in here about Ormin. [*Reading*] "The Austrian Red Cross medical convoy, under the leadership of Royal University Professor Rudolf Ormin, is departing Vienna by express train at eight-twenty this evening, to board the Austrian Lloyd steamer *Amphitrite* for Japan at noon tomorrow in Trieste, and will leave from there for the theater of war."

[*He hands her the newspaper and watches her while she gazes into it.*]

Must not be bad.

[*He sits down.*]

KLARA [*still standing*]: You were also involved in something like that once.

ECKOLD: You mean Bosnia? There's no comparison.

KLARA: It was also a kind of war, after all.

ECKOLD: Not just a kind of war—a very real one. You could've gathered that from the pages of my diary. Why, I did give them to you to read, at the time. You do remember, after all?

KLARA [*smilingly*]: I certainly do remember.

ECKOLD: They were firing at us from up on the cliffs. They took damned little heed of the Red Cross. Yes, they were definitely shooting at us medical people in particular. [*In a different tone*] But that's the sort of thing that comes with a leadership position—such as Ormin is in now. And in those days I was a very young doctor, just graduated. And today I probably wouldn't be of use any longer. It simply requires more resilience, more idealism, more youth.

KLARA: Ormin is two years older than you. And furthermore he's got something wrong with his heart, they say.

ECKOLD: Ah, years don't matter, not even health. It's success, recognition, fame, that keep a person young.

KLARA: If you'd pursued an academic career—

ECKOLD: Oh well, the difference in talents may not've been so enormously great, after all. It just had more to do with other things. I know that very well. Above all, Ormin had internal agility. That was it. That internal buoyancy, so to speak. Not to say a certain superficiality as well. One has to be born with such things.

KLARA: And he never had to drum up a practice.

ECKOLD: Neither did I. And, by the way, things didn't go much better for him materially speaking than for me, when we were both young doctors. Not at all. To be perfectly honest. Even he had to worry and struggle.

KLARA: But just for himself alone.

ECKOLD: His worries started with a vengeance when he got married. Only he always bore them lightly. Why, it's due to that. Always. If he dies today or tomorrow, Frau Melanie won't be especially well off, I tell you.

KLARA: She probably has a pension, after all, since legally they're not divorced.

ECKOLD: Pension—! Roughly two thousand crowns! Our good Melanie should go far with that. No doubt she's spent that much just on gloves and hats. At least she did before—

KLARA: People have no doubt said much nastier things about her than she deserved. They're always particularly hard on the wives of great men.

ECKOLD: Great—? Let's say—famous men. Well, thank God you've certainly been protected from that unpleasantness. Well—

[*He starts to exit on the right.* PROFESSOR ORMIN *enters, approximately fifty, gaunt, finely chiseled face, clean shaven.*]

ORMIN: Good afternoon. I hope you didn't wait dinner for me.

[*He kisses* KLARA*'s hand, extends his hand to* ECKOLD.]

KLARA: Unfortunately that wasn't possible for us.

ORMIN: Naturally, I've already—

KLARA: But a cup of coffee—?

ORMIN: If I may.

[KLARA *rings for* ANNA, *who comes right away; she gives her instructions.*]

ECKOLD: I'm glad to see you once more, before you depart. So, this evening, on the *Amphitrite*?

ORMIN: Yes.

ECKOLD: It's here in the paper too. I hope you'll have a good trip. Now that it's June.—When are you to arrive at your destination?

ORMIN: In four weeks. No doubt it'll take us considerably longer to arrive at the actual theater of war.

ECKOLD: Who knows if it mightn't all be settled before you get there.

ORMIN: Settled?—Why, it's hardly started. And, by all appearances, the matter's getting a bit drawn out.

[ANNA *brings the coffee;* KLARA *pours;* ANNA *exits.*]

ECKOLD: You're taking one of your interns along?

ORMIN: Yes, that Marenzeller. Kleinert will act as my substitute here at the clinic. [*Drinking the coffee*] By the way, do you know who's boarding ship with us in Trieste at the same time? Also on the *Amphitrite*? Our good old Flödling.

ECKOLD: Flödling?—Oh well, in time, he too is getting old, after all—but "good"? He may just fail at that.

KLARA: What's Flödling going to Japan for?

ECKOLD: Isn't he a correspondent, after all?

ORMIN: Certainly. For the *Rhineland Herald,* as he writes me.

KLARA: You correspond with him?

ORMIN: Not exactly on a regular basis. But since we were together a couple of weeks last summer—quite by chance—after long years—why, I told you that, after all—

KLARA: We just don't hear anything from him anymore. If you hadn't brought us his greetings from Helgoland—

ECKOLD: Why should we hear from him? He's been gone ten years now.

ORMIN [*to* ECKOLD]: He speaks of you as if you'd been the best of friends.

ECKOLD: Friends? I really don't know if I've ever had any close friends. [*To* ORMIN] Have you, perhaps?

ORMIN: Oh yes, some. You're probably setting your standards too high.

ECKOLD: What good would that do? I've seldom seen even a single standard fulfilled.

ORMIN [*gently joking; to* KLARA]: What's the matter with him, then? [*Trying to remember*] Ah yes. Your little daughter! By God, I miss her too. Have you had any word from her yet? No, that's hardly likely.

KLARA: Oh yes. A wire just came.

ECKOLD: From Innsbruck.

KLARA: Tomorrow they're in Zurich, in Luzern the day after.

ORMIN: Well—and in four weeks you'll have her here again.

KLARA: Unfortunately not. They're taking up residence in Berlin right after returning from their honeymoon.

ORMIN: So? Wörmann's so urgently needed in Berlin?

KLARA: Since his predecessor was appointed associate professor at the University of Breslau—

ORMIN: Yes, that's right! By the way, that son-in-law of yours will make a career for himself, he will! With twenty-eight research assistants at the Physiological Institute—and, most deservedly so, as I've got to say—

KLARA: Why couldn't it have been *here*?

ORMIN: It's not that far from Berlin to Vienna, after all.

KLARA [*to* ORMIN]: Just think, the day before yesterday, she was still sitting there. Seventeen years she sat at that place.—And now—all those rational considerations won't do any good.—It's such a gaping hole!

ORMIN: I wouldn't have thought you'd be taking it so hard. All fathers and mothers must be prepared for such a thing eventually.

KLARA: What good does it do to be prepared for that?!

ECKOLD: Why, I tell you, it would be better not to have had children.

KLARA [*almost frightened*]: How can you say that?

ECKOLD [*inscrutably*]: Well, I'm just saying it.

ORMIN: So— [*Pausing*] As far as formalities, I also wanted to tell you something else. Frau Melanie Ormin will also be among the Red Cross nurses going with my convoy to Japan.

KLARA: Ah!—

ECKOLD: Your wife?!

ORMIN: My—former wife, yes.

ECKOLD: Why, then you'll ultimately come back remarried?

ORMIN: I don't regard that as very likely.

KLARA: Give Melanie my warmest greetings.

ORMIN: You have such kind memories of her?—

KLARA: I always found her so likeable. You know that.

ECKOLD: Please send my regards as well. And don't forget to greet Flödling for me. You can also tell him that it's especially uncouth of him not to have been in touch, when we were such "friends" as he claims.

ORMIN: You demand more than you give. After all, you repudiated him yourself just now.

KLARA: And yet he liked him very much.

ECKOLD: Liked? He interested me. He was an amusing so-and-so. Malicious and sentimental.

ORMIN: Not a rare combination among aesthetes whom nature has otherwise so meagerly endowed.

ECKOLD: Meagerly endowed—because he limped a little? In return, he had such nice blue eyes.

ORMIN: That wouldn't be the most disturbing contradiction in his being. Worse yet that he possesses such a poetic soul, but no poetic talent. That would seem to ruin his character.

KLARA: I've seen some of his lovely verses.

ORMIN: There's nothing to object in that, up to a certain age. But he keeps on doing them. Last summer, on the North Seashore, he even recited several to me.

KLARA: Well?

ORMIN: The surf was strong. I really couldn't judge.

[*The* SERVANT *enters with a visitor's card.*]

ECKOLD [*taking it*]: You'll excuse me, Ormin. But now I'm afraid I must—The golden practice, you know. But perhaps you'll still be here?—

ORMIN: I hardly think so. There's various things to attend to before I set off.

ECKOLD: Still, you'll keep my wife company for another fifteen minutes, won't you? And perhaps you can send for me before you leave. Why, we can't have you leave just like that, without any ceremony at all—so, auf Wiedersehen!

[*He exits to the right.*]

KLARA [*quickly resuming the conversation*]: I think it's nice Melanie's coming along with you.

ORMIN: Not with me. She's simply coming along.

KLARA: But otherwise it just wouldn't have occurred to her.

ORMIN: One cannot know that. Just think of all the things she's already tried in her life, and even partially accomplished, now that she's been away from me.

KLARA: Wasn't she living in Vienna until recently?

ORMIN: That's not been the case for a long time. Just three months ago she came back from Madeira—where she was managing a hotel for foreigners.

KLARA: I thought she'd been living in America.

ORMIN: That was some time ago. Do you know, she was playing in the theater there? English. I just found that out. She's even said to have had some skill.

KLARA: A remarkable person. One day perhaps you'll be happy with her again!

ORMIN: But—

KLARA: Fifteen years ago you probably weren't mature enough for marriage.

ORMIN: Oh, but I was. Actually, I was always mature enough. I just should've found the right woman. [*Quite plainly*] But I met her a few years too late.

KLARA [*smiling*]: You would've run off on her, just like your Melanie.

ORMIN: But why? And I didn't run off on Melanie. That's an erroneous perception on your part. One day, Melanie as well as I just began making our little trips, each of us for ourselves. From a distance, that may easily seem like running off. By the way, I don't believe it was due to me. I myself was born loyal, as least as far as domestic life, even if you doubt it. I, of all people. I, much more than Karl, for example.

KLARA: More than Karl—you—?!

ORMIN: Surely. There's definitely something other than domestic life hidden in him, why, something of an adventurer.

KLARA [*smiling*]: In Karl?

ORMIN: Yes, in your husband, the general physician, Dr. Eckold, with daily office hours from three to four.

KLARA [*shaking her head*]: No doubt you regard yourself as a great judge of human character?

ORMIN: One just has to take that on oneself. It's not always pleasant, I assure you. But, to speak quite seriously, each of us has lived contrary to our nature, Karl just as much as I. For I, I actually yearned for peace, for inner peace, all my life. Had I found it, I probably would've accomplished more.

KLARA: Still, I think you can be satisfied.

ORMIN: Satisfied? Ah, you're thinking about my so-called career, I'm a doctor and even a professor—As if that were so important! But I might well have gone even further, in a more peaceful situation.

KLARA: More peaceful—?

ORMIN: Well, let's say, in the peace of a home, even if that may sound a bit corny. But that just wasn't given me.

KLARA: Perhaps it wasn't meant to be given you.

ORMIN: Meant? I doubt it, for I know very well that, in a different situation—I might've been able to find that peace. [*In a warmer, but very plain tone*] We both know it, Frau Klara.

KLARA [*softly shaking her head*]: Just what's getting into you?

ORMIN: Why, after all, before saying good-bye, one can reflect one more time.

KLARA [*smiling*]: But not talk about it.

ORMIN [*seriously, but not gravely*]: If one senses one's never said it with the right words, perhaps, and may not have another opportunity very soon—

KLARA [*smiles, without looking at him*]: I hope you don't have any bad premonitions?

ORMIN: I've never suffered from that. Of course, that doesn't prevent me from weighing the probabilities.

KLARA: But I have premonitions. And mine are—I know—nothing will happen to you.

ORMIN: Now I'm not excessively apprehensive either. Nobody's forcing me to leave for regions of war and pestilence. Why, we're ultimately subject to unfathomable, sure decrees everywhere—more of them with each year, as it were.

KLARA: You're still so young.

ORMIN: I?—Look, one should say that about Karl rather than me.

KLARA: Yes, one can say that about him too.

ORMIN: He's remained more vigorous than I. Really, for me, he still has his student face. Why, he's had better luck too.

KLARA [*smiling*]: In spite of his adventurer's nature?

ORMIN [*remaining serious*]: Perhaps even in his profession.

KLARA: But after all, you'll not envy him for that?

ORMIN: Why not? Is mine perchance of a higher kind?—I assure you, sometimes there's something downright tremendous in being called to an unknown house and being introduced—not to some person, but to a sick stomach. At least Eckold gets to know his patients, after all—

KLARA: As if that's so particularly—

ORMIN [*interrupting her*]: Yes, the livelihood of a general practitioner has its own, very special appeal, all right. Especially when one can draw on a sure fund of general human kindness.

KLARA: Do you regard Karl as a good person?

ORMIN: Hmm, there you're putting me before a difficult question. Good—no doubt he's good. Why, we all are, more or less. But kind—? I don't quite know.—Hear me well: kindness, to be specific, that's something very high and rare. One can sin out of kindness—even commit crimes.

KLARA: Something like that just can't happen with good people.

ORMIN: Quite right. Good people get into petty meanness, at most.

KLARA [*smiling*]: That's—that's actually what Flödling could've said.

ORMIN: Do you think so? Well then, I'd better take it back.

KLARA [*somewhat embarrassed*]: It seems our old friend didn't succeed in getting you to like him.

ORMIN: We were together daily in the summer. And people on vacations reveal themselves even more than they usually do.

KLARA: I ask myself if he didn't behave differently toward you from what he really is. Perhaps that's just his manner. If your view of him is correct, he must've changed a great deal.

ORMIN: One certainly doesn't change, Frau Klara. One dissembles, one lies about something to other people, even to oneself now and then; but, in one's deepest being, one always remains who one was.

KLARA: If only one knew exactly where this deepest part would hide itself.

ORMIN: No doubt we agree about that. There, where our wishes sleep or appear to be sleeping.

KLARA: What counts in the end is only what we've done and lived—and not what we wished or longed for.

ORMIN: Quite right, Frau Klara. All the less may we imagine we know a person, as long as their features blur behind the foggy haze of so-called experiences.

KLARA [*smiling*]: And your gaze reaches behind those foggy hazes?

ORMIN [*earnestly*]: Now and then. Thus the incidental circumstance of your strolling through existence as the solicitously loyal wife of my old friend Karl Eckold has never been able to deceive me about the fact that deep within you slumbers the soul of a great lover.

KLARA [*turning pale*]: Of a great lover, no less? [*Smiling*] You're flattering me. I love Karl, certainly. I've always loved him. But surely there's nothing great about that.

ORMIN [*seriously*]: You know very well I didn't mean it that way.

KLARA [*with equal seriousness*]: I've never wished myself a different fate. Never. I may say of myself that I did all that lay within my powers to brighten up the arduous life, filled with difficulties, of a person dear to me above all others. That wasn't always easy—but, after all, one knew what one was in the world for.

ORMIN: Yes, I well believe that—Karl needed you.

KLARA: As I needed him.

ORMIN: Really, Klara? You've always been convinced that just Karl Eckold, he alone, was to signify the meaning and purpose of your life?

KLARA [*tartly*]: He and Bettina.—Yes.—The meaning and purpose.

ORMIN: Beg your pardon!

KLARA: What am I to pardon?

ORMIN: Perhaps I didn't succeed in maintaining the proper tone today, like a hundred other times, when one [*standing up*] could end by saying, "Until the next time, tomorrow—or the day after, my lady!"

KLARA [*smiling*]: Until—that day six months from now!

ORMIN [*as gently as possible*]: Let's hope. But now—

[*He wants to say good-bye, awaits a motion from her.*]

Oh please, better not to send for Karl after all. Why, we've already said good-bye. And—however much I like him—my last impression from this house— [*Interrupting himself; plainly*] Farewell, Klara!

KLARA: Farewell!

[*They are at the door together, he holds her hand in his.*]

KLARA: Ormin!

ORMIN: Klara—?

KLARA: Evidently you have the feeling of having failed to accomplish something—through some fault of your own.

ORMIN [*ambiguously*]: Failed to accomplish—Who hasn't?

KLARA: Before you go, however, I'd like to reassure you about that, at least as far as I'm involved.—So, dear friend, believe me, you don't have the slightest cause to blame yourself.

ORMIN: I really don't understand—

KLARA: Even if you'd been more ardent or adroit than you were in those days, I mean ten years ago, you would have failed in making me part of your collection.

ORMIN: Hmm.—But Frau Klara, I really don't understand the intent behind your choice of words—

KLARA [*interrupting him*]: Oh surely I would have been one of the more noble specimens, I've no doubt about that. But it couldn't be. It shouldn't be.—To be specific, I didn't love you.

ORMIN [*after a little pause*]: Oh—oh, how stupid of me!

KLARA [*with a weak smile*]: You do yourself an injustice. I repeat: it really wasn't due to you. All the effort would have been in vain. Had I loved you less, I could have become yours—perhaps. But you would have—been more than my lover. You would have become my destiny. That's the reason it shouldn't be.—And not just my destiny.

ORMIN: What would it have mattered? For *us*, it would have been happiness. How many people are granted something like that? Happiness—! We would have experienced it.

KLARA: For six months, for a full year perhaps. And, even in that brief interval, we wouldn't have enjoyed it in purity.

ORMIN: It could have become pure. With time, it would have become pure.

KLARA: Never.

ORMIN: —Bettina—?

KLARA: Not just for her sake.

ORMIN: Him?—What could he mean to you—in those days?

KLARA: What he was for me—what he remained for me—always remained. Never did I know so well that I belong here—belong to him—than in those days.

ORMIN: Precisely in those days?

KLARA: I never knew it so well.

[*Pause.*]

ORMIN: Pardon me, but, if I remember well—it seems to me your relationship with Karl left a great deal to be desired, precisely at the time we're just talking about.

[KLARA, *taken aback, looks at him.*]

ORMIN: Oh, that wasn't hard to notice. No material is probably more transparent than that from which marriages are made. An individual may well dissemble, if necessary, but there are no masks for human relationships.

KLARA [*after a brief hesitation*]: We were estranged from each other in those days, I don't deny it. But despite that, yes, that's precisely why— [*Interrupting herself; more warmly*] You can't understand it! Why, you've never found out what a marriage means, what a marriage can mean. You don't know the kind of threads a common existence is able to knit, an existence lasting for years—and ours was truly common, years on end. The threads are stronger than all those that passion has the power to knit between a man and wife. All sorts of things may tug and erode, the threads don't tear. A couple simply belongs together. And one never senses it more deeply—

ORMIN: Than when one would most like to separate.

KLARA: You just don't know the truth of what you are saying there. In mistrust and agony, they still belong together—just as much as earlier—and perhaps later—in devotion and tenderness—more firmly still, more irretrievably! I never could have left him, never should have left him. In those days less than ever. Now do you understand [*with a soft smile*] that all your efforts would have been in vain and that you really don't have to blame yourself?

ORMIN: It probably doesn't matter anymore whether or not I understand. But the fact you're telling me that only now—

KLARA [*without looking at him*]: Sometime or other I had to.

ORMIN [*rather gently*]: But you seem to have some doubts whether, in a year or two, I'll have the privilege of sitting across from you like this, here, or somewhere else, and—

KLARA [*quickly*]: You shouldn't leave with a false picture of me.

ORMIN [*lightly*]: Into eternity.

KLARA: To distant shores.

ORMIN: And does it give you great satisfaction that out there, abroad, I'll be preserving within me the picture of a saint, instead of that of a woman?—

KLARA: I'm not a saint. The word applies to me a great deal less than you suspect.

ORMIN: Let's not take the words too hard and weightily.

KLARA: Take them as weightily and literally as you will. I'm no more a saint than I was ever a great lover. I'm a woman like hundreds and thousands of others, believe me. Perhaps not worse, but quite certainly not better than thousands of others.

ORMIN: Why, that sounds— [*Moving closer to her*] Is there one more secret, Klara?

KLARA: No more for you, Ormin, in this hour.

ORMIN: No more for me?

KLARA: None.

ORMIN: Do I understand you rightly, Klara?

KLARA: I surely believe that you understand me rightly.

ORMIN: But it's to remain a secret, after all—?

[*Pause.*]

KLARA: A name—is that so important?

ORMIN: I'm not asking.

[*Pause.*]

KLARA: There are peculiar junctures, Ormin. By this time tomorrow, you'll probably be walking up and down on the deck of the *Amphitrite* in his company.—

ORMIN: In his—What are you saying there? Him? Why, that's—

KLARA: It was him.

[*Pause.*]

ORMIN: And in this case there was absolutely no danger of it becoming a destiny?

KLARA: Why do you ask? [*Looking pointedly around her*] Why, here you have the answer.

ORMIN: Which you couldn't have foreseen in those days.

KLARA: Perhaps, however.

ORMIN: You'll never persuade me you entered into such an experience with calculation. There has to be some explanation why he, of all people—

KLARA [*smiling*]: And probably one has to be a man, and a bit vain, to keep seeking an explanation for a case which simply isn't that unusual, when one just hasn't been—

ORMIN: Been the lucky one.

KLARA: The lucky one?—

ORMIN: You loved him.

KLARA: I don't deny it.

ORMIN: More than me.

KLARA [*with a spontaneous smile*]: *Less* than you.

ORMIN: But he could have become your destiny after all.—Yes, even he! It didn't lay in your power after all.—If he'd clung to you, if he'd not let you go, if he insisted on his—rights—

KLARA: Rights?—He didn't ask any more than I was ready to give. Life hasn't spoiled him—unlike others.

ORMIN [*softly to himself*]: Unlike others!

KLARA: He'd been—really lonely, even from his youth. He'd not even—known the peace of a parental home.

ORMIN [*smiling*]: And thus one could also be a little bit sister and mother.—

KLARA: One was lover and beloved.

ORMIN [*always plainly*]: And the first ray of heaven in a dreary existence! The great, the one and only happiness of a life—

KLARA: That's what one was.

ORMIN: Or at least had every reason to delude oneself with that idea.

KLARA: That's what I was to him. And more than happiness perhaps. I certainly don't know what life has made of him. It certainly hasn't granted him everything he might hope, that he might perhaps demand. But I know what he was in those days. You certainly didn't know him. Nobody knew him. Who took the trouble to look into that defiant and lonely soul? I did. That's why I could be the first of all people to be something for him. And I was everything to him in those days—and I didn't have to destroy anyone else.

ORMIN: And what is more, an adventure—a little bit of which also comes into consideration, after all.

KLARA: Adventure?

ORMIN: An experience! At an hour when, for all sorts of reasons, you'd simply become ready for that kind of thing.

KLARA [*shaking her head*]: I could've foreseen it, no doubt.

[ORMIN *makes an inquiring expression.*]

KLARA: That now my features would blur for you. Yes, even you. What you claimed earlier—about others—is true: the picture of my soul blurs from your sight behind the clouds of experiences. [*After a light sigh*] I shouldn't have said anything, Ormin.

ORMIN: But Klara, surely you're not regretting? Why, I'm so grateful to you! It was well and good that you—that we both—have finally spoken the truth in this hour.

KLARA: Are we really so sure of that?

ORMIN: Klara!—

KLARA: Oh well. Perhaps.—If it hasn't been words.

ORMIN: Those words—we'll forget them. Why, it doesn't depend on them. Why, they're just—

[ECKOLD *enters from the right side.*]

ECKOLD: Well, you're still here.

KLARA: I was just going to send for you.

ORMIN [*starting to say good-bye*]: Dear friend—

ECKOLD: I thank you for having had such patience.

ORMIN: Nevertheless, it's time to leave now.

ECKOLD: I don't want to keep you any longer. So, once more—pleasant journey.

[*They shake hands.*]

By the way, I can't conceal I envy you a little in departing.

ORMIN: Honestly? Well, come join us. Leave your practice for a couple of months and travel with us.

ECKOLD: What am I supposed to do in your group? Surgery isn't my specialty.

ORMIN: That shouldn't be an obstacle. Perhaps we can also provide help against the pestilence. But that doesn't seem to especially attract you either, does it?—

ECKOLD: Why, it wouldn't work after all, even if it attracted me. I've never gotten further than yearning to do that.

ORMIN: Isn't he being a little unfair toward his fate?

KLARA: Sometimes I tell him that.

ECKOLD: Well—So, may things go well for you, heal as many people as possible, and see that you return healthy yourself.

ORMIN: Let's hope so. So, adieu. Think of me every now and then. Auf Wiedersehen, Frau Klara.

[*He gives them both his hand and leaves. Silence.* ECKOLD *looks at the clock, rings for the* SERVANT, *who enters.*]

ECKOLD: Has anyone else come meanwhile?

SERVANT: No, Herr Doctor.

ECKOLD: Has the coach come already?

SERVANT [*at the window*]: Not yet.

KLARA: It's only four-thirty.

[*She has slowly walked to the window.* ECKOLD *sits down and reads the newspaper.*]

KLARA [*turning around toward him*]: You wanted to say something to me?

ECKOLD: There'll be time for that tomorrow just as well.

KLARA: Because of Bettina, isn't it? The payment of her grandfather's inheritance? Are there some difficulties? Why, you were at the notary's office today.—

ECKOLD: Yes.—That too. The business with the inheritance is going quite smoothly. Everything will be wound up in a couple of weeks. Besides, that detail's not important for Bettina now. Indeed—but—actually I wanted—Tell me, no doubt you really yearn for her?

KLARA: And you?!

ECKOLD: Of course. But I, after all, I have my profession. I think it'll be harder for you to get used to Bettina no longer living here at home.

KLARA: Well, I was prepared for that.

ORMIN: Despite that. Why, your whole existence, at least over these past few years, was completely filled by Bettina. You'll feel a terrible emptiness.

KLARA [*smiling faintly*]: No doubt there are some other things too—or aren't there?

ECKOLD [*rigidly*]: Still, if you felt like moving to Berlin, perhaps—I, for my part—I'd not withhold my consent.

[KLARA, *taken aback, looks at him.*]

ECKOLD: I'd certainly have nothing against it, by any means; all the less, since Bettina's no longer here, there's really no more necessity for us to continue living in the same house.

KLARA: I don't understand you.

ORMIN: Why would that be so difficult?

KLARA [*increasingly taken aback*]: You want—you mean—I should move to Berlin?

ECKOLD: It's a suggestion. We'll have to talk further about the details. But, all things considered, I believe—

KLARA: What does that mean? What kind of sudden notion is this?

ECKOLD: Sudden? It just seems that way to you. I've just not spoken about it until now. That would've been premature. I like to talk about things only when they've become relevant. But I can assure you it's a very old idea of mine that, after Bettina's marriage, we could dissolve our—our common household.

KLARA: Our common—

ECKOLD: Yes, a very old idea, a favorite idea. I could also tell you how old, I could tell you almost to the day. It's been ten years now. Last May, it was ten years—to the day. Do you understand me?

[*He stands facing her; they look each other in the eye. Pause.*]

KLARA: And ten years you've kept silent?

ECKOLD: Yes I have. But I'm not asking for your admiration. It was much easier than you believe. One must simply know exactly what one wants. And I just knew. As long as our daughter was living in her parental home, it would've been most impractical, why even immoral, to interrupt the externally calm course of our existence, to provoke such a far-reaching upheaval of our living conditions. And now that Bettina is no longer in the house, it would be just as immoral for us to continue living together.

KLARA: Did you force yourself to keep silent for ten years?

ECKOLD: Why after all, I knew this day had to come. I lived toward it, as it were.

KLARA: Did you live ten years for this day? I don't believe it. I don't think anybody's capable of such self-control, you least of all.

ORMIN: You always underestimated me, I know that. The two of you did.

[*Pause.*]

KLARA: Why didn't you send me away *in those days*?

ECKOLD: I could, with the same right, ask the same: why didn't you *go away* in those days?

KLARA: I could answer the question for you. Because I believed my home was here. Because my home was here—always—despite everything.

ECKOLD: There are a number of things to be said for that perception, above all, its extraordinary convenience.

KLARA: It was also your perception.

ECKOLD: Oh—

KLARA: Yes, that it was. Otherwise you could've thrown me out. Why, that would have only been your right, by common opinion. But what prevented you—in those days—was simply the feeling—that essentially nothing had changed in our relationship.

ECKOLD: Ah!

KLARA: That, precisely in those days, hardly anything else could basically change between us through *facts*—

ECKOLD: I don't quite understand—

KLARA: We were distant from each other—in those days. That's essentially the way it was. And anything else that happened would mean little, compared to the estrangement that had set in between us!

ECKOLD: Estrangement? What time are you talking about? What do you call estrangement?

KLARA: Well, don't you know anymore? Don't you recall what made everything else possible? Should precisely that have faded from your recollection?

ECKOLD: Ah, well now I have an idea. You're speaking about the gloomiest time of my life, the time of my gravest worries and struggles, the time when I had to give up my academic and scientific dreams once and for all, when it was settled for good that, for no lack of personal ability, I was destined and condemned to remain a laborer in my field, instead of attaining what fell into others' laps. I'll readily concede to you that I was in a rather bad mood in those days. One can imagine a wife standing at the side of her husband in such a grave period, supporting him, seeking to compensate him at home for all the viciousness he must fight out there in the world. But, in any case, you're trying as you did in those days to make my gloominess into a kind of fault, and the so-called estrangement was nothing but a welcome excuse for you to seek [*with disdain*] your happiness outside home.

KLARA: You're being unfair. I did my genuine best in those days to help you get over all the disappointments and bad experiences. I may well have lacked the strength. Perhaps I got tired too quickly. But it never occurred to me to count your unfortunate temperament as your fault, as you call it. The estrangement was probably nobody's fault, yours as little as mine. It may well be that human relationships are subject to illnesses—as are human beings themselves. You no doubt had to feel that, as did I. And that's why you also knew that the fact itself—the deception, as it's customarily called, couldn't mean very much. Why, otherwise you wouldn't have—accepted it, as you did, after all.

ECKOLD: You think so? Well, no doubt then I must explain to you why I could accept it. I was prepared. I saw the misfortune drawing near. Why, one always sees that. Some shut their eyes. I didn't. And I was smart enough to anticipate you there. Do you understand? You just have to credit my vanity. I didn't wait that long, until [*disdainfully*] your fate and mine had been fulfilled. I saw it approaching, it wasn't to be delayed, and thus I simply anticipated you. It would be amazing if you hadn't even suspected anything! How little you must've been concerned about me, and I made absolutely no secret of it. He especially, your—lover, was very well informed. Didn't he even hint it to you? That would be peculiar. Perhaps you've forgotten it. Well, that's just the same.—In any event, it wasn't so hard to bear—the misfortune—especially when one had definite plans for the future.

KLARA [*in a calm tone*]: It would've been tidier to throw me out.

ECKOLD: And tidier of you, in any case, to leave—at the right time. Such things are just never very tidy. But it wouldn't have been wise if we'd separated in those days, no matter who initiated the thought of such a separation.

KLARA: And today, today it should have become so wise an idea, all of a sudden?

ECKOLD: Why, it's in fact the only possibility today.

KLARA: You certainly don't believe that yourself.

ECKOLD: Why not? Would my resolve seem more reasonable to you, were I to roll my eyes, raise my hand against you, and rage around like a madman? That's how it would've been played ten years ago, if I'd been a fool. You can't, however, ask that of me today.

KLARA: We don't have any witnesses, Karl. You'll regard me as intrusive as little as I regard you as—

ECKOLD: Well?

KLARA: As a dilettante who doesn't want to have his comic scene ruined. So, let it go at that. You wanted your triumph, you've gotten it. May that suffice for you. As you can no doubt imagine, I'll be at Bettina's just as often as possible. That's certainly my own wish. But why everything else? Why dissolve a joint arrangement in which, as good as nothing, nothing more is left today to give meaning to such a belated punishment and vengeance? What I've been to you these last few years—and you to me, we could well be for each other from now on. Why, you've not been acting out a comedy all these years! After all, that would go beyond human strength. You've perhaps not admitted that you pardoned me inwardly long ago. Oh, earlier, much earlier—long before we became nothing more for each other than good friends.—

ECKOLD: Good friends?—That's a word too. Of course one has all sorts of things to talk about, when one's living under the same roof, when a relationship consists merely of various common interests of everyday life, and a child besides. If it pleases you to call such a situation friendship, may it not be denied you. It's never hindered me, for my part, from keeping my existence separated from yours in the depth of my soul, and from living for the hour which has finally arrived.

KLARA: But then you've been living for it only since we've really been nothing more for each other than housemates. For at one time, it was different.

ECKOLD: It was never different.

KLARA: It was different!—Just remember! Why, another time came, after that terrible time of estrangement, of lies, if you will—a better time—that time in which we found each other again!

ECKOLD: Both of us—each other again—?!

KLARA: We both knew what we'd suffered, even without saying it to each other. And a lot of things became good again. Everything! Why, just remember. We were happy again, happy as earlier, happier than we'd ever been. You can't get rid of that. Just think about our trip—soon afterward. About the wonderful days in Rome, in Naples we spent together. You weren't acting out a comedy for me *in those days*! I'd let you have everything else, for all I care. But that time we came back to each other from our experiences and we knew once more what we meant for each other, that wasn't a lie and wasn't self-deception. Just remember. Certainly it's hard to talk about that today. But I know it and you know it too. I'd never been so entirely yours, never, even in our earliest years together, I'd never been so very much your lover as precisely in those days, when we found each other again.

ECKOLD: That's—that's simply a mistake.

KLARA: That can't be a—

ECKOLD: Oh yes! You were neither my wife nor my lover in those days—as little as you've later become my friend. You could no longer be all that for me.

KLARA: Karl!—

ECKOLD: Yes—I remember. That time had its charms too. But you weren't my lover—at most—

KLARA [*passionately*]: Don't say what could never be made good again.

ECKOLD: Who has anything to make good now? You became what you simply could be for me under those circumstances—

KLARA: Karl!—If that's true—

ECKOLD: It's true.

KLARA: Then you ought to have said it to me, before you took me again. You had the right—perhaps—to throw me out, perhaps even to kill me. But you did not have a right to hide the punishment which it pleased you to inflict on me, you did not have that right. You've deceived me worse and in a thousandfold more cowardly ways than I deceived you. You've humiliated me more deeply than one person may humiliate another!

ECKOLD [*triumphing*]: Is that how you feel? Is it? Are you aware of that? Oh, that feels good. And it was worth the effort to await this hour for ten years, if you really feel your humiliation today as deeply as I felt mine in those days.

KLARA: I never humiliated you.

ECKOLD: Yes you did! Humiliated, mocked, and covered with disgrace!—If it hadn't been him, I almost believe that I would have been able to forget, to pardon. That the waves of my wrath would have dispersed long ago, my hatred extinguished some time ago.

But what filled my heart with bitterness against you was that it was precisely him to whom you gave yourself, him, to whom everything came so easily, from youth on, everything which was denied me, no matter how desperately I tried. That it was him, the one who always fancied himself the greater one, just because nature had given him a more agile mind.—But that also gave me the patience to let my hatred grow within me, without bursting my breast.

KLARA: Him? What came so easily to him? Who is so fortunate in the world that they can be spoken of in such words?

ECKOLD: Don't you want to hear his beloved name once more? Ormin's name, the name of the magnificent, of Ormin, the superior, Ormin, the favorite of the gods—

KLARA [*as if benumbed*]: Ormin?! But that's certainly . . . ! Ormin?!—And—and, if all that just weren't true?

ECKOLD: What's gotten into you all of a sudden?

KLARA: Where is your proof? Where is it?—

ECKOLD: Your brilliant idea occurs to you a bit too late. You could have betrayed yourself ten times, a hundred times in this hour, had that even been necessary. But could the two of you ever really imagine that his renting a room for your love nest under a false name would have taken care of everything and that all precautions would have been met? The investigations were made a little more difficult by the ingenious pseudonym of Ernst Mayer, but they led to the goal, even if only at the last moment. Had you already broken off your relations on May tenth instead of the day after, I wouldn't have any factual proof in my hand. Because the next day the two of you mustn't have felt entirely secure after all, Herr Ernst Mayer had departed, set off to destination unknown—and your dream of love was at an end. I'm well informed, isn't that so? And how splendidly everything has come to pass for all of us. Had I also seen you disappear into that house the very next day—

KLARA: Well?

ORMIN: It might be possible that your illicit hour might well have ended badly after all. For a piece of fool is really hidden within each of us—the Ormins as well as the Eckolds. But that's how I gained time to reflect, which I used; and thus I resolved to keep silent until today.

KLARA: And, as far as he's concerned, even today . . .

ECKOLD: What do I care about him?! That sentimental dandy who, upon aging, travels across the ocean, because his skills are beginning to fail, even in surgery, as they claim here? Into pestilence and danger of war, to be united again with his worthy wife, in a melodramatic conclusion—?

KLARA: You shouldn't revile him.

ECKOLD: Why not? Hasn't his whole life been nothing but a revilement of me?

KLARA: If you feel that way, then you ought to have said so to him at least once today, to his face.

ORMIN: Do men have to talk seriously and fully about such things? I've never kept secret from him what women mean, have meant to me, from a certain moment on, the others just as much as you. Just as he's always known I see through him, down into the bottom corners of his tastefully decorated soul.

KLARA: There's nothing to see through in him! He's never playacted a comedy as you have. He's always been real.

ECKOLD: Does the charm still have its effect, even today? You're starting to make me feel sorry.

KLARA: There's no cause for that. I've been happy. Just as happy as a woman can be on earth. I'm still happy today, that once I was his—and you can't take that, nobody can take that from me! It was just him and no other. I can't avail you there. And I loved him unspeakably. Unspeakably!—do you understand me? As nobody else in the world! Oh—and I'll never forget it, that I spent good times even in this house and that I was so intensely, closely connected with nobody else but you through many years—and even you will—remember again, later one day, soon, only when you've become calmer. But what was everything that life presented me, what was peace at home, the happiness of motherhood—compared to that short interval of bliss in which I was his—his—in which I—was Ormin's lover!

ECKOLD: You saw him today for the last time. Do you know that? He won't be coming again.—Did he tell you that?

KLARA: He knows it?

ECKOLD: It's not been kept from him, as far as I'm aware. Now perhaps you'll also comprehend that I preferred to forgo a dispute with him.

KLARA: I comprehend. Oh, I comprehend everything. And I comprehend everything so well that I—will leave your house this very evening.

ECKOLD: We're certainly in agreement. Why should it happen this very day? I'll give you time, as long as it pleases you.

KLARA: I'm going today. It'll still be ten years too late.

[*Pause.*]

ECKOLD [*shrugging his shoulders*]: You know I'm of a different view. Even I am not completely ungrateful for those first years of our marriage, which . . . But—today the hour came to talk about everything else. Angry words aren't to be avoided in such cases. [*Looking out the window*] Still, I don't think it's out of the question that, later on, we can talk calmly with each other. You've nothing more to say to me?—Well—until—until this evening.—Why, it's obviously necessary to discuss certain external, formal points.—Now I must go.—I must . . . [*Hesitating; then*] Adieu.

[KLARA *is silent,* ECKOLD *leaves.* KLARA *is alone a while, quite still and rigid. Then, as if awakening, she goes into the room on the left, comes back in hat and coat, hesitates, then sits down at the little desk on the right, takes a piece of paper, and begins to write; then leaves off.*]

KLARA: For what? To nobody. Words lie.

[*She stands up.*]

Bettina? She no longer needs me.

[*She rings.*]

ANNA [*coming in*]: My lady?

KLARA: I'll be coming home somewhat later on today. Don't wait with supper.

[*She leaves.* ANNA *gazes after her, somewhat taken aback.*]

[*Curtain*]

~ BIBLIOGRAPHY ~

The following items treat Schnitzler in general, rather than specific plays. Like the plays in this volume, they are intended to be accessible to anyone, including those unfamiliar with German language or literature. My apologies for any omissions, which are purely unintentional. I wish to thank Mary Barbosa-Jerez of the Reference Department in the Ekstrom Library at the University of Louisville for guiding me through the bibliographic labyrinth. I am most indebted to my colleague in humanities, Professor Karen Gray, for her exemplary patience, understanding, and helpfulness throughout innumerable computer crises. Special thanks as well to my colleague Réné Djoumo, whose expertise with a new computer has been a veritable godsend.

— W.L.C.

Alter, Maria P. "Schnitzler's Physician: An Existential Character." *Modern Austrian Literature: Journal of the International Arthur Schnitzler Association* 4, no. 3 (1971): 7–23.

Beller, Steven, ed. *Rethinking Vienna 1900: Austrian History, Culture, and Society*, vol. 3. New York: Berghahn Books, 2001.

Daviau, Donald G. "The Reception of Arthur Schnitzler in the United States." In *The Fortunes of German Writers in America: Studies in Literary Reception*, edited by Wolfgang Elfe and Gunther Holst. Columbia: University of South Carolina Press, 1992.

Garland, H. B. "Arthur Schnitzler." In *German Men of Letters: Twelve Literary Essays*, edited by Alex Natan. London: Oswald Wolff, 1963.

Gay, Peter. *Schnitzler's Century: The Making of Middle-Class Culture, 1815–1914*. New York: Norton, 2001.

Kann, Robert A. "Arthur Schnitzler: Reflections on His Image." *Wisconsin Studies in Contemporary Literature* 8, no. 17 (1967): 548–55.

Kuna, Franz. "Vienna and Prague, 1890–1928." In *Modernism, 1890–1930,* edited by Malcolm Bradbury and James Walter McFarlane. Atlantic Highlands, N.J.: Humanities Press, 1978.

Liptzin, Sol. *Arthur Schnitzler*. Riverside, Calif.: Ariadne Press, 1995.

———. "Remembering Arthur Schnitzler." *Modern Austrian Literature* 25, no. 1 (1992): 1–6.

Lorenz, Dagmar C. G., ed. *A Companion to the Works of Arthur Schnitzler.* Rochester, N.Y.: Camden House, 2003.

Reichert, Herbert W., and Herman Salinger, eds. *Studies in Arthur Schnitzler: Centennial Commemorative Volume*. Chapel Hill: University of North Carolina Press, 1963.

Roberts, Adrian Cliug. Riverside: Ariadne, 1989.

Schlein, Rena R. "The Motif of Hypocrisy in the Works of Arthur Schnitzler." *Modern Austrian Literature: Journal of the International Arthur Schnitzler Association* 2, no. 1 (1969): 28–37.

Schorske, Carl E. *Fin-de-Siècle Vienna: Politics and Culture.* New York: Vintage Books, 1981.

Seidlin, Oskar. "Arthur Schnitzler in Retrospect." In *Festschrift für Detlev W. Schumann zum 70. Geburtstag,* edited by Albert R. Schmitt. Munich: Delp, 1970.

Swales, Martin. *Arthur Schnitzler: A Critical Study*. Oxford: Clarendon Press, 1971.

Tax, Petrus, and Richard H. Laws. Someps. *Arthur Schnitzler and His Age: Intellectual and Artistic Currents.* Bonn: Bouvier, 1984.

Urban, Bernd, John Menzies, and Peter Nutting. "Schnitzler and Freud as Doubles: Poetic Intuition and Early Research on Hysteria." *Psychoanalytic Review* 65 (1978): 131–65.

Viereck, George S. "The World of Arthur Schnitzler." *Modern Austrian Literature: Journal of the International Arthur Schnitzler Association* 5, nos. 3–4 (1972): 7–17.

Weiss, Robert O. "The Human Element in Schnitzler's Social Criticism." *Modern Austrian Literature: Journal of the International Arthur Schnitzler Association* 5, nos. 1–2 (1972): 30–44.

———. "The Psychoses in the Works of Arthur Schnitzler." *German Quarterly* 41, no. 3 (1968): 377–400.

Yates, W. E. *Schnitzler, Hofmannsthal, and the Austrian Theatre*. New Haven, Conn.: Yale University Press, 1992.

———. *Theatre in Vienna: A Critical History, 1776–1995*. Cambridge, Eng.: Cambridge University Press, 1996.